Enhancing Early Emotional Development

Enhancing Early Emotional Development

Guiding Parents of Young Children

by

Jean Wixson Gowen, Ph.D.

and

Judith Brennan Nebrig, L.C.S.W.

·PAUL·H·
BROOKES
PUBLISHING CO

Baltimore • London • Toronto • Sydney

Paul H. Brookes Publishing Co.
Post Office Box 10624
Baltimore, Maryland 21285-0624

www.brookespublishing.com

Typeset by Barton Matheson Willse & Worthington, Baltimore, Maryland.
Manufactured in the United States of America by Versa Press, Inc., East Peoria,
Illinois.

Numerous real-life examples are presented throughout the book of parent guides
working with parents and their babies and toddlers using the relationship-based
reflective model of parent support and guidance. The names of family members
and parent guides have been changed to protect the privacy of the people with
whom the authors and their colleagues have been privileged to work. Real names
are used by permission.

Epigraph on page xi from Schorr, L.B. (1997). *Common purpose: Strengthening
families and neighborhoods to rebuild America* (p. 43). New York: Anchor Books
Doubleday; reprinted by permission.

Library of Congress Cataloging-in-Publication Data

Gowen, Jean Wixson.
    Enhancing early emotional development : guiding parents of young chil-
dren / by Jean Wixson Gowen and Judith Brennan Nebrig.
        p.   cm.
Including bibliographical references and index.
ISBN 1-55766-531-1
    1. Emotions in infants.   2. Infant psychology.   3. Parent and infant.
4. Child rearing.   I. Nebrig, Judith Brennan.   II. Title.

BF720.E45 G69   2001
649'.122—dc21   2001037535

British Library Cataloguing in Publication data are available from the British Library.

Contents

About the Authors

Jean Wixson Gowen, Ph.D., served as Associate Director of the Family, Infant and Preschool Program in Morgantown, North Carolina, from 1987 to 1997. Before that, she was Senior Researcher at the Frank Porter Graham Child Development Center at the University of North Carolina at Chapel Hill and Director of the Children's Center at the University of South Florida. Dr. Gowen has written several articles on child neglect, infant–mother attachment, mother–child interaction, and symbolic play and has taught graduate courses in child development and early childhood programs. She received her doctorate degree in educational psychology from the University of North Carolina at Chapel Hill and master of arts in psychology from the University of South Florida. The mother of four grown children and grandmother of one grandchild, Dr. Gowen is retired and lives in Athens, Georgia, where she divides her time between community work and catering to the whims of her cat, Yoshitaka.

Judith Brennan Nebrig, L.C.S.W., is Director of the Child and Family Services Division of Trend Community Mental Health Services in Transylvania and Henderson Counties, North Carolina. She served as the Director of the Family Resource Program, an early intervention service for infants and toddlers at developmental risk, from 1978 to 1998. In addition, Ms. Nebrig has co-authored two journal articles and presented at several national conferences. She received her master's degree in social work from the University of North Carolina at Chapel Hill and her master of science in education from Virginia Commonwealth University in Richmond. Ms. Nebrig and her husband have three children and two grandchildren; they live in Brevard, North Carolina.

Acknowledgments

We are especially grateful to the families who have shared with us their struggles and accomplishments. From them, we have learned a great deal about the needs, strengths, and courage of families as they parent their young children. We have also gained valuable insights about working with families from many of our colleagues at the Infant Toddler Services of Trend Community Mental Health Services and at the Family, Infant and Preschool Program. We appreciate the encouragement and support extended to us by colleagues and friends as we have worked on this book. Our understanding of both early emotional development and relationship-based work with families has been greatly enriched by the writings and presentations of numerous professionals who are cited throughout the book. The comments on an early version of the manuscript by three anonymous reviewers were very valuable and greatly appreciated as well. We would be remiss if we did not mention the extent to which this book has profited from the gentle and helpful feedback from our editors, especially Heather Shrestha and Janet Betten.

A special word of thanks goes to our children and grandchildren. Much of what we know about parenting babies and toddlers has come from our own experience raising our children and from our now-grown children sharing their parenting challenges with us. Some of them have kindly read and responded to portions of the text as well. Watching our grandchildren progress through the early stages of emotional development has been informative and delightful—and sometimes challenging! And last, but certainly not least, we thank Fred Nebrig for his support. I, Jean, am especially grateful for his warm hospitality and good humor as I descended upon his household time after time for yet another writing weekend; and I, Judy, for his unfailing confidence that we could actually complete this project.

To our children and grandchildren

"There has to be a string from my heart to theirs; then when they tug on it, I'm there."

—Anonymous home visitor

I

Nurturing Babies, Toddlers, and Their Parents

1

It's All About Relationships

Principles for Guiding Parents

Celeste, Helen, and Katherine gave special attention to emotional development when they worked as parent guides for five troubled mothers. Maureen, frustrated by her inability to soothe 5-month-old Victor, angrily described him to Celeste as "a devil child." Lisa fought back tears as she told Helen just how lonely and inadequate she was feeling as a new parent. Lynette wanted to parent her children well, but her physical and emotional illnesses compromised her ability to do this. Linda struggled to stay in recovery from her substance abuse so that she could properly parent her children. Samantha, a teenage mother of two young children, worked with Katherine to overcome the effects of childhood abuse on her parenting. Over the ensuing months, Celeste, Helen, and Katherine provided guidance and support to help these mothers feel—and be—more confident and competent in their efforts to parent their babies well.

Our society is becoming increasingly aware of the importance of healthy emotional development. This awareness has been prompted in part by distressing stories in the media about children shooting other children, teen parents abandoning or killing their newborns, and adolescents using illegal

3

drugs or committing suicide. And these are just the stories that make the headlines; parents, teachers, and people who work with children and families know children with behavior problems, children who have given up on themselves, and children who are frenetically trying to prove their worth—all difficulties that can arise from problems in emotional development.

People with healthy emotional lives have the ability to control their impulses and delay gratification. They can motivate themselves, persist in the face of frustrations, regulate their moods, keep from being swept away by distress, empathize with others, and feel hopeful (Goleman, 1995). These abilities have their beginnings in parent–infant relationships that are warm, sensitive, and responsive. The importance of these early relationships to emotional development cannot be overstated. The foundation for healthy emotional lives is laid in the early years, as important connections among areas of the brain that affect emotions and behavior are formed. How these connections are formed and whether emotional development gets off to a good start depend largely on the quality of parents' interactions with their babies. Many parents sense this, as shown by results of a national poll in which parents expressed a desire for more information about children's emotional and early brain development (Melmed & Ciervo, 1997).

Professionals who work with families of young children can, and often do, play a major role in guiding and supporting parents in their efforts to enhance the emotional development of their children. This book presents an approach to providing this support and guidance that has proven especially effective with parents whose parenting is challenged by various personal and family difficulties.

THE RELATIONSHIP-BASED REFLECTIVE APPROACH TO PARENT GUIDANCE AND SUPPORT

Parent guidance and support that are relationship based are focused on the quality of the relationships of everyone involved—the parent–child relationship, the professional–parent relationship, and the relationships among other key players such as family members and community helpers. Relationships are key both to emotional development in children and to effective parent guidance and support. Although there are ways that parents enhance early emotional development, such as responding to their babies' cries and setting limits for their toddlers, the quality of these relationships is most influential. The same is true for professionals in their work with parents. The professional–parent relationship is the vehicle for providing information and guidance to parents about emotional development and for offering concrete assistance to the family to meet their needs. The quality of that relationship matters as much as the specific information, guidance, and assistance that is offered. Parents learn to be warm, sensitive, and responsive with their children by experiencing warmth, sensitivity, and responsiveness in their relationships with other significant people in their lives.

The approach to parent guidance and support presented in this book is also reflective. Building and sustaining nurturing relationships between both the parent and the child, and the professional and the parent, is an ongoing process that requires continual reflection about what is happening within these relationships. Parents and professionals do this by wondering to themselves and sometimes exploring with each other why certain things are happening and what might be done to help. Being reflective helps parents and parent guides be responsive rather than simply reactive.

Another characteristic of the relationship-based reflective approach is its emphasis on highlighting the strengths of parents and their children. A review of interventions to develop secure infant–parent attachments (an important aspect of early emotional development) found that the more effective programs fostered individual strengths and self-sufficiency rather than focusing solely on needs and problems (Egeland, Weinfield, Bosquet, & Cheng, 2000). Noting that individuals come to intervention programs with diverse characteristics, strengths, and needs, Egeland et al. (2000) also recommended that programs to promote early emotional development be sufficiently flexible to assess and address individual characteristics and needs and that they begin early enough and be of appropriate intensity and duration to meet the needs of each family. The relationship-based reflective approach requires that parent support and guidance be given in ways that are flexible and tailored to the needs and strengths of individual parents, children, and their families.

When, Where, For Whom, and By Whom

In this book, the term *parent guides* is used to refer to the people who provide relationship-based reflective guidance and support. Chosen because it denotes the way in which someone following this approach works with families, parent guides offer parents support, information, reflection, and guidance as they accompany them on a portion of their parenting journey. This term also reflects the fact that this approach is suitable for use by a variety of professionals.

Although most of the examples presented in this book describe work done by infant-toddler home visitors with individual families, the relationship-based reflective approach to parent guidance and support can be used effectively by a variety of professionals in any program or environment that serves parents and their young children. These professionals can include early interventionists; infant-toddler specialists; service coordinators; pediatric nurses and doctors; parent–infant psychotherapists; child protective service (CPS) workers; and staff of substance abuse treatment programs for parents and children, teen parent groups, child care centers, homeless shelters, domestic abuse shelters, and family resource centers. The basic principles that govern this approach to guiding and supporting parents can inform the work of these professionals, and many of the strategies presented in these chapters can be adapted by them. Even professionals whose sessions with parents and their children are focused on specific issues (e.g., physical therapy) or whose contacts are relatively brief and less frequent (e.g., well-baby visits) can find their work with families enriched by following these guiding principles. Messages, both verbal and nonverbal, conveyed by people viewed as authority figures can have profound effects on parents, especially new parents who may be uncertain of their parenting skills and parents whose histories have left them unsure of themselves. In some sense, all interactions with families are interventions.

Who Can Benefit   Because emotional development occurs within relationships, the relationship-based reflective approach is especially effective for helping parents and other caregivers enhance this aspect of early development. When emotional development is at risk, such guidance and support can make an important difference in the lives of these young children. For instance, a greater percentage of babies from high-risk families developed secure attachments (an important aspect of early emotional development) with their mothers by age 15–18 months when their families received regular home visits during their first year of life (Gowen & Nebrig, 1997; Lyons-Ruth, Connell, Grunebaum, & Botein, 1990). Nurturing emotional development should be emphasized for children with developmental disabilities. The need to focus on physical, sensory, and cognitive development of children with disabilities can sometimes cause emotional development to be overlooked.

Although this book focuses on promoting emotional development during the child's first 2 years, the guiding principles and many of the strategies presented can be used effectively with parents during pregnancy. There are many good reasons to begin this work during pregnancy:

> Mothers, especially first-time mothers, may feel particularly vulnerable, and therefore open to outside support during this period. Pregnant women may be less likely to interpret such offers of help as criticism of their parenting abilities, as their children have not yet been born. (Egeland et al., 2000, pp. 69–70)

In addition, by addressing factors that can interfere with good parenting (e.g., maternal depression, lack of social support, substance abuse, domestic violence) early, the baby will have a better chance of being born into a healthier caregiving environment.

Fathers Are Parents, Too   For scheduling and other reasons, home visiting programs and other parent guidance services often do not involve fathers. Even when fathers are invited to participate, they sometimes decline, saying that raising the kids is the mother's job. Nevertheless, parent guidance programs are well advised to try to meet with the father on the first visit, whether he is the biological father, the stepfather, or the mother's current live-in partner who is serving as a surrogate father. During this visit, the parent guide can let the father know how important he is to the child and make an effort to genuinely involve him in the discussions. Arrangements can be made to include him periodically in visits with the family, and he can be given the parent guide's number to call when he has questions or concerns of his own.

GUIDING PRINCIPLES FOR PARENT GUIDES

The three principles that guide the work of professionals using the relationship-based reflective approach are derived from the rationale for this approach. The first guiding principle states that parent guides must cultivate caring, trustworthy relationships with the parents and, when possible, with the children's other primary caregivers. According to the second guiding principle, parent guides need to be reflective in their work with parents and children and to help parents be reflective in their interactions with their children. The third guiding principle recognizes the importance of parent guides' highlighting the strengths of parents and their children, for it is only by building on strengths that positive changes occur.

Principle 1: Cultivate Caring, Trustworthy Relationships with Parents

> *Maureen is a mother in her late twenties. She lives with her son, Victor, and her partner, Howard. Howard works to support the family; however, he is minimally involved with the rearing of Victor, Maureen's child from a previous marriage. Maureen revealed her history of physical and emotional abuse and her conflict-ridden relationships early during her relationship with Celeste, an infant-toddler specialist who was Victor's parent guide for 2½ years. Maureen was referred to this home visiting program by her pediatrician because she shared with him her frustrations about how difficult her baby was.*

The key to successful support and guidance of parents lies in the quality of the relationships that guides form with parents. Parents nurture the emotional development of their babies and toddlers by being warm, sensitive, and responsive to them. Parent guides, in turn, nurture parents' ability to do so by being caring, sensitive, and responsive to the parents. All parents benefit from working with parent guides and other professionals who are supportive and caring. After all, who would not prefer to work with a professional who treats people with respect, is attentive to their needs, appreciates their positive attributes, and helps them gain additional skills? Parents who did not have positive emotional experiences during their own childhoods are especially in need of guides who relate with them in warm and caring ways. Due to their childhood experiences, these parents may have developed insecure attachments with their parents and unhealthy views (internal working models) of themselves, others, and relationships. Parents who experienced troubled childhoods often have more difficulty being warm, sensitive, and responsive in interactions with their children. Therefore, they have a particular need for relationships that are warm and caring, attentive and responsive, and consistent and trustworthy. Over time, these *corrective attachment experiences* can often help parents modify their internal working models so they have more positive feelings and views of themselves, others, and relationships (Lieberman & Pawl, p. 430). This, in turn, can help them to be more sensitive, responsive, and affectionate with their babies and toddlers.

Cultivating caring relationships is sometimes a challenging task for parent guides. Some parents, due to their histories and current circumstances, may appear hostile, passive, or unmotivated. Their behaviors may provoke feelings of frustration, anger, helplessness, or sadness in the professionals working with them. For example, Katherine, the parent guide of a mother, Samantha, found herself feeling as if no matter how much she did, Samantha would ask for more, often in a demanding, critical way. As a result of her troubled childhood, Samantha was very needy and at the same time very aggressive in her interactions with helping professionals. When this happens, parent guides must attend to and learn from, but not succumb to, their emotional reactions to parents. Katherine sought help from her supervisor in dealing with such feelings in order to be responsive and to establish healthy boundaries with Samantha. Even parents whose childhoods were more benign than Samantha's may be challenged by current life events or feel unsure of themselves as they embark on the parenting journey, especially with their first children. They, too, can appreciate and benefit from positive, caring relationships with their parent guides.

Parallel Process   People learn how to be with others by experiencing how others are with them. This is how one's views and feelings (internal models) of relationships are formed and how they may be modified. Therefore, how parents are with their babies (warm, sensitive, responsive, consistent, available) is as important as what they do (feed, change, soothe, protect, teach), and how parent guides are with parents (respectful, attentive, consistent, available) is as important as what they do (inform, support, guide, refer, counsel). The choice of how to be with parents is determined by how guides want parents to be with their babies and toddlers. Jeree H. Pawl, Director of the Infant-Parent Program at San Francisco General Hospital, referred to this parallel process as the platinum rule: "Do unto others as you would have others do unto others" (1994–1995, p. 23). Guides teach parents how to be with their young children by how they are with them rather than by simply modeling parenting behavior with the child. Although there are times when it is appropriate to demonstrate some technique (e.g., how to position a child with cerebral palsy), in general, modeling is to be avoided especially with insecure parents. It can appear to them that the guide is the "better" parent and leave them feeling discouraged and inadequate.

In all of her interactions with Maureen, Celeste tried to follow the platinum rule and practice parallel process by being with Maureen the way she hoped Maureen would be with Victor. She was sensitive and responsive to Maureen's indications of need, such as when Maureen described Victor as "a devil child" and complained that he was fussy and demanding. Maureen's feelings of inadequacy in dealing with Victor were manifested in the tense and irritable way in which she interacted with him. Celeste observed these interactions, listened to these complaints nonjudgmentally, and responded with sensitivity—she did unto Maureen as she would have Maureen do unto Victor. She respected Maureen's experience even though her own observations were different, and she joined with Maureen in finding ways to soothe this hypersensitive baby.

Sometimes, parents' troubled feelings relate to some aspect of their children (e.g., a spirited temperament) that the parents need help to perceive more clearly and to relate to in a more helpful fashion. Parents' troubled feelings may also stem from their childhood experiences and the disturbing feelings and painful memories that their own children evoke for them. In either case, the problem is real, and the solution lies not in blaming the parent but in trying to understand and help the parent resolve the problem. This is parallel to what parents need to do with their babies—that is, to understand that when their baby or toddler cries it is not that the child is simply being bad but that there is something wrong that needs to be addressed (even if it is a toddler's tantrum that needs to be understood but perhaps ignored at the moment).

Existing in Another's Mind   On one occasion, when Celeste asked her to say something about what was helpful about their weekly home visits, Maureen said, "When you come to my house, I know you are really *there* for me." When Celeste listened to Maureen, she listened fully, encompassing Maureen in her mind, caring about what she was communicating. When Celeste returned week after week, commenting and building on what had gone before, it became apparent to Maureen that Celeste thought about her and cared about her in her absence—that she existed in Celeste's mind. For some parents, this is a new experience, for as children they too often felt

> Like little billiard balls, careening about from someone else's impetus, responding to that impetus, but left wholly on their own . . . until the next, unexpected external thrust. This will rarely have anything to do with what they want, or what they need. It is in that sense a nonorganic, episodic, lonely existence, and they are held in no one's mind. (Pawl, 1995, p. 5)

As Celeste caught and held Maureen in her mind, Maureen was better able to hold Victor in her mind—to be more truly there for him.

Celeste revealed her caring for Maureen and Victor in many ways. She showed the genuine interest that she felt in Maureen's feelings and thoughts about her past and her present. She listened nonjudgmentally to Maureen's complaints about Victor and helped her to understand the source of those feelings. She demonstrated trustworthiness by being honest, dependable, and consistent. Maureen could count on her being there as promised, on time (or apologetic if unavoidably late). She was attentive to Maureen so that her responses matched where Maureen was and could help her move forward according to her growing ability. Because she existed in Celeste's mind, Maureen's sense of her own capability and value grew and flourished; it was observable in her increasingly sensitive responses to Victor.

Principle 2: Be Reflective

Parent guides hold parents in their minds when they reflect on their experiences with the parents. They wonder about what they see and hear the parents do and say. Celeste wondered why Maureen described Victor as "a devil child." What feelings and thoughts, conscious or unconscious, were evoked by Victor that caused his mother to make such a devastating pronouncement? Celeste tuned her antenna to listen sensitively with her "third ear" to pick up signals that would help her understand the dynamics of the relationship unfolding before her. She contemplated the possible connections between Maureen's feelings of failure when she could not soothe her baby and her feelings of failure when, as a young child, she could not please her mother. Celeste continued to reflect as she observed patterns that confirmed this connection; these reflections helped her better understand what she observed. Because Maureen had the courage, desire, and ability to be self-reflective, Celeste was able to discuss these issues with her over the course of their work together.

Knowing that people tend to project feelings and perceptions from past relationships onto current relationships, Celeste examined the ways in which Maureen interacted with others, especially with Victor and with her, to gain a sense of any ways in which Maureen's early experiences affected her current relationships. Celeste also tuned in to her own feelings and reactions so that, with help from her supervisor, she could clear away any of her own baggage that might be interfering with her developing a relationship with this family. These phenomena, known as *transference* and *countertransference*, are present to some degree in most encounters among people, not just in psychotherapeutic relationships. "If left to unravel, unbridled by insight, transference and countertransference can undermine effective working relationships between parents and professionals" (Foley, 1994, p. 20). The goal for parent guides who are not clinically trained is not, as it is in many psychotherapeutic relationships, to analyze and explain transference and countertransference reactions but rather to recognize and manage them so they do not interfere with their work with the families (Foley, 1994). Being reflective is a major way to accomplish this. "Reflective consciousness involves maintaining an awareness of the multiple meanings that may motivate parents' feelings and reactions. Rather than reacting spontaneously to a parent's 'unreasonable' anger, we try to respond in a more self-possessed and considered fashion" (Foley, 1994, p. 20). Awareness of and reflection on one's feelings, reactions, and behaviors are also needed in order to give supportive and helpful responses. This may include an examination of one's history to understand and manage one's countertransference.

Janet, a young parent guide, was on the verge of tears when she came to her supervisor for support and guidance before going to a scheduled home visit that afternoon. When she had called to confirm the appointment, the mother had lashed out and shouted at her. She had accused her of trying to say she was not an adequate parent, in spite of Janet's careful attempts to provide concrete and emotional support. In her session with her supervisor, Janet was invited to explore her emotional response to the mother's behavior, including her feelings of rejection, a desire to retaliate, and identification with the child. She was also encouraged to consider how salient aspects of her own situation (e.g., her desire to have a baby herself) might relate to her feelings in

this situation. Through reflective questions, her supervisor then pro-
vided support for her to understand the mother's projection of her in-
ternal models of people and relationships so Janet would not take the
mother's anger so personally. They then discussed how Janet would try
to relate to the mother during the visit that day. Janet came back to her
supervisor after the visit and reported that, as a result of their discus-
sion during supervision, she had been able to see this mother differently.
"And we had our best visit yet," she reported.

Promoting Reflective Parenting   Parent guides need to be reflective
in their work with parents not only to enhance their ability to understand
and respond to parents more appropriately but also to help parents be
more reflective in their interactions with their children. Forming an ability to be reflective about one's thoughts, feelings, and experiences and
about the behavior, ideas, and feelings of others is an important part of
emotional development. This development is fostered by parents' being
reflective with their children. Parents do this by reading and reflecting on
their babies' cues to understand their needs, interests, and feelings and by
responding in ways that help them get their needs met. As their children's
cognitive and language skills develop, parents should talk with them about
their thoughts and feelings. To do these things, parents must be reflective
themselves. Parents vary in their ability to do this (Belenky, Clinchy,
Goldberger, & Tarule, 1997), and some will need considerable help from
their guides in learning to be reflective not only with their children but
also in their other relationships and in dealing with various life situations.

In the reflective model, parent guides wonder to themselves about
what they observe in order to understand parents and parent–child relationships. They also respectfully and carefully wonder out loud with parents and ask questions, not just to gain information, but also—in fact,
especially—to help parents discover things about themselves, their children, and their relationships. With these discoveries, parents are better
able to make adjustments that help their children develop optimally as
well as encourage self-reflection in their children.

Principle 3: Highlight Strengths

Recognizing and highlighting families' strengths is important in several
ways. First of all, highlighting parents' strengths for them enhances their
sense of self-efficacy, and a feeling of self-efficacy is one of the most important resources a parent can have (Gowen, Nebrig, & Jodry, 1995). For

instance, mothers who feel more effective as parents t
more appropriate caregiving (e.g., are more sensitive,
and engaged) than mothers who feel less effective (Gowe
Gelfand, 1991). Very few people are motivated to make
someone points out their shortcomings and mistakes; ins
able to do things differently. Many parents of young children, even those
who experience competence in other areas, have doubts about their ability to be good parents. They often need someone who will very carefully
observe and highlight for them instances of good parenting behaviors
(e.g., an instance of their reading their baby's signals accurately, responding in a sensitive way, and the baby's grateful response). When professionals highlight both the parent's behavior and the positive outcome
(e.g., baby's response), parents can become more aware of the effects of
their positive behaviors. Such observations, made over and over again, are
like food for hungry parents, giving them energy to keep on learning and
nurturing their children. Furthermore, when parents feel confident about
their actions, they are more likely to ask for help when they need it (Klass,
1996, 1997).

Parent guides must also constantly look for and highlight *for themselves* the strengths of the families with whom they work. They need to remember always that strengths are the building blocks for successful parenting and family functioning. While it is important to recognize certain
problems and needs, solutions come only from identifying and building
on the family's strengths and capabilities to overcome those problems and
meet their needs. Celeste built on Maureen's strengths—her intelligence,
capacity to articulate concerns, and ability to engage with helpers—by listening nonjudgmentally to Maureen's complaints and by helping her seek
and use other helpers, and marshal the social supports she needed. As they
continued to work together, Celeste used various strategies (see Chapter
3) to nurture Maureen's emerging strengths of sensitivity and responsivity in her interactions with Victor.

The strengths of families and their individual members come in many
forms including attitudes, beliefs, and values; problem-solving and coping
skills; personal skills and competencies; a willingness to communicate with
others and to seek help; and social and material resources (Dunst, Trivette, & Deal, 1988). Even behaviors that are dysfunctional (i.e., do not
function well for the parent) can be seen as "adaptive attempts gone awry"
(Waters & Lawrence, 1993, p. 66). The mother who self-medicates with
street drugs to dull psychic pain stemming from a childhood of abuse and
neglect is acting out an adaptive striving in an unhealthy way. In their
competence model of therapy, Waters and Lawrence stated that, "Believing that healthy seeds are always at the center of maladaptive patterns,

we look to symptoms as information about underlying strivings" (1993, p. 10). When the underlying strivings are recognized, parents can be helped to find healthier pathways to meet their needs.

One of Lynette's "adaptive strivings" was her commitment to take good care of her two children. She did this, however, by overusing medical care rather than changing some of her personal and familial patterns. Helen, her parent guide, built on Lynette's adaptive striving by guiding, assisting, and supporting her in obtaining a home of her own (away from a problematic relationship) and child care for Jeffrey, the older of the two children.

Strengths-based guidance also includes using parents' strengths strategically to overcome or compensate for limitations they may have. For example, Maureen had not been very good at taking care of herself emotionally (e.g., using street drugs and alcohol to self-medicate, getting into abusive relationships) but had demonstrated an ability to be assertive with professionals when she got a social worker to facilitate a parent support group in her community. Building on that strength, Celeste later encouraged her to enlist the help of other members of her Alcoholics Anonymous (AA) group in getting a baby sitter so she could attend AA meetings, thereby taking better care of herself by addressing her addiction.

2

Laying a Strong Foundation

The Building Blocks of Emotional Development

Fifteen-month-old Caitlin is sitting on the living room floor, happily playing with her toys while her mother, Sharon, sits nearby reading the newspaper. Caitlin is cranking the handle of a jack-in-the-box. When the clown figure pops up, she turns quickly toward her mother and laughs in glee. Sharon shares in her delight and says, "Wow, you made Mr. Clown pop up, didn't you!" After several unsuccessful attempts to stuff the clown back into the box, Caitlin becomes frustrated. She starts fussing angrily and again turns to her mother. Sharon comes over and shows her how to close the box. Caitlin repeats the sequence of cranking the handle and laughing with her mother when the clown pops up. This time, though, her hand gets caught under the lid when she tries to close it. She cries and holds out her hand to her mother who comes to her, kisses her "boo-boo," and comforts her. After a few minutes, Caitlin becomes interested in the new toy her mother hands her, and Sharon returns to reading the paper.

Caitlin has successfully accomplished the major emotional development tasks of a baby's first year. She is able to experience and appropriately express the full range of emotions available to a 15-month-old. She laughed

15

with delight when the clown popped up and wailed with pain when she was hurt. She concentrated on the task of trying to stuff the clown back into the box but fussed angrily when she was unsuccessful in her attempts. She freely expressed her feelings and needs to her mother—her delight when the clown popped up, as well as her need for help when frustrated and for comfort when hurt. She also demonstrated that she is able, with the help of her mother, to remain organized and keep from being overwhelmed by her intense feelings. This is an important step toward the development of the ability to regulate her own emotions. The secure attachment that she has developed with her mother allows her to explore her small world with confidence that her mother is available for comfort, protection, and assistance when needed. Caitlin's confidence and well-balanced emotions were shaped over this first year primarily by her day-to-day experiences with Sharon and with her father, Frank. Through these daily interactions, Caitlin is beginning to develop internal models of her parents as loving, caring, and dependable and of herself as worthy of love.

During her second year, Caitlin and her parents will build on this secure foundation as Caitlin faces new challenges. Conflicts will arise as her emerging sense of self and need for autonomy clash with her parents' need to set limits on her behavior. These conflicts are challenging for Sharon and Frank as well, but they provide important opportunities for helping Caitlin gain additional skills for regulating her own emotions and for controlling her behavior. By recognizing and adjusting to Caitlin's spirited temperament, her parents are better able to guide her development. Throughout these first 2 years, her brain and nervous system continue to develop in ways that both affect and are affected by her emotional experiences.

This chapter presents an overview of the major ingredients of emotional development (infant–parent attachment, internal working models, and emotion regulation) and of the roles that temperament and early brain development play in this process. Subsequent chapters illustrate with real-life examples how parents can nurture this development during the first 2 years and how professionals and paraprofessionals can support and guide parents in this important endeavor.

FORMING SECURE INFANT–PARENT ATTACHMENTS DURING THE FIRST YEAR

The formation of secure attachment with one or a few select people is a major achievement in emotional development during the first year (Bowlby, 1973, 1980, 1982). Babies develop a strongly felt need to know that their parents are psychologically and physically available and that they will protect them and attend to their needs. (The term *parents* is used to refer to those people who are the babies' primary caregivers.) Human babies have a prolonged period of dependency on others for their nurturance and protection. Attachment to those who care for them arises from this basic survival need. It is no wonder then that these attachments are imbued with such strong feelings.

Babies typically develop attachments with a small group of people involved in caring for them (Rutter, 1997). Ideally, these attachments yield a sense of security arising from their dawning realization that they are protected, loved, and well cared for; however, babies usually become attached to their parents even if the care they receive from them is not very sensitive, loving, or responsive to their needs. It surprises people sometimes to see a young child who has been abused by his mother cry when separated from her. Babies who receive less than adequate care, even some who are abused and/or neglected, usually become attached to their parents, but the quality of their attachments are different. These babies are more anxious and insecure because they cannot depend on their parents for comfort, protection, and love to as great a degree as the babies who develop secure attachments. Babies who are institutionalized, grossly neglected, abused, and/or subjected to a chaotic array of caregivers may not develop an attachment to any caregiver. If left untreated, this becomes a serious disorder. (This and other attachment disorders are discussed later in this chapter.)

The type of attachment that a baby forms with one caregiver may differ from the attachment that he or she forms with another. For instance, some babies develop a secure attachment with one parent and an insecure attachment with the other (Cox, Owen, Henderson, & Margand, 1992; Main & Weston, 1981; Steele, Steele, & Fonagy, 1996). This is good news because it means that a baby may develop a sense of security with one parent that may mitigate some of the problems arising from an insecure attachment with the other parent.

Assessment of Attachment

To assess how securely attached babies are with their parents, Mary Ainsworth and her associates developed a procedure called the Strange Situation (Ainsworth & Wittig, 1969). Although this procedure is not suitable for assessing individual infant–parent dyads for clinical purposes, its use in research has yielded rich information about the characteristics of infant–parent relationships that lead to the different types of attachment as well as the consequences of insecure versus secure attachment for the child's later development. This information is put to practical use by parent guides who work with families of babies and toddlers who are at risk for, or have formed, insecure attachments (Rutter, 1997).

The Strange Situation procedure is conducted when the baby is 12–18 months of age and usually is not used with babies with neurologi-

cal problems. The eight episodes that comprise this procedure are intended to be mildly to moderately stressful for the baby in order to assess
how the baby uses (or does not use) the parent to deal with stress. The
procedure takes place in an unfamiliar environment and includes the baby
playing with some toys in the presence of the parent who is joined shortly
by a stranger. In one episode, the parent leaves the baby with the stranger
and in another, the baby is left alone. The assessment is stopped if the baby
becomes too upset or if the parent requests that it stop. The security of the
baby's attachment to the parent is assessed by examining various aspects of
the baby's behavior during the procedure such as the ease with which the
baby separates from the parent to play and explore and the ease with which
the baby is comforted by the parent when distressed. Of special significance is the behavior of the baby during reunions with the parent.

Observers code the babies' behaviors during the procedure, and based
on the coding, babies are initially classified as having a *secure attachment*
relationship (Group B) or one of two forms of insecure attachment: an
anxious/resistant attachment (Group C) or an *anxious/avoidant attachment* (Group A). Later a fourth category of attachment, *disorganized/
disoriented attachment* (Group D), was added. In the hands of highly
trained coders, this procedure is a reliable and valid instrument for research on attachment with samples of babies ages 12–18 months. As noted,
it is not appropriate to use this procedure as a diagnostic tool with individual babies (due to the risk of misclassification) or with babies with
developmental disabilities. For instance, some of the behaviors that are indicators of *disorganized/disoriented attachment* are very similar to behaviors exhibited for very different reasons by some children who have neurological problems (Pipp-Siegel, Siegel, & Dean, 1999).

Types of Attachment

Understanding the behaviors that are indicative of quality of attachment
can help parent guides recognize infant and parent behaviors that are revealing about the dyads' attachment process. Parent guides do this not to
diagnose or classify but to gain information to augment their other observations so they can design appropriate ways to address any issues they
discern. (Chapters 4, 5, and 6 describe what to look for in infant–parent
relationships that help parent guides understand the attachment process as
it develops during the first year and what to do to help parents promote
this development. Chapters 7 and 8 include examples of problems in toddlerhood, many of which stem from children's insecure or disordered
attachments with their parents. Again, suggestions for helping these
parent–toddler dyads are presented.)

Secure Attachment   During the Strange Situation procedure, babies who are securely attached will typically separate easily from their parents and become absorbed in playing with the toys while their parents are still present. Because the stranger is not intrusive when she enters, these babies are usually not wary of her presence, though they may check with their parents to see how the parents are responding to this person. Secure babies may show distress when their parents leave, but even if not overtly distressed, they may signal their awareness of their parents' absence by glancing at the door and by playing in a more subdued manner. If they are distressed by the separation, they go immediately to their parents when they return, actively seek comfort (e.g., cling to or sink into them), and remain there until they regain calm. If they are not unduly distressed by the separation, they happily greet their parents and seek psychological if not physical contact through showing them a toy, "talking" to them, or establishing eye contact. They clearly prefer their parents more than the stranger even though they may accept contact with the latter. In studies of low-risk populations, the proportion of infants classified as secure ranges from 57% to 73%. These percentages are lower in studies of high-risk infants (Spieker & Booth, 1988). Caitlin, from the case study at the beginning of the chapter, gives every indication of being a securely attached child.

Anxious/Resistant Attachment   Babies who are classified as having *anxious/resistant attachments* with their parents (about 7%–15% in American nonclinical samples; Cassidy & Berlin, 1994) are not as ready to explore their new environment during the Strange Situation procedure, even when their parents are present. They are quite distressed by separation from their parents and cannot be calmed by the stranger. Of particular interest is their behavior when reunited with their parents. "They may stiffen the body, kick, push away, bat away offered toys, and squirm to get down only to cry for pickup again" (Sroufe, 1996, p. 183). (Due to this behavior, this category is sometimes referred to as *anxious/ambivalent attachment*.) These babies are not able to use their parents effectively to regain composure.

Anxious/Avoidant Attachment   Babies who are classified as having *anxious/avoidant attachment* (about 20% in American samples; Cassidy, 1994) behave quite differently in the Strange Situation from the babies with *anxious/resistant attachment*. They separate easily from their parents with hardly a backward glance. They show little or no wariness when the stranger enters. Even though they may show distress at being left alone, they usually settle down when the stranger joins them. They show little or no interest in the return of the parent. Indeed "they may ignore or pointedly look away from, turn away from, or move away from the parent"

(Sroufe, 1996, p. 183). The avoidance behavior they show their parents is not typically indicated in their behavior with the stranger. Although some of these babies may not look distressed when separated from their parents, physiological measures (e.g., cardiac measures, cortisol level) indicate that most really are—they just do not show it except in somewhat dampened exploration and play behavior (Spangler & Grossmann, 1993).

There are several other indications that their show of independence in the Strange Situation is a façade. When observed at home, they tend to exhibit approach-avoidance behaviors with their mothers. For instance, they may approach the mother but touch her for only a moment before withdrawing. If they do achieve close physical contact (e.g., climb up onto her lap), they rarely respond positively (e.g., sink into and relax against the mother's body; Ainsworth, Blehar, Waters, & Wall, 1978). Children with avoidant attachments also tend to be highly dependent on their preschool teachers (Sroufe, Fox, & Pancake, 1983).

Disorganized/Disoriented Attachment   A number of researchers found it difficult to fit all of the babies that they assessed into one of the three groups (A, B, and C) that Ainsworth identified. This situation was especially true when researchers assessed babies who had been maltreated. Therefore, Mary Main and her colleagues identified a fourth category that they labeled *disorganized/disoriented attachment* (Group D; Main & Solomon, 1990). These babies look very disorganized and disoriented in the presence of their parents during the Strange Situation. They exhibit behaviors such as

> Approaching the parent with head averted; rocking on hands and knees following an abortive approach; moving away from the parent to the wall when apparently frightened by the stranger; screaming for the parent by the door on separation, then moving silently away on reunion; or rising to greet the parent on reunion, and then falling prone to the floor. (Main & Hesse, 1990, p. 164)

Their behavior often is a strange mixture of the behaviors of children in the other three categories, for instance, seeking proximity with the parent then avoiding him or her or resisting contact if it is attained (Main & Solomon, 1986).

Attachment Disorders and Disturbances

Charles Zeanah, a child psychiatrist who has studied attachment and who directs intervention programs for at-risk children and their families, has described seven types of clinical disorders of attachment (Zeanah & Boris, 2000; Zeanah, Boris, Bakshi, & Lieberman, 2000). When the behavioral signs of an attachment disorder are only somewhat or sometimes evident, then they are more indicative of an attachment disturbance rather than a full-blown attachment disorder. According to Zeanah (1996), it is likely that only a small proportion of insecurely attached children meet criteria for clinical disorders of attachment.

In two of the types of attachment disorders/disturbances described by Zeanah and his colleagues (*nonattachment with emotional withdrawal* and *nonattachment with indiscriminant sociability*), the child does not develop an attachment with anyone. In the other four types, the children do develop attachments with one or more caregivers, but they exhibit behavior problems such as self-endangerment, extreme inhibition, hyper-vigilance and hyper-compliance, or role-reversal. A seventh type, *disrupted attachment disorder*, can occur when a child experiences the sudden loss of an attachment figure. (Characteristics of each disorder are presented in the appendix at the end of the book. Screening for these disorders is discussed in Chapter 6.)

Research on these disorders is in its infancy and criteria for assessing them continue to be revised and refined as new data become available. Only trained clinicians should assess children for the purpose of diagnosing an attachment disorder; however, parent guides can screen for attachment disturbances and disorders and refer children as needed for further evaluation and intervention. Although some behavioral signs of attachment disturbances/disorders appear as early as 9 or 10 months of age, the diagnosis of an attachment disorder is typically not made until after age 12 months. Therefore, further discussion of these disturbances/disorders is reserved for Chapter 6.

Caregiving Behaviors Associated with Security of Attachment

Babies develop feelings of security with parents who are warm, caring, sensitive, and responsive (De Wolff & van IJzendoorn, 1997). Like Caitlin, these babies are fed when hungry, comforted when upset, and helped to relax and sleep when tired. Their parents talk and smile at them and give them interesting things to look at and play with when they are awake and alert. They are protected by their parents, and harmful and frightening experiences are minimized. When they smile or fuss or look wistfully at a just-out-of-reach toy, their parents often notice and respond to these signals. Of course, any parent will on occasion be grumpy or inattentive, but if the preponderance of babies' day-to-day experiences with their parents are loving and nurturing, they learn that their parents can be counted on to care for them, and this usually leads to development of secure attachments with their parents. Some parents, however, face challenges to their ability to provide this kind of caregiving.

Challenges from Babies   Some babies offer special challenges to parents who are striving to help them feel comfortable and secure. For instance, babies with spirited temperaments tend to be emotionally intense and sensitive to various kinds of stimuli, and some are slow to adapt to change (Kurcinka, 1991).

The cues of some babies and young children are more difficult to read than those of others. This is especially true of children with autism and some other developmental disabilities and delays (Walden, 1996). Fortunately, there is evidence that a number of parents are able to compensate for their babies' disabilities in ways that lead to secure attachment (Lederberg & Mobley, 1990; van IJzendoorn, Goldberg, Kroonenberg, & Frenkel, 1992). Parent guides working with families of children with disabilities need to be especially sensitive to the effort that this requires and to support parents in these efforts. Although it is beyond the scope of this book to discuss how parent guides can respond to specific needs engendered by specific disabilities, the principles and strategies that comprise the relationship-based reflective model will be helpful for parents of children with disabilities as well as other parents. Of particular importance is the need to listen carefully and empathetically to their thoughts and feelings and to help them obtain the resources they need, especially respite care.

Even babies who appear to be developing typically may be difficult to "read." Nan told Diane, her parent guide, that Jimmy, her 3-month-old, just didn't like to play with her. Dianne watched as Nan shook a rattle for him. He expressed mild interest by looking at the rattle, so Nan, hoping to get more of a reaction, shook the rattle even harder. After a few moments, Jimmy started to cry, and Nan, looking dejected, turned to Dianne and said, "See, he just doesn't want to play with me." Dianne had noticed a blank look on Jimmy's face shortly before he started crying, which may have been his cue that he had had enough of the rattle shaking. Many babies this age would have signaled their need for a break by looking away, but Jimmy's cues for engagement and disengagement were more subtle. Dianne helped this mother "read" her baby by responding, "It seemed as if he was enjoying the rattle, but I noticed that just before he cried, his face went kind of blank. I wonder what that meant." When the mom did not respond, Diane continued, "You know, maybe it was his way of saying, 'I need a little break.' Babies this age do that when they're playing— they need little moments now and then to calm down. Let's watch him next time you're playing with him and see if we can see him 'say' that."

Babies whose chronic pain cannot be alleviated even by the most nurturing parents offer a special challenge to parents attempting to help them feel secure and safe. Anthony had serious and chronic ear infections throughout infancy and toddlerhood. His mother became frustrated by her inability to soothe his distress and began to think he was angry with her. In situations like Anthony's, parents need help not only with their attempts to find ways to soothe their babies but also with ways to avoid blaming themselves or their babies.

Challenges from Parents and Their Caregiving Environments The life circumstances, both past and present, of some parents make it difficult for them to care for their babies in ways that help them feel comfortable and secure. Some parents are so depressed, distracted, or distressed that they are simply not there for their babies much of the time or they may treat them harshly or fail to meet their needs in a reasonably consistent manner. All of these situations put development of secure attachments at risk. The various circumstances (e.g., substance abuse, mental illness, spousal abuse, lack of social support) that make it difficult for parents to parent well are described in Chapters 9, 10, and 11. The ways in which these circumstances may affect caregiving are described, and ways in which parent guides can help these parents are presented through a number of real-life examples.

Outcomes Associated with Security of Attachment

The types of attachments babies form with their parents can have important consequences for their later development. Securely attached babies tend to become cooperative, compliant, and sociable toddlers and resilient, socially competent, compliant, and self-controlled preschoolers (Cassidy & Berlin, 1994). However, babies with *anxious/resistant attachments* are apt to be somewhat withdrawn and dependent as toddlers and lacking in confidence and assertiveness as preschoolers (Erickson, Sroufe, & Egeland, 1985). Preschoolers who as babies have anxious/avoidant attachments tend to be highly dependent, noncompliant, and unskilled in social interaction with peers and often are described by their teachers as hostile, impulsive, easily defeated, and withdrawn (Erickson et al., 1985). Finally, classification in infancy as having a *disorganized/disoriented attachment* predicts aggression at age 5 years (Shaw, Owens, Vondra, Keenan, & Winslow, 1996) and deviant levels of hostile behavior toward peers as preschoolers (Lyons-Ruth, Alpern, & Repacholi, 1993).

The behaviors seen in these insecurely attached toddlers and preschoolers derive not only from their sense of insecurity but also from the coping strategies they developed to deal with the ways they were treated by their parents and other attachment figures. For instance, babies who are frequently rejected when they seek comfort learn to avoid these parents in times of distress to reduce the pain of further rejection. These are the babies who usually are classified as having *anxious/avoidant attachments* with their parents (Ainsworth et al., 1978). Such coping behaviors may be adaptive in the immediate situation but maladaptive in the long run (Crittenden, 1988). Some of the troubling behaviors encountered in parents may be derived from similar coping behaviors that they developed during their childhoods. For example, Maureen, whom we met in Chapter 1, tries to take charge and be in control of others. This may be a strategy she developed early on as a result of her childhood experiences of being rejected.

Secure attachments with their caregivers may also buffer children from having elevated levels of the steroid hormone cortisol during stressful situations (Gunnar, Brodersen, Nachmias, Buss, & Rigatuso, 1996). Adverse or traumatic events (e.g., encounters with unfamiliar people, separations from the mother, inoculations) can elevate the baby's cortisol level. These researchers found, however, that over time, young children in secure attachment relationships tend to exhibit less elevated levels of cortisol when under stress than children who are insecurely attached. This information is important because the amount of cortisol in the system affects metabolism, the immune system, and the brain. Excessively high levels of cortisol alter the brain by making it vulnerable to processes that destroy brain cells and, just as important, by reducing the number of connections in certain parts of the brain (Shore, 1997).

INTERNAL WORKING MODELS OF SELF, OTHERS, AND RELATIONSHIPS

Through countless moments of day-to-day interaction with their parents (diapering, soothing, playing, feeding) babies begin to form feelings about themselves as well as expectations of the significant others in their young lives. These internal representations of self, others, and relationships were termed "internal working models" by Bowlby (1973, 1982).

Who Are You, and What Can I Expect from You?

Babies begin acquiring answers to the questions "who are you?" and "what can I expect from you?" during their first months of life. Expectations of others evolve from babies' experiences with their parents and the manner in which their parents meet their needs. Babies who are well cared for, like Caitlin, expect to be fed when hungry, comforted when distressed, and played with when they are alert and ready for interaction. Caitlin is learning that the important people in her life are responsive, caring, reliable, and loving—people she can depend on to meet her basic social and emotional as well as physical needs. This provides her with a sense of security. When she toddles forth to explore her small world, she does

so with assurance that should she encounter something frightening, per-
plexing, or difficult, she can turn to her parents—her secure base—for
protection and assistance.

Babies who experience countless moments of joyful, sensitive interactions with their parents begin building internal models of intimate relationships as warm, loving, and pleasurable. When Maureen returned Victor's smile (see Chapter 1) and then gazed lovingly into his eyes, Victor
experienced all of the components of this event—his own motor movements including his smile, the image of his mother's smiling face, and his
inner feelings of joy (Stern, 1989). (It is also important to note that these
components were being registered in Victor's developing brain.) Celeste,
Maureen's parent guide, reinforced this interaction by speaking through
Victor so that Maureen would be encouraged to repeat this activity often
in the days and weeks ahead. When most of their interactions yield experiences of comfort, protection, and pleasure, babies develop an inner
sense that close relationships are love oriented, trustworthy, and nurturing
rather than power oriented, untrustworthy, and neglectful or hurtful. This
model is what these babies come to expect from relationships and, therefore, what they oftentimes seek from intimate relationships in the future.

Babies whose cries for help often go unheeded begin to feel that the
people they depend on are unreliable. Babies who look into their mothers'
faces and find only blank stares will begin to develop models of relationships as empty, distant, and unfulfilling rather than close, loving, and joyful. These mothers may love their babies very much, but their depression
or distress or alcoholism may make it difficult for them to express this love.
Other babies may come to view relationships as harsh and hurtful when
they receive this type of treatment most of the time from their parents.
These negative internal models of relationships with significant others
begin to shape the social expectations and behaviors of these young children. For example, Jane grew up in a substance-abusing household. Her
mother was inconsistently available to her and unable to protect her from
her abusive father. By the time she was removed from her home at age 8
years, she was aggressive toward her mother and her peers, disruptive at
school, was very angry in general, and had a very low frustration level.

Who Am I?

During the first year, the seeds of the baby's sense of self are also sown.
Not only are babies developing an inner sense of others and of attachment
relationships, but within these relationships, they are also beginning to
form complementary internal working models of themselves. Babies who
are loved view themselves as lovable. Babies whose needs are met feel wor-

thy of attention and care. When babies' attempts to figure things out and make things work are supported, they develop competence and confidence; their budding sense of self-efficacy and worthiness propel them into even greater efforts at mastery. Their open, comfortable relationships with others prompt them to seek assistance when needed. Babies whose cries of distress are ignored, whose bids for attention are met with harshness, and whose needs for joyful interactions are unfulfilled develop a sense of self as unworthy, lacking in value, inept, and unlovable. When their parent guides first met them, Lisa was too depressed to have joyful interactions with her son, Ethan, and Maureen was so frustrated that she often responded harshly to her son, Victor. These parents needed all of the support and guidance they could get in order to overcome obstacles to being able to nurture the development of positive internal working models in their young children. Often this involved some modification of their own models of self, others, and relationships.

Early on, a person's internal working model begins to affect how they behave with others. The following example illustrates how two children reacted very differently in similar situations, suggesting dissimilar internal working models:

> A child approaches another and asks to play. Turned down, the child goes off and sulks in a corner. A second child receiving the same negative reaction skips on to another partner and successfully engages him in play. Their experiences of rejection are vastly different. Each receives confirmation of quite different inner working models. (Sroufe, 1988, p. 23)

Creating Their Own Worlds

The two children in the previous example are, in a small way, creating different worlds—different sets of experiences—for themselves. The first child has begun to create a personal environment of isolation from support and interaction. Her separation may further reinforce her internal model of others as being unavailable, which in turn may cause her to reject others before they can reject her, thereby confirming her belief that she is on her own in a hostile environment. By continuing to act on this belief, she creates the environment she has come to expect. On the contrary, if the second child continues to act as though she expects people to accept her, she will probably enjoy an active social life.

As illustrated in the previous example, perceptions and expectations stemming from internal working models often become self-fulfilling prophecies, in large part because these expectations lead individuals to act in ways that elicit certain reactions from others. The following example demonstrates how this phenomenon sometimes happens in preschool classrooms.

A study by Sroufe and Fleeson (1988) found that children with insecure attachment histories tended to elicit from teachers either controlling and angry reactions or undue nurturance. Which reaction depended on the particular quality of the children's early relationships (i.e., the nature of their attachments as infants with their mothers) that in turn affected their behavior in the classroom. The teachers were more controlling but had fewer expectations of compliance with the insecurely attached children than with those with histories of secure attachments. With children with histories of *anxious/resistant attachment*, teachers were highly engaged and very nurturant, whereas with children with *anxious/avoidant attachments* they tended to express more anger. Not all teachers, however, reacted in these ways. They may have been the ones who could see a wounded soul beneath a child's surface persona. Sometimes parent guides are in a position to help others (e.g., child care providers, foster parents) change their perceptions so that they see wounded souls in need of healing rather than just bad behaviors in need of correction.

Internal working models continue to affect how people feel about themselves and relate to others throughout the life span. These deep assumptions about self and others generate perceptions and expectations that then influence behavior. This knowledge is useful for helping people who work with families understand not only some of the troubling behaviors of children but of the parents as well. The behaviors of the parents with whom parent guides and others work are also governed by their internal working models of self, others, and relationships. Parents who were let down and disappointed time and again by their parents and others in their lives may have a very hard time expecting anything different from their parent guides or other professionals. They will often perceive rejection when none was intended and have difficulty believing signs of acceptance. Take the case of parents in Project STEEP (Steps Toward Effective and Enjoyable Parenting) who consistently missed appointments for home visits and group sessions but later (because their parent guides managed to stay the course) thanked them for not giving up on them as everyone else had (Egeland & Erickson, 1990). It would have been easy for the parent guides to have simply dismissed these parents as unmotivated, but they did not. When parents behave in ways that are frustrating, disappointing, and even irritating, it is often difficult to avoid being pulled into their models of what relationships are like. It is imperative, however, that parent guides and other professionals break these patterns by not responding in the ways the parents, due to their past experiences, expect. In so doing, professionals provide important opportunities for these parents to experience different, healthier relationships. In time, this may help them modify their internal working models of self, others, and relationships in ways that can benefit their relationships with others, including their children. When parent guides observe troubling behaviors in either parents or children, they can wonder what internal working models are causing those behaviors and how they can provide, and help parents provide, corrective emotional experiences.

Changing Internal Working Models

Helping parents promote positive internal models within their children often involves helping the parents modify their own internal models. These internal representations of self, others, and relationships are called *working models* because they are works in progress (Bretherton, 1985). Although it is usually a slow and difficult process, especially for adults, these internal models can be affected by new experiences and thus altered. Because of their childhood experiences, Maureen, Lisa, and Lynette developed many negative internal representations that interfered with their enjoyment of life, as well as their ability to parent well. Using relationship-based reflective strategies, Helen and Celeste kept delivering the message to them: "You are a worthy person; you have many strengths (and here's what they are). I care about you and your child." Eventually, they began to act in ways that suggested that just maybe they were starting to believe it.

REGULATION OF EMOTION

Lisa, in her anxious desire to "do it right," would try to feed Ethan as soon as he showed any signs that he might be waking up, a practice that often resulted in Ethan's falling back to sleep after a few sucks. Helen, her parent guide, helped Lisa understand that it was okay, in fact preferable, to wait until Ethan was fully awake before feeding him so that he could finish his meal before going back to sleep. In this way, Lisa was soon able to establish much smoother feeding and sleeping routines with Ethan. These routines are basic to the establishment of physiological regulation—the first step in establishing emotion regulation.

A beginning ability to regulate their emotions is another important development for children during their first 2 years. With appropriate parent support and guidance, they grow in their ability to experience a wide range of emotions in adaptive and flexible ways. Transitions among mood states become smoother. They learn to tolerate more intense feelings without falling apart as well as gain skill in modulating the intensity and duration of emotions. They also increase their ability to recover from strong emotions and regain equilibrium. These developments are important because the ability to experience strong feelings enhances lives. Few of us would elect drab, colorless lives of flat affect in which we did not experience peaks of joy, moments of great enthusiasm, and the motivation that springs from outrage over acts of injustice. However, unregulated intense arousal such as explosions of rage and attacks of incapacitating panic can wreak havoc. So, the goal of emotional development is to gain the ability to fully experience a wide range of feelings but to do so in a regulated manner.

Initially, the responsibility for children's emotion regulation rests entirely with their parents, as when a mother reduces her baby's hunger-induced tension and distress by feeding her. As babies' abilities increase, they play more of a role in joint efforts with their parents to modulate their own emotions. When Caitlin could not stuff the clown back into the box, she coped with her frustration by turning to her mother for help. By the end of the second year, most children have developed several strategies for self-regulation; however, parents, other caregivers, and teachers need to continue guiding this process for years to come as children become better able both experientially and biologically to regulate their own experience and expression of emotions. (For instance, the frontal lobes of the cerebral cortex, which play an important role in the regulation of emotions, are not fully developed until early adolescence.)

Emotion Regulation Strategies

Coping by seeking help from someone, as Caitlin did, is just one of the strategies for regulating emotions described by Ross Thompson (1994), a research psychologist who has studied early emotional development. Several of these strategies (e.g., redirecting attention, using coping resources) are presented in this section. How parents promote the development of some of these strategies during the first 2 years and how parent guides can support these efforts are topics for the five chapters in Section II. Parent guides will observe parents as well as children using many of these strategies, sometimes in healthy ways and sometimes in maladaptive ways. When apparently inappropriate or dysfunctional behaviors are observed in parents or in their children, it is useful to wonder what emotion regulating function those behaviors might be serving. A mother may shield herself from painful memories by tuning out her baby's cries. Parents who abuse alcohol or other drugs may be trying to numb their psychic pain.

Redirecting Attention   A mother talks to her baby in "motherese" with a soft, sing-song voice, looking into his eyes. The baby responds with a bright-eyed gaze and a smile. The mother increases the excitement a bit, and the baby's smile widens as he coos and wiggles his arms and legs. In a few moments, baby looks away, and the sensitive mother pauses, sits back, and gives him time to calm. In this instance, the baby is regulating his emotions by turning his attention away and thus "managing the intake of emotionally arousing information" (Thompson, 1994, p. 32). Parents capitalize on the emotion-regulating effect of changing their baby's focus of attention when they introduce a new toy or carry an upset baby to the window to look at the dog playing in the yard. It should be noted, though, that distraction may not be calming for babies who get overly stimulated by new things, which is sometimes the case with babies who were exposed to cocaine in utero (Mayes, Bornstein, Chawarska, Haynes, & Granger, 1996). Other techniques such as swaddling may be more effective in these situations.

Gradually children learn to use the strategy of distraction for themselves. For instance, in a study of 24-month-olds, children who distracted themselves by playing with toys in a mildly stressful situation (e.g., while waiting to open a brightly wrapped gift) were less distressed than children who did not do so (Grolnick, Bridges, & Connell, 1996). As children develop, redirection of attention becomes internal as well as external. For instance, they attempt to regulate their emotions by thinking of pleasant things during a distressing event or by focusing on positive outcomes. Children can also redirect their attention in ways that help them cope at the moment but that are maladaptive in the long run. For instance, children who develop *anxious/avoidant attachments* with their parents tend to divert their attention away from the parent to avoid the pain of the rejection they so often experience when they come to their parents for comfort (Main & Solomon, 1986). This tendency to avoid seeking comfort from others will not serve them well, however, in other areas of their lives.

Interpreting Emotion-Arousing Events   Emotional responses to events are also governed by how these events are construed. To help them regulate emotions, parents often reinterpret events for their children starting when they are babies. For instance, a 6-month-old starts crying when the sudden loud barking of a dog startles him. His mother picks him up, comforts him, and says in a soothing voice, "Oh, that scared you, didn't it? It's just a dog barking at a squirrel in the tree. He won't hurt you." The baby does not understand the mother's words, but her soothing voice and calm manner reinterpret the situation from a frightening to a benign event. As cognitive and language skills develop, the verbal interpretations parents give of initially distressing situations become increasingly important. They provide children the tools with which they can reframe situations for themselves.

Babies also check in with their parents in unfamiliar, novel situations to see how the parent is responding. If the parent looks relaxed and positive, babies are more likely to approach, or at least not back off from, the unfamiliar toy or person (Feinman & Lewis, 1983). For example, baby Ellie was sitting in her car seat when Carla, her mom, stopped to speak to two friends at the side of the street. At first, Ellie smiled at the two who were strangers to her but began to be distressed as the two leaned closer and continued to talk, look, and smile at her. She turned with a worried expression to her mother who smiled and murmured, "I'm not going to leave you; these are my friends, and they won't hurt you, sweetie." Ellie smiled warmly at her mother and looked again toward the two strangers.

Parents sometimes unintentionally frame situations for their babies in ways that distress them. When 10-month-old Christopher was dropped off at child care for the first time, his mother felt very anxious about leaving him and could hardly keep her tears back. Her behavior interpreted this departure as a dreadful event for little Christopher who buried his head in his mother's shoulder when the child care worker reached out for him. He then looked at his mother who was biting her lip. Christopher again buried his head in his mother's shoulder and had to be taken crying from his mother's arms. In situations like this, child care staff need to take time to gently and persistently reassure the child and relieve his or her distress. Reassuring the mother so that she communicates a more comforting message to the child is also important; some parents need help in dealing with their own anxiety over separating from their little ones.

Using Coping Resources   Various coping resources, both material and interpersonal, are used by children and adults alike to help them manage emotional arousal (Thompson, 1994). In fact, this is a primary method of regulating emotions for infants and toddlers, and the coping resources most often used are attachment figures. In healthy parent–infant relationships, babies can count on their parents to comfort them when they are distressed and to help them calm down when they become overly excited. Babies cry out for their parents when they are hurt or upset, and toddlers seek out their parents when distressed, just as Caitlin did when she hurt her hand on her toy. Sensitive parents respond to their children's solicitations by providing physical comfort (e.g., holding, stroking) and reassuring them in a soothing voice. When parents are not this responsive, parent guides can help them as Dianne did when Cory whimpered and went to his mother, Amy, when he heard thunder. Speaking for the baby, Dianne said, "Hold me, Mommy, I'm scared." Amy held and comforted him.

Not only do infants and toddlers seek comfort from their parents to lessen arousal, but they also turn to them to share joy and pleasure. Parents enhance these positive feelings through their playful interactions, taking care to avoid overstimulation. Parents are also a resource in helping babies calm down and go to sleep with lullabies, rocking, and other soothing routines and procedures such as infant massage.

Babies also gain access to material coping resources. Many babies learn to soothe themselves by sucking their thumbs or pacifiers, by stroking the edges of their blankets, or clutching their teddy bears. Taking their favorite blanket or stuffed animal with them to child care or a foster home often helps alleviate some of the anxiety arising from these new and unfamiliar situations.

A variety of coping resources are employed by parents for themselves as well as in the service of their children. Parents turn to others for comfort when upset, for advice about emotionally disturbing events, and for enhancement of pleasure. This is one reason why having an adequate and satisfying social support network is so important for parents. Among the other coping resources used by adults are exercise to reduce stress and caffeine, alcohol, and other drugs to either heighten or dull feelings and emotional arousal. Obviously, some resources are more healthy than others.

Selecting, Creating, and Controlling the Environment   Another way in which emotions are regulated is through both the selection and creation of living circumstances and through attempts to control and manage the emotional demands of one's everyday environments. Parents do this for their children when they avoid placing them in overly stressful situations and otherwise shield them from intensely arousing events. Unfortunately, for parents who live in violent neighborhoods this is a major challenge. Other parents who themselves lack adequate emotion regulation expose their children to distressing emotional situations within the home.

Children cannot and should not be protected from all stressful situations; however, exposure to such situations must fit the child's ability to deal with stressful circumstances. Separation from their parents is a common stressful event for young children. Sensitive parents try to ease the distress caused by such separations in a number of ways (e.g., by familiarizing the child with the substitute parent, letting the child take a favorite stuffed animal or other toy into the new environment). Several strategies for easing the stress of separation are presented in Chapter 12.

Parents also use this emotion regulating technique for themselves. They may avoid certain situations or people or try to manage a stressful situation by rehearsing what they will say or do beforehand, as Angela did when she practiced with her parent guide, Helen, how to request food stamps in English. Some parents remain in very distressing situations instead of moving toward more benign ones in apparent contradiction of this strategy; however, leaving an abusive spouse or getting away from a life on the streets may be more anxiety producing than staying with the familiar, especially for people who have developed feelings of helplessness from their life experiences.

Expressing Emotions   Emotional development includes learning to regulate the expression of emotions as well as the regulation of the emotions themselves. Helping children learn ways to appropriately express their feelings is a major parenting responsibility that starts during infancy. It includes letting children know that their feelings are valued even when the behaviors used to express them may not be acceptable. When parents ignore or punish the expression of certain emotions by their children (e.g., neediness, anger, fear), they may develop a constricted range of expressed emotions. But when all of their emotions are acknowledged and accepted, then they learn to express their feelings openly and freely. This does not mean that parents must accept all of the behaviors with which their children act out their feelings. As children become more mobile and expand their repertoire of behaviors during their second year, most parents recognize the need to set limits and redirect behavior, but children can learn that their feelings are acknowledged and accepted even though there are limits on the ways in which they can express those feelings.

Parents who were not given this kind of guidance while growing up may experience difficulty handling and expressing appropriately a full range of emotions and in accepting their children's expressions of certain feelings. If they are uncomfortable with anger, for instance, they may have trouble dealing with their children's anger. Marie's mother became very distressed when Marie appeared angry, due perhaps to her not having been allowed to express anger when she was a child.

The ways in which emotions are expressed can also have consequences for further regulation of feelings. If emotions are expressed in ways that result in satisfactory outcomes, then the person generally feels good about the experience; however, if emotions are expressed in ways that engender stressful, hurtful, or otherwise unsatisfactory outcomes, then the results are apt to lead to further emotional upheaval.

Self-Reflection   Self-reflection is of vital importance in the regulation of emotions. "The reflective self knows that the self feels, perceives, reacts, and so on" (Fonagy, Steele, Steele, Moran, & Higgitt, 1991, p. 202). Being able to reflect on the fact that one is feeling angry or unloved is distinct from simply feeling angry or unlovable. Being self-reflective affords children—and parents—opportunities to not only regulate their experience and expression of feelings but also to think about what is causing these feelings. Parents help their children develop this valuable skill in the same way that parent guides help parents become more reflective—by being reflective with them. Amy, with Dianne's guidance, was helping Cory take a first step toward being self-reflective by naming for him what he was feeling when he heard the thunder.

As cognitive skills develop, self-reflection can develop to include an awareness of how the views of others influence one's self-perceptions. Children who are often criticized may become super sensitive to criticism. As adults, they can reflect on how it came to be that they are so reactive to criticism and then use this self-reflection to modify their internal models of themselves and others.

TEMPERAMENT

Parents of multiple children often remark that their children seemed so different right from the start. A mother of four children said that each of her children arrived in this world with his or her own distinct personality. She described her first child as being very easygoing. "As a tiny baby, if she started to awaken during the night after her midnight feeding, a gentle rocking of her bassinet eased her back to sleep." Her second child, however, was described as highly reactive to sights, sounds, and movement. Being gently placed on a padded surface for diaper changes elicited a startle reaction, and being completely undressed and eased into a nice, tepid bath was out of the question for many weeks.

During the heyday of behaviorism, newborns were viewed as blank slates—tabula rasa—on which their personalities would be sketched by their environments. Now it is acknowledged that babies arrive in this world with biologically based predispositions to behave in certain ways, and that development is interactive between "nature" and "nurture" from the beginning. This means that parenting needs to be different for every child. Parenting provides a good fit when it is appropriately tailored to these unique predispositions or temperaments of babies. When parents and parent guides view babies' behaviors in this way, it makes it possible to normalize what is happening and to move toward establishing a good fit (Carey & McDevitt, 1995).

Temperament Styles

Some babies develop regular sleep and feeding schedules quickly, take to most new foods easily, smile at strangers, adapt easily to new situations, and accept most frustrations with little fuss. Children with these characteristics are aptly labeled *easy* children. In contrast, some children tend to have irregular sleep and feeding schedules; are slow to accept new foods; take longer to adjust to new routines, people, or situations; and express both positive and negative feelings loudly and intensely. Because many parents find these children difficult to handle, they were originally labeled *difficult*, but this type of temperament is now termed *spirited* (Kurcinka,

1991) in recognition of the many positive attributes of these children. A third group of children resemble the easy children in their quickness to become regular in their biological functions and the relative mildness of their emotional reactions, but they are much slower in adapting to new people and situations. They are generally referred to as *slow-to-warm-up* children.

These temperament groups were identified in a ground-breaking longitudinal study of 130 middle-class babies and their parents (Thomas, Chess, Birch, Hertzig, & Korn, 1963). As pediatricians who were seeing babies and their parents on a regular basis, Stella Chess and Alexander Thomas became skeptical of the then-popular behaviorist notion that the personalities of children are shaped almost entirely by their experiences, so they observed babies and interviewed parents at regular intervals during the first 3 years, beginning when the babies were 2–4 months old. From this study, they identified nine dimensions of temperament: activity level, rhythmicity (regularity in biological functions), approach/withdrawal, adaptability, sensitivity, mood, intensity of reactions, distractibility, and persistence. When factor analyzed, these nine dimensions formed the three clusters: easy (40% of the children in their sample), difficult (10%), and slow-to-warm-up (15%). (The characteristics of 35% of the children in their study did not come together in ways that fit well into any of the three clusters.)

The Chess and Thomas study has prompted an avalanche of temperament studies since the 1960s. Chess and Thomas defined temperament as the "how of behavior" (1996, p. 32), different from ability (the "what and how well" of behavior) and from motivation (the "why" of behavior). Different investigators have described temperament in a variety of ways. Some have focused more on the approach/withdrawal aspect of temperament and termed children who tend to approach novel and unfamiliar situations and people as *uninhibited* and those who tend to withdraw as *inhibited* (Kagan, 1996). Others have looked not only at tendencies to approach new experiences and to be fearful or inhibited in certain situations but also at how the child behaves when frustrated (Rothbart, Derryberry, & Posner, 1994). Others have focused on mood and have found a relationship between activity in the frontal lobes of the brain and this aspect of temperament (Dawson, 1994; Fox, 1994). Because irritability is a mood characteristic evident in some newborns, studies have examined the relationship of infant irritability and the development of infant–parent attachment.

Although different investigators have identified different (but often similar) ways of describing different aspects of temperament (Kohnstamm, Bates, & Rothbart, 1989), most agree that temperament has a biological basis influenced, in part, by genetic factors (Kagan, 1996). Recognition of the biological basis for temperament differences has brought temperament researchers and investigators of early brain development together in a new field called *affective neuroscience* (Gunnar, 1998). Research in this field is beginning to suggest ways in which some of the differences in temperament are rooted in biological differences. Knowing this, the parent guide can say to the parent, "Jenny is a spirited child. She came that way. She might be challenging because she is persistent and is intense in her reactions to things, but she also is likely to stand her ground and fight hard for things she needs. That's a good thing, isn't it? In the meantime, she may also need you to help her manage those little things that bother her so much like new foods, new clothes, and that annoying tag in the back of her shirt."

When parents are helped to understand how their babies respond to stimulation, they can plan ahead and arrange an environment that encourages the positive parts of temperament. The parent guide can ask questions such as "what is your temperament," "how do you fit with your baby's temperament," and "how could you plan ahead to avoid temperamental outbursts?" This can help parents who are having difficulty understanding—and accepting—why this baby is acting so differently from their last baby or their friend's baby.

Some Effects of Temperament Differences   In a previous section, we discussed how the children's developing sense of themselves (their internal working models of self) can lead them to create their own environments. The same can be said about temperament. For instance, children ages 2–5 years were observed during the first couple of sessions of a playgroup (Gunnar, 1994). The more inhibited children regulated their arousal levels by engaging in more familiar, solitary activities and using the teachers as sources of security and comfort. The more uninhibited children, however, ventured forth to socialize with other new children and sample the exciting elements of this new situation. It is interesting to note that the more venturesome children had higher levels of cortisol (a measure of stress) than did the inhibited children who played it safe, so it is not that the uninhibited children were immune to the stress of this new adventure, it is just that their temperaments led them to approach rather than withdraw from novelty.

Differences in temperament also influence the reactions children evoke from others. Parents and teachers alike will tailor their responses to differences in children's reactions to threats of punishment and expressions of disapproval. A teacher might know, for example, that to prompt 2-year-old Ben to stop climbing on the table, she need only say, "Ben, get down," in a firm voice. To elicit the same response from James, however, she must not only go to him and say the same thing but also help him down. Toddlers who throw fierce tantrums when frustrated are going to elicit different responses compared with those who only fuss a little. It will be harder for their parents to follow the pediatrician's suggestion to ignore the child than it would be for the parent of the child who fusses only a little. Children with strong approach systems who love to try new things may bump up against more sanctions than more reticent children do. For example, Matthew, the risk taker and intrepid explorer, heard "no, no" much more frequently than his more cautious sister did. Children like Matthew may begin to see themselves as bad because they hear "no" so often unless their parents view exploration as a positive behavior, arrange plenty of opportunities for safe adventures, and share their children's joy in discovery.

Irritable Babies   From birth, some babies fuss and cry more often than others. Even very responsive parents may end up responding to a lower percentage of their babies' distress signals than parents of less irritable babies who make fewer demands for response. Because parent responsiveness to distress is associated with development of secure attachment, are irritable babies more apt to become insecurely attached? A Dutch scientist addressed this question by observing a group of mothers and their babies from birth to age 12 months (van den Boom, 1989). This study found that the irritable babies did receive less maternal responsiveness and were more apt to be insecurely attached with their mothers at age 12 months.

Temperament Is Not Destiny

Although temperament influences a child's experiences (both those they create and those they evoke), it does not determine the child's outcomes. The environment, especially the nature of the child's relationships with primary caregivers, exerts a strong influence on how a given temperament is expressed (Calkins & Fox 1994; Kagan, 1994; van den Boom, 1989). For instance, in a follow-up study, another group of Dutch mothers of irritable babies were taught how to be more sensitive and responsive with their babies (van den Boom, 1989). More of their babies became securely attached than did irritable babies of mothers who did not receive intervention. Mothers in the intervention group learned to read their babies' signals and to back off when their babies turned away. They were encouraged to imitate their babies' positive behaviors (especially vocalizations) and to sooth them when they cried. The intervenors also coached mothers in how to play with and enjoy positive interactions with their babies.

Goodness of Fit   Chess and Thomas (1996) have found through their studies and their clinical practice that the extent to which parents' caregiving practices are harmonious with their children's temperaments is crucial. This *goodness of fit* between the child's temperament and the parents' temperaments and their expectations, beliefs, and values regarding child behavior is more important than any particular temperament characteristic. A sociable, energetic parent who wants to dash off to a gathering of other parents and their children will probably feel frustrated by her slow-to-warm-up child's reticence but experience a good fit with a spirited child who is also adaptable (which not all spirited children are). The intensity of spirited children is unnerving for some parents, whereas other parents accept the more robust temper tantrums and delight in their children's exuberance. These same parents may perceive the easy baby as being somewhat unresponsive.

When working with families of young children, parent guides can help parents recognize when challenging behaviors appear to stem from their children's temperaments. Often this alleviates the guilt and anxiety (even anger) some parents feel over their children's troubling behaviors. The parents who have been wondering what they have done wrong (or have been berated by family members) because Jamie will not sleep through the night as "she should" or because Casandra spits out all new food that's offered to her, can now see that these are simply temperamental differences. Temperament should not become an excuse, however, for letting difficult behaviors persist. It will be worth the extra efforts it will take to help Jamie develop a regular sleeping routine and Casandra to learn to accept new foods.

When parents are concerned about behaviors of their children that might be related to temperament, parent guides can first help them discern whether the problem might derive from mismatched temperaments. Parent guides do this by exploring with parents the characteristics of their own temperaments. How would you describe the energy and activity levels of both you and your child? How comfortable are each of you in new situations and meeting new people? How do you feel about being interrupted when you're right in the middle of something? How easily does your child adjust to change? How strong is your reaction when you are upset or excited about something? How about your child? The next step is to help the parent accept both the child's temperament and his or her own. Parent guides can explain that temperament differences are normal—part of what makes each of us special and unique. They can also point out the positive aspects of the different temperament types as described later in this chapter. The third step is to work with the parent to figure out how these two temperaments can live well together. They can begin by examining the situation that prompted this discussion and then explore other situations that may be influenced by the temperament characteristics of each of them as described by the parent.

In discussing temperament and behavior with parents and when observing them and their children, parent guides should be alert to the possibility that what they are seeing and hearing about may represent something more than just temperament. For instance, if the child's activity level is beyond being just spirited (suggesting the possibility of attention-deficit/hyperactivity disorder) or the child's lack of social responsiveness is not simply a matter of being slow-to-warm-up (suggesting the possibility of Asperger syndrome or autism), the guide will refer the child for evaluation.

Children with spirited temperaments are usually the most challenging to their parents. When the positive aspects of their unique characteristics are recognized, however, spirited babies can also be some of the most delightful children (Kurcinka, 1991). Charisa, a spirited child who adapts slowly to new people and situations, is fortunate to have a mother who provides many opportunities for her to confront the unfamiliar in ways that help her to adjust and feel secure. While shopping with her grandmother when she was 4 years old, Charisa was able to say, "I'm shy" to the saleslady who kept insisting that she reveal her name. This awareness and acceptance of her own temperament helped her transcend her own shyness so that by the time she was 6 years old, she would approach new children on the playground and engage them in play.

In their studies of inhibited and uninhibited children, Kagan (1996) found that inhibited infants whose mothers consistently protected them from all minor stresses were more likely later to retreat from strangers and unfamiliar events than children whose mothers had been accepting but had also made age-appropriate demands. Depending on their own temperaments and life experiences, some parents will need help recognizing and doing this.

Two-Sided Coins   Each of the nine temperament dimensions identified by Chess and Thomas has both a positive and a negative side (Carey & McDevitt, 1995). For instance, a baby who is highly distractible is usually more easily soothed. Later on, this child may have difficulty concentrating on tasks but be very observant. The child who, on the contrary, is low in distractibility may be oblivious to important signals but may be able to work efficiently in noisy places. A toddler who is very persistent (stubborn, the parent might say) may drive that parent crazy, but that same characteristic can serve the child well later in school. Parents may need help in seeing the positive side of some of their children's temperament characteristics. (Parent guides may also find it helpful to look for the positive aspects of the temperaments of some of the parents with whom they work.)

The Biology of Temperament

Findings from a number of studies provide evidence of the biological underpinnings of temperament. From an early age, temperament differences can be observed in children's reactions not only to novelty (new situations, unfamiliar people) but also to frustrations, threats, and opportunities to explore and experience interesting and pleasurable activities. These differences are thought to arise from differences in the ease with which various emotional systems in the brain are activated. Three systems have been described: the approach system, the frustration/rage system, and the fear/inhibition system. The baby who gleefully goes after the new, interesting-looking object on the coffee table appears to have a highly reactive approach system. The toddler who throws a huge fit when not allowed to grab the new object on the coffee table demonstrates a highly reactive frustration/rage system. The child who backs off when offered a strange new toy probably has a highly reactive fear/inhibition system. These differences are attributed to varying thresholds for activation of certain circuits within the brain (Rothbart et al., 1994).

EARLY BRAIN DEVELOPMENT

Like temperament, the development of infant–parent attachment, internal working models, and emotion regulation are closely linked to the early development of the brain. Metaphorically people tend to view the brain as the domain of intellectual activity ("he's a brainy person") and locate emotions elsewhere in the body—in the stomach (butterflies in the stomach, a gut-wrenching experience) or the heart (heartfelt gratitude), but the brain plays an enormously important role in the development and expression of emotions. Although there is much still to be learned, the research thus far underscores the importance of sensitive and responsive parenting during the early years to the healthy development not only of the brain but of the whole biological system of which the brain is a very important part. Four key reasons why such early nurturing experiences and their effects on brain development are critical to children are that

- Childhood experiences determine many of the connections that are formed and retained in the brain

- Development of pathways in the brain lays the foundation for infant–parent attachment and for internal working models

- Sensitive caregiving during this time of brain development helps children become more resilient to stress and develop other aspects of emotion regulation

- Effects of early trauma and neglect are significant and often long lasting

Use It or Lose It

Newborns' brains are immature at birth but undergo rapid development during their first few years. At birth, a baby's brain weighs only 25% of its eventual adult weight but makes rapid gains by tripling in weight from the child's birth to age 3 months (Chugani, 1994). Babies are born with around 100 billion brain cells, so the weight gain is due primarily to the tremendous increase in connections among them (the synapses) that accounts for the astonishing early development of babies' brains. When babies receive the kind of sensitive and loving care that Caitlin does, these connections form the basis for healthy emotional development.

During childhood, the brain is alive with activity as trillions of connections (synapses) are formed and traveled before some are discarded as not worth keeping. It is as though the brain is holding its options open until it knows what pathways it needs to retain. As a 2-year-old, Caitlin has as many synapses as she will have as an adult (approximately 500 trillion, 10 times what she had at birth). This number will double by age 3 years and remain at that level for a decade. After this, there will be a gradual decline in synapse density, and by the time she is in late adolescence, the number will be reduced by half through a process called pruning and remain at approximately this level (500 trillion) through adulthood (Shore, 1997).

Pruning does not occur equally in all parts of the brain nor does it all occur during adolescence. For instance, there is rapid neuronal growth between age 2 and 4 months in the part of the brain that processes vision (the occipital lobe). Pruning of these synapses begins as early as age 12 months, much earlier than in most other regions (Huttenlocher, 1994). Knowing this, surgeons now remove congenital cataracts as early in infancy as possible. The most dramatic amount of pruning appears to be in the cerebral cortex, where roughly 33 synapses are eliminated every second. Despite this loss, a section of an adult brain no bigger than a match head contains about a billion connections (Restak, 1995).

Through the rapid development of synapses during the early years, rich sets of connections are formed in the brain. Each neuron has several dendrites that pick up signals (nerve impulses) from surrounding neurons and an axon that, with the help of neurotransmitters (e.g., epinephrine, serotonin, dopamine, endorphins), sends signals on to other neurons. Each neuron forms up to 15,000 synapses during the early years (Shore, 1997). The increase in the number of synapses is aided by the development of spines on the dendrites that provide more receptors for accepting signals (Sylwester, 1995). Through these synapses, connections are formed among various sources of stimulation. Sensations coming from the outside world (sights, sounds, tastes, textures) are associated with internal sensations (feelings of pleasure, hunger, tension). Feelings become associated with experiences. When Victor's mother smiled back at him, the image of his mother's smiling face was associated in his brain with his internal sensations of pleasure and of his own smiling.

Neurons that are connected frequently tend to form groups that are favored when similar stimuli are encountered. They become like a pathway formed across the grass from one sidewalk to another. Once this group begins to resemble a path, it becomes the preferred route. Typically, the connections that are used most frequently are the ones that survive the pruning process. Shore describes this as a "use it or lose it" process, as follows:

> When some kind of stimulus activates a neural pathway, all the synapses that form that pathway receive and store a chemical signal. Repeated activation increases the strength of that signal. When the signal reaches a threshold level (which differs for different areas of the brain), something extraordinary happens to that synapse. It becomes exempt from elimination—and retains its protected status into adulthood. (1997, p. 20)

By the age of 3, the brains of children are two and a half times more active than the brains of adults—and they stay that way until adolescence. These early years when synapses are developing and there is a lot of brain activity afford wonderful opportunities for shaping the child's brain and hence emotional as well as intellectual development.

All of these factors point to the importance of childhood experiences because they determine to a great extent what connections are formed and which connections are retained. Connectivity is a crucial feature of brain development because the neural pathways formed during the early years carry signals and allow us to process information, including emotional information, throughout our lives (Shore, 1997). As Victor looks into his mother's smiling face and hears her voice responding to his cooing, these sensations become linked with feelings of joy. When Victor experiences this and similar occurrences repeatedly over days and months, well-developed pathways are formed that link sensations of his mother with those of comfort, pleasure, and security. The foundation is laid in his brain circuitry for a positive internal working model of his mother and for a secure attachment to her. Although these early positive experiences are extremely important, all is not lost if they do not occur as frequently as one might hope. Due to the flexibility in the development of the brain especially throughout the childhood years, later corrective relationship experiences can apparently strengthen otherwise weak initial connections regarding positive relationship experiences. Nevertheless, negative experiences during the early years appear to have deleterious effects on brain development and consequently on emotional development.

Effects of Trauma and Neglect

The experience-dependent nature of early brain development makes young children especially susceptible to the effects of emotional, cognitive, and physical neglect and abuse. Samantha, a teenage mother of an 18-month-old girl, Penny, and a newborn baby, Katrina, had been severely abused physically, emotionally, and sexually as a child. She felt unable to control her sudden emotional outbursts when Penny did something that irritated her. Samantha was probably experiencing what Daniel Goleman (1995) termed "emotional hi-jacking," a phenomenon that occurs when raw emotional responses are not modulated by the thinking part of the brain. The tendency to experience emotional hi-jacking is thought to be the result of early experiences that affect brain development in ways that influence the development of emotion regulation.

The limbic system, which is roughly in the middle of the brain, plays an especially important role in emotional development and behavior. This system can act like a rapid response team receiving a 911 call. A part of the limbic system called the amygdala is an important member of this team. There are two routes by which information can reach the amygdala (Goleman, 1995). One way routes information directly to the amygdala from the area of the brain that receives sensations from the outer world (the thalamus). This action permits a rapid response to a threatening situation; however, the amygdala's ability to judge situations on its own is pretty unsophisticated. The other route goes from the thalamus up through the thinking part of the brain (the cortex) and then to the amygdala. This provides an opportunity for a more reasoned analysis of the situation. At the zoo, people may see a rattlesnake and feel apprehensive (the amygdala kicking in), but they know that the snake cannot hurt them, so they calm down a bit (the cortex telling the amygdala to cool it).

Well-socialized behavior depends on the ability of the later maturing cerebral cortex to modulate the more primitive, reactive, reflexive outputs of the lower parts of the brain. This aspect of development goes awry if the lower regions (the midbrain and hindbrain) are overdeveloped and/or the connections between the limbic system and cortical areas are under-developed. Samantha's traumatic childhood apparently left her with an underdeveloped ability to activate the cortical processes that can keep emotional responses in balance.

Bruce Perry of Baylor University has studied numerous traumatized children, including those who escaped from the Branch Davidian compound in Waco, Texas. He maintains that when traumatic stress persists, the neurophysiology of the brainstem and midbrain tends to become overdeveloped leading to anxiety, impulsivity, poor emotion regulation, and motor hyperactivity. Furthermore, children raised in unpredictable, chaotic, violent environments often adapt by developing hypervigilant, hyperreactive arousal systems (Perry, 1997). The quick response system involving just the direct connection from the thalamus to the amygdala may be useful in the immediate situation, but overdevelopment of this more impulsive mode of reacting does not serve the individual well in the long run; this appears to be the case for Samantha.

Traumatic stress for babies is often accompanied by emotional neglect. In fact, having an emotionally unavailable parent is in itself a source of stress. Emotional neglect contributes to the underdevelopment of the forebrain (e.g., the cerebral cortex and its links with the limbic system). This, in turn, affects the development of such things as empathy and problem-solving skills. It is not surprising, then, that so many of the children whose mothers were emotionally unresponsive and unavailable during infancy were classified as insecurely attached at age 18 months and showed major signs of maladaptation at subsequent developmental stages (Egeland et al., 2000).

This chapter describes the development of infant–parent attachment; positive internal working models of self, others, and relationships; the emerging ability to regulate emotions; the role of temperament in emotional development; and the developments within the brain that support these important ingredients of emotional growth. These developments are profoundly affected by the quality of the interactions young children have with their parents and other people who play significant roles in their lives, such as child care providers and grandparents. The next chapter presents an approach to supporting and guiding parents and other caregivers that can help them as they strive to promote healthy emotional development during these important first 2 years.

3

Heart to Heart

Strategies for Guiding and Supporting Parents

Lisa looked dejected and awkward as she sat holding her first child, Ethan. The shades were drawn, and the lights were off. Lisa's expression was flat, her movements were slow, her hair was not combed, and tears welled up in her eyes several times during the visit. Helen tuned into the nuances of this picture and worked hard to understand and be completely there for Lisa. Helen, a social worker with training in infant mental health, was accompanied on her first visit with this young mother by the health department nurse who was concerned about Lisa and how she was caring for 1-month-old Ethan.

Helen knew that her work on behalf of Ethan would need to be guided by the three principles of the relationship-based reflective model of intervention described in Chapter 1. First, the work would be done primarily through Helen's carefully built and tended relationship with Lisa. Second, Helen would be intentionally reflective rather than directive in her work with Lisa and Ethan. In this way, she would keep Lisa "in the driver's seat" by helping her discover for herself ways to parent that would nourish Ethan's healthy emotional development. Finally, Helen would be vigilant in her efforts to highlight Lisa's and Ethan's many strengths, knowing that doing so would build Lisa's feel-

ings of self-efficacy and, in turn, enhance her awareness of her baby's positive attributes.

This chapter describes the skills and strategies parent guides use as they put these principles into practice in order to help parents promote the healthy emotional development of their babies and toddlers.

SKILLS FOR GUIDING AND SUPPORTING PARENTS

It is critical for parent guides to possess the following skills: assessing parent–child relationships, looking for and highlighting family strengths, being reflective about and with parents, and focusing on the quality of the relationships they are forming with families. To practice these skills effectively, parent guides need to develop the ability to

- Look and listen nonjudgmentally and read the other person's nonverbal clues

- Develop hypotheses rather than jumping to conclusions about what is seen and heard

- Empathize and be willing to be informed and taught by the parent and child

- Be fully present in the moment with the family while maintaining a broad and deep perspective

- Stay focused, especially in the midst of chaotic situations

- Communicate clearly, honestly, respectfully, and positively

- Relate with people of varying ages, cultures, and educational levels, and do so in a wide range of circumstances—with a mother making tamales in her kitchen, a toddler in his child care center, a father drinking beer on his front steps, a physician in his office, and a judge in the courtroom

- Work on the behalf of families in collaboration with a whole team of helpers

The relationship-based reflective approach relies more on guiding parents than on direct teaching: "Imagine yourself standing behind your client and peering over his shoulder and see what he sees" (Berg, 1994, p. 53).

STRATEGIES FOR ASSESSING AND PLANNING

Knowing where to focus at any given time depends on keen and insightful ongoing assessment of the parent–child relationship and factors that seem to be affecting that relationship. The characteristics of each family (strengths, needs, aspirations, expectations, and concerns) determine the specific ways in which parent guides apply the principles of the relationship-based reflective model and the strengths-based approach in their work with families. The process begins when parent guides meet with parents to discuss what they hope to accomplish and what they can expect from one another.

Clarifying Expectations

There are many reasons why a professional might enter into a relationship with a family: to offer support and information to new parents and parents of babies with developmental disabilities, to provide health care, and to protect the child's physical and psychological safety. When parents initiate the contact, they usually have expectations of what they will gain from the relationship and what their role will be. For instance, when they take their babies to the pediatrician, they expect that the doctor will help them with the health care of their children. When the contact is initiated by a professional, however, the expectation may not be this clear. Professionals have the responsibility, then, of helping parents to understand their role. For example, a nurse may offer support and information services to first-time parents; a CPS worker may assess a family's need for help in protecting their child's safety; and an early intervention specialist may contact a family with a very premature baby to offer guidance on special handling in order for the baby to develop optimally.

In their initial contacts, these professionals explain and offer their services, stress that parents have a choice (if they do), and invite questions from parents. They allow parents to think about their offers, and they make further contacts when invited to do so. In these further contacts, professionals clearly describe what they can (and cannot) do, and what their expectations are for the families. They also demonstrate with their behavior that parents can expect respect; for instance, they ask permission before entering the family's space or picking up the child. Parents are informed when certain assistance is provided that will not be provided on an ongoing basis, such as taking the parent to her first parent's group meeting. Some parents may be uncertain as to what they might request of their parent guides. J.H. Pawl, who works with parents, once told a parent in this situation, "I will take care of myself, and I will always tell you if I feel that something is too much. It is not your responsibility to worry about; it is mine" (1995, p. 5).

Future problems can sometimes be avoided by being clear at the beginning about appointments. "You can count on my being here on time and letting you know as soon as possible if something prevents me from doing so. I need for you to be here at the times we agree on and to let me know as soon as you can if you can't be here then." If the parent doesn't have a telephone, options for notifying each other (e.g., leaving a message with a neighbor) can be discussed. Parent guides especially need to also have clear agreements with families regarding how long their visits will be.

Although they lay out these expectations for families, some programs find they need to have some flexibility regarding no-shows. In one program that had a policy of not dropping mothers due to missed appointments, some mothers later told their parent guides that this was

> Their first experience with someone who 'hung in there' with them, and some even ... admitted later that they 'tested' their facilitator early in the program to see what she would do. In one mother's words, 'She was the first person who ever thought I could come through.' (Erickson, Korfmacher, & Egeland, 1992, p. 504)

Some parents, due to past experiences, have difficulty trusting that anyone truly cares about them—they may need repeated demonstrations of caring to penetrate this wall of mistrust. Therefore, some parent guides have an understanding with parents that they will keep coming back unless the parent states that they do not want them to come anymore. When a parent misses a couple appointments in a row, the guide can wonder with them about what is going on, thus acknowledging that there is an issue but also conveying a willingness to work it out with them.

Another scheduling issue parent guides sometimes face is when a parent raises a new, significant-sounding issue just as their parent guide goes to the door at the end of the scheduled 1-hour visit. When this happens, the parent guide can offer to make a note of it and promise that they can talk about it at their next visit. If it seems to be something that the parent needs to discuss sooner, the parent guide can offer a time when they can discuss it by telephone. When they do meet again, the parent guide may want to wonder aloud with the parent why he or she waited until the last moment to bring it up, that perhaps the parent wanted to discuss it but felt uncomfortable doing so for some reason. The parent guide should also question whether he or she had so controlled the visit that the parent did not get a chance to bring up the concern earlier.

In dealing with parents who test the boundaries, parent guides do, of course, have to deal with their agencies' constraints and the desire to balance the needs of families with the reality of often limited resources. They will be helped in this balancing act by holding onto the principles of being relationship-based (How can I gain this mother's trust?) and reflective (I wonder why she is testing our relationship in this way?).

Identifying Strengths, Needs, Concerns, and Goals

Through careful assessments of the parent–child relationship and of factors that can affect that relationship (e.g., characteristics of the child, the parent(s), and the caregiving environment), parent guides can begin to identify ways to help parents promote their children's emotional development. Such assessments are especially important during the early stages of their work together, and they continue to be an essential part of the ongoing intervention. The initial assessment process starts with information from the referral source and continues through the use of both formal and informal assessment procedures throughout the course of intervention.

Referral Information   Beginning with information parent guides receive from referral sources, they should look for strengths that can enhance parents' interactions with their babies and toddlers as well as needs that they may want to address with the parents. Information such as "the parents are interested in receiving information and assistance," "the baby's senses are intact," and "there is evidence of family and/or community supports," point to some strengths that can be relied on to help parent–child relationships. If strengths such as these are not noted, the guide should ask questions of the referring agent in order to identify strengths with which to connect at the beginning of the relationship with parents. The referring agents can also be asked about any additional issues that may need to be addressed. In the example of Lisa, the health department nurse was concerned about Lisa's apparent depression and its effect on her parenting. She reported that Lisa often left Ethan for long periods of time in the care of her former neighbors.

Interviewing Parents   By asking parents to identify their own and their children's needs and strengths, the parent guide not only elicits this information but also communicates to parents that they are the experts on their own children and that they are in charge of their own lives. The message from the guide to the parent is: I am here to help you achieve *your* goals. Sometimes parents' goals may be straightforward, and it is clear how guides can help them achieve them. Parents may want to learn how to care for their babies, to understand how babies learn, to get good child care so they can go back to school, or to get support (e.g., respite, answers to questions, material resources) when they need it. At other times, parents' goals are not so straightforward or their goals and the goals of the referring agent are not the same—as when CPS refers parents for help with parenting skills after an investigation of alleged neglect or abuse. In this situation, parents often feel they are doing the best that can be expected and that what they really need is help getting basic needs met and "getting CPS off my back." The guide's challenge is to decide with parents on goals and activities that will help them feel supported, which may well include doing what it takes to assure CPS—and themselves—that their children will be safe and adequately cared for. Parent guides can work with the parents and CPS staff to develop service plans that state measurable outcomes relevant to the issues that brought the children into CPS care. (This topic is revisited in Chapter 12 in the section on children removed from their parents due to maltreatment.)

Interviewing parents about pregnancies and their children's births and early weeks or months can help parent guides identify strengths and needs, as well. For instance, mothers who have lost a baby in the perinatal period may experience relationship disturbances with babies born subsequently (Heller & Zeanah, 1999). With these mothers, parent guides may want to explore with them their feelings about their loss to determine if they seem to have resolved feelings of guilt or fear related to the loss.

Asking about the pregnancy, birth, and early weeks of the present child is also helpful. Celeste asked Maureen to tell her more about Victor, starting with the pregnancy, explaining, "It will help me know how to help if I know as much as I can about him and his family and how you all do together." As Maureen gave the account of a typical but stressful pregnancy and delivery, Celeste encouraged her by asking open-ended questions for clarification and accepting information neutrally, neither reacting strongly nor trying to minimize the difficulties. When Maureen said Victor was angry from the moment he arrived, for example, Celeste nodded and waited for Maureen to continue. Maureen then went on to describe how Victor seemed to cry angrily from the beginning and how angry she was feeling about not being able to quiet Victor now. The Working Model of the Child Interview (Benoit, Zeanah, Parker, Nicholson, & Coolbear, 1997) presents several questions that might be used to explore with parents their thoughts and feelings about their babies:

- What was your reaction to having a boy/girl? Your husband/partner's reaction?

- How did you decide on your child's name?

- How would you describe your child's personality?

During the early interviews, Lisa shared with Helen her feeling of success and accomplishment in her job at a fast-food restaurant. The contrast between her feelings of competence in this job and her feelings of inadequacy as a mother were readily apparent. Helen acknowledged to Lisa that it can be frustrating to be successful in one area and then to be placed in a situation where it feels that nothing you do quite works. She went on to share that she had worked with other parents who had experienced this frustration, for example, a mother who was an attorney and felt much more competent defending her client in court than she did taking care of her baby at home. Not only did Helen help Lisa to realize her feelings were typical by sharing the experiences of other mothers, but over time she also built on the information Lisa shared about her feelings of competence in her job to help Lisa regain some of her sense of self-efficacy.

Listening to parents tell about their lives, both as children and as adults, is an important way to gain information about factors that may influence their parenting behavior in both positive and negative ways. Parents vary in their tendencies to talk about their past and current situations. Some parents may share their stories more with their behaviors than with words, as in the case of the mother described by Selma Fraiberg and her associates, "We see the baby in her mother's arms screaming hopelessly; she does not turn to her mother for comfort. The mother looks distant, self-absorbed. She makes an absent gesture to comfort the baby, then gives up. She looks away" (Fraiberg, Adelson, & Shapiro, 1975, p. 391). When the staff later discussed this incident, they said to each other incredulously, "It's as if this mother doesn't *hear* her baby's cries!" (Fraiberg et al., 1975, p. 392). As they continued to work with this mother and her baby, they learned that the mother's cries as a child went unheeded. These lingering effects of childhood experiences on parents' behavior with their own children are, in Fraiberg's words, "the ghosts in the nursery." Listening as parents tell their stories in both words and behaviors can be an intervention as well as an assessment, especially for parents, like the mother in this example, whose own childhoods were troubled.

Important information about what families view as their needs can be gained by using a checklist of family concerns such as the Family Concerns Indicator (Project AIMS [Attachment, Intervention, Mastery, and Support], 1990). Using this tool, the parent can indicate whether any of the listed concerns have occurred within their family and whether any of them are of concern at that time. The list contains items such as hospitalizations, legal problems, housing or transportation difficulties, problems with alcohol or drugs, and job or work difficulties. Although the parent may not wish to share this information initially, use of the list lets them know that these are things that the parent guide is willing to help them get assistance with, and they may decide to share this information at a later time.

Structured Observation   Using a checklist of infant and caregiver behaviors that are indicators of their type of interaction offers another way of identifying strengths and needs in parent–child interaction. Using the AIMS Family Observation Checklist, Celeste noted that Victor made eye contact with his mother from time to time and that he brightened when his mother put out her arms to pick him up in response to reading his cues correctly. She noted that Maureen responded to Victor's satiation cues when feeding him and that she smiled in response to his broad smile. Celeste also looked for instances when Maureen described Victor in positive ways (Maureen described him negatively in initial contacts). Checklists such as this one help guides become aware not only of what they see but of what they don't see occurring in parent–child interactions.

Ongoing Assessments   While initial assessment procedures are important for launching the intervention process, ongoing assessments reveal the changing and emerging needs and strengths of the child and family. These ongoing assessments focus on the everyday behaviors of babies, toddlers, and their parents that naturally occur during home and office visits. Sometimes the parent guide will suggest things that the parent may try or prompt some behavior through the various strategies suggested later in this chapter. Informal assessments occur each time the parent guide meets with the children and their parents. They are often cyclical in nature, beginning with sensitive observations and active listening followed by reflection (sometimes with the parent) on what is or is not seen and heard, and then, if called for, some intervention followed by more observation and reflection. "Through a cycle of intervention and reevaluation—by putting into practice the ideas or hypotheses raised by the initial assessment procedures—more information will be acquired that can serve the dual purpose of refining assessments and enhancing interventions" (Meisels, 2001, p. 6).

These interventions that stem from parent guides' observations and reflections may involve coaching parents as they interact with their children, as Celeste does when she engages Maureen and Victor in floor time (described later in this chapter), or they may be simple comments such as the one Celeste makes in the following example. Celeste observed that, in the initial assessment, Maureen did not make any positive statements about Victor. A few weeks later, Celeste observed Maureen bouncing Victor on her leg, playing "horsie." Her intervention was simply to comment on Maureen's pleasure; Maureen responded with, "He has good balance for his age," the first positive comment about Victor that she had said to Celeste. Celeste responded, "He sure does, doesn't he," thus reinforcing not only the mother's positive comment but also her ability to recognize developmental accomplishments. Throughout the course of their work together, Celeste continued to identify strengths that could enhance the interaction between mother and child, as well as to determine barriers to this interaction. The material and examples presented throughout this book can act as a guide for informal assessments. More structured guidelines are presented in the AIMS indicator, The Ounce of Prevention Scale (Meisels, 2001), and the Developmental, Individual, Relationship-Based (DIR) Approach (Wieder & Greenspan, 2001).

Setting Joint Goals and Work Plans with Parents

Parent guides and parents need to agree on long- and short-term goals to pursue together and to delegate responsibility to each person for working toward these goals. For example, the parents of 15-month-old Samuel were concerned because he was not sleeping through the night. During a home visit, Samuel's mother and the parent guide agreed that the parents would keep a sleep record for the following week to get a baseline for how long Samuel was sleeping each night. The guide's responsibility that week was to research print and video information for suggestions about how to help babies develop the ability to self-soothe during the night. These tasks and the parties responsible for doing them were written down, and the list was checked off during the next home visit.

When parents have many things, past and present, that impinge on their ability to set and meet goals, such clarity and agreement on between-visit responsibilities are critical. The Intensive Home Visiting 2000 program in North Carolina used a visit form that helped provide this clarity. The form, used each visit, included feedback about activities decided on during the previous visit, told what the family and parent guide agreed to do between visits, and outlined plans for the next visit. This format helped the parents learn about structure, served as a tool for parents to form the concept of future orientation, taught the practice of goal setting, encouraged the completion of goals, and signaled the end of the visit.

When Parents and Professionals Do Not See Eye to Eye   Parent guides sometimes have concerns about the child that are not acknowledged by the parent.

Freida's parents, Martha and Arnie, were heavy smokers who remained unconvinced by Freida's pediatrician that their child's frequent respiratory illnesses were related to their smoking in the house. At one point, they confessed to Dianne, their parent guide, that they had not restricted their smoking to the bathroom and outdoors as they had told Freida's doctor they would. When Dianne asked them if they thought their smoking around Freida had anything to do with her respiratory illnesses, they each responded, "No."

Their flat denial posed a problem for Dianne—what should she do to protect the health of this child? Should she report the parents for medical neglect? The health professionals all agreed that Freida's health was compromised by this exposure to second-hand smoke. If Dianne reported that the parents were still smoking, she would only anger them. What if Freida were removed from her parents' custody? Would the result create even greater problems for her? Because the situation for Freida was not immediately life-threatening, Dianne decided that a more concerted effort could be made over the next few weeks to convince the parents not to smoke, at least not where Freida would breathe the smoke. Perhaps by acknowledging how difficult it is to quit and give up the positive effects of smoking, Dianne could interest the parents in trying other ways of achieving some of those effects—such as using nicotine patches. Another approach would be to simply override their denial, appeal to their obvious love and concern for Freida, and offer them information about the effects of second-hand smoke. As Dianne reflected on these various options, she also wondered why Martha continued to smoke even though it led to her serious health problems. Had she, at some level, given up on life?

When professionals' concerns are ignored or denied by the parents, as in the case with Freida's parents, it is especially challenging for professionals who want to help parents promote their children's development. These situations can include ways in which parents relate with their babies and toddlers (e.g., being punitive or emotionally unavailable), unsafe and unhealthy caregiving environments (e.g., no childproofing of house, second-hand smoke, violence in the home), and lack of treatment for personal conditions (e.g., substance abuse, mental illness) that interfere with their ability to parent well. Obviously, when a child's immediate safety is at stake, professionals must act to protect the child, but in situations where there is not imminent danger, parent guides should work to understand and help parents remedy the situation.

It is best to start by assuming that parents want what is best for their children, even if their behavior seems to contradict this. The next step is to wonder what is causing the behavior or condition that concerns the professionals. Is it lack of information, a carryover from a troubled childhood, some source of stress in their current lives, or simply that they know what is expected of them and do not agree with professionals, as in the case of Freida's parents? The strategies for assessing the needs of children and their families will help parent guides discover some of the answers to these questions. The foundation for successful implementation of these strategies, however, is the quality of the relationships formed between parent guides and parents. When parents trust their guides and have faith in their guides' knowledge and commitment to their welfare, they are more apt to follow their guides' suggestions.

Being trustworthy means being honest, and this sometimes means confronting parents' behaviors or beliefs. Beverly had 15-month-old Zeke with her when she came into Helen's office to talk with her about difficulties with her older child. When Zeke became a little fussy, Beverly pulled a piece of gum from her purse, unwrapped it, and gave it to him. As Zeke started to put the gum into his mouth, Helen said, "It must be the grandmother in me, but I get worried when I see him do that. I'm afraid he'll choke on it." Beverly replied, "Oh, he's used to it. He never chokes," but after a pause, she said to Zeke, "Here, give me that—you're going to make a mess," and took the gum from him. (Because Zeke was not making a mess, she may have said this to save face while responding to Helen's concern.) Helen then handed Beverly a toy to use to distract the child and said, "Thank you, mommy," speaking for the baby. Beverly could take this remark any way she wanted to—as thanks for taking the gum away or as thanks for the toy.

Another parent might not have taken the gum away from the child, perhaps to demonstrate that the child would not choke. Then, the guide could gently say to the parent, "Can I tell you why I am so concerned? I would like to tell you a story about a child who did choke." The parent guide could then tell a story about a child who almost died because he choked on something. "So when I see a baby who this might happen to, I want to give information to parents because I know that parents really want their babies to be safe." It would have been quicker for Helen to have simply said to Beverly, "Do you know that Zeke could choke on that?" and taken the gum away. This action would have prevented Zeke from choking, but it could have damaged her relationship with Beverly and might not have stopped Beverly from giving Zeke gum in the future. By using "I" messages and handling the situation in a nonjudgmental way, she showed her concern, provided information, expressed her belief that the mother wants her child to be safe, and allowed the mother to find a way to save face.

When Parents Spank A sticky situation often arises when parents hit their children. As in many situations with parents, there is no simple one-size-fits-all response. When it is the first occurrence that the guide has witnessed, he or she might say, "Wow, I never saw you do that before; what's happening?" The point is to keep the discussion open so the issue can be explored together. If the parent replies that he or she needs to spank to teach the child to behave, this conversation might follow:

Guide: How does that work for you?
Parent: Oh, it works! She stops doing it.
Guide: Do you mean she never does it again or just that she stops right then?
Parent: Well, it doesn't really stop her from doing it again.
Guide: Would you like her to really learn not to do that?
Parent: Well, yeah.
Guide: Okay, let's talk about some things that might work better in the long run than hitting her.

When parents strike their children in front of professionals, the professionals should wonder why the parents are doing it. It may be that this is just how they interact with their children, and they don't think anything of it, especially if they are in their own homes; however, it is worth wondering if they might be communicating something by these actions, especially if they have had trouble with CPS. Perhaps they are saying, "Help, I'm overwhelmed, and I'm about to lose it" or they may be testing the professional with the message, "I know you don't approve of this, so what are you going to do about it?" They could also be thinking, "Can I trust you to be honest with me?" or "Can I count on you to stop me when I get out of control?" As in other situations, parent guides need to pay close attention to the parents' demeanor. Do they seem matter of fact? At their wit's end? Enraged? Defiant? Parent guides also need to tune into their own reactions and any issues they may have about corporal punishment. Of immediate concern, of course, is whether the parent's behavior appears to be a threat to the child's safety. If so, then that must be handled. If the child's safety is not threatened, the parent guide can work with the parent over time to move toward more effective means of discipline while, at the same time, addressing any underlying issues that may be present. The bottom line is the communication of sincere concern for the welfare of both the parent and the child. Because hitting children is harmful to their development (Straus, 1994), parent guides should be prepared to help parents find more effective and less harmful ways to discipline their children.

Lack of Follow Through   Whether the needs and goals are identified primarily by parents or developed with input from parent guides, some parents may present a further challenge—not following through on agreed-to actions. This situation should not be viewed as a failure on the part of either the parent or the guide but should be used to identify barriers and make adjustments. For instance, Angela, who had agreed to sign up for food stamps, admitted during the next visit that she had not done so. Helen, her parent guide, acting on the assumption that this mother wanted what was best for her child, asked, "What kept you from doing that?" Angela explained in Spanish that she did not go because she was afraid she would not be able to communicate what she needed in English. Helen and Angela then figured out that Angela could overcome this barrier if Helen wrote out phonetically what she would need to say. They then role played what Angela would say and do until she felt comfortable that she could handle getting the food stamps on her own.

In some instances, parents may not follow through because even though they say they support the agreement, they are not really convinced about it. Martha and Arnie told Freida's doctors they would stop smoking around Freida. In reality they had not adhered to this agreement because they were not convinced it was necessary. However, they were honest with Dianne, which gave her the opportunity to continue pursuing this concern with them. When a parent does not respond favorably or is difficult to engage, it is tempting to simply walk away and view the parent as resistant or unmotivated (Greenstein, 1998). The same professional, however, would not consider it appropriate for parents to give up on their babies if the babies do not respond in the way they desire!

Hidden Agendas Versus Joint Goals   Parent guides may witness any number of troubling parenting behaviors, such as rough handling of a baby, hostile remarks to or about children, and unresponsiveness to a baby's bids for attention. Addressing these behaviors, even when they are not explicitly named as concerns by parents, is not the same as having a hidden agenda for the family. For instance, parents may spank their children because they want their children to be safe and to learn proper behavior. In this case, the parent guide joins with the parents' goal by helping them learn a more effective and less harmful way to achieve these results. When professionals have hidden agendas for families, they determine what the family's needs and goals should be and then attempt to manipulate the family toward fulfilling those needs and reaching those goals. When, however, parent guides partner with parents, they seek to understand the parents' underlying needs and goals and then use their professional knowledge to help parents reach those goals in the most beneficial ways. As professionals, parent guides should seek to keep themselves informed about best practices, but they should also learn from history and realize that the "best practices" of one era are sometimes considered the "worst practices" at a later time. Parent guides should share with parents their knowledge and observations in ways that respect parents' rights to disagree and disregard their advice, as long as the child's psychological and physical safety are not in jeopardy.

The model of parent guidance introduced in this chapter has been developed over many years in the practice of early intervention to promote healthy emotional development. The three foci of this model are 1) nurturing parents, 2) enhancing parent–child interaction, and 3) strengthening the caregiving environment of the child. Although each focus is described separately, the foci are most often used simultaneously, and some strategies can be used to address more than one of these foci. Strategies for nurturing parents and enhancing parent–child interaction are presented in this chapter. Ways in which parent guides can support and guide parents, while helping them gain access to needed services and resources to strengthen their caregiving environments, are addressed in Section III.

STRATEGIES FOR NURTURING PARENTS

Parents come to the task of parenting with different natures and temperaments. They differ in childhood experiences as well as the situations surrounding their becoming parents. This section describes and illustrates eight strategies for nurturing parents: listening and following the parent's lead, highlighting and building on strengths, providing concrete assistance, promoting use of formal and informal supports, teaching coping and solution-finding skills, helping parents tell their stories, setting limits, and being consistent and trustworthy. The importance of nurturing parents cannot be overstated. As previously noted, a major impediment to the ability of some parents to nurture the emotional development of their children stems from the negative emotional baggage they bring from their own troubled childhoods. Nurturing these parents provides them much-needed corrective emotional experiences.

It quickly became apparent to Helen that Lisa needed support and emotional refueling. Lisa's sense that she was unable to please her parents while growing up left her with very little self-confidence to draw on as she faced this new challenge in her life—caring for her newborn son, Ethan. Ethan was 1 month old when referred to a home-based early intervention service. Lisa, a single mother, was described as depressed, and medical providers were concerned because she frequently asked others to care for Ethan. They were also concerned about the way she provided for Ethan's basic needs. For instance, she fed Ethan when he was half-asleep, and she had left him for several hours and even overnight with her former neighbor. Currently, Lisa had almost no social support. Ethan's father lived in a nearby county and was not involved with Lisa at the time of birth. Lisa's mother lived 1,000 miles away, and Lisa did not have a telephone. Her only source of social support had been her neighbors and her co-workers at the fast-food restaurant in which she had worked until the day of Ethan's birth. She expressed a sense of loss about having to stay home after Ethan was born. The strategies used to nurture and support Lisa as she struggled to care for Ethan illustrate some of the major ways that parent guides and other professionals can nurture parents.

Listening/Following Parents' Lead

Listening and following the parent's lead is the cornerstone of nurturing guidance for parents. It begins at the first contact.

On Helen's fist visit with Lisa, she literally sat at Lisa's feet because Lisa was sitting in the only chair in the room. Her observations of the dimly lit room and Lisa's appearance and demeanor confirmed the signs of depression that had been reported. Helen listened intently as Lisa first said that she did not know of anything that would help her. Following her lead, Helen backed off, giving Lisa the time she needed. Later, when Lisa tearfully said that she did not know how to take care of a baby, Helen validated her feelings nonjudgmentally, commenting on how nice it would be if babies came with instructions and wondered, "What are some of the things you're not sure about?" Lisa replied, "Most of the time, Ethan falls asleep while he's feeding, then he wakes up again in a little while, wanting to be fed again." Her eyes filled with tears when she said this, and her body posture communicated a sense of burden.

Wondering to herself what might be making these typical new mother experiences so overwhelming for Lisa, Helen asked her to tell about Ethan's birth and first month so she could get to know Ethan. Lisa told Helen how she worked at the fast-food restaurant. Co-workers guessed when she might have the baby and how soon she would be able to be back at work. When she noticed that Lisa brightened significantly as she told this story, Helen realized that Lisa had enjoyed the status and companionship at work and that others had perceived her as being valuable there. Helen reflected this observation aloud, and Lisa confirmed her sense of competence in that job. Helen commented, "It must be really different for you being home alone with Ethan after working at a place that you really liked." (Following parents' lead often means being with them in their sadness, rather than moving quickly past it to solutions.) Lisa tearfully agreed that she missed being around her co-workers.

Lisa went on to volunteer that she did not know how to be a parent. She talked wistfully about her competence at work and how alone she felt being with Ethan without transportation or a telephone. Helen commented that it must be really different now learning this new job of parenting, especially when babies do not communicate with words. Lisa responded with an example of how Ethan lets her know when he is hungry. Helen then wondered aloud what else Lisa was learning from Ethan. During this brief conversation, Helen noticed that Lisa was now looking at her, was not tearful, and had good observations about her son. Helen highlighted these observations, naming them as strengths that help parents know how to respond helpfully to their baby's needs. Helen was intentional about each response she made to Lisa because just as building a healthy relationship with her baby would happen in many small responsive interactions every day, so the parallel relationship between Helen and Lisa was being built through many small but significant interchanges, beginning in this first meeting.

Highlighting and Building on Strengths

The parent guides for Maureen, Lisa, Lynette, Linda, and Samantha continuously looked for and built upon the many strengths that these mothers brought to their parenting role. Maureen's courage and ability to be self-aware and self-reflective enabled Celeste to talk with her about her issues and early experiences in ways that helped Maureen to gradually free herself from many of the ill effects of her past. Helen was able to build on Lisa's strong social skills by bringing her to a parent–child group where Lisa gained support and companionship that helped her move out of her depression. In spite of her physical and mental illness, Lynette often demonstrated her enormous desire to give and care for other people. Helen highlighted these acts of generosity and caring and built on this characteristic trait as she and Lynette worked together to strengthen Lynette's ability to care for her children and for herself. As long as Linda was in recovery from her substance abuse, she exhibited many positive parenting practices. She read to and played with her children, established expectations for their behavior and set firm limits without being harsh, and responded to their needs appropriately. Her parent guide was quick to highlight these strengths for her as a way of putting emotional "money in the bank" for Linda to draw on when she became overwhelmed by psychic pain from her troubled past and was tempted to drink. Samantha's strong desire to give her children a better childhood than she had experienced combined with her intelligence and interest in gaining parenting information were strengths that her parent guide highlighted and built on as they worked together to accomplish Samantha's parenting goals.

It is important for guides to be vigilant in order to find these moments of success or strength to highlight and build on. Helen used highlighting to reinforce Lisa's good observations of her son during the first home visit. She also looked for and found a moment when Lisa was successful in holding Ethan in a comfortable way and quickly commented on it by speaking through the baby, "There, your Mama's figured out how you like to be held." Lisa can use that feedback both to guide future parenting behaviors and to help her experience self-efficacy. By commenting on the positive effects of Lisa's behavior on Ethan, Helen not only helped Lisa feel good about her behavior but also increased Lisa's awareness of the connection between what she did and Ethan's response.

Sometimes one must look very hard to find behaviors related to their children that can be pointed out to parents. In these instances, strengths may be found in parenting behaviors that are not directly related to interactions with their children (e.g., choice of the child's clothes or toys, attention to the child's room). Parents' strengths that are not directly related to their children can also be highlighted. For instance, at the playgroup, Helen highlighted Lisa's remembering to bring the plastic bags as she had promised. For parents like Lisa who have few parenting successes on which to build a sense of competence, it is important to discover and highlight strengths in any area of their lives. All of us need to be reminded of our capabilities from time to time, but for parents whose sense of self is diminished because of their own histories or because of particular challenges of their baby, it is crucial.

Highlighting parents' strengths is also important for parent guides themselves because it focuses their attention on parents' competencies. It can be difficult at times for parent guides to persist in finding and highlighting strengths in parents whose difficulties seem overwhelming; sometimes they need help from their supervisors to discover them. One supervisor, for example, asks each parent guide to begin any discussion about a parent by naming the strengths of that parent. This procedure is a regular reminder that parent guides can assist parents in their goal of parenting their children well only by building on the strengths and capabilities of families.

Providing Concrete Assistance

When parents lack fundamental necessities, having someone offer to help them obtain these necessities serves two important functions. First, it puts parents in a position to focus on their relationship with their child rather than on how they will feed, clothe, or house the family. Professionals are sometimes frustrated when parents do not follow through with suggestions they have made that will help their children develop. Further observation and listening may reveal that parents lack sufficient food, shelter, or safety. When these needs are addressed, parents are more empowered to attend to their children.

Second, providing concrete assistance when needed communicates to parents in a very basic way that someone cares about them and that they are worthy of care. When parents feel inadequate in their parenting role or overwhelmed by a particularly challenging child, they need care demonstrated in very concrete, tangible ways. For example, Helen took Lisa and Ethan to their first playgroup. Doing so let Lisa know that she was important, something she was not convinced of at the time. If Helen would have continued to drive Lisa on a regular basis, however, she would have fostered Lisa's dependence and feelings of inadequacy.

Parents who have internal working models of themselves as incapable and unworthy of care often have difficulty seeking and accepting the assistance that is available to them in their communities. Their lack of trust in others and in themselves may make them appear unmotivated and sometimes hostile to others from whom they need assistance. Parent guides can help parents feel comfortable asking for and accepting help. They do this by first withholding judgment and demonstrating that the parent is of value, has capabilities, and is worthy of help. Then, they can tune into the parent's unique situation and style to determine the right amount and type of assistance to offer. Guides can sometimes smooth the way for parents by helping other providers understand the parents and their needs and strengths. In this way, they increase the possibility that parents' attempts to use their resources will be successful and that these experiences, in turn, will enhance the parents' sense of competence and self-worth.

Timing and amount of concrete assistance are very important for guides to consider because they can vary from individual to individual and from day to day. For instance, a mother who has untreated depression may be quite capable of getting to an appointment one day but be totally overwhelmed with getting her baby and herself ready to leave the house the next day. The guiding principle for giving appropriate help is to assist in ways that promote, not undermine, the parent's sense of efficacy. This is best done by recognizing and building on the parent's existing competencies and by providing just the amount of support needed at the moment. It also entails being patient and allowing parents to proceed at their own pace.

When Leane told her parent guide, Dianne, that she had been thinking about pursuing her general equivalency diploma (GED), Dianne was delighted because she had been concerned about this mother's depression and self-imposed isolation; however, she suppressed her urge to jump in and offer to find a class for the mother, child care for the child, and so forth. Instead, she said, "Sounds like that's something you have been thinking about for a while. Do you have some ideas about how you would like to do it?" Leane said that she knew they offered GED classes at the community college but that she would not feel comfortable being around "smart college kids," and she did not know of any other classes. Dianne offered to obtain information about other classes and then helped Leane determine how she wanted to proceed. At Leane's request, she rehearsed with her the questions she would ask when she met with the teacher of a class in town. Although that meeting went well, Leane wasn't ready to attend a class outside of her community. During the ensuing months, Dianne continued to be supportive, but it remained Leane's project—she controlled the steps and the pace as she proceeded toward her goal. Eventually she not only enrolled in a class but was instrumental in getting the class started in her own community, and she earned her GED.

Promoting Use of Formal and Informal Supports

An important part of the parent guide's role is to help parents strengthen their ability to seek, maintain, and use formal and informal sources of support. During their first session, Helen repeated some of the concerns she heard Lisa share and then described the particular services that she thought Lisa might enjoy and benefit from. By then, Lisa was beginning to trust that Helen was interested in her as a person; that she, Lisa, had some areas of competence; and that feeling overwhelmed was probably not unusual, given the changes in her life. She decided that she would like to attend the parent–infant playgroup on Friday (3 days away), and that she would like to have a therapist for herself as well as a parent guide who could help her and Ethan get off to a good start. Even though Lisa could have used Medicaid transportation services, Helen offered to take her and Ethan to the playgroup because she knew that parents usually have a hard time going alone to a new place where there are people they do not know. As mentioned earlier, this also demonstrated to Lisa that Helen thought she was worthy of this special attention.

Lisa and Ethan were ready when Helen came to take them to the parent–infant playgroup. At the group, Lisa demonstrated one of her strengths—her social skills—while interacting with her peers. She shared with them that Ethan had slept for several hours the past night, and she offered ideas about topics to discuss in future group times. When Helen commented that they needed plastic bags to line the trashcans, Lisa volunteered to bring some the next week. Helen expressed her appreciation for Lisa's helpfulness as a way to highlight and reinforce Lisa's self-efficacy and positive internal model of self. The following week when Helen arrived to take them to the group, Lisa met her at the door with hair carefully styled, dressed in a crisp skirt and blouse, and with Ethan carefully dressed and safely in his car seat. To Helen, she looked like a different woman than the one she had met just 10 days earlier. On the way, Helen repeated a comment another parent had made after the playgroup the previous week, "I hope Lisa comes back; I really liked her." The power of the group to be a place of support and information increased significantly in that moment!

Lisa's depressive symptoms lessened noticeably even before she began formal therapy and received medication. The informal support she received from other mothers and the formal support she received from Helen, her parent guide, augmented each other to help Lisa make and maintain her gains. Helping parents strengthen their informal support systems is an important task for parent guides (see Chapter 11).

Teaching Coping and Solution-Finding Skills

Within the relationships intentionally built by parent guides there are many opportunities to nurture parents by teaching them coping and solution-finding skills. Helen did this with Lisa when Lisa began thinking about getting back together with Ethan's father 3 weeks after Helen's initial visit. He was visiting Ethan weekly at his mother's house, and on one of those visits he told Lisa that he was interested in getting back together with her. Lisa shared this with Helen and said, "I'm going to move real slow on this. I told him that he hurt me bad, and I am going to be careful about thinking about what's best for me and Ethan." Helen reinforced her cautious approach and then asked her some questions about what she thought would be best for her and Ethan.

These questions were not designed to give Helen information but to help Lisa reflect on her situation and discover for herself how to solve these problems and make plans on behalf of herself and Ethan. So, for example, Helen asked her what were some pros and cons of being in the town where she was developing friendships and services versus moving fifty miles away to be with Ethan's father. She asked her what Ethan's father might do to demonstrate to her that he had really changed. She wondered what Lisa would do for a back-up plan if things did not work out, and she asked if Lisa had talked to her mother and what her mother had said. The questions she asked were attuned to Lisa's ability to explore new possibilities, just as Lisa was learning to be attuned to Ethan's emerging abilities and needs. In helping parents gain skills in finding solutions, it is important to remember that the purpose is not simply that they will solve the immediate problem, though this is a worthy endeavor, but also that they will be able to use solution-finding skills in the future to help them figure out what they and their children need and how they can provide for those needs.

Parent guides are in a better position to help parents cope and find solutions when they can view matters from the parent's perspective, identify and highlight the parent's strengths, and understand the parent's shortcomings. In her book, *Family Based Services: A Solution-Focused Approach*, Insoo Kim Berg (1994) presented some ways of doing this:

- Have an open mind about the parent and be prepared to give him or her the benefit of the doubt.

- Put yourself in the parent's shoes and try to look at everything from that point of view.

- Figure out what is currently important to the parent, and see these as valuable assets that may have served the parent well over the years, although these very points of view may now create problems for the parent.

- Check how realistic your expectations for the parent are, given his or her limitations and circumstances.

- Help parents identify their successes, however small, ordinary, or insignificant. Ask how they have accomplished them and what it would take for them to repeat or expand these to other parts of their lives.

- Look for positive motivations behind the parent's behavior and comment on them.

To assist parents to gain skills in finding solutions to their problems, parent guides can begin with Berg's guidelines. With this foundation, guides can then help parents take the following specific steps: 1) describe the problem or goal, 2) describe what it will be like when the problem is solved or the goal is reached, 3) identify what it will take to get there, 4) break this down into small, doable steps, and 5) agree to review progress during subsequent visits. This is what Dianne did with Leane when she decided she wanted to earn her GED.

Helping Parents Tell Their Stories

Three very important things happen as parent guides and other professionals help parents tell their stories. First, they learn more about what has
happened to the child and the child's family and how these events have
affected them. Using this process, they can discern patterns or themes
that can help them understand each family more fully. They can learn
what areas to explore with the parents as they get to know each other better. Second, they build trusting relationships with the family. As the parents experience the genuine, respectful, nonjudgmental interest of these
professionals, they begin to believe that their guides care about their well
being and that of their families. "Parents need to know that we care before they care what we know," explained Klass (1997, p. 1). Intentionally
helping parents tell their stories is a powerful way to let them know you
care. Finally, by listening to parents' stories, parent guides help them
make discoveries and connections for themselves. Lisa, for example, knew
she was feeling very sad and overwhelmed and that she liked to be at
work; however, she may not have realized before hearing herself tell about
her experiences that there was a connection between how she was feeling and the big change that had just happened in her life. As Musick explains, "Language, whether spoken or written, puts a psychological space
between feeling and action. It encourages reflection and self-awareness,
thinking before automatically doing" (1993, p. 230). In addition to listening to parents tell their stories, parent guides can structure opportunities for parents to keep a journal and to write poems, letters (sometimes
to the babies), and stories. This technique has proven to be especially effective with some teen parents (Musick, 1993).

In order to help Lisa tell her story, Helen leaned toward her slightly
and asked an open-ended question in a nonjudgmental way—she asked
Lisa to tell her about Ethan's birth and first month so she could "get to
know him a little." From Lisa's perspective, there was no right or wrong
answer to this question, so she didn't have to be afraid of making a mis-
take. She knew a lot about it and had some vivid memories and strong
feelings. She could tell as little or as much as she wanted; she was in control. By showing with their body language and facial expressions that they
are sincerely attending to the parent's story, parent guides help parents tell
their stories. As Lisa told about the details surrounding Ethan's birth,
Helen also listened with interest, without judging, and asked additional
questions to keep the story going. She noticed the feelings that were expressed verbally and nonverbally.

Often parents tell their stories not so much with words but with their
behaviors—with the "language of interaction" (Trout, 1987b, p. 15).
The previous example of the mother who seemed not to hear her baby's

cries is a powerful example of this. The awkward way in which Lisa held Ethan reinforced her words about not knowing how to be a parent. Asking her neighbors to keep Ethan for hours at a time could be understood as part of her story too—perhaps the part about being so far away from family or about Ethan's father not coming to the hospital when Ethan was born. The ways in which parents tell their stories can also reveal the nature of their attachments with their own parents. (This topic and its significance for working with parents will be discussed further in Chapter 9.)

When professionals help parents tell their stories, it is important that they honor the fact that the parents have entrusted their stories to them. They must be worthy of that trust by receiving the stories with respect and by using them only in the service of helping the families to grow. Parent guides who are not trained in psychotherapy need to be cautious in their use of this technique. They should avoid interpreting stories for the parents and pushing for more information or expression of feelings than parents volunteer. When parents reveal current or past traumas that seem unresolved or are flooded with intense feelings as they tell their stories, parent guides can listen with compassion and offer these parents referrals to appropriate therapists and groups (e.g., psychotherapists, parent–infant psychotherapists, sexual abuse survivors groups, Al-Anon groups, grief support groups). Guides also need to examine their own reactions to parents' stories with their supervisors.

Project STEEP employed the following strategy in a parenting group to help parents get in touch with messages and feelings from their pasts that may have been influencing their parenting (Egeland et al., 2000). In this exercise, written messages are placed on a table (e.g., you're so cute, I can't believe you would do that). These are messages that a child might hear from a parent, either through overt statements or implicit in the parent's actions. Parents are asked to choose the messages they remember hearing as children. Their choices are discussed with a focus on the feelings, both positive and negative, that are evoked by these messages. Then, the parents are asked to choose messages that they *wished* they had heard. Finally, they are asked to choose the messages they want to pass on to their children; in doing so, they symbolically discard messages from their pasts that they do not want to repeat (Egeland et al., 2000). They are subsequently encouraged to practice conveying these positive messages to their own children.

Setting Limits

Just as parents do not do their children a favor by never setting the kind of limits that help them feel secure and protected, so professionals do not do parents a favor when they fail to set limits with parents. For instance, they need to respond to parents' behaviors that are harmful to themselves or their children as discussed in the previous section on spanking. Parent guides also need to have clear boundaries for their own roles in the lives of the families they serve. Lisa, for instance, was offered a ride to the playgroup for the first two sessions. At the second session, Helen asked her if she could make arrangements with the Medicaid transportation coordinator for the third and following sessions. Lisa was able to do that. Limits that are appropriate for one parent may not be appropriate for another parent. For example, if Lisa had lived far away from a telephone, Helen would have offered to call the transportation coordinator and arrange for weekly transportation; or, if it took a mother more than 2 weeks to demonstrate that she was ready to arrive at the playgroup by herself, the limit of 2 weeks would not be appropriate for her. Reading parents' cues is as important as the parents' reading those of their babies.

Setting appropriate limits includes being clear about one's own role as a parent guide. Unlike family members or friends, a guide's role is to work him- or herself out of a job by helping parents find their own way, using new skills and informal and formal supports available to them along the way. When Lisa ran out of diapers before her check came one month, Helen, in addition to helping her find resources to purchase diapers, problem solved with her about how to prevent this from happening in subsequent months. Rule of thumb when answering the internal question, "Should I do this?" is to ask two more questions: "Will it help parents gain more skills and confidence?" and "Will it help them be clear about our work together?" When Lisa struggled to get Ethan strapped into his car seat, Helen waited patiently rather than jumping in to help. When another parent, who had agreed to be home for weekly visits, failed to call and inform the parent guide that she was going to help her friend move at the time of their scheduled visit, the parent guide did not fit her in that week but saw her the next week at the regularly scheduled time.

Parent guides clarify their roles and the work that they intend to do together with the parent through their behavior as much as through their words. When Yolanda, who left the television on all of the time, started watching the television program during a home visit, Helen did not assume the role of babysitter but actively engaged Yolanda in conversation and baby watching. However, when Helen visited another mother who made tamales for a living, she sometimes sat in the kitchen and talked with the mother while she prepared the tamales and her toddler played on the floor nearby because this mother was able to focus on their conversation, her toddler, and her work simultaneously. At times, however, when parents do something that distracts them from their interactions with their parent guides, the parent guides might wonder to themselves whether the parent is feeling uncomfortable or wanting to avoid talking about something. Depending on the circumstances and the relationship the parent guide has developed with the parent, the parent guide might say something like, "You seem to have something on your mind (or as if something is troubling you). Is it something I might be able to help with (or something you want to talk about)?"

Some parents become overly dependent and too demanding on their parent guides. When Samantha began services, she was overwhelmed with the care of her new baby and her toddler, so people were worried about her and bent over backwards to provide assistance. As the weeks went on, she became quite demanding: "I can't stand it; I need more time [meaning more child care]." On other days, she would call demanding that someone take her right then to her doctor's appointment or grocery shopping. Responding to these demands would not have helped Samantha grow. Her help providers (e.g., parent guide, therapist, social worker) met as a team to decide how to assist her in getting her needs met in ways that would help her develop her own competence and confidence without communicating rejection of her. This was especially touchy for Samantha given her history of rejection and neglect. Her parent guide then let Samantha know, "We want to be helpful, but we need to work out a plan for how you are going to get the things you need." They then worked out an agreement about how much respite care would be provided to Samantha, how transportation would be arranged, and so forth. They also helped her to strengthen and utilize her informal social support systems. This is an important way in which parent guides help parents become less dependent on formal services (see Chapter 11).

Being Consistent and Trustworthy

Parent guides should do what they say they'll do. They should come when they say they'll be there, leave when they have been there the agreed on length of time, and interact with families in similar ways from visit to visit. Helen arrived when she said she would to pick up Lisa and Ethan for the playgroup. Each week at the playgroup, the room was ready when the parents arrived, and the general schedule was the same each week. In her work with Lisa and Ethan, if Helen were unavoidably late (and she could not call because Lisa did not have a phone), she made a big deal about her being late—it was not a little thing. It is not unusual for parents to have a long history of people not being there for them consistently. The platinum rule reminds parent guides that, if they want parents to be consistent with their babies, they must be consistent with the parents. Trust then gets built on both lines of the parallel.

Conclusion

As illustrated throughout this section, nurturing parents is not simply a matter of giving "warm fuzzies." Rather, it means being with parents in ways that not only promote good feelings about themselves (e.g., by highlighting their strengths and reinforcing positive behaviors), but by helping them further develop their strengths and sense of self efficacy. In so doing, parent guides assist parents in gaining skills and attitudes that they can use to enhance their interactions with their babies and toddlers. They nurture parents so that the parents can nurture their children.

STRATEGIES FOR ENHANCING PARENT–CHILD INTERACTION

Four-week old Caitlin begins to fuss so her mother picks her up, cuddles her for a moment, then changes her and nurses her. Eight-month old Victor squeals with delight as he pulls the small blanket from his mother's smiling face. Fourteen-month-old Ashlin looks at her dad who smiles reassuringly as she regains her balance. Gabriel's mom lets him sit with her a while before joining in the toddler music class activities, sensing that this is what his slow-to-warm-up temperament requires. Through these moment-by-moment interactions with the important people in their lives, babies and toddlers develop their feelings and perceptions of themselves and what it is like to be with and depend on others. Parent guides carefully observe these little but oh-so-important interactions for they reveal the nature of the developing parent–child relationship that is the foundation and context for the child's emotional development. The "baby watching" that parent guides do on their own and with parents is the foundation for their helping parents enhance their interactions with their babies and toddlers.

Reflective Developmental Guidance

The term "developmental guidance" is used to describe both what parents do with their babies to promote their development and one aspect of what professionals do with parents to promote good parenting skills. Through reflective work with families, the authors have come to an understanding of developmental guidance that combines these two traditional understandings. The use of the same term for both processes is indicative of the parallel process involved.

It is the role of parents to guide and support the overall development of their children including their emotional development, which affects all other areas of development and occurs within the parent–child relationship. Caregiving that guides and supports healthy emotional development within this relationship looks for and builds on the child's strengths and strivings, responding with contingency, sensitivity, and consistency to cues that the child gives. Children's cues and responses change rapidly during the first 2 years; therefore, guiding and supporting this development is challenging to all parents some of the time, and to some parents most of the time.

The parallel role of the parent guide is to guide and support parents so that they can guide and support their children. Not surprisingly, such guidance and support develops through regular interactions between parents and guides. Intervention that supports and guides parents in their role within this relationship looks for and builds on strengths and strivings of parents and responds with contingency, sensitivity, and consistency to verbal and behavioral cues given by parents. Within this parallel process, *developmental guidance* is guiding and supporting parents in a way that enhances their ability to guide and support the development of their children.

There are a number of strategies for providing this kind of developmental guidance effectively. Five are illustrated here: anticipatory guidance, speaking through or for the baby, wondering and reflective questioning, floor time, and videotaping parent–child interactions. Successful implementation of these strategies depends on parent guides' knowledge of typical development of babies and toddlers and ability to appreciate the unique characteristics of the individual children and parents with whom they work. (Chapter 2 and Chapters 4–8 provide information regarding emotional development during the first 2 years and illustrations of how to provide developmental guidance specific to each stage of this development, using these strategies.)

Anticipatory Guidance   Anticipatory guidance is a form of developmental guidance used to help parents anticipate typical developments that are on the horizon so that they can be prepared. This is especially beneficial when the upcoming developments are apt to be challenging. Dr. T. Berry Brazelton (1992) has developed the concept of *touchpoints* to underlie anticipatory guidance. Touchpoints are the universal spurts of development and the trying periods of regression that accompany them throughout childhood. Anticipation of these touchpoints can be used as windows into the future to help parents understand and prepare for their children's behavior so they can interact in ways that promote healthy development. For instance, parents can be alerted to the fact that most babies between 3 and 12 weeks of age develop fussy periods in the late afternoon. "If they can understand the infant's need to fuss at the end of each day between three and twelve weeks of age, they won't have to feel so responsible for the fussing" (Brazelton, 1992, p. 62).

As Victor approached his first birthday, Celeste used anticipatory guidance so that Maureen would not be so overwhelmed by the typical toddler negativism that was on the horizon—another one of the touchpoints described by Brazelton (1992). Brazelton stated

> If I can use the one-year visit . . . to alert them to the reasons why a compliant infant will turn into a stubborn, resistant toddler, they do not feel so guilty and helpless. Otherwise, they take her negativism personally and try to restrain or control it. (1992, p. 147)

Many parent guides see families more often than pediatricians do and many have opportunities to observe more extended parent–child interactions in their homes. Therefore, these parent guides not only inform parents about touchpoints in development, but also assist and support those parents who need more than information in order to help their children during these times.

As Celeste described these typical toddler behaviors to Maureen, she also commented on Maureen's growing enjoyment of Victor and on the hard work she had done to get to this place in their relationship; she reminded her of the things she had already learned about interacting with Victor. Highlighting these strengths contributed to Maureen's sense of efficacy that, in turn, helped her negotiate this time more successfully.

Speaking Through or For the Baby   How information and guidance are given to parents is often as important as the information itself, especially with vulnerable parents. When parents are relatively confident in their parenting efficacy and are forthcoming with their requests for information about infant development and parenting issues, developmental guidance can be given in direct, straightforward ways; however, when parents are unaware of their need for guidance, are insecure in their role, or have difficulty trusting others, they may interpret well-meant information or advice as critical and threatening to their sense of efficacy. Speaking through or for the baby is one strategy that helps parents hear needed information more easily and is an effective way to reinforce parents for instances of good parenting. This strategy is easy to use with parents, one that is often done quite spontaneously by people interacting with young children and their parents. For instance, a mother might say to her toddler, who joyfully greets his daddy at the door, "Boy, you're sure glad to see your daddy, aren't you?" This is an example of speaking *through* the baby—the person says something to the baby that is intended for the parent's hearing. When speaking *for* the baby, the person says what the baby might if the baby could talk, often as a way of highlighting what the baby's nonverbal cues are saying. For instance, a nurse might say as she hands a newborn to her mother, "Oh, Mommy, I know your voice!"

Speaking through and for the baby was a strategy used by Celeste toward the primary goals she and Maureen had for their work together. This strategy is good for conveying information that can help parents reframe their perceptions of their babies' behaviors. When Victor was learning to feed himself with a spoon, Maureen was frustrated that he kept dropping his food on the floor. She interpreted the behavior as being naughty and making more work for her. Celeste reframed Victor's behavior by speaking for him: "I'm learning about gravity, Mom, and I sure like to practice dropping things. Do you have anything else I can drop besides food?"

Speaking through and for the baby also can be used to reinforce instances of warm interactions that might not be noticed and appreciated by parents who do not think of themselves as able to make good things happen. For example, when Victor and Maureen were taking turns making noises Celeste said, speaking through Victor, "You and your Mommy sure look like you're having fun together!"

These examples show speaking through and for the baby in incidental times during individual visits with families. Guides can also combine this technique with videotape viewing, inviting parents to take turns with them in speaking for their babies. In this reflective situation, both the guide and the parent may see opportunities for reading and giving words to baby's cues that they might not have been able to capture at the time. Speaking for the baby has been developed even further as a technique to use with groups of teen parents. First, they take turns speaking for babies who are on videotape and later apply this technique with their own babies, both while watching videotapes of their interactions and as they interact. Sometimes the teenagers speak for another parent's baby, being careful to follow the ground rule of only saying positive things. This group activity has been found to be effective in increasing the sensitivity of response by these young parents (Carter, Osofsky, & Hann, 1991). Parent guides should be careful when using this technique so they do not convey criticism of some action the mother has just taken. For example, a parent guide should not say for a baby, "I don't like it when you yank my toy away like that."

Wondering and Reflective Questioning Wondering and reflective questioning are techniques that date back to Socrates. By wondering aloud about things and asking questions that encourage reflection, parent guides help parents explore possibilities and discover potential solutions for themselves. For example, when Maureen asked Celeste's advice on whether she should send 11-month-old Victor to visit his father for a week, Celeste did not give direct advice, even though it was requested. Instead, she wondered aloud what it might feel like to Victor to be away from his mother when he was in the middle of forming an attachment with her. Because she knew how badly Maureen wanted this break from parenting, she also wondered what it might be like for Victor if his mother were very stressed because she really needed this respite. As Celeste encouraged this reflection, she helped Maureen find a way for Victor to visit with his father without sending him away and to swap babysitting with another mother so each could have some periods of respite.

When parent guides "wonder" about something rather than asking direct questions, stating opinions, or giving advice, they help several important things to happen. First, the parents do not feel on the spot to answer but are invited to do so. Second, guides communicate that they are not the only ones who can figure things out—parents have unique contributions to make to their own problem-solving efforts. Third, the guides model reflective thinking as a useful way to respond to situations. Wondering is one form of reflective question-asking and includes questions that start with phrases such as "I wonder what would happen if . . . ?" "I wonder why she . . . ?" and "I wonder how your husband (or baby) might respond if you . . . ?" Examples of other reflective questions are: "What things have you tried in the past when . . . ?" and "How did you figure that out?"

These strategies can also be used to help parents wonder and reflect on what is happening with their baby or toddler. When Maureen picked Victor up to comfort him when he fussed, Victor pushed on his mother's chest, arched his back, and continued fussing. Maureen looked confused and frustrated, so this conversation followed.

Celeste: I wonder what he's trying to say. What do *you* think he's trying to tell us?

Maureen: He's saying he's mad at me.

Celeste: I wonder what would help him handle being mad?

Maureen: Well certainly not me holding him.

Celeste: I wonder what has helped at other times when he doesn't let you hold him.

Maureen: Sometimes he really likes it when I just lay him on his back and leave him alone for a little bit.

Celeste: Do you want to try that now? Maybe it will work—of course, maybe it won't this time, and we'll have to think of something else. I've seen a lot of babies do this, and different things work with different babies at different times.

Celeste guided Maureen in reflecting on what might be happening with Victor, what he might need at the moment, and what things have worked in similar situations in the past. She also helped Maureen realize that the situation was typical ("I've seen a lot of babies do this . . .") and added that parents often have to try different things before they find what works.

Wondering and reflective questioning can also be used successfully in combination with the strategies of floor time and videotaping. Parent–infant psychotherapists sometimes use a similar technique called "watch, wait, and wonder" to help parents make connections between what is currently happening with their babies and what has happened to them in their own childhoods (Muir, 1992).

Parent guides also wonder to themselves and with their supervisors about what they are observing and experiencing with families as a way to generate hypotheses rather than jumping to conclusions about the relationships unfolding before them. These hypotheses can suggest actions to try with families. Celeste wondered with her team in the beginning of her work with Maureen what might explain the difference between the baby she observed and Maureen's description of him. One team member suggested, "Perhaps Maureen is more relaxed when she feels the support of your presence and, therefore, Victor is more relaxed when you are there?" They also wondered how Maureen's feelings of parenting inadequacy affected her perception of her baby, saying, "Might it be that she can't see herself as capable of having an easy baby?" and "Maybe Maureen's mother's negative comments about Victor are bringing back old feelings of failure from her childhood?" Celeste kept these hypotheses and reflections in mind as she continued her work with Maureen and Victor.

Floor Time   Floor time is described by its author, Dr. Stanley Greenspan, as both a philosophy and a technique (Greenspan & Greenspan, 1989; Hanna, Wilford, Benham, Carter, & Brodkin, 1990). As a philosophy, it says that young children are usually on the floor; so if parents and other caregivers want to really be with children, they need to be literally on the floor with them. Floor time as a technique is a very effective way to help parents tune into their babies and interact with them in ways that foster their sense of self-worth and self-efficacy. During floor time, the parent starts by sitting on the floor with the baby. There are five discrete steps in the process: observe, engage, follow baby's lead, extend the drama, and close the circle of communication.

Celeste used this strategy of developmental guidance with Maureen and Victor many times. One example was when Victor was about 7 months old and needed help to explore and to extend the length and complexity of his play with his mother. Celeste had observed that they had some trouble getting "in synch," and Maureen was missing Victor's subtle cues. Celeste suggested floor time and explained that it was a different way of playing with babies that many parents found fun and helpful. She said she would coach Maureen by sitting near her and whispering from time to time because this was a new way of playing that might not feel natural at first. She then briefly explained the five steps of floor time so Maureen would know what to expect.

She began by asking Maureen to sit on the floor with Victor, observe him, and watch for an opportunity to join him in play (Steps 1 and 2). Maureen watched Victor pick up a plastic ring and bang it on the rocking spool, so she picked up another one, and did the same; Victor grinned and banged harder. Celeste whispered, "Nice following of his lead!" (Step 3). Shortly, Maureen began to guide Victor's hand, so he would put the ring on the spool, thus attempting to control the game. Celeste whispered, "Remember, follow his lead or expand" (Step 4). Maureen went back to Victor's game and said, "You're playing a drum, aren't you!" She then tapped the ring on the floor and rolled it a little; Victor tried to imitate. Celeste whispered, "Nice expanding." After a few more moments, Victor looked away, and Celeste whispered, "It looks like he's had enough of this game" (Step 5). This guided interaction helped Maureen to tune in to Victor and to use his cues to extend and elaborate their play together. Maureen was learning to read her baby, a skill she would use in many different situations.

Videotaping Parent–Child Interactions   A camcorder is a valuable piece of equipment for parent guides. When videotaping is a regular part of home visits or office visits of parents and guides, it can be a good way to offer developmental guidance. To reinforce a parent's strengths, the guide can first review the videotape of a session and select instances of the parent responding in appropriate ways to the child and then highlight these instances while viewing the tape with the parent. For instance, the guide might say, "Look at him smile! He must really like it when you lean down and talk to him like that." This entails not just praising but commenting in a manner that nudges parents to make connections between their behaviors and their children's responses. Sometimes parents discover for themselves what they have done. In a videotape of a home visit with Maureen and Victor, Celeste saw Maureen respond to Victor's babbling with, "Oh, yes, you are telling me something very important" followed by Victor babbling again to his mother. Because Maureen usually ignored such attempts at engagement, Celeste wanted to highlight this in order to encourage Maureen to do it more often. As they watched the videotape together at the next contact, Maureen discovered for herself the positive effect her response had on Victor. She seemed to need the opportunity to observe when she was not in the situation in order to really reflect on what was happening. If she had not discovered for herself by just watching, Celeste would have remarked about it herself, calling attention to Maureen's helpful response.

When videotaping is used regularly, it can also provide a way to help parents notice when their interaction with their child is not helpful. For example, in a videotaped interaction, Barbara was blowing bubbles for her baby, Sandra. At first, Sandra followed the bubbles with her eyes and squealed as she waved her arms and kicked her feet. After a while, though, she looked away, communicating that she had had enough. As Barbara continued to blow the bubbles, Sandra began to writhe and then to whimper. When Dianne, the parent guide, watched the video with Barbara later, she asked, as she usually did, what the mother noticed about her baby in the video. Barbara said, "She didn't like me blowing bubbles. She doesn't like playing with me as much as she likes playing with her father." Dianne rewound the videotape, and they watched a portion again. Dianne asked Barbara to notice when Sandra changed her behavior. Barbara could, with the instant replay, notice that Sandra had, in fact, enjoyed the bubbles for a while and then tired of them. This experience helped this mother discover a valuable and critical parenting skill—reading her baby.

By taping often, parents and children get used to having the camcorder in the room. At first, it is common for parents to concentrate on how their hair looks, how they sound, or how heavy they have become; this passes with regular use. Sometimes parent guides find transporting video equipment a bit of a nuisance, but its value clearly outweighs the trouble.

Infant Massage

When 23-month-old Rosalinda felt she was getting upset, she would go to her mother and say, "'Ssage, Mommy!" Several months earlier, Lisabeth, a certified infant massage instructor, had taught Rosalinda's mother, Andrea, how to massage her. Rosalinda was a hyperactive child with low tolerance for frustration. Massage was introduced to help her release physical and emotional tension—it accomplished this and much more for this single mother and her baby.

Andrea had felt overwhelmed by the challenge of caring for Rosalinda who, from the beginning had been a spirited child. Andrea had a history of abusive relationships and received no support from her family—just occasional scolding for not whipping Rosalinda when she misbehaved. The massage instruction was embedded within the relationship-based reflective intervention she received during home visits from Lisabeth, her parent guide. She received support for her parenting and was introduced to a play-group where other mothers provided much-needed social support and interaction for both her and Rosalinda.

The massage was an important addition to these interventions with benefits for Andrea as well as for Rosalinda. Andrea found that doing the rhythmical massage strokes and focusing on Rosalinda's reactions to the strokes were very calming for her as well as for Rosalinda. Lisabeth also taught Andrea to use breathing as another way to help Rosalinda calm down. Andrea would hold Rosalinda firmly with her back against her own chest and take slow, deep, even breaths; this, too, calmed both her and Rosalinda. Research has found a number of benefits from massage for babies. For instance, low birth weight babies who were massaged briefly three times a day for 10 days after birth gained 47% more weight than equally low weight babies who received standard care, even though the groups did not differ on caloric intake (Field et al., 1986).

In addition to the benefits to both parent and baby of the massage itself, infant massage provides another avenue for helping parents tune into their babies' cues. Massage sessions start with the parent putting massage oil on her hands and rubbing them together in front of the baby while asking the baby's permission to start the massage. Some parents may think this step is weird because little babies do not understand this question, but they can be helped to see how quickly babies begin to understand these signals. When parents pay attention to their babies' responses to the cues—the smell of the massage oil, the sound and sight of their rubbing their hands together—parents can see that their babies are telling them whether or not they want the massage. As the massage continues, parent guides can help parents continue to notice their babies' responses to different strokes and when their babies signal that they are ready for the massage to end.

Lisabeth was teaching the mom, dad, and grandmother of 4-month-old Tanya how to massage her. Tanya had had four surgeries on her ears and had to wear hearing aids that irritated her. The family agreed to try massage to help Tanya calm down in the midst of this discomfort. When it came time for Dad to have his turn massaging Tanya, he began appropriately by asking Tanya's permission and then started massaging her leg. Tanya, who was tired of the new procedure by then, turned away, clenched her fists, and tried to withdraw her leg. The following conversation occurred.

Lisabeth: How are you going to know when she's had enough?
Dad: I think she's had enough already.
Lisabeth: How is she telling you that?
Dad: She's pulling her leg away.

Lisabeth: Anything else?

Dad: Yeah, she's turning away and squirming. She doesn't look like she's enjoying it.

Lisabeth: It really does seem like that. Great, you can really read your little gal!

Then, Lisabeth explained that it takes a few sessions before some babies get used to having massage and that it's fine to stop whenever the baby indicates that she's had enough even if they haven't done all of the strokes.

The strategies presented in this chapter for assessing and planning with parents, for nurturing parents, and for enhancing parent–child interaction can be used to help parents enhance the early emotional development of their children. The specific behaviors of parents and children that parent guides will focus on at any given time will, however, vary depending on the child's age and stage of development. The next five chapters discuss how the basic elements of early emotional development described in Chapter 2 are expressed and developed over the first 2 years. Ways in which parent guides can use the strategies presented in this chapter to help parents promote development at each age and stage are discussed and illustrated with numerous real life examples of guides working with parents and their children. How parent guides can assist parents in dealing with the personal and family factors that challenge parents' abilities to promote these developments is addressed in Section III.

II

Promoting Emotional Development During the First 2 Years

4

Getting to Know You

The First 3 Months

Sharon immediately awakens when she hears Caitlin stirring in the bassinet next to the bed. She glances at the clock reading 3 A.M. and groans. After just 3 hours of sleep, she lightly rocks the bassinet because sometimes this helps Caitlin go back to sleep. But Caitlin starts fussing in earnest, and Sharon gently picks her up, cuddles her in her arms, and murmurs, "Sounds like you're a hungry little girl. Let's get a diaper change, then you'll be ready for chow time again." Caitlin's father Frank talks quietly to Caitlin as Sharon changes her diaper. Then, he rolls over and goes back to sleep as Sharon begins nursing Caitlin. Sharon feels a pang of resentment that Frank can so easily return to sleep when she feels so desperately tired herself. It has been a rough night. Earlier, there had been a stretch of time (it seemed like hours) when nothing that she or Frank did could calm Caitlin, who fussed and cried until she finally fell asleep. But, as Sharon gazes down on Caitlin who is now eagerly sucking at her breast, a warm glow of tenderness engulfs her. Caitlin stops suckling for a moment, and Sharon softly murmurs, "You were really hungry, weren't you, little pudding?" They gaze into each other's eyes for a moment, then Caitlin begins sucking again. After a while, she drifts off to sleep and her lips curve into a fleeting smile. Sharon, too, smiles and says to herself, "Now you're happy that your tummy's full." She carefully lays Caitlin back in her bassinet, curls up next to Frank, and goes back to sleep.

Sharon and Frank are assisting Caitlin in accomplishing the first step in the development of emotion regulation by helping her establish smooth feeding and sleeping routines. They are doing this by responding promptly to her needs and providing a consistent environment. They are able to care for Caitlin in this way because they are fortunate enough to have sufficient resources—both internal and external—to do so. They have adequate financial resources to provide for their needs and to allow Sharon to stay home with Caitlin until they, as a family, feel comfortable with making alternative part-time care arrangements. Frank and Sharon have a mutually supportive and caring relationship, and they receive additional support from family and friends. They were both raised in sufficiently nurturing families so that their attachment relationships as they grew up helped them construct positive internal working models of self, significant others, and relationships. Although Caitlin is a spirited child, which creates challenges for Sharon and Frank, she nevertheless is healthy, as are Frank and Sharon. Many parents, however, are not as blessed as Sharon and Frank. This chapter describes the emotional needs of babies during the first 3 months and the caregiving that these needs demand, including some of the challenges that hinder parents in their efforts to parent well and how parent guides can help them address these problems.

Caitlin and her parents are off to a good start in addressing a major developmental task of the first 3 months, the establishment of physiological regulation. This first step in the development of emotion regulation occurs as babies form smoother feeding and sleeping routines and develop periods of quiet alertness. Parents help their babies develop physiological regulation by learning how to comfort them when they are distressed and how to engage them when they are ready for interaction. Getting to know their babies and what works with them helps strengthen the parent–infant bond that, in turn, provides the foundation for the development of babies' secure attachments with their parents. Both the development of physiological regulation and the parent–infant bond are aided by the special abilities the baby brings to these tasks as well as by the quality of caregiving the baby receives and the resources available to the parents.

ESTABLISHING PHYSIOLOGICAL REGULATION

At birth, babies leave an environment in which their physiological needs are typically well met. During pregnancy, mothers meet fetuses' basic needs by maintaining good health and not subjecting them to unnecessary risks (e.g., cocaine). Once fetuses leave the womb, however, their caregiving demands increase dramatically. Hunger, fatigue, and an awesome array of stimuli create arousal of the newborn's immature nervous system. Sensitive and responsive parents facilitate physiological regulation right from the beginning by responding appropriately to their babies' cues of hunger, fatigue, and other sources of discomfort and by providing suitable opportunities for stimulation and interaction when their babies are ready for them. As parents gain skill in these areas and as they learn their babies' rhythms, smooth routines for feeding, sleeping, and playing can be established and physiological regulation begins to develop. Tuning into the baby's need for consistency and predictability is a good starting point.

Helping Babies Tame the Booming, Buzzing World Outside the Womb

Newborns come into the world equipped with an ability to pick up patterns of familiarity, demonstrated by the marked preferences they show for familiar sights, sounds, and odors. Soon after birth, babies turn more frequently toward their mothers' breast pads than toward breast pads of another mother (MacFarlane, 1977). They also prefer the already familiar voices of their mothers more than the voices of other females (DeCasper & Fifer, 1980; Mehler, Bertoncini, Barriere, & Jassik-Gerschenfeld, 1978). Nurses can give new mothers the gift of seeing this preference if they hold their newborns so they can turn their heads then ask the mother to speak from her baby's side. Most babies will slowly turn their heads to the familiar sound of the mother's voice. The nurse can then frame this as the baby's special interest in the parent. This procedure can help the parent bond with the baby—a process that may be at risk with some parents.

Babies also prefer to listen to melodies that they heard sung by their mothers while they were in the womb more than melodies they hear for the first time after they were born (Panneton & DeCasper, 1986; Swain, Zelazo, & Clifton, 1993). The same is true for stories heard prenatally (Cooper & Aslin, 1989; DeCasper & Fifer, 1980). They also prefer their mother's native tongue to other languages even when the languages are spoken by the same person (Moon, Cooper, & Fifer, 1993). Within a few days after birth, babies show a preference for their mother's face compared with that of a female stranger (Bushnell, Sai & Mullin 1989; Field, Cohen, Garcia, & Greenberg, 1984). Parent guides who have an opportunity to work with families both before and after the birth of their babies can help parents appreciate these phenomena.

Demonstrating to parents that their newborns will turn toward them when they speak is just one of the procedures in the Neonatal Behavioral Assessment Scale (NBAS; Brazelton, 1992). This scale not only provides parents and health professionals a wealth of information about the baby, but it also delights parents as they observe the many fascinating things their babies can do. This observation can help them get off to a good start with their little ones. In fact, studies have shown that after participating in this assessment with their babies, "the mother and father are significantly more sensitive to their own baby's behavioral cues at one month, and they remain more involved throughout the first year" (Brazelton, 1992, p. 32). The nurse in the hospital, the pediatrician in the clinic, and the parent guide can all take advantage of this fact by asking parents what they have noticed that their babies are doing and by highlighting for them things that they observe. "Just look at the way she gazes at you! She just knows that you're her mommy (or daddy)." "Have you noticed what she does when you stroke the outer side of her sole?" (The baby will spread her toes in the Babinski reflex.)

Importance of Consistency   Perhaps it is because babies have an ability to detect patterns of familiarity that they seem to derive comfort from having consistent and predictable caregiving. This was demonstrated in a classic study in which each newborn in a group received consistent care from a specific nurse so that they both became familiar with each other. The importance of this consistency in care became evident when the babies were switched to different nurses after 10 days. An immediate and persistent increase in crying and other distress signals, such as gagging and turning away during feeding, occurred over a period of several days (Sander, 1975). By providing responsive and reliable care, the parent can capitalize on the baby's sensitivity to familiarity to help the baby recover from distress and establish physiological regulation.

Some parents, due to past or present severe life stresses or lack of support, are not able to provide reliable and consistent care during these crucial early months. Other family members may be able to help such parents provide an island of calm and predictability for their babies. Intervention in the form of concrete assistance or emotional support can be offered in addition to informal family support. When substitute care must be given to a baby, parents should share information so that the caregiver can learn the baby's routines, familiar smells and sights, and how the baby is best soothed. A simple thing such as using the same detergent to wash the baby's crib sheets and the same baby care products can provide continuity in odors that baby experiences. (Suggestions for easing transitions to care by others are presented in the section on child care in Chapter 12.)

Comforting the Baby

Hunger and other sources of discomfort create tension and distress for the baby. The most beneficial role for parents is to help their babies find relief from this distress and reduction of this tension. In order to respond appropriately when their babies are upset, parents must, first of all, realize that their babies are in distress, and then be able to relieve that distress. The first step is often easy because, fortunately, babies are born with the ability to emit lusty cries when they feel distress, cries that grab the attention of adults within hearing range. These cries and other signs of distress signal high arousal—a nervous system that is overly excited by hunger and other sources of discomfort and pain. Most parents are highly motivated to discover ways to respond quickly and effectively to alleviate their babies' distress and stop the crying. A baby's cry elicits a physiological response from most listeners. Nursing mothers tend to "let down" milk when they hear their babies cry. Both parents (Frodi, 1985) and nonparents (Murray, 1985) responded to the typical cries of babies with significant increases in blood pressure and heart rate.

Many parents talk freely about when and how much their babies cry and what they think and do about it. This discussion is an opportunity for parent guides to describe what is happening with their babies and what the babies can learn from their parents' responses to their cries. When babies cry and someone promptly appears to lovingly change, feed, or simply comfort them, their arousal levels and feelings of distress lessen. These babies experience a pattern of distress followed by relief—they cry, someone attends to their needs, and then they feel better. This experience, repeated countless times over the course of days and months, lays the foundation for the development of attachment and a sense of self as efficacious and lovable. Parent guides, when spending time with babies and their parents, can observe and describe, using speaking for the baby, how babies express tension and signal their needs by crying and then calming down with the help of their parents. Then, guides can go on to explain how important this cycle is to emotional development.

When Caitlin cries, her parents wisely pick her up and try to do whatever is needed to relieve her distress. In a classic study, Mary Ainsworth and her colleagues (Bell & Ainsworth, 1972) observed a number of babies and their mothers monthly in their homes. They found that babies of mothers who responded promptly and appropriately to them when they cried during the first 3 months cried less during the last quarter of the year than did babies of less responsive mothers. At age 12 months, the babies of more responsive mothers tended to rely more on facial expression, gesture, and vocalization to communicate their intentions and wishes to their parents. This information is welcome news to those mothers who fight the urge to hold and comfort their crying babies because they have been told that they might spoil them if they keep picking them up when they cry. Comforting a distressed baby does not reinforce crying; it reinforces a sense of security.

Mothers often report feeling greatly distressed when they try to adhere to misinformed advice from other family members or friends to let their babies cry for fear of spoiling them. The parent guide can support the mother by saying, "You know, people who study lots of babies found out something you might not expect; when babies are picked up and soothed promptly, they actually cry less as time goes along, rather than more. You don't make your baby spoiled by attending to her needs." The parent guide can explain that when little babies cry, they are just letting people know that they need something. "They may be in pain, hungry, tired, bored, uncomfortable, or just blowing off steam at the end of a stressful day. Sometimes you can recognize which of these is the problem just by the way they cry. Crying is their way of telling you what's wrong." The parent guide can then explore with the mother how she might inform other family members of this information without alienating them. When appropriate, the parent guide can offer to meet with the mother and the family member who has this concern, as Helen does with Julia and Jackson in the following example.

Julia was a victim of abuse by a boyfriend who had also severely abused their baby daughter. When she remarried and had a second daughter, Julia could not tolerate even a little fussiness from her, although her husband, Jackson, thought it was okay for their baby, Kate, to fuss a little before picking her up. This disagreement caused strife between the parents and inconsistent care of Kate. Their parent guide, Helen, encouraged them to discuss in her presence their different feelings when they heard Kate cry. During this discussion, she helped Jackson learn why Kate's cries caused such strong reactions in Julia. The parents were then able to negotiate, with help, a compromise that they both could accept. Jackson was able to appreciate how hard it was for Julia to hear Kate cry for even a little while, so he was more able to support her in picking Kate up more quickly than he would have otherwise. Kate actually cried less with this response, and nothing more needed to be said.

Not All Parents Respond Alike   Most parents have experienced the feeling of powerlessness and failure that occurs when, for whatever reason, they cannot console their baby. Although parents differ in how they respond in these situations, most can benefit and generally appreciate some support and help in figuring out how to comfort their babies. When that feeling of failure leads to anger at the baby, help is definitely needed.

After having two children placed in foster care because of her substance abuse, Linda (now in recovery) feels a great need to be a "perfect parent." She finds herself getting angry at her baby, Sheryl, when she is not able to soothe her. The parent guide speaks through the baby to express the healthy strivings of Linda: "Sheryl, your mommy is trying so hard to figure out how to help you feel better right now. She's really hanging in there because she loves you and hates to see you uncomfortable." After a few more minutes of Sheryl's crying, she speaks for Sheryl, saying, "Mommy, it's not your fault. I'm just having a hard time calming down right now. If I could tell you what's the matter, I sure would!" These interventions were done within the larger context of a comprehensive intervention with Sheryl, Linda, and other family members that addressed factors such as Linda's recovery and the family's difficulties with protective services as well as factors within the mother–child relationship.

Sometimes feelings from the mother's childhood experiences may be triggered by her baby's crying. This situation was the case for the mother who seemed not to hear her baby cry, as described by Selma Fraiberg (see Chapter 3). It was also the case for Samantha who could not tolerate Katrina's crying—she would rush to pick her up at the slightest whimper. This action was a source of conflict between her and her boyfriend, Katrina's dad. Samantha explained to her parent guide, "I'm doing that because no one was there for me when I cried." Katrina's crying may also have set up a tension in her that she could not tolerate, given her background.

Parents with histories of abuse or neglect may be particularly affected by their babies' crying, as Samantha was. Although it is typical for a parent or for anyone to experience physiological arousal and some feelings of discomfort when they hear a baby cry, some parents experience more profound reactions due to their own histories as well as to their present circumstances. Abusive mothers exhibited greater increases in heart rate to a baby's cries than did nonabusive mothers (Frodi & Lamb, 1980). The baby's cry may threaten the parent's defenses against revisiting painful feelings and memories. Excessive exposure to crying or exposure to especially aversive crying may tip vulnerable parents' motivations from altruistic to egoistic, that is, from concerns with their babies' distress to desires to alleviate their own discomfort in listening to the cries (Murray, 1985). Such a shift might involve avoidance of the crying infants or even abusive outbursts to stop the babies from crying. Often the explanation given for shaking a baby is that the baby just would not stop crying. In one study, excessive crying was given as the most common reason by parents who had battered their babies (Weston, 1980). One mother confessed to her guide that she would cut herself to reduce tension, "so I won't hurt the kids," a revelation that prompted her parent guide to refer her for therapy.

Mothers experiencing depression are often challenged by their baby's need to be soothed. Lisa, the depressed mother we met in Chapter 3, was totally overwhelmed when Ethan woke up and cried at night. The only thing she knew to do was to put a bottle in Ethan's mouth. Doing that whenever Ethan cried for any reason meant that Ethan was not being helped to establish routines in his feeding, and Lisa was left feeling even more overwhelmed and depressed. In addition to helping her with Ethan's feeding routine, Helen addressed Lisa's depression. Because it was caused, in part, by the sudden isolation of being a single parent and not working, she was helped by attending a parent–infant playgroup, through which she had contact with other mothers of babies in a supportive environment. Therapy, including medication, helped to lift her mood, and she was then more able to read her baby's cues with confidence and to figure out effective soothing responses. While the depression was being treated, her guide continued to provide support and gentle developmental guidance.

Levels of Response to a Baby's Cries   Crittenden (1993) identified four levels of reasons for parent's unresponsiveness to their babies' signals of distress. At the deepest level, parents, like the one described by Selma Fraiberg (see Chapter 3), appear unaware of their babies' signals. At the next level, parents recognize that there are signals but misinterpret them. At a third level, they interpret the signals correctly but do not know what to do about them, and at the highest level, they have a pretty good idea about what to do but for various reasons (e.g., being depressed or distracted) they do not respond. Each of these levels or reasons for the mother's unresponsiveness can call for a somewhat different intervention.

When parents appear unaware of their babies' signals (the first level), parent guides can first try amplifying the babies' cries for these parents: "Somebody sounds uncomfortable, doesn't he?" If the parents still dismiss their babies' needs, parent guides can ask what they think their babies are trying to communicate. Parent guides must really listen to what the parents say and then may offer some alternatives for them to consider. So, for example, if the parent says, "He just wants to be picked up," the parent guide might say, "He really does like to be near his mommy doesn't he?" Now the mother is encouraged to consider her baby's cries in a different way than she did a moment ago. If amplifying their babies' cries and reframing their meaning does not seem to make a difference in the parents' responses, further efforts into what is interfering with their responsiveness are warranted, as in the example from Selma Fraiberg. Parent guides must listen with ears and eyes and feelings to what parents' actions (or inactions) may be telling them about their stress or their childhood experiences of not being heard when they were crying out.

Guides can then respond with sympathetic listening, sensitive acknowledgement of their feelings, and, if necessary, referral to a parent–infant psychotherapist or other mental health therapist.

At the second level, when parents hear their babies' signals but misinterpret them, parent guides can help the parents attribute different, more accurate meanings to the cries. For instance, a parent guide might hear the parent say, "She gets mad at me because I can't always make her feel better; she just doesn't like me." The parent guide will try to deal sensitively with the feelings of inadequacy that are being communicated by this statement, as Celeste did with Maureen. The parent guide might also speak for baby with comments like, "I really like to have you pick me up; I feel so good in your arms!" In this way, the parent is encouraged to reframe the meaning of baby's cries so that he or she can respond more appropriately.

The third level, parents interpreting their babies' signals accurately but not knowing what to do, is especially likely when babies' responses to parents' ministrations are confusing or do not match parents' expectations. For example, premature babies with underdeveloped nervous systems may respond adversely to being stroked. Parents of such babies will appreciate information about other ways to soothe them than those they have tried before. Parents may not know what to do because they lack information, have mental retardation, or do not understand their babies' temperaments. Using strategies presented throughout this book, parent guides can help these parents develop appropriate responses to their babies.

When parent guides encounter parents who demonstrate at times that they know what to do in response to their babies' cries but do so inconsistently (the fourth level), they can help them acquire the resources needed (e.g., therapy for depression, respite care, treatment for alcoholism) so they can be more available for their babies. For example, Joan is a parent who knows what to do but is unable to respond consistently because of her mood fluctuations. She has depression and schizo-affective disorder. She takes psychotropic medications and when her medications are at the right level, she can respond to her daughter Susie's signals very sensitively. On other days, when she is feeling angry and frustrated or depressed, she does not have the energy to move outside of herself to attend to her child. Her parent guide, Dianne, works collaboratively with Joan's physician to regulate her medications so that she can have more days of feeling stable and being appropriately responsive to her baby.

Not All Babies Cry Alike Some cries seem more irritating than others even to the average listener. Babies' cries differ in pitch and "rhythm" (i.e., the duration of the cries and the pauses between the cries). Cries with a higher pitch are typically perceived to be more arousing and aversive than cries with a lower basic pitch (Lester, Boukydis, Garcia-Coll, Hole, & Peucker, 1992; Zeskind, Klein, & Marshall, 1992). Cries of infants who have been rated as having spirited ("difficult") temperaments contain longer pauses both within and between cry sounds than cries of infants who have been rated as having "easy" or "average" temperaments. When unrelated mothers listened to tapes of temperamentally different infants (as assessed by their own mothers), they rated cries of "difficult" infants as sounding more irritating and spoiled than cries of "easy" or "average" infants (Lounsbury & Bates, 1982). Cries of infants with a high number of pre- and perinatal complications are rated as more urgent, grating, and aversive (Zeskind & Lester, 1978). Cries of many preemies are perceived as particularly aversive, and preemies are typically overrepresented among abused children (Frodi, 1985; Frodi et al., 1978).

Parents can be very relieved to learn that some babies' cries are more spirited than others due simply to the temperament with which they were born. As parent guides spend time with parents and their babies, they can observe in the moment how the babies cry and how their parents react to the sound of the cries. They then have an opening for wondering if the parents have heard about different temperaments in babies and discussing with them how temperament differences are manifested in various baby behaviors including the intensity of their cries. If parents of preemies seem especially upset by their babies' cries, they too can be helped to understand that often a premature baby's cries are different and can be especially upsetting. They can be reassured that this is typical and that it will not last forever. In the meantime, ways to calm their babies can be explored with them. Reminding parents that these babies with their immature nervous systems can tolerate only stimuli that are at a very low level, guides can suggest that parents hold or rock or look at their babies, but only introduce one of these at a time (Brazelton, 1992). They can also provide information for parents from Dr. Brazelton's experience that low-keyed environments (e.g., decreased noise, light, and other stimulation) will help their premature babies gain and maintain well-regulated arousal levels.

Some babies are fussy and irritable because they are hypersensitive to sights, sounds, touch, and movement. Care must be taken not to overwhelm them with stimuli. Brazelton (1992) recommended that parents slowly introduce just one stimulus at a time. The sequence might include picking up and cuddling the baby, then looking down at his face, then crooning to him, and finally rocking, singing, and looking at him at the same time. The secret is to take each step slowly and wait until the baby relaxes before introducing the next stimulus. Feeding, diapering, and putting a hypersensitive baby to sleep are best done in a darkened, quiet room. Even playing with the baby works best in a quiet place, free from distractions. Over time, such calm care can help many hypersensitive babies become better regulated. In some cases, the cause of hypersensitivity appears to be the use of certain drugs (illegal or prescription) during pregnancy; in other cases, the cause is unknown. If the cause is organic (i.e., a physical impairment in the brain), the treatment will have to continue over many years (Brazelton, 1992).

Some parents respond to their babies' irritability by blaming themselves or taking it personally. For instance, they may feel as if the baby is trying to drive them crazy. In these situations, parent guides can support parents by exploring with them possible reasons for their babies' irritability (e.g., temperament, hypersensitivity) and helping them find ways to calm their babies. The guides may also want to consider whether something in the parent's past or present situation is contributing to their reactions to their babies.

Engaging the Baby

Babies not only come equipped with ways to signal distress, they also soon demonstrate interest in their surroundings (especially other people) through their facial expressions, body movements, and eye gaze. In this way they indicate that there is more to life for them than simply sleeping and eating. As we noticed with Caitlin, babies usually take little breaks during nursing known as the burst–pause pattern (e.g., suck-suck-suck-pause). Often mothers jiggle their babies during these pauses in attempts to get them to resume feeding; however, babies tend to pause longer when their mothers do this as if to savor these moments of interaction (Kaye, 1982). Observers have noticed that, just as Sharon did, some mothers begin looking at and talking to their babies during these pauses and then become quiet again when their babies resume nursing (Brazelton, 1992). Because young babies tend to focus best at a distance of about 8–10 inches, the nursing position is ideal for these moments of mutual gazing. Extremely long periods of mothers gazing at their babies are common during this stage and, when not nursing, mothers tend to vary their facial expressions to keep their babies' interest (Stern, 1974). Over these first few months, babies begin to develop longer periods of quiet alertness between the times when they are sleeping, feeding, or fussing. These times are precious moments for most parents who are thrilled by their babies' attention to them—they are special moments for brain development, as well. Babies' budding interest in their surroundings corresponds with the period of intensive activity during the second and third months in the parts of babies' brains that process vision (occipital lobe); touch and bodily sensations (parietal lobes); and hearing, speech, and language development (temporal lobe).

As parent guides and parents watch babies together, parent guides look for ways to help babies teach their parents about their developing interests and increased awake times. For example, talking through the baby, the parent guide says, "I see you just looking and looking at your Mommy. Pretty soon you'll be cooing and smiling, just carrying on a regular conversation with her, won't you?" and "Before long you'll be awake more during the day and will be so much company for Mommy and Daddy!" Professionals who do not have opportunities to observe these interactions and thus help babies teach their parents in these ways, can still ask questions of parents about their babies' interests and awake times, and can stress the importance of this interest in the world.

Helping babies teach their parents about their developing interest in social interaction is more difficult if the parents typically do not hold their babies so they can have eye contact with them. Such was the case with Victor and his mother, Maureen. Noticing Maureen holding Victor with his back to her most of the time, their parent guide, Celeste, commented in a low-keyed manner, "I wonder what he will do if you hold him so he can see your face?" Fortunately, Victor then was able to teach his mother by brightening and making eye contact. Then, Celeste reinforced the pair with, "You like seeing Mommy smack her lips, don't you?" If after a few instances of this type of intervention, parents still do not hold their babies so they can have eye contact, parent guides need to wonder with the parents how it is for them when they hold their babies this way and then to respond with sensitivity and support to their responses. Some parents may feel threatened by this level of intimacy and need to move gradually toward this.

Even when held facing their parents, some babies still do not make eye contact. Melanie, a parent guide, said when she observed this, "I notice he looks away when you hold him face to face." When asked, the mother said that she had noticed this as well and wondered about it. Melanie then suggested some ways to engage the baby's visual response: vocalizing, gently touching the baby's nose and then slowly moving the finger back to the parent's eye. The possibilities are endless. The important aspect of this intervention is for parent guides and parents to work together and for parent guides to look for ways to acknowledge and encourage parents' discoveries of what helps. If after a week or two, Melanie's intervention does not work, she might suggest that the baby's vision be checked.

Partners in the Dance   Being locked into each other's eyes with soft, open expressions is an intensely moving experience that deepens the bond between parents and their babies. Often parents and their babies interweave their behaviors in a delicately timed synchrony of interchanges. Babies are usually so compelling with their engagement behaviors that their parents can learn "the dance" with them. Typically babies gaze intently at their partners who smile and nod and talk to them in relaxed, high-pitched voices. The babies react with smiles and coos and make active pre-speech movements of their lips and tongue combined with hand, arm, and leg movements (Trevarthen, 1993).

Over the first few months, these periods of mutual attentiveness tend to last longer and become enriched by enhanced eye-to-eye contact and the babies' smiles and vocalizations (Emde, 1989). Babies begin to spend more time gazing into their partners' eyes (Maurer & Salapatek, 1976). During these periods of sustained mutual gaze the mother's positive facial expressions stimulate and amplify positive affect in the baby, which is then communicated back to the mother. These exchanges generate an elevation of arousal that supports heightened levels of interest and enjoyment that in turn generates development of parts of the brain associated with pleasure.

When the Dancers Are Out of Step   By age 2 months, the interactions of well-attuned baby–parent dyads begin to resemble a refined, delicately synchronous dance in which each partner responds to the nuances of the other's expressions (Reddy, Hay, Murray, & Trevarthen, 1997). Evidence of this comes from experiments in which the mothers' behaviors do not match what the babies have come to expect.

In one study, mothers and their babies communicated with each other via a closed circuit television or double video system. Babies responded to the images of their mothers on the video screen as they typically did when actually in her presence. For some of the babies, however, the presentation of their mothers was delayed slightly so that their behaviors were out of sync with their babies' behaviors. These babies rapidly appeared confused and eventually became avoidant (Murray & Trevarthen, 1985).

The importance of having a responsive partner in the dance was also demonstrated in studies in which mothers were asked to cease communicating with their infants and to adopt a still, expressionless face similar to the unresponsiveness that babies of depressed parents often experience (Cohn & Tronick, 1989; Tronick, Ricks, & Cohn, 1982). The babies responded by becoming quickly disturbed. Initially they protested by looking at their mothers, frowning, thrashing their arms about, and making effortful negative vocalizations. As the still-face presentation continued, they tended to look away and become withdrawn, darting occasional glances in their mothers' direction as though to check to see if their mothers were becoming available again. Babies do not respond in this way if their mothers simply cease their interaction with them to turn and talk with another person (Murray & Trevarthen, 1985).

Parent guides who have the honor of watching parents and babies synchronize their movements in this "dance" can hardly keep from commenting, "As I watch you two, it's like watching two people dance together; doesn't it feel like that to you?" They can then talk about how much babies learn in these moments of synchrony—about themselves and about other people. It is almost painful to see a parent and baby who seem to be out of step in the dance. The parent might be emotionally unavailable or intrusive, overstimulating, or confusing as a partner, or the baby may be responding with poor rhythm to the parent's attempts. Finding out what is inhibiting the couple is primary to guiding intervention. The parent guide needs to observe, ask open-ended, nonjudgmental questions, form and check out hypotheses, and use this information as a guide to helping the couple get in step.

Marisa and her 2-month-old son, Freddy, were such a couple. Freddy had been in foster care for a month, and they had supervised visitation once a week. Freddy arched his back when being held, and his mother struggled to find a way to hold him that was comfortable for both of them. The parent guide first acknowledged how hard it must be to try to understand what your baby is saying when you only see him once a week. Then, she offered a rocking chair and coached Marisa to try only one thing at a time to help him settle and go to sleep—either rocking or patting, not both as she had been frantically trying to do. Fortunately for all involved, it worked! Freddy soon relaxed in his mother's arms and fell asleep. With a nod and a smile, the parent guide congratulated Marisa on learning the steps to this dance.

Self-Regulation of Emotion

Although the primary responsibility for emotion regulation falls to parents and other caregivers during these early months, babies typically do begin developing some self-regulation techniques during this stage. By the time they are 2 months old, babies typically learn the self-regulating technique of averting their gaze when they become overstimulated during social interactions. This helps them lower the intensity of this emotional arousal and regain equilibrium—but only if the parent is sensitive to their cues and backs off to allow them this respite. Three types of gaze aversion at this age have been identified. Babies may avert their gaze with a neutral expression when they simply turn away to look elsewhere. They also turn away, usually with a more distressed expression, to escape intrusive and insensitive demands for interaction from their partners. A third type of gaze aversion sometimes occurs as early as age 10 weeks when, following a greeting or renewal of pleasant contact with their partners, babies smile deeply and avert their heads and gaze briefly, then turn back to their partners (Reddy et al., 1997). This may function to briefly control the strong positive affect aroused by the initial greeting and eye contact.

Another emotion regulation strategy that babies use to regain calm when they are distressed is sucking on their thumbs, fingers, or pacifiers (Stifter & Braungart, 1995). Some parents fear that this practice will eventually deform the baby's teeth; however, results of a study by dentists demonstrated very little difference in the need for braces between children who did and those who did not suck their thumbs (Brazelton, 1992). Some babies also use rooting around in their cribs, rocking their heads, hand clasping, hair fingering, and other self-manipulations as self-comforting devices.

When the parent guide observes the parent responding to the baby's gaze aversion by pausing a little in whatever they are doing with the baby, the parent guide (who has been watching for this opportunity) can then comment, "Your Mommy understands when you need a break, doesn't she. You're a lucky guy!" When the parent does not respond by backing off a bit, the parent guide can use speaking through the baby to help the parent notice the ways in which the baby uses gaze aversion and appreciate what this means. For example, the parent guide says, "You're getting a little excited looking at Daddy like that, so you're taking a little break, aren't you?" Then, the parent guide turns to the father and says, "It's so good that he is able to do that—then he doesn't get overwhelmed and fussy." The same strategy can be used when thumb sucking is observed or reported, after first listening to the parents' feelings about this issue.

When babies look away, parents sometimes assign negative meanings to this. A parent with a low sense of efficacy is particularly likely to say something like, "She doesn't want to be held" or "He doesn't like me." Parents making comments like these may be helped by responses like, "How is he telling you that?" Parent guides then have opened the possibility of finding out more about how the parents are feeling about themselves and their parenting and can then provide support and reframing of their babies' signals. Depending on the parents' responses, they might explain that because interacting with their parents is so enjoyable, babies often have to take little breaks so that they do not become overly excited.

Sometimes parents respond to baby's gaze aversion by increasing the stimulation. For example, if a baby averts his gaze, his mother might pull him closer to her face to reengage him. Usually, the baby will then escalate to a fussy state, and the mother will feel that she has failed. When the parent guide observes or the mother reports this occurrence, talking

through the baby may be helpful: "Oops, Mommy thought you were getting bored, but maybe you just needed a little break." Then, the guide can
say directly to the parent, "Let's see what he does if you wait a minute and
try again; that's how babies handle input from their world."

When family members insist on not letting the baby suck on a thumb
or pacifier, the parent guide, very carefully and with respect for their
experience, can wonder what they have experienced or heard about the
dangers of thumb sucking or pacifiers. Acknowledging parents' and other
family members' healthy striving (e.g., not having child suck thumb in
school, not hurting child's teeth later) and providing information for their
consideration may allow family members to consider alternative ways of
responding to this situation. For example, parents can be told that many
pediatricians (e.g., Dr. T. Barry Brazelton, 1992) view thumb sucking as
a healthy self-comforting pattern. Even fetuses suck their thumbs, and
newborns come equipped with the hand-to-mouth (Babkin) reflex that
makes thumb sucking come naturally. Many babies use thumb sucking as
a way of comforting themselves when they are upset or trying to settle
down. Because thumb sucking is such a handy way (no pun intended!) to
comfort themselves, babies who make use of it are often easier to live
with. Brazelton reports that if parents ask him about the relative merits
of thumbs versus pacifiers, he points out the obvious: "a thumb is always available" (Brazelton, 1992, p. 66). After saying this much, however,
Brazelton then turns the issue back to the parents. He knows that preferences and feelings about thumbs and pacifiers have deep roots in family
history and culture.

GETTING ACQUAINTED

Over these first few months, parents typically get to know their babies—
their unique characteristics, interests, and needs. Through trial and error,
they find what usually works to comfort their babies when they are upset
and to engage them when they are ready for interaction. In so doing, the
parents develop a sense of efficacy and satisfaction from their growing
ability to comfort and engage their babies (Sroufe, 1996). Gradually, trial
and error learning gives way to ideas of what works and to the feeling of
confidence that they know what their babies need and can specifically
meet those needs (Sander, 1975). By responding promptly and effectively
to distress signals, they help their babies find relaxation and surcease of
discomfort and begin to develop smooth routines of feeding and sleeping.
With this regulation of physiological functions, their babies begin to develop emotion regulation.

In order to discuss with parents what they are finding that works and to reinforce their efforts to discern this, parent guides can request, "Tell me about life with Tasheka?" or "What happens in a usual day with Jenny?" Asked in this open-ended way, parents can provide information that parent guides can then explore further with the parents and reinforce their efforts to discern what's working. During parents' accounts of how it is with their baby, parent guides should be alert for opportunities to provide information about the importance of developing smooth routines of feeding, sleeping, and playing, and that it will take some time to do so. It is so important that these invitations for parents to share intimate information about life with baby communicate genuine interest and respect for parents' knowledge about their babies.

Because mothers are usually the primary caregivers for their babies, the task of finding out what works generally weighs more heavily on them than on fathers; however, a number of fathers are becoming more involved in the caregiving of their babies—and with good results. Babies whose fathers participated in bathing, feeding, diapering, and other routines of physical care were more socially responsive and scored higher on the Bayley Scales of Infant Development than babies who did not receive this care from their dads (Parke & Sawin, 1975; Pruett, 1997). There is also evidence that nurturing fathers are less likely than less-involved fathers to sexually abuse their own or anyone else's children later in life (Parker & Parker, 1986). Even when performing many of the same functions, fathers generally interact differently with their babies than mothers do, and babies at an early age show that they anticipate these differences (Pruett, 1997). Fathers also play an important role by providing emotional and instrumental support to their partners. Parent guides should encourage and reinforce positive contributions from fathers.

When learning about life with baby, the parent guide might learn about feeding or sleeping problems. Respectfully, parent guides offer themselves as partners in problem solving with the parents. "What concerns do you have? What remedies have you already tried? What has been suggested by family members or friends? By your doctor?" The key to effectiveness is to keep parents in the driver's seat, to ask questions in order to help parents discover options for themselves. Then, they are more committed to trying these options, and they are more likely to succeed with them. In follow-up visits, parent guides can ask how things have gone with regard to the problems raised earlier and can then reinforce parents' success in finding solutions or can continue the problem solving with them.

Sometimes feeding or sleeping problems arise due to unresolved problems from the parent's past that can sometimes influence parenting behavior in insidious ways. Such was the case with Yolanda whose daughter Keesha was diagnosed with nonorganic failure to thrive when she was a few weeks old. When asking Yolanda to reflect on her own experiences of being parented as a child, Helen learned that Yolanda had been rejected as a child by her mentally ill mother because she was overweight. As they explored this further, it became apparent that Yolanda had derived an internal model of herself as unworthy and incapable of love, which existed to the present time and interfered with her ability to read and respond appropriately to Keesha. When the parent guide invited and listened with sensitivity to Yolanda's story about her childhood as well as her experience as a new parent, Yolanda began to view herself as more worthwhile and competent. Within a short time, she reported that Keesha was taking more formula and gaining weight. (The pediatrician corroborated this report.) Ongoing reflective relationship-based intervention with Yolanda and Keesha ensured that Yolanda could continue to support Keesha's psychological as well as physical growth.

States of Arousal

By understanding how their babies transition among various states of arousal, parents can better help their babies achieve physiological regulation. There are six states of arousal that babies cycle in and out of every 3–4 hours. Deep, regular breathing, tightly shut eyes, and very little if any movement characterize the deep sleep state. During this state, most babies can shut out nearly all environmental stimuli. During light, or rapid eye movement (REM), sleep, however, babies are more vulnerable to outside influences. In REM sleep, babies may suck with or without fingers in their mouths, move in a writhing way, and startle once or twice. Newborns typically sleep (either deep or REM sleep) 16 to 17 hours per day (Dahl, 1996). The indeterminate state is a disorganized, short-lived one that occurs when babies rouse or return to sleep. They may squirm, move jerkily, open and sleepily close their eyes, frown, and whimper.

It is during the wide-awake, alert state that parents can most profitably engage in interactions with their babies. In this state

> The baby's bright face and shining eyes demonstrate his open receptivity. His movements are contained. If he moves, he moves smoothly and can even achieve a goal, such as bringing his hand to his mouth or holding one hand with the other. His breathing fits itself to the stimulus. With an exciting stimulus, his breathing is deep. For a negative one, it is shallow and rapid. One can see his responsiveness on his face and in his entire body as he attends to an interesting noise or a familiar face. His face, his breathing, his body's posture—all convey interest and attention, or else a

desire to withdraw and turn away from an overwhelming stimulus. (Brazelton, 1992, p. 60)

The fussy alert state often follows the alert state. In this state, babies' movements are jerky and their breathing is irregular. They fuss and may thrash about. This is a time for parents to try to calm their babies and help them become organized again; however, in spite of their best efforts, the babies may transition into a full-blown crying state.

States of arousal can be described for parents and illustrated by observing their babies with them. Babies are such powerful teachers! It can be quite helpful for parents to recognize their babies' states of arousal. When babies are awake and it is time for their feeding but if they are still in the indeterminate state, parents might be encouraged to change them or provide mild stimulation by talking or moving them so that they transition to the wide-awake, alert state before they start the feeding. They are then more likely to finish eating before falling back into light sleep. Lisa was helped to do this with 1-month-old Ethan who kept falling back to sleep when Lisa tried to feed him before he was more fully awake.

If parents are trying to get their babies to look at a toy and the babies are in the fussy alert state, parent guides can observe aloud that their babies seem to need help calming down and getting organized again before they can respond visually. When parent guides observe babies in the wide-awake, alert state, they can comment for baby, "Boy I'm ready to play, Mom." Being able to match interactions with babies' states of arousal can be quite fulfilling to both parents and their babies and is worth careful observation and gentle comments by parent guides to raise parents' awareness of their babies' states.

Smooth transitions among states of arousal are more difficult for babies living in chaotic households. Parent guides who want to help babies by addressing their environments have a formidable task (see Section III). They can begin by deciding who in the baby's life is able and willing to help make changes. It might be the mother who is open to this challenge. The parent guide can help her problem solve, being careful not to alienate her from needed supports in the family, and can then support actions toward less chaos in the household. This may involve helping the mother herself achieve a more predictable, calm household routine, using a calendar and a "to do" list, and setting limits on comings and goings of other adults in the home. If the parent guide frames the need for the baby to have a calm environment as something that will help prevent behavior problems in the future, the mother may be more motivated to make the difficult changes that are called for.

A chaotic household is a serious problem for hypersensitive babies. Given that one cause of hypersensitivity is maternal drug use during pregnancy, these babies are at risk for living in disturbed environments. If their mothers continue to use drugs or live with people who do, these babies are probably exposed to too much stimulation, too little routine, and too many caregivers. Such is the case for some of the children of substance-abusing parents who are described in Chapter 10.

Blowing Off Steam   For many babies, the fussy state becomes prolonged toward the end of the day between about 3 and 12 weeks of age. Some pediatricians no longer refer to these fussy periods as colic, but view them as the result of an increasingly overloaded, immature nervous system cycling in shorter and shorter sleep and feeding periods and finally "blowing off steam" at the end of the day (Brazelton, 1992).

When parents report that their babies have become colicky or very fussy, the first thing they need is empathy. They are likely to feel guilt, fatigue, and anger—probably in that order. To be told that this is typical for most babies and that they usually outgrow it in a few weeks is true but does not take away those feelings. Parent guides can help parents arrange respite for themselves so they can rest, regroup, and feel okay again in order to help their babies have a better developmental course. Arranging respite also involves helping parents understand that it is not selfish or neglectful to get respite, but rather a positive step toward helping their babies through this period. When respite cannot be provided by another person, a parent guide may help the parent discover ways to find some relief each day at home by listening to relaxing music, taking a warm bath when the baby is sleeping, talking with a friend on the telephone, or doing some breathing and stretching exercises.

Some parents do not try to help their babies when they are "blowing off steam," and some get angry and overly frustrated during these fussy times. These reactions are a challenge for small infants, and they need someone to speak for them. When such responses are observed or reported by parents, parent guides need to ask the question, "What might help this go better for you?" It helps parents move on to doing something different when they feel that their feelings are validated. Often the question itself allows parents to think about the situation in a solution-focused way. Parent guides can then help them describe how they experience the fussiness and find ways of dealing with these feelings that are not harmful to their babies.

Sometimes a baby's mother reports that her partner gets really angry with the baby during these fussy times. Such a report will trigger a risk assessment by the parent guide who will question the mother about circumstances in which her partner becomes angry with the baby, what he does or says when he becomes angry, and whether there is any history of violence on the part of the partner. If the mother's answers to these questions indicate a high level of risk to the baby, the parent guide will need to report this situation to CPS or support the mother in protecting the baby in some other way, such as moving out. If the risk does not seem that great, the parent guide can arrange a time to meet with both of the parents, explaining to the father (or surrogate father) that she wants to meet with him because he is an important part of the baby's life and she would like to learn from both of them what it is like to be parents of this new baby. In the meantime, the parent guide can explore with the mother ways in which she could feel more comfortable about her baby's safety. For instance, Nancy, the mother of 2-month-old Samuel, told her parent guide that if she left Samuel and her husband, Robert, alone, Robert usually called her after a short while asking her to come home because he could not get Samuel to be quiet. Listening carefully to Nancy, the parent guide understood that Nancy really needed to have little breaks from child care and needed Robert to make this possible. Together they explored what the situation might be like for Robert and how to help him feel more confident with Samuel. Nancy was guided so that she intentionally did not jump in to soothe Samuel when she and her husband were both with Samuel, but instead she reinforced Robert's attempts to do so. This restraint was quite hard for Nancy because she had a strong need to be a good parent (and perhaps to be a better parent than Robert). Although the parent guide was not able to arrange a meeting with both parents, she did continue to support Nancy in her efforts to support Robert. Soon Nancy was reporting that Robert was "being a really good daddy," meaning that she felt comfortable leaving Samuel with him while she visited a friend.

Temperament

Babies' temperaments are revealed in the ways they move in and out of these states of arousal. Some babies do so quickly, others more slowly. The task for parents is to learn their babies' styles and especially ways to comfort them when they are in the fussy or crying states. Understanding how babies manage their environments can also inspire within parents a respect for their babies' competence—especially when, as suggested in Chapter 2, the positive aspects of different temperaments and styles are emphasized.

Parents also differ in their styles and temperaments. One of the authors observed a mother of a premature infant handle her baby roughly—she picked her up quickly, put her in the car seat with rough movements, and put a bottle in her mouth hastily so that the baby had difficulty grasping the nipple. These movements were not angry or hostile, just rough.

The mother's complaint that her baby was irritable gave the parent guide the opportunity to wonder if she would be less irritable if she were moved slowly and very gently because of her immature nervous system. The mother was able to pick up on this suggestion about special care for her premature infant rather than perceiving it as criticism or instruction that would have generated resistance and feelings of failure on her part.

When babies appear to have spirited temperaments, it is helpful to assess the match between these babies and their parents—what is the fit between baby's temperament and that of the parent? When babies move quickly and jerkily among states of arousal, can their parents help them make these transitions, especially from fussy alert to the quiet alert state by their own calmness, or are the parents' temperaments similar to their babies'? Do they become jerky and quick in their movements at these times, also? When observing or hearing about parents' responses to spirited temperaments as revealed in state transitions, parent guides can provide information that helps the parents realize how common their difficulty is and can offer alternative ways to respond to babies that parents can try. For example, if a parent begins to feel tension when trying to calm her baby who is in the fussy alert state, the parent guide can suggest that she ask another adult to take over until she has a chance to calm herself down. Reassure her that this is in the baby's best interest and is not selfishness or weakness on her part. If no other adult is available, the parent can be encouraged to lay the baby down in a safe place and walk away for a moment, breathe deeply, or whatever else she has learned that helps her to organize and calm herself. Then, she can try again with the baby. Samantha, whose childhood abuse left her overreactive to her children's fussing, learned to use techniques like this to calm herself when she felt herself becoming tense.

Baby's Special Abilities

Fortunately for the beleaguered parents, the end-of-the-day fussy periods described earlier are balanced by periods of quiet alertness during which babies' propensities for social interaction reward the parents who are physically and psychologically available for these moments of intimate interactions. Babies come equipped with visual and auditory systems specially designed to attend to human faces and voices. Newborns hear quite well in the typical pitch and volume range of human speech, and when awake, they naturally turn toward sounds. So, parents who talk and croon to their babies are rewarded by their attention. Newborns are very attracted to the perceptual characteristics of human faces such as the areas of sharp contrasts (e.g., the pupils of a person's eyes; Slater & Butterworth, 1997). Babies also attend to movement, which may be why people tend to bob their heads when talking to an infant. Very young babies often play very close attention to mouth movements when someone leans toward them and talks to them (Kugiumutzakis, 1986; Slater & Butterworth, 1997). Often they will stick out their own tongues after carefully watching someone who, within their range of vision, sticks their tongue out a few times (Jones, 1996). By around 10 weeks, babies also begin to notice their mothers' different facial expressions of happiness, sadness, anger, and surprise and respond accordingly (Field, Woodson, Greenberg, & Cohen, 1982; Haviland & Lelwica, 1987).

Watching the babies together with their parents or asking, "What's baby been doing since I last saw you?" can focus attention on what the babies bring to their interactions with their parents. Parent guides can notice examples of babies' attending to their parents' movements and facial expressions. They can highlight these either directly to parents or by speaking for or through their babies, depending on the needs of the parents and the relationship the parent guide has with them. For example, "Have you seen your baby try to stick his tongue out when you stick yours out? It's amazing that little babies can do that!" or "You may have noticed that he sometimes looks sad when you are sad—babies seem to pick up on your feelings even at this age." The parent guide can add that this is a time of increased activity in the part of their babies' brains (the right parietal lobe) that takes in and processes information about faces (Restak, 1995). Multiple connections (synapses) are being developed that help them recognize faces and facial expressions and associate them with other sensations such as how they feel.

Once the subject is open, parent guides can help parents notice other examples of what their babies bring to their relationships. Then, parent guides can suggest little games that parents can play to encourage their babies to show off their talents: sticking out their tongues slowly and watching to see if their babies follow suit, getting eye contact and then moving slowly to one side and see if their babies follow with their eyes, crooning softly, and watching babies' movements and eyes. After focusing parents' attention on these abilities of their babies, parent guides can then reinforce instances of parents' noticing and responding to these things during this and subsequent visits.

In these suggestions, it is assumed that parents are able to focus on what their babies can do, but what about those instances when parents appear disinterested in what their babies can do, even when helped to focus on this? The intervention strategy used will depend on the apparent reason for what seems like parental disinterest. A characteristic of adolescence is a focus on self as teenagers work to establish their identities. This self-focus as well as other adolescent issues may interfere with the other-focus needed for parenting. Other parents may seem disinterested in what their babies can do due to depression, substance abuse, or stressful family situations. Postpartum depression especially may be a problem for some mothers during this period. These issues and more are addressed in Section III.

Attributing Meaning

Right from the beginning, most parents tend to attribute meaning to their babies' behaviors. Parents treat the babies' coos, arm waves, gazes, and smiles as though they were intentional attempts to communicate. The wise mother ignores, as Sharon did, information that the smile that flits across the sleeping newborn's face is merely a physiological reaction. It is far more satisfying for most mothers to see this smile as affirmation that they are fulfilling their babies' needs and making them happy. The meanings that parents give to their babies' behaviors can tell parent guides much about the quality of the mothers' relationships with their babies (Cramer, 1987; Miller, 1995). Parents vary greatly in the meanings that they attribute to virtually identical infant behaviors.

> Parents constantly submit each of the infant's behaviors to influences stemming from their own private set of expectations, ideals, prohibitions, predilections, and so on. Through this process, various aspects of the infant's repertoire are selected and enhanced, while others are censored and extinguished. In this way, cultural and personal sets of values will be transmitted. (Cramer, 1987, p. 1044)

Parental attributions of meaning deserve special attention because they play such a crucial role in determining the parent's interactions with the baby. Many parental attributions are positive, or at least benign, and reflect the parents' personal and cultural values. When these seem to be associated with positive, healthy interactions with their babies, they can be simply highlighted as a way to raise parents' consciousness about them. When, however, such attributions arise from distorted parental perceptions of their babies, they can lead to actions that hinder their babies' development.

While Lynette (Jeffrey's mother) and newborn Jeffrey were still in the hospital, Lynette spoke of how much like his father Jeffrey was. She worried then about his becoming aggressive like his father. She continued to view Jeffrey this way, attributing typical assertion as being "stubborn, just like his Daddy" and later on as "mean," again like his father. From the beginning, Jeffrey had a hard time being seen as a person with his own unique qualities; instead, his appearance and behaviors were cast in the likeness of his father. When Lynette worried about his growing up to be like his father, her parent guide, Helen, helped her identify ways she was parenting Jeffrey differently from the way she knew her husband had been parented. As evidence of how this was working, Helen pointed out Jeffrey's many demonstrations of gentleness; she noticed and commented on how affectionate he was to his mother and marveled at how he could self-soothe using his thumb. In these ways, she offered an alternative way to view Jeffrey and his possibilities.

Reading Their Babies   It is a boon to effective caregiving that parents strive to see meaning in their babies' behaviors. Healthy socioemotional development depends on parents' abilities to accurately read their babies' signals of need, interest, and desire and to respond promptly and effectively to those signals most of the time. Parent guides can help parents tune into their babies' cues either as they are happening or later while watching videos together. They can ask parents if they are beginning to notice the different cries of their babies: the piercing, painful-sounding cry; the demanding, urgent cry; the bored, hollow cry; and the rhythmic but not urgent cry that occurs when a baby is tired or overloaded with too much stimulation (Brazelton, 1992). As they babywatch together, they can notice how babies also signal with their facial expressions and body postures and movements. Newborns show distress by grimacing, arching their backs, and throwing out their arms. Over time, babies' signals become more refined just as their emotions become more differentiated. The following are some baby signals and what they mean as described in Partners in Parent Education (PIPE; available from www.howtoreadyourbaby.com):

- Furrowed eyebrows indicate anger whereas raised eyebrows can show surprise.

- Eyes may be bright, shiny, and focused, indicating that babies are tuned in and alert, or they may be dull and unfocused, revealing that babies may be tired or overloaded and need a break.

- When babies look away, it can be their way of saying, "Time out!" but looking away in situations in which babies are not getting stimulation may signal boredom.

- Newborns sometimes indicate that they need to be swaddled by hugging themselves when things are too much for them.

- When babies put one hand to the mouth, sucking on their fingers or fist, and put the other hand to their ears or hair, it is a sign that they are comforting themselves.

- Pulling at their ears may indicate earaches.

- While yawns can indicate sleepiness, they also occur sometimes when babies are feeling a little stressed.

When parents miss most of their babies' signals or when they seem to be grossly misinterpreting babies' meanings, they deserve to have parent guides available to help them learn more about their babies. Physicians are in a particularly good place in parents' lives to provide intervention when they observe problems in this area. They can ask parents what their babies have been telling them with their bodies, and they can reinforce and extend these observations. They can have on hand printed materials or videotapes to loan that will help parents discover, in the privacy of their own homes, more of the wonders of babies and ways they can respond to them. Follow-up can then occur at the next well-baby check-up. If concerns still remain, physicians can refer the parents to a new-parent support group or home visiting program that can provide ongoing supportive counseling and information. Providing even a small amount of information and support very early can make a large difference in the trajectory of the interactions babies and their parents enjoy, and in the healthy emotional development of the babies.

Parents who can successfully read their babies' cues and respond effectively to meet their needs feel more confident in their parenting roles. Their babies are more apt to achieve sufficient physiological regulation and to enjoy periods of awake alertness in which they can get to know their surroundings and the people who care for them. They and their parents are ready for the social games of the next stage.

5

Let the Games Begin

3 to 7 Months

"Where's my little guy?" Christy, a single mother, calls out as she comes into her parents' house after work. She rounds the corner into the kitchen, and 4-month-old Tony squeals with delight when she greets him. She swoops him up out of his baby seat and carries him into the living room, calling over her shoulder, "I'll help with dinner in a minute, Mom. I've got to play with this little rascal first, though." Christy sits on the couch and lays Tony down next to her. He gazes intently at her as she leans toward him. "Soooo, what have you been up to today, hmmm?" She pauses, and Tony gives a little wiggle. Her eyes widen as she continues, "Oh, is that so. You really worked hard, huh?" She pauses again, and Tony wriggles more and coos. Christy's voice rises, and she draws out her words, "Yes, tell me all about it. Tell mommy all about it." The corners of Tony's mouth begin to turn up. "Oh, I see that smile. I see a smile coming on." Pause. "Come on now. Give mommy a big smile." Tony smiles more broadly, and Christy responds with enthusiasm, "That's a wonderful smile!" Tony waves his arms and kicks his feet. Christy does a little shimmy with her shoulders and exclaims, "Oooh, you're glad to see your mommy, aren't you, and I'm glad to see

*you." With that, Christy scoops him up and gives him a hug and a kiss.
When she lays him back down, he turns his attention away from her.
Christy leans back and smiles down at him while he recovers from the
intense excitement he just experienced.*

SOCIAL GAMES

Playful, loving social games such as this one are used more often and expand in their complexity during this period from age 3 to 7 months. They
start with the baby and parent gazing intently and lovingly into each
other's eyes. From this interaction, simple, playful interactions develop.
The parent smiles. The baby coos, and the parent exclaims, "Oh, you
don't say!" The baby wriggles. By age 7 months, the games have become
much more extended, and elaborate and traditional games such as Peekaboo have been introduced. This is the "falling in love" period—babies are
getting to know their parents and are on their way to developing attachments with them. It is a time of experiencing varied and sometimes intense feelings and learning in a rudimentary way how these feelings are
regulated. During the second and third months, these social games build
on the rapid development of those parts of the brain that process vision,
touch, bodily sensation, hearing, speech, and language development. As
Christy and Tony interact, important connections are being formed between what Tony sees and hears and how he feels.

Developing the Game

By age 3 months, babies and their parents typically begin to adjust to one
another and feeding and sleeping routines become a bit smoother (although there are still some challenges). As this happens, babies develop
longer periods of quiet alertness during which they are attentive to their
surroundings and are ready for interaction. The sharp increase of activity
in the cerebral cortex between the second and third months makes this a
prime time for visual and auditory stimulation (Shore, 1997).

   The Eyes Have It   Babies start paying attention to their parents' eyes
by the end of the second month (Maurer & Salapatek, 1976), and by age
17 weeks, the eyes have won out over the mouth as the most interesting
feature of the parent's face (Caron, Caron, Caldwell, & Weiss, 1973). In
well-attuned dyads, parents respond with delight to this attention, and
baby and parent develop many moments of gazing lovingly into each
other's eyes—an intensely felt experience for them both. Most parents are
captivated by babies' gazing intently into their eyes and by the social
smiles that begin to emerge around this time. By age 3–4 weeks, babies

smile in response to high-pitched voices, and by age 4–6 weeks they smile to a nodding face, but it is not until about age 3 months that they develop true social smiles. A month or so later they add laughter to their repertoire of interactive behaviors that include coos, gurgles, wriggles, and smiles. Not only do parents delight in their babies' smiles, but babies prefer looking at happy faces, and the greater the intensity of the smiling face, the more it is looked at (Kuchuk, Vibbert, & Bornstein, 1986). Many parents also talk to their babies during these social games, an important step in fostering language development. By age 3 months, babies can distinguish several hundred different spoken sounds. By 6 months, their auditory maps are different depending on the language, or languages, in their homes, and by 12 months they are babbling in their own language.

There are some ways that parent guides can steer this development, working through the parents. Before the babies are 3 months old, parent guides, watching the babies with their parents, can look for opportunities to give advance notice that their babies will soon be staying awake for longer periods and will be delighted by social games with their parents. They can also share information with parents about the importance of these games to baby's brain development. At each visit, then, the parent guide can ask the parent: "How long does Anna stay awake during the day now?" "Would you show me how you and Eric play together now that he is awake more?" Then, in observing them, the parent guide can notice how baby is looking at his parent and can say, "Ooh! He is certainly enjoying your attention! He seems to love it when you hold him so he can look at your eyes, doesn't he? . . . . How does that feel to you?" These questions call attention to the importance of mutual eye gazing, and help parents see the connection between how they hold and look at their babies and their babies' smiling responses.

When helping parents look for baby's interest in eye-to-eye social games does not seem to be enough and when parents do not hold their babies so that there can be mutual gaze, parent guides need to find ways to explicate this need of babies. Their stance is always, "Help me learn more about your baby." For instance, a parent guide might say, "What happens when you hold Shakita on your lap, facing you?" If the parent answers verbally, she responds with, "I'd like to see that; would you show me?" Now she has an opportunity to exclaim, a little or a lot, depending on her reading of the parent, about what she is seeing the baby do now that the baby is able to look into the parent's eyes. Again, it is important to also ask parents how these experiences feel to them. Sometimes the parent guide experiences a baby's gaze as engaging and delightful, but the parent experiences it as too intimate and too demanding. By asking nonjudgmentally what it feels like to the parent, the parent guide learns more about what kind of help the parent might need.

Getting in Tune Although babies of this age will attend to toys, especially ones that move or make noise, they are most readily engaged by another person. People not only move and make sounds, but they often do so in ways that are responsive to the baby's behavior. For instance, a baby looks at the mother's face, smiles and makes a "brm" sound. Magically, mother's face changes as she smiles and says, "Brm, brm to you!" When the baby waves his arms and kicks his feet, his mother shakes her shoulders in rhythm with his movements. Such imitations often occur and are fun for both baby and parent. When the parent guide observes an interaction in which the parent highlights the baby's behavior by imitating it, she can encourage the repetition of this behavior by commenting on how good it is for baby's development: "Her little brain is developing good connections every time you tune in to her like you just did," and later, "You are really helping her regulate her feelings when you do that; it's like you're a mirror in which she and her world are reflected in a way that helps her make sense of them," or "It's little games like this that help her become more attached to you—to know that you are her safety and security in this big world she's come into!"

Even parents who enjoy caring for their babies and have sufficient opportunities for doing so may need some guidance in ways to interact that assist their babies' developmental goals. Some parents may need help in understanding the importance of this type of interaction. For example, a mother may enjoy holding, rocking, and cuddling her 3-month-old but may not engage in face-to-face interactions that facilitate eye gazing. Some parents may find it difficult to read their babies' cues and adjust their play with their babies in response to those cues.

Beth needed a little help in modulating her play with Kevin. During parent–infant playgroup, they were both enjoying a playful episode of Beth touching Kevin's nose, mouth, ears, and toes. Kevin showed his pleasure by smiling broadly and making happy gurgling sounds. Enjoying this and wanting to continue the play, Beth touched his nose with her nose and then tickled his stomach with her hair. Beth appeared not to notice that Kevin looked startled and then a little distressed as she continued this new version of the game. Helen nearby did notice, however, and said to Beth through the baby, "Gee, Kevin, I think you were enjoying it more when Mommy touched you with her finger—then you could see her smiling face!" Beth quickly returned to using her finger and hand rather than overwhelming Kevin with more intrusive play. He rewarded her with a delightful giggle.

Videotaped interactions are a good tool for helping parents hone their skills of reading and getting in tune with their babies. In the example of Kevin, the parent guide and Beth would watch a videotape together, with the parent guide asking open-ended questions such as, "What do you think he would say here if he could talk?" "What part of the game do you think he was enjoying most? How could you tell? Why do you think that was?" These kinds of questions can help parents discover for themselves what their babies want and need and can thereby gain the confidence to expand their abilities to read their babies.

Another challenge to getting in tune occurs when the baby's temperament is not well matched with the parent's temperament. Sometimes this occurs when both the baby and the parent have similar temperaments. For example, Victor (whom we met in Chapter 1) was a slow-to-warm-up baby. He needed persistence from his mother in order to be engaged in social games. His mother, Maureen, was also slow-to-warm-up and needed more feedback than Victor was able to offer in order to stay engaged with him. An observer would think of two ships passing in the night when watching their attempts at social game playing. Their parent guide, Celeste, described Victor's temperament style as typical and offered guidance to help Maureen pursue Victor playfully, first when he was sitting in his infant seat, and then while holding him face to face on her lap, using whispers and soft, sing-song tones. In the conversations that ensued over several weeks, Maureen felt safe enough to make the comparison between her baby's style and her own. She appreciated her baby more, and this appreciation motivated her to try harder to get in tune with Victor.

When direct intervention such as this is not effective after a few weeks, further inquiry is needed to determine how to help the dyad. Sometimes parents do not tune into their babies and engage them in social games because they are simply emotionally unavailable to them. This problem can occur for a variety of reasons (e.g., depression, substance abuse, illness). When this emotional unavailability takes place on a regular basis, good supplemental care for the baby may be needed so these babies can receive the benefits of playful interactions while their parents are being treated. The parent guide's role is to assist with appropriate referrals and to support and monitor the interaction between baby and parent in regular contacts.

Variations on the Theme   Many parents soon learn how to keep the game going by being attentive and responsive to the nuances of their babies' behaviors just as Christy did in her interaction with Tony. They learn how to vary their smiles, movements, exclamations, and touch to keep their babies engaged. In this way, babies begin developing the ability to attend to an activity for increasing periods of time; their attention spans begin to stretch. Under the guidance of a sensitive and playful parent, these social games become more elaborate and extensive over the next several months. In addition to the type of interaction enjoyed by Christy and Tony, many parents begin introducing various traditional games such as Peekaboo and nursery songs as well as games created especially for and by the dyad. By 6 months of age, babies respond with eager enthusiasm to these familiar games and routines. The baby's developing cognitive skills enhance these social games. Building on their ability to detect familiar patterns (see Chapter 4), babies as young as 3 months can begin anticipating the next step in a familiar playful routine. In one study, 3-month-olds were shown pictures to one side or another. When the pictures were shown in a regular pattern (for instance, left, left, right), they quickly caught on and anticipated (looked for) the next picture in the expected position (Canfield & Haith, 1991). This ability can be exploited to the delight of both the baby and the parent in such games as Peekaboo.

When the parent is not sensitive and does not know how to play, the social games do not become more elaborate and extensive, and baby's development is impeded. Such was the case for Leon and his mother, Corrine. Her mild mental retardation and her lethargic temperament combined to inhibit her ability to play with her baby. When asked by the parent guide, Joanne, to play with him as they usually do, Corrine looked at Leon in his infant seat and repeated "Le-on" over and over in a monotone voice. This was her only attempt to get his attention and play with him. He looked at her at first, but when there was no variation in her attempts to play with him, Leon turned his head and stared blankly in another direction. When Joanne was talking with Corrine about her experience, she said, "He doesn't like to play with me." This gave Joanne the opportunity to offer the technique of floor time as a way to respond to Corrine's desire to have Leon want to play with her. Because of her need to have some of Joanne's attention directed to her, the sessions were structured with Corrine's half hour first then a half hour for learning to observe, engage, extend, and close circles with Leon. (These are the steps of floor time, the technique described in Chapter 3). Corrine and Leon made progress in the next few months with this concrete, structured intervention paired with continued attention to Corrine's personal emotional needs.

Another challenge to variations on the theme is found when parents want to keep their babies young and cuddly. Parents who really enjoy their babies' dependence on them might have this desire. The parent guide's challenge is to learn more about these parents so interventions can be tailored to the individual parents. Some of these parents may need help identifying other ways of getting their own needs met, rather than relying on their babies to do that. The parent guide can invite parents to talk about what it will be like for them as their babies get older and can do more things on their own. This discussion may reveal some of the unspoken fears or beliefs that threaten these parents. Here again is an example of parallel process. Just as babies need their parents to be attentive and responsive to their nuances, so too do the parents need the parent guides to be attentive and responsive to theirs and to look for ways to "vary the theme" with them to extend their abilities to do the same for their babies.

As we saw with Victor and Maureen, some babies are difficult to engage in ongoing social games. Parents of these babies need extra encouragement and support if they are to continue helping their child to play these games. Maureen's guide, Celeste, offered to join her in being detectives to figuring out what would work with Victor, given his temperament, and Celeste was diligent in noticing and highlighting those glimpses of pleasure in Victor when responding to his mother, so that Maureen could be fueled by them to continue the pursuit.

ON THE ROAD TO ATTACHMENT

In the context of these games as well as through all their other interactions day in and day out, babies build their relationships with their parents and other special caregivers. By the end of this period, they will show a marked preference for a select few. They will turn to them for help and comfort and will honor them with special smiles and greetings. Early in their lives, the part of the brain primarily responsible for recognizing faces (the right parietal lobe) undergoes rapid development (Restak, 1995), and by age 5 months, babies begin showing marked preferences for familiar faces. There is even evidence that babies as young as 6 months can distinguish pictures of their mothers from pictures of strangers (deHaan & Nelson, 1997). During the early months, even though babies indicate a preference for the familiar faces of their parents, they often smile in response to just about anyone who interacts appropriately with them. (Stranger anxiety does not occur with most babies until about age 7–8 months, although some begin to manifest this as early as 5 months.) By around 5 or 6 months, when the mother (or another beloved figure) appears, she is now greeted with a special show of delight just as Tony displayed when Christy came into the kitchen. Mothers may elicit greetings from their 3-month-old babies, but babies this age seldom display unelicited greetings. By age 6 months, however, spontaneous greetings are as common as those elicited by their mothers (Kaye & Fogel, 1980).

Remembering that promoting the developing attachment between infant and parent is the primary aim, the sensitive parent guide should be very intentional about highlighting babies' special attention to their parents. Comments such as, "Did you see her turn toward you when you spoke just now?" and "Have you noticed that he seems to prefer you to unfamiliar people more and more?" can help parents notice and appreciate this development in their babies. As parents are invited to think of other instances of this happening, the parent guide can introduce the fact that, in a few months, this preference will be shown by their babies' distress when confronted with strangers. They can be reassured that this is a typical and positive behavior and can be encouraged to be ready to assist their babies by being close by and comforting them when they become distressed.

Learning the Language of Emotions

In the social games of this period, babies are beginning to learn how to dialogue with another person. There is a give and take in the interchanges that portends the turn taking of intentional communication in the next stage (Reddy et al., 1997). In Christy's play with Tony, she responded to his wriggles, coos, and smiles in various ways. Then, she would pause and give him a chance to respond to her. Although these interactions often have the structure of a dialogue, at this age, they have more the character of a social dance than a conversation about a topic. Baby and parent are dancing to the music of their emotions; music that builds to a climax then subsides only to build again. Through this dance babies are learning the language of emotions—the facial expressions and body movements that portray nuances of feelings. During this stage, parents typically imitate many of their babies' behaviors. During the next stage, they engage more in affective attunement (Stern, 1985). That is, they tune into their babies' feelings and behave in ways that reflect and express those feelings. Still later, when these babies as toddlers venture forth to explore their world, they can turn to their parents when they encounter something novel or puzzling and read their parents' body language to determine whether it is something to fear and back away from or to enjoy and pursue.

   Although babies become especially familiar with the emotional language of the special people in their lives, by this age they are sensitive to the emotional messages conveyed by the tone of voice and facial expressions of unfamiliar people, as well. In one experiment, 5-month-olds heard both approving speech (e.g., a phrase such as "You're so good!" said with the phrasing and intonation of exaggerated praise used in infant-directed speech) and prohibiting speech (e.g., "You're so naughty!" again uttered with the appropriate phrasing and tone of voice). These messages were given in four different languages (English, Italian, German, and Japanese). The babies tended to respond differently to these messages (e.g., smile or brighten when hearing the approval messages) for each of the languages except Japanese. (The authors speculated that there were no differential responses to Japanese because in that language, even in infant-directed speech, the phrasing and intonation are not as exaggerated; Fernald, 1993). In another study of 5-month-olds, the babies reacted differently to photographic slides of happy faces and angry faces of strangers (Balaban, 1995).

A compelling way to provide information about how babies can read emotional messages in facial expressions and tone of voice is for parent guides and parents to watch videotapes together of babies and caregivers. These videotapes could either be of the dyad itself or of other babies. After watching and talking about what they saw, most parents can recall examples of their baby reading their emotions, as well. The parent guide then can describe how their babies will look to them later on when they encounter something strange in order to see from their parents' facial expressions whether it is okay or not.

When parents are generally or intermittently unavailable emotionally, they give their babies no language of emotions to learn. Intervention needs to target two things: parents must be helped to become more emotionally available, and because babies' emotional development cannot wait for parents to achieve this, good supplemental care of the babies by caregivers who are able to be emotionally available must be provided. Optimally, this supplemental care will be part of the day, so that there is ample time for parents to have adequate time with their babies, and if the supplemental care is center-based, each baby needs to have a primary caregiver. Interventions with the parents include treatment if there is mental illness or substance abuse, as well as parent–infant relationship work. Parent–infant interventions might include helping parents tell their stories, so that early experiences affecting the present relationship can be addressed. Following the principle of parallel process, parent guides working with the families need to be emotionally available to the parents. This availability is often communicated by providing concrete assistance and encouragement for positive steps taken and by coaching with parent and baby together. Coaching involves observing, asking open-ended questions, finding and pointing out instances when the parent is emotionally available, and then informing the parent frequently about the importance of what he or she is doing. In the parent guide's work with Lisa and Ethan, described in Chapter 3, this type of coaching was used. When parent guides use this style of coaching, they help parents stay in control of their lives, and they make it possible for parents to be the first to make new discoveries about their babies and their role as parents.

Sometimes parents' emotional language to their babies is negative, hostile, or rejecting. The intervention guidance given for working with parents who appear unavailable can also be used in these situations. During parent–infant work, the parent guide will find it helpful to speak for the baby as much as feasible. For example, in a videotaped session of a young mother and her 7-month-old baby from the Infant-Parent Institute (Trout, 1987a), the mother squeaks a toy close to her baby's face, obviously scaring the baby. The baby turns away and puts her arm up in defense, whereupon the mother repeats the squeaking "game," laughing at baby's distress. The parent guide speaks for baby by saying, "Mommy, that's scaring me." Then, she represents the baby's feelings more directly with the mother by asking, "How do you think she feels about that game?" The video clip expands on the scenario, describing significant issues in the history of the dyad and in the mother's situation, all of which are being addressed in the comprehensive intervention in addition to the direct work with the dyad.

Even when parents are trying to respond with sensitivity to their babies' cues, they may misread these cues and then respond in ways that do not help their babies build a coherent language of emotions. For example, Sheryl, about whom we have talked before, is in a playgroup with her mother, Linda. Sheryl has been easily distressed in the past and her mother has been worried about her ability to be a good parent. When Sheryl kicked her feet in tune with her mother's singsong words and head swaying, Linda interpreted this as discontent and immediately changed her behavior by picking Sheryl up so she would not be distressed. Sheryl, then, did not experience her mother's response as part of a dialogue of shared emotions. The parent guide, who had built a trusting relationship with Linda over the past few months, said, "It seems like she loved hearing you sing to her; did her kicking make you think she was getting upset?" Then, she and Linda were able to talk directly about Linda's interpretation, with the parent guide accepting Linda's healthy striving to keep Sheryl happy but also helping her to consider another view of Sheryl's response.

EMOTION REGULATION

Physiological regulation continues to develop during this period and becomes important to the development of emotion regulation both in its own right and as it is needed to provide the periods of quiet alertness needed for the social games to occur. These games, as well as other situations, provide a context for babies and their parents to work on a major emotional development task of this stage—caregiver-guided regulation of tension (Sroufe, 1996). At this stage, babies appear to be for the first time capable of learning characteristic styles of dealing with tension (Sroufe, 1996). Through both routine activities (e.g., feeding and bathing) and social games, parents help their babies begin to develop the ability to stay organized during heightened arousal and to do so for increasing periods of time. Across this age period, babies' interactions with their mothers consist of increasingly positive encounters in which high rates of maternal expressions of joy and interest are associated with increases in the baby's joy and interest (Malatesta, Grigoryev, Lamb, Albin, & Culver, 1986), a process that continues into the next stage. These interactions frequently begin with mutual smiling. "One partner increases a smile's intensity, eliciting an even bigger smile from the other partner, which ups the level yet again, and so on, producing a positive feedback spiral" (Stern, 1985, p. 102). This stage also brings new experiences such as teething and, for some children, child care that often creates distress and tension requiring parents' help with emotion regulation.

Physiological Regulation

Sleeping and feeding are two major areas in which parents can help babies develop physiological regulation. The 3- to 7-month period is a good time for babies to consolidate the establishment of regular sleeping and feeding routines.

   Sleeping   Typically babies (and adults as well) cycle between deep and light (REM) sleep about every 90 minutes. As babies come to light sleep, they are apt to cry out and move about in their beds. If they have developed some self-comforting behaviors (e.g., thumb sucking), they can generally calm themselves back into deeper sleep. Babies with active, intense temperaments may have more difficulty with this. The more pronounced 3- to 4-hour cycles of states are more challenging and parents often pick up their babies to feed them at these times; however, over time parents can help their babies back to sleep even if they become more fully awake at these points in the cycle. By about age 4 months, babies' nervous systems have matured enough for them to sleep for 12 hours with only one awakening. Events of the preceding day, however, can affect the baby's sleep pattern. Even babies who have learned to calm themselves back to sleep, may require comforting if they have become overstimulated or experienced many strange, unfamiliar events during the day (Brazelton, 1992). For example, 4-month-old Brennan was held and played with by several loving relatives during a holiday visit. That night she cried on and off for several hours and had difficulty falling asleep. She needed the most familiar face, voice, and movement possible to help her recover from the excitement and settle into sleep.

   How their baby is sleeping is of great importance to most parents, and they are usually frank in discussing this. As parent guides are learning about "life with baby" in this area, they can share some of the myriad of print resources that are available in various formats and languages. Then, they can discuss further how this information fits with what the parents have been told by other family members or friends and how they feel about their babies' behavior. Asking open-ended, nonjudgmental questions can help parents reflect on what is working for their families, both in the present and for the future. For example, if the parent is focused on getting to sleep because she has to go to work the next morning, she may prefer bringing her baby to her bed when he cries out rather than trying to help him get back from light sleep to deep sleep in his own bed. As the parent guide explores with this parent the possible outcome of having a hard time a year or two later getting her baby to sleep through the night, she is encouraged to reflect on the future as well as the present implications of her decision. If the parent guide frames with sensitivity the question of how the parent's response will contribute to the baby's developing self-regulation—something of importance beyond just sleeping patterns—she contributes even more to helping the parent promote the baby's physiological and emotion regulation.

> *Teenage Rene and her baby, Charlene, lived for a short time with Rene's mother, Sarah. Rene wanted to give Charlene a bottle in the evening and afterward put her in her crib to sleep, letting her fuss just a little if she needed to before falling asleep. It bothered Rene that her mother insisted on holding Charlene as she sat talking or watching TV with others until Charlene fell asleep. Although Charlene appeared to be adjusting to this stimulating environment, Rene's parent guide, Marie, wanted to support Rene's efforts, so she gave her information to justify her actions: "Your idea of having a regular calm bedtime routine for Charlene—giving her a bottle and then putting her to bed—will help her in her development." She went on to explain that developing regular routines for sleeping and eating lays the groundwork for babies' developing the ability to be more regular later in their emotional development. "They don't tend to fall apart as easily later when they hear the word, 'No' or when they get real excited about something," she added.*

It was easy to give Rene some developmental guidance about the importance of developing a sleeping routine because she brought up the issue—she did not like her mother interfering with the routine she wanted to establish for Charlene. When the parent does not complain about the baby's sleeping pattern but there appears to be a problem, intervention takes more finesse.

There are marked cultural differences regarding where babies and young children should sleep. In some cultures, young children traditionally sleep with their parents until school age. For instance, Charisa, who lives in Japan, slept with her parents (as is the tradition in her country) until just before turning 5 when she announced to her parents that she would like to have her own bed in her own room, an idea she picked up from some American children's stories.

Nancy reported that her 3-month-old, Samuel, was sleeping through the night. "He wakes up around 4 A.M. I put a pacifier in his mouth, and he goes back to sleep." The parent guide knew that Nancy was eager for Samuel to get older because of the demands she felt he made on her. The parent guide was concerned about whether Samuel was getting fed often enough. She asked, "When does he usually go to sleep?" (11 P.M.). "Does he eat just before he goes to sleep?" (Yes.) "He had a check-up last Monday, how did the doctor think he was doing weightwise?" (He gained 4 ounces.) Nancy then volunteered, "He gets 24 ounces a day; the doctor said that is what he needs." The parent guide responded, "I'm glad you're paying attention to how much he eats as well as how he sleeps." In their subsequent visits, the parent guide continued to monitor Samuel's weight and sleep patterns, both for information and to continue encouraging Nancy to reflect on her baby's needs, not just her own.

Establishing physiological regulation is challenged when the family life is very chaotic. In some families, the baby's needs get lost in the confusion of multiple caregivers, locations, sounds, smells, and visitors. In these situations, parent guides must work quickly to build enough trust with the parents to enable them to act as advocates for the babies. Often the chaos is typical for parents; they need someone to talk with them about their babies' needs for regularity of routine and handling. Depending on the parent, this concern can be framed as helping baby go to sleep more easily at night now or as a way for the parent to be less stressed. Always, beginning with the belief that parents want what is best for their babies and stating this for the parents allows the parent guide to partner with these parents on behalf of their babies. If parents and their infants are, of necessity, living with extended family or friends, and the chaotic family is all the support the parent has, intervention may include helping the parent find alternate sources of social support.

Feeding   During this period, babies can also begin to develop more regular feeding schedules. Parents' attempts to help them do so are often challenged by the fact that, for a period of a few weeks around age 4 months, babies often display an "exciting cognitive burst of interest in the environment" (Brazelton, 1992, p. 85). This often occurs right in the midst of mealtime, much to the consternation of many parents. Brazelton warns that "mothers who have been savoring the warm, uninterrupted intimacy of breast-feeding often feel deserted at this time" (p. 89). These parents may need help in understanding that their babies' sudden spurt of interest in their surroundings will subside a bit after a week or so and feeding can become more regular and less interrupted again. Parent guides can also help parents to appreciate the benefits of their babies' growing interest in things as an indication of cognitive development. Babies whose temperaments are highly reactive to stimuli will show the most striking changes in behavior at this time, which may cause concern on the part of the parent. In addition to understanding their baby's cognitive burst, parents of these babies may want to diminish the amount of distracting stimuli in the environment during mealtimes.

The introduction of solid foods, which usually occurs around age 4–6 months, can cause further disruption of the feeding process. The transition from sucking to eating solids takes some time for the baby to master, and some parents need help understanding that when babies spit out some of their food, it is just a part of the learning process. Babies also love to play with their food, the spoon, the bowl—the whole works. Parents who can relax and enjoy their babies' exploration and cognitive development have an easier time during this transition period.

Before solid foods are introduced, parent guides can use anticipatory guidance to inform first-time parents about the early feeding experience and explore with them how they may want to handle this. Letting parents know that the necessary fluids for digestion are not activated unless the baby has a pleasant time at feeding (Brazelton, 1992) may encourage them to find ways to make mealtime enjoyable. Parent guides can share some of the ways other parents have made mealtime more pleasurable for everyone, such as giving the baby one spoon to bang on the tray while the parent feeds with another spoon or telling themselves, "The most important thing at this moment is my baby's tummy. I can clean up any mess that's made after she's finished!" Babies who have the temperament characteristic of being slow to adapt to new things will also pose a challenge to parents at this time. Guides can help these parents understand that when their babies make a sour face and turn away from new food it is just their cautious temperament coming into play.

Regulating Emotional Arousal

As parents extend their social games, they often build the emotional intensity of the exchanges in positive ways until the games erupt in a burst of mutual joy. In this way, parents help babies experience increasingly more intense emotions and remain organized while doing so. The key is to remain organized. Accomplishing this organization helps prepare babies for the next stage of development in which they will encounter more and more situations that elicit strong feelings as they attempt to master various challenges. Parents and other caregivers help babies manage these periods of intense positive arousal by observing babies' cues that they are becoming overstimulated (e.g., arching their backs, averting their eyes or heads, looking distressed) and by backing off to give them time to calm down a bit before either resuming the interaction or switching to another, calmer activity.

When parent guides have the opportunity to observe parents and their babies enjoying these interactions, they can share in the delight and also help parents appreciate the significance of these times together. "That fun little game is so important to her! She's getting experience with happy intense emotions. That will help her deal with strong emotions, both positive and negative, as she gets older—such as when she wants to climb on the TV and you tell her 'No'." The discussion can then proceed to other examples that the parents have, so they can see how what they are doing now with their babies prepares them for what is coming up.

Some parents tend to alternate between intruding in their babies' space and missing their cues for engagement. This type of interaction is frequently seen with depressed parents. When Jeffrey was a baby and his mother, Lynette, was experiencing a bout of depression, she would often hug him tightly when she needed warmth or reassurance, unaware of his arching his back at times. She also tended to ignore his signals when he showed mild distress and even when he smiled. In situations such as this, parent guides need to support parents in obtaining treatment for their depression. Then, to support baby's ongoing development, they need to look hard for any exceptions to the intrusive-ignoring pattern and reinforce times when parents seem to respond to their babies' playful gestures. They should then highlight such exceptions, amplify the babies' positive responses, and add, "You must do this together when I'm not here because he seems to enjoy it." They should also add a comment about how this will help the baby in coming stages of development.

When excitement builds in this way, parents must be able to read their babies' signals and know when a moment of respite from the game is needed. Babies at this age often signal that they need a break by looking away or turning away, as Tony did. Christy did not take Tony's turning away from her as a personal rejection but correctly read his signal and simply leaned back and relaxed, giving him time to regain his composure. This time allowed Tony's arousal level to lower and for him to regroup before becoming reengaged. Had Christy pushed him to continue, Tony would have become overstimulated, and joy would have turned into distress. By granting him the respite he needed, she was helping him to learn that he could tolerate high levels of emotional arousal without becoming disorganized:

> Understanding that infants need to modulate their own level of tension, the responsive parent remains relaxed when they break contact and comes in again when they are ready. Sensing the importance of such interchanges, or simply enjoying them, the responsive parent stays involved with the infant . . . and the total encounter becomes . . . greater in length and more rich and varied. (Sroufe, 1996, p. 164)

When parent guides observe parents pausing, as Christy did to give Tony time to regroup, they can reinforce this by highlighting what the parent did and then add, "You're helping your baby regain composure, so he'll be able to tolerate even more emotional excitement without 'losing it' and getting upset."

Some parents respond to their babies' turning away by trying harder to keep them engaged. When this behavior is observed, parent guides need strategies for balancing both the babies' and the parents' needs. In the example presented in Chapter 3, the mother, Barbara, kept blowing bubbles at her baby, Sandra, after Sandra indicated a need for a break by turning away. Then, when Sandra started fussing as the bubbles kept coming, her mother interpreted this reaction as Sandra not liking to play with her. Their parent guide, Dianne, took this opportunity to assure Barbara that most babies act this way when they are getting too excited. Together Dianne and Barbara used direct observation and reviewed the videotape of this interaction and others to interpret Sandra's gestures, which were very subtle, so that Barbara could allow respite time and they could both enjoy the building of emotions in their games. Dianne pointed out to Barbara how important all this was to Sandra's future dealings with strong emotions.

Another type of challenge is when babies become easily overstimulated. Jeannie, whose mother used cocaine during pregnancy, had this problem. She was placed in foster care when she was a few days old. Her foster parents had had difficulty helping her with earlier physiological regulation, and now, at 6 months, they were challenged by her hypersensitivity to certain types of stimulation. When Jeannie was playing with her foster father and began getting excited, she rapidly became upset and started to screech. Her foster parents used infant massage strokes on her that they had learned. They also discovered what incremental rate of arousal Jeannie could tolerate in order to expand her capacity, albeit more slowly than they could with their older child who was not hypersensitive.

There are times, however, when any baby will become overstimulated or distressed. Most parents soon learn various ways to help their babies calm down. Young babies are often calmed by motion (e.g., rocking, being carried, going for a car ride). Redirecting the baby's attention to something novel or pleasant such as gently introducing a new toy or carrying the baby to the window to look at something interesting can also be helpful. When parents, because they have enough trust, show or tell the parent guide that they are having difficulty helping their babies calm down, the parent guide can share some of these emotion regulation strategies, adding, "These have worked for some parents I know." The parent guide encourages the parents to decide which strategies they think might work with their babies and then to try them. The next time they are together, the parent guide should ask the parents to share (and maybe even show) what has worked so the parent guide can then share this technique with other parents. The message being conveyed in this intervention is that caregiving is not about knowing what is the right way to do things but about learning what works for them and their baby. It also suggests that when parents discover something that works for them, they can share it with other parents. Such a message is, itself, an intervention to help increase parent's sense of efficacy, which is key to increasing competence.

When parents do not seem to be aware that they are having difficulty calming their baby but the parent guide observes a problem, the parent guide must be the one to initiate the interaction around this concern.

During a home visit, 4-month-old Tina quickly became overstimulated when her mother, Lynette, held her on her lap facing her while she talked with animation with Helen, their parent guide. Changing her position did not help. Offering the bottle did not help, either. Putting her in her swing (a suggestion offered by Helen) helped only for a moment, and having Helen walk her (Lynette's suggestion) did not help at all. After a few moments of Helen walking Tina, Lynette recalled that music sometimes helped her calm down, and she put on a classical music tape given to her at the neonatal intensive care unit in which Tina had spent her first month of life. Tina began to quiet down

and attend to the music. Helen congratulated Lynette for recalling this
and offered to bring more tapes, as Lynette said music also helped her
to calm down.

Important elements of this scenario include 1) the parent guide did
not have the answer—she and the mother discovered it together, 2) the
mother decided when she wanted the parent guide to assist by walking the
baby, and 3) the parent guide risked failing in front of the mother by
agreeing to do so. The next time Tina is overstimulated, Lynette is more
likely to play the music tape first. Helen will watch for this on subsequent
visits in order to reinforce Lynette's use of what has worked in the past.

Sometimes babies need help calming down, but their parents do
nothing to help. This situation might be so serious that it will require
careful, sensitive work with the parent and her baby. If the following interventions do not seem sufficient or the problem keeps reoccurring, the
parent guide should refer the mother for parent–infant psychotherapy or,
if that is not available, regular psychotherapy. Initially, the parent guide
can try speaking through the baby, to see if this intervention is enough
to call the parent's attention to the baby. The parent guide might say,
"You're needing your Mommy to help you right now, aren't you,
sweetie?" She can then look toward the parent to see if she responds to
this prompt. If she does, then the parent guide can reinforce her for helping her baby settle down. If she does not respond even with the prompt,
the parent guide can say to the parent, "It looks like you're so sad (or
worried or tired) yourself that you just can't figure out how to help baby
calm down. Is that the way it feels? What could I do that would help
right now?" By offering support to the parent in the moment, the parent
guide communicates her concern for the parent as well as the baby and is
then able to offer further assistance. This process should include learning
about the parent's own experience of being parented, his or her experience of life with this baby, the other stressors in the parent's life, and the
support people that may be available for the parent and baby. The parent
guide could help the parent arrange for supplemental care for the baby
until the parent is better able to respond to the baby's need to be calmed
when distressed.

As noted in Chapter 4, an early developing strategy for self-regulation
of emotion is gaze aversion to avoid becoming overly aroused. As parents
engage their babies more and more in social games, some may need help
in recognizing that playing with and stimulating their babies can sometimes be too much of a good thing. In a national poll of fathers and mothers (Melmed & Ciervo, 1997), 87% of the parents thought that the more
stimulation babies receive, the better off they are.

Distressful Experiences

Many working parents start leaving their babies with babysitters or at child care centers during this stage (some do so before the age of 3 months.) Although stranger distress generally becomes more intense around 7–8 months or age, some babies begin exhibiting this distress by age 5 months. As was noted earlier, even very young babies detect differences between familiar and unfamiliar patterns of care. Therefore, it is helpful if parents can help their babies become at least somewhat familiar with their new surroundings and caregivers before leaving them. Parents may feel hurt when they return and are greeted with fussiness instead of the hoped-for joyous reunion. It is not surprising, however, that some babies wait until they are in the arms of a beloved parent to release some of the tension accumulated throughout the day (Brazelton, 1992). (Several suggestions for easing the distress of being separated from their parents and placed in a new environment are presented in Chapter 12.)

Teething   Another new experience that causes distress, teething, may start for some babies toward the end of this period. Teething can be especially troublesome during feeding. When the baby sucks, blood rushes into the already swollen gums. Rubbing out some of the swelling before offering the bottle or breast may cause some initial crying but may ease the pain of sucking (Brazelton, 1992).

By helping babies regulate the emotions and tensions that arise during this period of development, their parents and other caregivers are preparing them for the challenges generated by new cognitive and motor skills over the next several months. In addition, by being emotionally available for playful interactions as well as helping them stay organized while experiencing intense feelings, their parents are facilitating within their babies a sense of security in their interactions with them. In these ways, parents promote the development of their babies' secure attachments with them and set the stage for the next period of development.

The social games of this stage serve as stepping stones to the next stage of development when babies begin to play more with objects. At first, their object play is simply supported by their caregivers, but by the end of the year, they engage in more interactive play with objects and their caregivers (Adamson & Bakeman, 1985; Bakeman & Adamson, 1984; Kaye & Fogel, 1980; Schaffer, 1984). The lessons Tony learns at this stage about regulating emotions during dyadic interaction will help him to develop the ability to remain organized in the face of the inevitable frustrations and moments of excitement that will occur as he attempts to master his expanding environment during the next developmental stage. His mother and other primary caregivers will continue to play an important role but one that differs from the one needed at this stage.

6

Expanding Horizons

7 to 12 Months

Seven-month-old Lateesha is sitting on the floor playing with a squish ball. She shakes it several times then sets it down and pats it exuberantly. She picks it up again, mouths it, then holds and carefully inspects it as she pokes at one of the colorful knobs. Her mother, Betty, who has been sitting next to her watching her play, says, "Hey girl, you're really getting into that squish ball, aren't you. Do you like that purple knob?" Lateesha looks at her mother for a moment then continues to play with the ball. When she sets it down again, Betty picks it up to look at it. Lateesha immediately fusses vigorously and reaches for it. Betty quickly returns the ball, "Oh, you weren't finished playing with it, were you! I am so sorry." For a few seconds, Lateesha continues fussing and furiously shakes the squish ball back and forth, but then she calms down and returns to playing with it. While she is engrossed with the ball, Betty quietly gets up and walks out of the room. Lateesha looks around for her mother, and when she does not see her, she starts fussing. She quiets and smiles when Betty reenters the room and speaks to her but starts fussing again when Betty does not return to her. "Oh my, you didn't want your mama to leave you." Lateesha continues to fuss and reaches toward her mother when she sits back down beside her. After Betty holds and com-

forts her for a moment, she returns to her play with the squish ball. When she drops it, it rolls out of her reach. Betty watches as Lateesha leans forward and tries unsuccessfully to reach the ball. She fusses, and Betty starts to get the ball for her, but just then Lateesha notices her toes and starts playing with them.

A couple of months later, Lateesha is again in the living room with her mother. She pulls herself to stand and cruises along the side of the coffee table where some of her toys are sitting. Holding on with one hand, she picks up a rattle, shakes it, then lets it drop to the floor. Next, she picks up a small rubber ball, mouths it, and watches it fall as she deliberately drops it. It rolls away from her, so she lowers herself to the floor and creeps after it. The ball rolls under a chair and when she is unable to reach it, she turns toward her mother and fusses. Betty retrieves the ball for her, then returns to straightening up the room. After this happens a second time, Betty decides to introduce a new toy that she has just gotten for Lateesha. "Look, Lateesha, what Mama's got for you." Lateesha watches as her mother unwraps a ring stack toy and dumps the rings onto the floor. Lateesha grabs one of the rings and starts mouthing it. Betty picks up the largest ring and says, "Look, Lateesha, you put the rings on the pole like this." She lets the ring slide onto the pole. Lateesha grabs the pole with her other hand and mouths it. Betty laughs, "No, silly, you're not supposed to eat it. You're supposed to put the rings on it. Here, you do it." She hands Lateesha the next largest ring. Lateesha drops the pole, takes the ring from her mother, and bangs it on the pole. "Okay, I can see that you're into banging. How about banging two of them together like this." Betty picks up two rings and clicks them together. Lateesha drops the ring she was holding, takes the two rings from her mother, and clicks them together. Just then the doorbell rings, and Lateesha watches as her mother opens the door and greets her new friend, Jennie. When she sees Lateesha, Jennie exclaims, "Oh, there's that precious baby I've been hearing about!" She rushes over, swoops up Lateesha into her arms, and gives her a big kiss. Lateesha starts wailing and reaches for her mother who takes her and comforts her.

Three major changes affect emotional development during 7–12 months of age: 1) babies' growing abilities to expand their horizons, 2) the development of attachments with their parents and other primary caregivers, and 3) further development of emotion regulation. Cognitive and motor developments during the second half of the first year bring many opportunities for babies to broaden their emotional experiences. Fundamental to these developments is the brain's growth during this period. At around 6–8 months, there is a flurry of activity in the frontal cortex, which is the primary site for critical thinking and problem solving. Then, around 8–12 months there is increased activity in the prefrontal cortex, the part of the brain that assumes major responsibility for planning and rehearsing future actions and connects with the limbic system to regulate emotions.

Babies' new skills coupled with a natural curiosity propel them to explore and attempt to master their ever expanding environment. These adventures bring not only the pleasure and excitement of new discoveries, but also many frustrating and distressing situations. In addition, new sources of woe (e.g., stranger distress, separation anxiety) arise in the wake of cognitive developments of this period. The role of parents is to help their babies grow in their abilities to remain organized while experiencing the full range of emotions and to do so in ways that foster the development of their babies' secure attachments with them. Throughout the first year, the type of caregiving babies experience shapes the kind of attachments they will form. By the end of the year, whether those attachments are secure or insecure can be assessed.

EXPANDING HORIZONS

Lateesha exemplifies the expanding interest in exploring things in the environment characteristic of babies in the second half of their first year (Adamson & Bakeman, 1985; Schaffer, 1984). More and more the main focus of their attention shifts from their parents to other aspects of their environment, especially objects that they can grasp, hold, and play with. Babies can now sit independently, which frees their hands and arms to pick up, hold, and play with toys. They soon develop a rich repertoire of object play behaviors that they try out on the toys and other objects they encounter, as Lateesha did (Piaget, 1952). They mouth, wave, shake, pat, drop, and bang them on the floor. In these ways, babies learn the properties of objects and what they can do with them. Before long, they select behaviors that produce the most interesting results, developing what Piaget termed *means–end thinking* (1952). They learn that balls roll when dropped, and rattles make sounds when shaken. Their motor skills also develop, which enables them to explore their environment as well as their toys. Although their interests have expanded to include more of their environment, babies in this stage still want their parents available as play companions with whom they can share their discoveries and to whom they can turn for help and comfort when needed. Toward the end of their first year, babies begin showing, pointing at, and giving objects to their parents and other playmates (Rheingold, Hay, & West, 1976). These activities soon expand into games of give and take and by the end of the first year, they may delight in teasing their parents by offering a toy only to playfully withdraw it before it is taken. The game is fostered by their partner's exaggerated and feigned dismay and disappointment over losing the toy (Reddy et al., 1997). All of these various types of play and exploration feed significant developments within the brain (Perry, Hogan, & Marlin, 2000).

Parents support their babies' play and exploration by interacting with their babies and by providing safe and interesting opportunities for these activities. Parent guides can help parents appreciate the importance of doing so by highlighting for them aspects of their babies' play and commenting on the developmental importance of these behaviors. For instance, while observing the baby for several minutes each week at home, a mother and parent guide have a wonderful learning lab in which to focus on the baby. The parent guide looks for examples of the baby's interest in exploring things, then comments on what she sees, thus focusing the parent's attention. The parent guide then can offer information about what babies learn from this type of play, including some comments about how play and exploration affect brain development. She can say, "She's really finding out what she can get that ball to do, isn't she? She's learning how to push and bang and roll things." After continuing to watch, the parent guide might add, "She's such a little scientist; she is finding out about what this toy can do and how she can make that happen. This is *so* important because this is the age when the problem-solving part of her brain is undergoing such significant developments." Later, the parent guide can ask, "What other things does she like to play with?" or "Sounds like she is really learning how to get things to make sounds and to move! Has she started dropping things and watching them fall yet?" The purpose of these low-keyed comments is to encourage parents to observe and reflect and to appreciate what they and their babies are doing that contributes to their babies' development. This reflection enhances their sense of knowing their babies and their feelings of parenting competence; these are important ingredients in the parents' ability to further support their baby's development through their relationship.

Supporting Play on the Floor and on the Fly

Babies need some time to play and explore on their own, but they also need their parents to enter into their play from time to time to reinforce their efforts, share their delights, assist with problems, and help them elaborate and expand their play. Sometimes this means literally sitting with their children and supporting their play by attending to and commenting on what they are doing as well as modeling and suggesting ways to extend and expand their play. Betty attempted to expand on Lateesha's play by demonstrating how to put the rings on the pole, but she did not insist on her doing so. Instead, she switched to a different, more appropriate game for a 7-month-old—banging the rings together. By following their babies' lead and supporting their efforts instead of taking control of the child's play, parents are facilitating the development of their babies' sense of efficacy and mastery.

When parents and other caregivers do this, they are engaging in floor time (see Chapter 3). Parent guides can encourage parents to be with their babies in this nondirective, supportive way by simply suggesting that together they might "watch baby" and "follow his lead like in a drama where baby takes the lead role, and you play the supporting actor." Depending on how well the technique works, the parent guide can acknowledge the baby's grateful response and encourage the parent to expand on baby's response or wait for another response, then "close the circle of communication" as Celeste did with Maureen and Victor in Chapter 3. Floor time is effective not only one-to-one with a parent–baby dyad but also with a parent group in which the parents share with one another as they do floor time with their babies. Child care workers can also use this technique with babies in group care to foster their development.

In addition to entering into their babies' play from time to time, parents can also support the play on the fly—that is, while they are doing other things. With their babies in a safe place close by, parents can be readily available for brief interactions as needed. By keeping a watchful eye and ear, sensitive parents can enter their children's play as needed to retrieve a toy that has rolled out of reach (as Betty did for Lateesha), to provide comfort when needed, or to simply give a smile of reassurance or appreciation when their babies look uncertain or want to share some discovery. These experiences enable babies to play happily and comfortably in the knowledge of their parents' accessibility and responsiveness to their needs.

Dipping into baby's play may happen in very brief episodes—sometimes just 30 seconds now and 30 seconds later. Parent guides can keep a watchful eye and ear and support parents in brief, responsive interactions to encourage parents to do the same with their babies. They can do this by indicating when they see parents supporting baby's play on the fly, thus highlighting these positive episodes as feedback for the parents. They can expand on their observations and comment on what babies are gaining from their parents' responses and how much babies appreciate these interactions. Speaking through the baby, the parent guide may say, "You just love it when Mommy notices what you're doing, don't you?

You're learning that she's there for you!" Positive feedback in turn builds parents' sense of efficacy and increases the chance that these positive behaviors will be repeated.

When parents make positive comments to their babies about what they are doing in their play, they provide positive reinforcement and promote language development in their children. Parent guides can speak through the babies to encourage parents to make these positive comments. For example, they can say to a baby, "You're trying so hard to get that ball. . . . There, you got it!" When the action is completed, the parent guide can say to the parent, "I was commenting on what I saw her doing as a way of helping her connect language with what she is doing. That kind of thing will help her eventually learn to talk. Do you do that sometimes?" This comment can begin a brief conversation about talking with babies even before they have words and how this might feel to parents. Some parents say, "I feel silly talking to a little baby who can't talk back!" The parent guide can respond, "It may seem a little odd to do that, but did you know that your baby's brain is working hard at learning language from hearing you and others talk to him?" The guide can then go on to explain that starting around age 2–3 months, development of the part of their baby's brain that processes language (the temporal lobe) accelerates. By age 6 months, babies' auditory maps are different depending on the language in their homes, and by 12 months they will be babbling in their own languages. Parents are more likely to talk to their babies when they understand how helpful this communication is to their babies' development. They may need to start out doing this activity when no one else is around, if that seems easier for them. At a later contact, the parent guide can ask how the technique is working for the parent and then acknowledge or expand as seems appropriate.

Problems in Parent–Child Play

Some parents play with their babies in intrusive and directive ways. In this case, wise parent guides follow the platinum rule and refrain from being intrusive and directive with parents. Instead, they *observe* the parents' styles and present moods in order to *engage* with them effectively. They can then *wonder* aloud if their babies are enjoying the play. If these prompts are not enough to facilitate change in parents' directive play, the parent guides may want to offer, "You have bought him such interesting things to play with. Let's watch him and see what he will do with this one." In these ways, parent guides offer themselves as partners with parents in observing, then engaging, expanding, and closing circles of communication with their babies. For some parents, watching a videotape of themselves playing with their babies helps them see the need to change their style of interaction.

Sensitive parents do not engage in activities with their babies that are belittling, scary, or mean, and they avoid being critical of their babies' attempts at mastery (e.g., saying "No, that doesn't go there" in an irritated tone when the baby puts the wrong ring on the ring-stack toy). Parents also have responsibility for halting inappropriate play others engage in with their babies. When parent guides observe insensitive play on the part of parents or other family members or friends, they have the challenge of advocating for the needs of the baby while maintaining a relationship that may be fragile with the parents. Within the context of an ongoing relationship, parent guides can describe babies' reactions and ask the parents what they think their babies are trying to tell them. The parent guides could then either agree with the parents' interpretations or describe what they see. For example, in response to a parent's behavior, a parent guide might say, "I noticed how she put her arm over her eyes and leaned back. I wonder if that means she's a little afraid of that loud, squeaky toy." Through a number of such brief interventions, parents can be helped to interpret their babies' behaviors and respond in more sensitive ways. If they do not respond to such guidance, further assessment and perhaps psychotherapeutic intervention, along with protection of the baby, may be necessary.

Sometimes parent guides observe parents who do not play with their babies. In these situations, parent guides first need to ponder what they are observing. Are the parents depressed? Are there some unusually stressful events affecting their responses to their babies? Do they engage with their babies in warm and nurturing ways in other situations (e.g., diapering, feeding)? Perhaps they simply do not know how to play with a baby or they may be embarrassed to do so while being watched. By asking themselves reflective questions, parent guides can start to sort out what seems the most likely reason, which in turn can help them determine what intervention to try first. To further help them understand the situation, the parent guide can try making comments such as the following to help parents reflect on their behavior:

- "It seems like stuff on your mind is making it hard for you to enjoy Danny right now . . . can I help?"

- "Hey Mommy, look at me! I just got to that ball!" (speaking for baby)

- "Wow! I've never seen him travel like that! He's sure trying to get over to where you are!"

- "It must feel kind of funny to have an audience when you are interacting with Danny. I'm pleased to be able to get to know the two of
  you better, though."

These are points of departure for exploring more fully the concerns
the parent guide has about the parents' lack of support for their baby's
play. If maternal depression or other factors (e.g., substance abuse, domestic violence) seem to be interfering with the parent's ability to enter
into the child's play, then interventions to address these factors need to
occur, with supplemental care provided for the baby during the time the
parent is being helped. (More about addressing such factors is presented
in Section III.) However, if the parent seems to interact well with the
baby but does not encourage exploration and play, floor time strategies
may be helpful. Print material and videotapes geared to the parent's ability and interest, as well as playthings for parents and their babies to explore together, are tools that can contribute to informing, encouraging,
and raising parents' awareness about the importance of their responses
in play.

Sometimes, it is helpful for the parent guide to enter into the play
with the parent and child. For example, Trisha was quite distracted by her
own pain of having her 11-month-old son, Robin, "taken away from her"
and was emotionally unresponsive to him in the new environment of the
playgroup where they were having a supervised visit. Robin stayed by his
mother's side and did not venture to explore the playthings in the room.
The parent guide, Patti, with whom Robin was acquainted, invited Trisha
to bring Robin and join her on the carpet. She then handed a busy box
to Trisha, suggesting that she help Robin push the buttons so he could
make the figures pop up. Patti expressed mild excitement to Trisha when
Robin made one of the figures pop up. She coached Trisha to help when
Robin was not able to do it or when he expressed distress when another
baby got in his space. In this way, she supported their interaction so
Robin could get as much as possible from his mother in this safe, though
brief, visit.

For a variety of reasons, some parents restrict their babies' opportunities for exploration and play with objects. For instance, one mother kept
her baby at this age cuddled next to her on the couch for hours at a time
while she watched television. Some other parents keep their babies in
playpens most of the time. These parents may not understand the importance of play and exploration for their babies' development or they may
be trying to protect their babies from getting hurt. For some, there may
be psychological reasons for limiting their babies' involvement in these
developmental activities. As with every other challenge, the first task for

the parent guide is to figure out what keeps these parents from letting their babies move about and explore and play with things.

As babies become more involved with other things, the role of parents shifts from being partners in the dance to sitting more on the sidelines to facilitate the play as Betty did with Lateesha. While many parents accommodate and even anticipate this shift (Kaye & Fogel, 1980), others have difficulty giving up "center stage." They may have needed that role to assure themselves that they were indeed worthy and important, at least to their babies, or for other reasons they may relish the intimacy of the one-to-one social games. When this seems to be the case, parent guides can invite the parent to get on the floor with the baby with some toys and suggest that they see what the baby does with the toys. If the parent keeps initiating social games rather than supporting the baby's play with the toys, the guide can explore with the parent their feelings about this. Having this discussion while they watch the interaction on videotape would be helpful. "You really seemed to be enjoying your interaction with Tommy, so how did it feel when he crawled away like that to play with his toys?" Parents may reveal during this discussion, or at other times when they are telling their story, feelings of loneliness or fears of abandonment which the parent guide can address directly and through referral for therapy when needed.

Parents who are overprotective of their babies and therefore restrict normal exploration do so for a variety of reasons. Parents of babies who were very premature or medically fragile and parents who have experienced the loss of a child are particularly vulnerable to being overprotective. Parent guides need to know enough about the family to gear intervention to the unique dynamic being presented. Has the parent experienced some loss, such as a miscarriage, a child with a disability (loss of the expected child), a divorce, or loss of custody of another child? Some parents need a lot of empathy and encouragement from parent guides in order to allow their children more exploration. Developmental guidance given as information rather than correction is more easily accepted. For example, Karen's baby, Hannah, was very premature and had respiratory difficulties for several months. The parent guide, Katherine, saw them every week, and when teenage Karen had difficulty letting Hannah crawl a few feet away from her, Katherine said, "It's hard to let her get away, isn't it?" Karen replied that it was hard because they had been through so much, and she was still not sure how to handle Hannah. Katherine acknowledged these feelings and how typical it was for mothers in her situation to have them. She expressed her confidence that Karen, who had done so many hard things already, would soon do this difficult task of letting Hannah explore her surroundings.

Actively listening to parents' feelings and worries in regard to their baby's exploration is important. For example, Ellen's older child was removed from her care when she was a year old, so Ellen really cherished the closeness she had developed with her son, Eric, during the first few months. When he was 10 months old and crawling efficiently, she described herself as overprotective and reluctant to let him out of her sight for an instant. As she talked with her parent guide about her experiences and her feelings about losing her older child, she discovered the source of her apprehension with Eric. This insight and the ongoing encouragement of her parent guide freed her to begin letting him move away a little and to enjoy it when he would come back to check in or get help.

Some parents restrict their babies' opportunities to explore (e.g., by keeping them in playpens) in an effort to keep them safe. This may be how they define good parenting. In these situations, parent guides can join with them in their desire to protect their babies and then help them find ways to develop safe environments for exploration, while also helping them understand the importance of such exploration for their babies' development.

Creating a Safe Environment   Parents support their babies' play at this stage by setting up safe environments with safe, age-appropriate playthings. Betty and her husband Leland childproofed their living room and closed off other rooms with baby gates and doors so that Lateesha would have a safe place to explore; play with her toys; and practice her crawling, cruising, and creeping skills. They used "what if" thinking to help them do this—for example, looking around the living room and thinking about what might happen if the baby grabbed, pulled, or poked available things or places. They were able to plan ahead and problem solve based on this "what if" thinking. In this way they continued to foster the development of secure attachment by helping Lateesha feel safe, secure, and protected.

Some parents put their babies in playpens for long periods of time, sometimes in another room. This can be a very sensitive subject for parents who may have been raised this way themselves, are being given advice by family or friends that support the use of playpens, or are worried about their babies' safety and see playpens as a way to be "good parents." The first step (again) for parent guides is to watch and listen to learn more about what meaning playpens have for these parents. Asking open-ended, nonjudgmental questions, such as "What are your thoughts about having babies in a playpen rather than spending some time on a blanket on the floor?" can provide the beginning of dialogue on this. If the playpen is in another room than the parent, the parent guide can look for opportunities to comment on how it might feel to babies to not be able to see or hear their parents when they might have something important to share with them. They might wonder aloud how the parents know when their babies have something to share with them or need their reassurance when they cannot see each other. These gentle questions can guide parents to think of other alternatives to the present situation. They also can open other areas that may need attention, such as a mother's need to have time for herself, that the parent guides can help the parents address.

In addition to a safe environment, babies need safe, age-appropriate toys or other objects such as pots and pans for play. When parent guides note the absence of playthings in the home, they can offer to bring some toys "to see if baby likes these." Also, most early intervention programs have playthings that they can loan to families, and some communities have toy lending libraries. Of course, the parent guide will want to avoid any indication that the parent has been remiss in not providing these play-things themselves. They can also reassure parents about any sanitation concerns they might have. If the parent does not seem to know what to do with the toys, the parent guide can use the floor time technique de-scribed previously to help them with this. With parents who enjoy making things, parent guides can share information about how to make some play objects out of household items.

Another safety and sanitation issue for some parents is babies' pro-pensity to mouth everything within reach. This behavior is an important way for babies at a certain age to explore things, but it is a practice that really upsets some parents. When parent guides notice this, they can first join with the parent by saying something such as, "He loves to put things in his mouth, doesn't he?" Then, they can add, "At his age, putting things in their mouths is the main way babies explore and learn about things." If parents continue to demonstrate an aversion to babies putting things in their mouths, parents guides can help by exploring with these parents what it is that bothers them about this behavior, using open-ended ques-tions such as, "Tell me what it feels like to you when he does that," or "Can you help me to understand?" Parents might have realistic fears about their baby's choking on something put in the mouth. One parent reported that she has always had a fear of choking because her brother had actually choked to death on a bean when he was a child. Reinforcing par-ents for having these concerns, the guide can offer ideas about having available objects that have no sharp edges and that are too big to get stuck in the baby's throat. For other parents, baby's mouthing even large ob-jects is felt to be "nasty" and wrong. Again, exploring these feelings in nonjudgmental ways and offering information about how helpful it is to baby's exploration may help. By the end of the first year, manipulation and visual examination become the more predominant means for learning about objects (Ruff, Saltarelli, Capozzoli, & Dubiner, 1992). Informing parents of this may help some parents tolerate a few months of mouthing.

Parents who let their babies explore in unsafe environments present a challenge to parent guides. The task here is to maintain what may be a fragile relationship with the parents without ignoring real or potential danger to their babies. Of course, the best time to address this possibility is before it happens with anticipatory guidance before the babies are crawling and cruising. At that time, a parent guide might comment on Susie's ability to scoot and say, "It won't be long before she's all over this house; would you like to talk a little about how to get the house ready for her?" When parent guides meet with families after their babies are already navigating in unsafe environments, they need to bring their creativity and finesse to bear on behalf of these babies. "I" messages can be helpful: "I'm worried about what will happen if he reaches that coffee table (with the cigarette lighter on it)" or "I wonder what she might do if she grabs that TV table (with the lamp on it)?" Through "I" messages, parent guides can articulate the "what if" situations for parents when they are not doing it for themselves. People with limited cognitive abilities, like Janice in Chapter 10, may especially need someone to help them think this through and will need information shared in direct, concrete, visual ways, repeatedly. If this help is provided, parents with mental retardation can keep their babies safe as they explore. (Suggestions for working with parents with mental retardation are presented in Chapter 10).

Often, parent guides hear, "He has to learn not to touch things. I'm not going to put everything out of his reach." The guide can respond, "Of course. How many things do you think it would take for him to learn not to touch things?" Then, "What if you left out that many things and put other stuff away, so that you won't have to be saying 'no' so much? Would that make your life easier while he is learning to leave some things alone?" Another possible response is, "Of course. How do you feel about having some of her things at her eye level, to help her leave the other things alone? Some parents have told me this makes life easier for them."

DEVELOPMENT OF INFANT–PARENT ATTACHMENT

As babies move into the last quarter of their first year, their preference for their parents and other primary caregivers is often demonstrated in the joyous greetings they bestow upon them as well as the distress they express when separated from them. The security of this attachment to a few select caregivers has been gradually built over the preceding months by the nature of the many interactions they have experienced with these caregivers. When these interactions have been characterized by sensitive, responsive, affectionate caregiving, the babies develop attachments that generate feelings of security. As they begin to turn the corner into their second year, this sense of security combined with increased mobility enables them to venture forth to explore their small world with confidence, knowing that they have a readily available source of comfort and protection should they need it as well as an appreciative audience for their many exciting discoveries.

At age 12 months, Caitlin (whom we met at the beginning of Chapter 2) and her father, Frank, were having a great time playing outdoors, but Frank decided it was time to come indoors. Caitlin had a different idea.

As soon as Caitlin's father picks her up and heads toward the door, she starts fussing, but Frank keeps walking, saying, "Oh, I know you want to stay outside. We had a good time out here, didn't we? But Daddy needs to fold the laundry now, so let's find you something fun to play with inside." Frank then sits on the floor with Caitlin, pulls a basket of toys over, and lifts out a bucket. Frank shakes the bucket, and it rattles. "What's this?" he asks. Caitlin stops fussing and reaches for the bucket. "I wonder what's inside—shall we look?" Frank lifts one edge of the lid, and Caitlin eagerly pulls the lid off and peers inside. When Caitlin is happily engaged in taking the plastic balls in and out of the bucket, Frank rises, moves to the other side of the room, and starts folding the clean towels.

A few minutes later, Caitlin spies one of her books lying on the coffee table while crawling after one of the balls that has rolled away. She pulls herself up to stand at the table and cruises earnestly along its edges until she reaches the book. She grabs it then turns toward her father and says, "Buh." Frank looks up, smiles, and says, "Yes, that's right. You have your book." Caitlin excitedly plops down on the floor and looks at the pictures in the book. Suddenly, Pixie, a visiting friend's terrier, trots into the room, licks Caitlin's face, then ambles away. Caitlin turns to her father, fusses, and holds out her hands to be picked up as Frank approaches her. Gently, Frank carries her back to his chair and snuggles her on his lap as he says in a soothing voice, "That scared you didn't it, when Pixie licked you? She was just being friendly." Upon hearing her name, Pixie runs over and stands, tail wagging, in front of them. As he reassures Caitlin, Frank reaches down and pats Pixie's head. Caitlin seems less afraid by this time. Then, Pixie's owner calls her back into the other room, and Caitlin clambers down from Frank's lap and resumes playing with her toys.

Caitlin is accomplishing one of the major developmental tasks of the first year, the development of secure attachments with her parents. In this example, she demonstrates the secure attachment she is developing with her father, just as the example in Chapter 2 illustrates her secure attachment with her mother. Throughout her first year she experienced her parents as being, for the most part, sensitive and responsive to her needs. When she was hungry, she was fed. When she felt distressed, she was comforted. When she was ready for playful stimulation, she received it, and when she was tired, she was helped to relax and go to sleep. Through all of these experiences, she learned that her parents were dependable, caring, and loving. She gained a sense of security from knowing that her parents were available emotionally as well as physically to interact with her, care for her, and protect her. This sense of security enables Caitlin to use each of her parents as a secure base from which she can explore her world. When the attachment process is not going well, it is revealed in both the ways in which babies explore (or don't explore) and the manner in which their parents interact with them as they do so.

Exploring from a Secure Base

The felt security of knowing that one of their attachment figures is available for comfort and protection allows the young child to focus on the important work of play with confidence and calm alertness. This security in turn enables the child to engage more fully and productively in the play activities that promote cognitive, socioemotional, and motor development, as Caitlin did. Once she calmed down and became interested in her toys, Caitlin played happily, exercising her developing cognitive and motor skills as she crawled and cruised, filled and emptied the bucket, and searched for one of the balls when it rolled out of sight. She focused on her play with confidence that her father was available to help if she should need him, and indeed he did come to her rescue when Pixie frightened her. Because her parents had successfully comforted her so many times in the past, Caitlin was able with the help of her father to fairly quickly get over her frustration from not being allowed to stay outdoors and her fear of the dog. The ease with which she was comforted attests not only to the security of her attachment but also to the healthy development of emotion regulation.

When parent guides working with parents observe any of these indicators of exploration and secure attachment, they have an opportunity to highlight for the parents their babies' ability to explore with confidence, as well as instances of babies' turning to them for reassurance, refueling, and comfort. They can do this through direct comments about what they observe, or by speaking to the baby so the parent can "overhear" positive comments. Using these ways of communicating to parents, parent guides can help parents see how their babies' ability to explore relates to the secure attachments they are forming with them and how that stems from their sensitive responses to their babies over the months.

As babies' motor skills develop during the second half of the first year, their interest and ability in exploring their environments increases tremendously. First, they are able to sit, which frees their hands for exploring and playing with toys and other objects. Then, they learn to crawl, creep, and cruise, which greatly expands the territories they can explore. Venturing forth into their small worlds is very exciting, but it can also be somewhat scary, especially for children with inhibited temperaments who are often wary of what is new and unfamiliar. The extent to which their parents provide safe environments for exploration and are available when they feel uncertain or distressed affects not only the nature of the babies' explorations, but also the security of the attachments they are forming with their parents.

If parents, for whatever reason, are unable to provide a secure base for their babies' explorations (e.g., be emotionally available when their babies feel uncertain or distressed), their babies' explorations may become inhibited or reckless, depending on their temperaments. One strategy that may be helpful in these situations is for a caring parent guide to amplify babies' bids for response from their parents. The parent guide might speak for the baby who is ignored by her mother when she looks to her for reassurance as she loses her balance and sits down suddenly by saying, "That was a little scary, Mom." Another strategy is to explore with parents their feelings when their babies seek their help only to be met with annoyance and sometimes rejection. For instance, when the baby crawls to the mother, pulls up, and leans against her leg, only to have the mother complain, "I wish you'd stop clinging to me. Go play." The parent guide can ask the mother, "How does it feel when he does that?" and then explore those feelings with her.

When such guidance does not seem to make a difference in parents' ability to provide a secure base, parent guides need to assess further to understand what is keeping these parents from responding to their babies. Are there current stressful events? In this case, their guides can provide emotional and instrumental support. Are the parents depressed or using street drugs? Then, the parents can be referred to the appropriate treatment and provided support and guidance for parenting as they continue in their treatment. Are the parents feeling loss because they see their babies moving away from them? Parent guides can listen to the parents' feelings and worries in this regard and help them identify the help they need to work through this barrier (as in the example of Ellen and Eric). If the parent–child relationship is seriously impaired (hostile, rejecting, struggling), substitute caregivers, such as family members, nurturing friends, or community child care, need to be identified. Quality supplemental care would help the babies receive the sensitive and responsive care they need while their parents are getting the therapy they need in order to parent their babies in ways that promote healthy emotional development.

EMOTION REGULATION

A number of developments converge to affect the growth of emotion regulation during the second half of babies' first year. By about 8 months of age, the frontal cortex shows increased metabolic activity (Shore, 1997). This increase is significant because the frontal cortex is associated with the ability to regulate and express emotion as well as to think and to plan. By this time, the generalized distress characteristic of earlier months has branched into anger, distress, fear, and disgust (Sroufe, 1996). Due to increased cognitive and motor skills, babies now have more opportunities to experience these varied emotions in different contexts.

During this stage, babies use what they have learned in the previous stage in order to play a more active role in regulating their emotions. If caregiving went well during the previous stage, babies learned that their parents are available to help them regulate their emotions without becoming disorganized and to assist them in recovering when they do. In the face-to-face social games of that period, they also learned to establish psychological contact with their parents so that they can communicate, at first nonverbally and later verbally, across space. Building upon these lessons learned, babies initiate more contact with their caregivers for the purpose of emotion regulation. They share their delight in discoveries, seek their parents' attention when distressed, and check in with their parents when confronted with uncertainty. The parent's role is to be available and responsive to these initiations and to continue to help their babies maintain or regain equilibrium while experiencing the varied and sometimes intense feelings that arise as babies enjoy peaks of joy and deal with new challenges such as stranger distress and separation anxiety.

Peaks of Joy

Although play with toys is a major activity for babies at this stage, there are still many important moments in well-attuned dyads of direct, face-to-face interaction (Bakeman & Adamson, 1984). Typically, mothers shift during this stage from simply imitating their babies' behaviors to engaging in responsive behaviors that reflect their babies' feeling states, a process that Daniel Stern (1985) called *affect attunement*. For instance, the mother may mimic the rhythm of baby's kicking in a sing-song: "Well, la de-dah te-dah!" The positive affect seen in the face-to-face social games of the earlier period becomes high intensity elation by age 9 months (Schore, 1994). In fact, at a later point, mutual gaze is often brief because its intensity can become almost intolerable (Kaufman, 1989). Throughout the second half of the first year, peaks of joy and excitement become higher and more frequent as parents help their babies experience increasingly higher levels of these positive feelings. These intensely positive experiences play an important role in the development of the baby's brain. For example, they stimulate increases in production of chemicals in the brain that are known to have rewarding properties and to mediate social affect (Schore, 1994).

Parents who are sensitive to their babies' cues will notice that with age and cognitive development, babies begin to laugh more in response to social and visual stimulation. In response, parents switch from relying just on the physical stimulation that used to elicit laughter in their 4-month-olds (e.g., kissing the baby's tummy, playing the "I'm gonna getcha" game) to provoking laughter by acting silly (e.g., pretending to suck on the baby's bottle, crawling on the floor; Sroufe, 1996). During the last quarter of the first year, babies delight in getting into the act by clowning (i.e., eliciting laughter and attention from others by doing such things as screwing up their face, walking, or breathing in a funny way; Reddy et al., 1997). Babies also initiate positive interactions through sharing with their parents their delight in such things as discovering what a toy can do or seeing something funny.

By sharing information about how these interactions help early brain development, parent guides can help parents appreciate the importance of these peaks of joy and of regulating them so that the baby does not become overly excited and fall apart. Information about how these enjoyable, well-regulated little interactions have positive, long-lasting effects can be offered through speaking for the baby and other techniques for highlighting positive interactions. For example, on one of her early visits with Lynette and Jeffrey when he was age 9 months, Helen watched as they engaged in a delightful game of Jeffrey's riding Mommy's leg as a horsie. After a few moments of this game, as Jeffrey squealed with excitement, Lynette had the "horsie" come to a walk, helping its rider get reorganized. Helen commented to Lynette, "You know, it's *so* important what you were doing with him just then! When you play together and he gets excited, then you calm things down before he gets too wound up, it actually affects how his brain gets wired. Things like this will help him be able to not overreact to things as he gets older." (Lynette had said one time that both she and Jeffrey's father have trouble with overreacting to situations.)

Floor time and coaching interventions are good strategies to use with parents who do not engage their babies in positive interactions or do not seem to enjoy their babies' responses. An open-ended question like, "What kinds of things do you do that he gets excited about?" followed by, "Would you show me how that looks?" may start the process. If, with such a prompt, the parent is able to elicit a joyful response, the parent guide highlights this and comments about its importance. If the parent responds with something like, "He doesn't get excited about much," the guide can first ask the parent to "say more about that" to learn more about what is happening and how the parent feels about it. Later, the parent guide can ask questions such as, "Have you ever tried riding him on your leg like a horsie?" or "What do you think she would do if you and she danced with Barney while he is on TV?" It is not necessary for parents to demonstrate these things for the parent guide, as they may feel embarrassed or unsure of themselves. Instead, parent guides plant these seeds and observe during their next visits after parents have had a chance to practice. Then, they will have an opportunity to highlight and reinforce what the parents have accomplished. The "seeds" might take some nurturing before progress is observable; for example parent guides might inquire about what happened during the week, for instance, "Did you have a chance to try that horsie game?" or offer to try some games with their babies to see if they respond. Their belief needs to be that parents do want what is good for their babies' development; they just might not know how to encourage it.

Although Corrine had learned some ways to interact with Leon, these interactions lacked a playful, joyful quality due to Corrine's very flat affect. When asked by her parent guide, Corrine acknowledged that Leon did not seem to get very excited about things, so they brainstormed about some things she could try. Then, her guide, Joanne, coached Corrine as she tried several new behaviors with Leon. At first, Corrine was a bit hesitant but gradually she began to enjoy such things as holding Leon and dancing around the room to music, playing Peekaboo and Pat-a-cake with him, and making silly sounds for him. It took several weeks to elicit joyful responses from Leon, but as his mother became more relaxed and her behavior seemed less strange to him (Corrine had never interacted with him in these ways before), he began to smile and even giggle during these play times.

When exploring with parents it may become clear that, even when some parents are appropriately engaging, their babies are not responding joyfully. After first acknowledging these parents' efforts and naming the discouragement or sadness they may feel, the parent guides and parents can get to work as detectives to determine what is impeding development (e.g., a sensory or cognitive difficulty, a temperament mismatch) and to seek ways to remediate or compensate. The solution may take other helpers as well (e.g., a physician, neurologist, audiologist). Then, the first time a parent guide and parent observe even a little "mound of joy," they can celebrate together and know that real "peaks of joy" may come later.

Managing Excitement   Parents not only help babies experience these many moments of positive feelings but they also need to help their babies modulate these affective experiences so that their emotions remain well-regulated and their behavior organized. Parents do this by taking care that their babies do not become overly excited, as Lynette did in the "horsie" game with Jeffrey. When peaks of joy border on hysteria, the sensitive parent helps the baby regain composure and a sense of calm rather than continuing activities that further excite the baby.

The suggestions for developmental guidance and response to challenges described with peaks of joy are also useful when helping parents manage the excitement. Questions such as "What kinds of things help her to not get so excited in play that she gets upset?" and "What do you do to help him calm down?" asked when baby is getting too excited can prompt a parent to notice a baby's state and to think about how to help him regulate. Then, when it works, the parent guide will acknowledge it and add a comment about how important that ability will be as he gets older and has to manage all kinds of excitement, both positive and negative.

For a variety of reasons, some parents overstimulate their babies. The parent guide needs to watch and listen to learn why this is happening and then gear intervention to that hypothesis. For example, if the parent is misreading baby's disengagement cues (e.g., arching, wide eyes) as positive excitement, the baby needs someone to speak for him: "Oops, I'm getting too much of a good thing here; I need to slow down a little, Mommy." If parents overstimulate because they have a higher threshold for stimulation than the baby does, they may not notice the baby's different response level. An observation shared with these parents could help: "He seems to have a temperament that is more easily excitable than yours; have you sometimes noticed that?" Pause. "Some babies are like that; they seem to need smaller doses of fun than we do. There's nothing wrong with that, just 'different strokes.' " Pause. "Watching him for those signs that seem to come just before he cries and changing to something calmer then will probably keep him happy." The parent guide can suggest videotaping and watching the baby together at the next visit, during which the parent and guide can be detectives together by videotaping an interaction between the parent and the baby, then watching it together to find out how the baby lets the parent know when he or she is about to go over the edge.

Negative Feelings

New challenges in the form of negative feelings such as stranger distress and separation anxiety also arise during this stage. Parent guides can use anticipatory guidance to alert parents to these developments and offer developmental guidance to help them deal with them when they occur.

Stranger Distress   During the preceding stage, babies began to differentiate strangers from familiar people and were sometimes wary of them. During this stage, due to increased cognitive abilities, this wariness intensifies and becomes *stranger distress*. How babies at this stage respond to strangers is influenced both by the baby's temperament and by the situation. Babies who have inhibited or slow-to-adapt temperaments generally respond more negatively than uninhibited, more adaptable babies. The circumstances in which the baby encounters the stranger also matters. If Betty's friend had not rushed over and picked up Lateesha, she might have gotten a more favorable reception. She could have simply joined Betty on the floor near Lateesha, watched their play and talked quietly with Betty for a few minutes, then joined their activity by playing with one of the toys in the way that she had seen Betty play with it. With her mother close by, Lateesha could have more easily handled her wariness, and she might have accepted this stranger if she had exhibited this more gradual approach and more familiar behaviors (Sroufe, 1996; Waters, Matas, & Sroufe, 1975).

Babies sometimes have their own ways of handling the tensions created by encounters with unfamiliar people. In one study of 10-month-olds, an unfamiliar adult would approach the baby in a step-by-step fashion (Waters et al., 1975). A number of babies responded by watching the approaching stranger with brief glances away followed by looking again. Recordings of heart rates of the babies taken during this experiment revealed that when the babies first looked at the stranger across the room, their heart rates decreased, indicating attention to something new, but as they continued to gaze at the stranger, their heart rates accelerated, demonstrating increasing arousal and tension. When they looked away, their heart rates dropped back only to rise again when they once more locked into watching the approaching stranger. By turning away for a few moments, they modulated their emotional response to this event.

Even someone who is not a complete stranger can sometimes evoke a wary response during this stage. When seeing families in home or office, parent guides can use babies' changing reactions to them as a way to support parents' efforts to help their babies during this developmental phase. The baby who had responded with interest to the social worker's friendly greeting a couple of months ago now turns toward and clings to father when the social worker appears. At this point, the social worker can comment about how "She's right on schedule, Dad; she now knows that she doesn't know me as well as she knows you. She'll probably watch us real closely for a while, to see if you think I'm okay; then she'll be able to believe it, too." Parent guides can reinforce parents when they effectively deal with their babies' reactions by commenting on how much that will help their babies as they meet more and more people.

Some people who interact with babies of this age do not understand the phenomenon of stranger distress. Like Betty's friend, they may upset the baby by being too intrusive and then may become offended by the baby's negative response. Parents can be encouraged to let people know that this is just what babies do at this age and that it does not mean that the baby does not like them—it is just that they need a little time to get used to them. When parents understand their babies' temperaments, they can also help others appreciate these unique characteristics of their babies with comments like: "Charisa's especially shy at this stage," or "Bobby is a spirited child, so don't be put off by his intense response."

Not only do babies at this stage begin to act somewhat afraid of strangers, but they show fear in other situations, as well. Some theorists see this as indicative of a level of cognitive development that enables them to appreciate fearful situations (Sroufe, 1996). This is demonstrated in experiments using the *visual cliff*. In these studies, babies are placed on a table that has a clear Plexiglas top, one side of which has a checkerboard surface directly underneath it (the "shallow" side), while the other side has a checkerboard surface several feet below (the "deep" side). Babies age 5 months indicate through differential attention that they recognize the difference between the shallow and deep sides. By age 9 months, they demonstrate fear of the deep side by acceleration of heart rate (Schwartz, Campos, & Baisel, 1973). These results support the notion that there is a shift in babies' reactions to fearful circumstances as their cognitive development permits a growing understanding of the meaning of such situations.

Separation Anxiety During this stage, babies frequently become distressed when separated from their parents as revealed both by their behavior (e.g., crying and clinging to the parent) and by physiological measures. For instance, significantly higher cortisol levels were noted after a 30-minute separation from the mother compared with the cortisol levels while playing with the mother present (Larson, Gunnar, & Hertsgaard, 1991). This separation anxiety appears to depend on certain cognitive developments such as the ability to discriminate the parent from other people and the understanding that the parent still exists even when out of sight. Babies who have mental retardation do not exhibit separation anxiety as early as other babies do. Certain games that babies enjoy playing with their parents at this age, such as Peekaboo and give and take with balls and other objects, employ a theme of withdrawal and return. Sigmund Freud and Rene Spitz speculated that these games may bear some relationship with the developmental task of dealing with the comings and goings of their parents (Emde, 1989).

Parent guides can help parents cope with and respond to babies' expression of separation anxiety by first explaining that this new behavior is typical and indicates cognitive growth. When parents wonder about their baby's reaction to being left at the church nursery or with a baby sitter, the parent guide can respond, "Yes, he's right on schedule. His mind has developed to where he can realize that you are separate from him and can go away, but he's not yet had enough experience or mental development to know for sure that you will come back. How do you think he'll learn that?" A discussion about continued development and ways to help baby with his anxiety in the meantime should then follow. Parents need to know that with most children, separation anxiety tends to peak around age 18 months and then subsides a bit but will continue in some situations for years to come. (Many parents can remember the homesickness they felt when they first went off to spend the summer with their grandparents or went to summer camp.) During the present phase of development, however, it is especially important to minimize the number and length of separations and to help the baby with separations so as not to turn normal stress into emotional trauma for the baby.

Parent guides can elicit from parents ideas about what might help their babies deal with separations and can suggest ways that other parents have found helpful. Some examples would be: 1) the parent remaining unperturbed at times of separation (this may take some preparation beforehand and self-talk at the time of separation); 2) the parent spending a few moments talking with the substitute parent so that the baby can experience that the parent trusts the other person; and 3) the parent leaving something with the baby that smells like the parent (a pillowcase, for example), especially if he has particular difficulty with separations or if the separation is longer than a day. (More suggestions are presented in the section on child care in Chapter 12, including ones that parents can use as their children become more verbal.)

Parents can be reassured by the parent guide informing them about the effects of temperament on babies' separation anxiety. For example, some babies have more difficulty with any change in routine, some have reactions that are stronger than those of other babies, and some warm up to new people more slowly than others do. Understanding their babies in this light might alleviate the parents' own anxieties, thus helping them help their babies with *their* anxieties.

Child care workers notice that some parents do not prepare or help their babies with separations. This behavior may happen with parents who are absorbed in their own goals, stress, or anxiety, or when they are unaware of their babies' particular needs at this time. Child care workers and other parent guides can speak for these babies when they ask, "It feels kind of scary when Mommy (or Daddy) leaves you, doesn't it?" If the parent does not respond to this prompt with some efforts to help the baby, the child care worker can comment, "Maybe it would help him if you stayed and talked with me a moment, so he can see that you think he is in a safe place." Anticipatory guidance may be needed so that the parent allows enough time for this.

Some babies are overly distressed by separations, while others show no outward signs of concern during separations. When these reactions are noted, the parent guide needs to consider whether the attachment process is going well for these babies and their parents. They may be forming *anxious/resistant* or *anxious/avoidant attachments* with their caregivers. If there are other indications that this may be the case (e.g., insensitive or otherwise troubling parent–child interactions), intervention would be directed toward increasing the security of their attachment, *not* toward giving more opportunities to practice separation. For example, a technique such as floor time can be used regularly to increase parents' abilities to read their babies' cues and respond in a sensitive manner. This is food for the babies to use to develop secure attachments, which will, in turn, help them manage separations. Coincident with this technique would be parallel interventions with the parents to address those characteristics or circumstances that impede their ability to be sensitive and responsive to their babies' needs at this time.

Whenever possible, long-term separations of babies from their primary caregivers should be avoided during infancy, especially during this developmental stage. The cost to the baby in terms of long-term development is simply too high. If such a separation must occur, either to prevent or respond to serious abuse or neglect or for some other compelling reason (e.g., hospitalization of the mother) careful safeguards must be put into place. (These are described in the section on out-of-home placements in Chapter 12.)

Other Negative Feelings Babies are bound to become frustrated at times as they become more purposeful in their attempts to figure out what they can do with their toys. These are opportunities for them to learn that they can experience and deal with frustration without falling apart or by recovering their equilibrium if they do. The parent's help is often vital at these times. By acknowledging and labeling these feelings and working with them in these situations, parents help them move on to reframing and problem solving rather than remaining stuck in their distress. Emotions thus become a source of motivation instead of a cause of disorganization. When Lateesha's ball rolled away from her, Betty did not rush in to help her but let her try to solve her own problem. When she was unable to do so, however, Lateesha expressed her frustration and turned to her mother for help, which was quickly forthcoming. During this stage, babies are beginning to learn with their parents' help how to keep or regain a sense of composure when they have experienced strong feelings of anger, frustration, joy, or fear.

Social Referencing

The visual cliff experiment has also been used to demonstrate how babies toward the end of their first year begin checking in with their parents when faced with a novel or ambiguous event. They look toward their parents to see how they are reacting to the situation and respond accordingly. Twelve-month-olds who were placed on a modified visual cliff were more apt to cross to the deeper side if their mothers posed joy or interest than if she posed sadness; few crossed if she posed anger or fear (Sorce, Emde, Campos, & Klinnert, 1985). In another study, 10-month-olds were more friendly with a stranger when their mothers reacted positively when the stranger entered than when the mothers' reactions were neutral (Feinman & Lewis, 1983). Babies will also look to their fathers for cues about how to respond in novel and ambiguous situations (Hirshberg & Svejda, 1990). They become quite upset, though, if they simultaneously receive conflicting signals from their two parents, as parents were asked to do in one study (Hirshberg, 1990). In the literature, this phenomenon of checking in with parents in these kinds of situations is referred to as social referencing. This strategy becomes important for babies to use to regulate their emotions as well as to guide their behavior.

When babies can check in with their parents and receive helpful and appropriate responses, it gives them confidence that their parents are there for them to support and guide them. This confidence helps them to feel more secure as their motor skills enable them to venture further away from their parents. It is also a major step forward in establishing a lifelong relationship in which they can come freely to their parents for advice and encouragement.

Parent guides can help parents reflect on the messages they are giving when their babies check in with them. For example, Juan is beginning to pull up; he looks toward his mother, Lupita, who looks alarmed and reaches for him although there is no danger. If this continues as a pattern, Juan will probably stop trying to pull up. The parent guide, Melanie, intervenes early by commenting to Lupita as soon as Juan starts to pull up, "See how he is checking in with you? He's looking for you to tell him it's okay to do this new thing. Are you okay with it?" Melanie can then learn how Lupita feels about it and help her to reflect on what Juan feels and needs from her.

Other parents may consistently ignore their babies' nonverbal requests for information on how to proceed when confronted with something strange. Samantha's younger daughter, Katrina, often found herself on her own, emotionally, as Samantha experienced a conflicted relationship with her other daughter, Penny, and with her own mother. While in a parent–infant playgroup with Katrina, then age 7 months, Samantha seemed not to notice Katrina's worried glance as another crawler came toward her. Katrina floundered as she tried, on her own, to respond to this novel event. Fortunately, the parent guide who was facilitating the playgroup did notice her nonverbal request for information. She spoke for Katrina to her mother, saying, "I don't think Katrina is sure what to do about Kevin. She may need you to let her know if Kevin is safe or not." Samantha, with this help, could attend to Katrina and help her proceed with Kevin. The parent guide then said, "Nice job, Samantha. Did you notice how she picked up on your calm smile and head nod?"

Children with different temperaments respond differently to novel events and unfamiliar people. Slow-to-adapt (inhibited) children not only check in frequently with their parents but often want to stay near them until they become more familiar and comfortable with a new situation. Children who have strong approach tendencies (i.e., are quick to adapt and uninhibited) may not check in with their parents nearly as often. Some babies, however, may not engage in social referencing with their parents even in situations that would normally call for it. For example, Robin typically did not look toward his mother, Trisha, when confronted with a strange or new situation. When parent guides observe this kind of behavior, they need to wonder about its cause. They might begin by saying to the parent, "Some babies at this age look to their parents when they come across something new or strange to find out if it's okay to play with it. Have you ever noticed your baby doing this?" If the parent answers "Yes," they can discuss situations in which this occurs, and the parent can be provided information about the importance of these interchanges both in the moment and in the future development of the baby and the parent's relationship with the baby. If the parent answers no, then the parent guide needs to investigate other possible explanations such as the baby's developmental status (e.g., cognitive delays, autistic tendencies, perceptual abilities). For instance, the tendency to engage in social referencing is closely linked to the babies' cognitive development and especially their understanding of causality (Desrochers, Ricard, Decarie, & Allard, 1994).

If the baby's developmental status seems to be on course, then the parent guide should consider the quality of the parent–baby relationship. The parent may have been so unresponsive, hostile, or rejecting to the baby's past bids for attention that the baby may have given up. This was the case for Robin, whose mother, Trisha, had bipolar disorder, personality disorder, and chemical dependency. Due to Trisha's severe and persistent mental illness, she was unable to parent Robin, so his grandmother had custody. Trisha visited him at the grandmother's house with supervision. Robin seemed to rely on himself alone when he was with his mother at playgroup. Robin had learned not to expect his mother to respond when he communicated with her, so he had stopped trying; he communicated only when his mother initiated the interaction. In addition to working with Robin's mother, the family's parent guide, Patti, worked with the grandmother to help her respond to Robin in ways that promoted Robin's use of social referencing with his grandmother and with his teacher at the child care center. Child care teachers can facilitate babies' use of social referencing with them by being especially expressive in their interactions with the babies (Camras & Sachs, 1991).

Lateesha and Caitlin, like many other babies during this stage, are developing ways to remain organized in the face of challenges and heightened emotions. Their parents have laid the foundation for this process by helping them establish smooth routines for feeding, sleeping, and regulation of arousal states as well as encouraging secure attachments by being sensitive and responsive in their care of them. Physiological regulation continues to play an important role in the development of emotion regulation. Parents assist this process during this period by helping their babies develop more regular (but not rigid) routines and schedules for eating, playing, napping, bathing, and sleeping. For instance, they avoid exciting games and try to minimize other distractions and stresses at mealtime, naptime, and bedtime. They avoid making an issue at mealtimes about such things as whether their babies are eating all of their food, how they hold their spoons, and whether they are making a mess. At naptime and bedtime, they may use massage to help their babies relax and go to sleep.

Although babies with responsive caregivers are on their way at this stage to being able to self-regulate their emotions, they still rely heavily on their parents to help them do this. Some of the ways in which parents help babies develop emotion regulation are illustrated in the example of Frank and Caitlin. For instance, Frank used distraction to help Caitlin recover from her feelings of distress and frustration over having to go indoors when she was having such a good time with her daddy outside. Although a certain amount of frustration is both inevitable and helpful to the baby's development, the overall amount of frustrating situations need to be kept to a manageable level as much as possible. Frank was sensitive and responsive to Caitlin's fear of the dog by comforting her and by helping her reframe her perception of the dog. Comforting babies who have become frustrated or upset (as Betty also did when a visitor upset Lateesha) can help them learn that they can regain composure under such circumstances. Emotion regulation is also aided when caregivers share positive feelings with their babies as Frank did when he smiled and verbally acknowledged Caitlin's delight in discovering her book on the coffee table.

Parent guides can provide developmental guidance by offering information to parents about how babies develop the ability to experience and regulate a range of emotions. (Information on this topic is provided in the section on emotion regulation in Chapter 2.) Although this information can be provided through reading materials, videos, and discussion/support groups for some parents, it is best done informally for many parents as the parent guide observes and interacts with them and their babies together in groups or individually in their homes or other settings. Then, babies can assist the parent guide in guiding and supporting their parents' efforts to help them establish emotion regulation.

When parent guides observe parent behaviors that help babies develop emotion regulation, they can reinforce these efforts. For instance, they might speak for the baby: "Mommy, thanks for helping me calm down just now. I feel much better now." They can also verbally highlight such things as the parents' labeling their babies' feelings and point out how this practice will give their babies a way to be in touch with their feelings and to communicate them to others. Parent guides can expand these observations by commenting about how babies' temperaments seem to be influencing their ability to regulate emotions. For example, Davey is a healthy 1-year-old who is very spirited in his movements and expressions of feelings. He is intense with a range of emotions and actions. A caring parent guide can help him and his parents by describing this as his unique style and suggesting that his parents need not be surprised if he needs more help than his older brother did at this age when he gets too excited or angry or even overly fatigued. The parent guide can then help his parents find things that work to help Davey calm down and also to appreciate his exuberance and vitality. The goal is not to "fix" Davey for he is not broken, he is just Davey. By normalizing this, the parent guide helps the parents understand Davey's uniqueness and accept suggestions as to how they might give him a little more or different help in regulating his emotions.

The development of emotion regulation is fostered by parents' acceptance of the full range of feelings expressed by their babies even in situations where they may need to set limits on how those feelings are expressed. Some parents may accept and help regulate their babies' expressions of excitement but become anxious with expressions of anger and aggression. Others may be uncomfortable when their babies express fear or dependency needs, whereas some may have difficulty with extremes of any sort. There can be many reasons for this, but the parent's own childhood experiences are a likely source of their discomfort with certain emotions. Encouraging parents to reflect on their own life experiences with an empathetic parent guide can help them accept a wider range of emotions so they can help their babies fully experience and regulate the full emotional spectrum. In some situations, it may be enough simply to wonder aloud what seems to be making it hard for the parent to see her baby express a particular kind of emotion or feelings about certain situations. For example, Maureen was okay with Victor expressing dependency needs, but she had a hard time tolerating any expression of Victor's that she interpreted as anger. When Celeste would wonder out loud with her about that, Maureen would say something like: "I can't please him. He's mad at me, and I can't figure out what he wants." One time when Celeste observed this, she said, "It really seems to get to you when Victor fusses. Am I right about that? Is that how it feels to you?" Maureen responded, "Yes, it really does." Celeste then asked, "I wonder, do you think this has anything to do with what you told me earlier about never being able to please your mother?" Maureen thought for a moment and then replied, "Yes, his fussing is like my mother all over again, letting me know she's disappointed in me."

Parents' abilities to help their babies develop emotional regulation are diminished when they do not typically regulate their own affect but become overwhelmed or use blunting, a defense mechanism that prevents the person from feeling the full emotional effect of the circumstance, to ward off effects of strong emotions. If other caregivers in the family are not able to compensate for what this parent is unable to provide at this time, an intervention to provide supplemental care in a quality setting should be provided. While the babies receive this direct help, their parents could be helped by individual counseling, by a psychoeducational group, or an intervention such as Dialectical Behavior Therapy (Linehan, 1993) depending on the nature of their dysregulation.

Children need to learn that their feelings are accepted even when the way they are expressing these feelings is not acceptable. Some parents have difficulty with making this distinction. For example, 9-month-old Tina was angry because her 2-year-old brother, Jeffrey, took a car she was playing with. In her anger, she hit her brother on the arm. Her mother scolded, "Stop being mad; you have to learn to share!" Helen, who was sitting near them, intervened by saying through Tina, "It's hard when somebody big takes your car; isn't it?" and to Lynette, "What would be a good way for her to respond, do you think?" This comment prompted her to reflect on the situation from Tina's perspective and to think of alternative ways to respond. Together they identified ways Tina could express her anger without hurting Jeffrey.

On another occasion, Tina began to cry in frustration when she could not retrieve a toy from under the table and her mother ignored her distress. Helen spoke for Tina, saying, "You're so frustrated, aren't you, Sweetie? What do you need Mommy to do to help you right now?" She then waited expectantly for Lynette to respond to the amplified cue. Lynette retrieved the toy saying affectionately, "Here you go, Punkin."

Social Referencing and Emotion Regulation   Babies and parents also use social referencing as an emotion regulation tool. By the end of the first year, babies have become quite mobile and understand much more of what is said to them. They can now move away from their attachment figures but still maintain contact with them through verbal communication and eye contact. In this way, they partner with their parents to modulate their emotions. When these joint efforts are successful, they develop confidence in their ability to experience more intense emotions without falling apart. Being readily available and responsive to their babies' attempts to check in with them is just one of the many ways in which parents and other caregivers help babies establish secure attachments with them, develop positive internal working models of self, others, and relationships, and begin development of emotion regulation. Toddlers also frequently use social referencing during the second year as they check in with their parents to determine what is and is not prohibited.

Emotion Regulation and Attachment

Babies tend to develop open, flexible emotional expression when they have parents who, like Betty, Sharon, and Frank, tend to respond with sensitivity to the full range of their emotional signals—the negative as well as the positive (Cassidy, 1994). Babies who are classified as securely attached tend to express their wishes directly and freely through eye contact, facial expression, vocalizations, and the showing and giving of objects (Grossmann, Grossmann, & Schwan, 1986). They share their feelings as well as their toys with their parents. When these babies become frustrated or frightened, they can express these feelings fully and turn to their parents for help, as Lateesha did when her ball rolled out of reach and Caitlin did when she encountered Pixie. Through these ameliorative responses from their parents, babies learn that they can handle intense feelings and can thus feel more secure. "The experience of security is based not on the denial of negative affect but on the ability to tolerate negative affects temporarily in order to achieve mastery over threatening or frustrating situations . . ." (Cassidy, 1994, p. 233). As noted in Chapter 2, securely attached children also tend to have lower levels of cortisol when in stressful situations than do insecurely attached children (Gunnar et al., 1996) indicating that they are feeling less stressful. Babies of sensitive, responsive parents also turn to them to share positive emotions such as the joys and pleasures of discoveries and accomplishments. In this way, they are building an inner sense that intimate relationships offer companionship as well as comfort and assistance. When babies enter their second year without the foundation of secure attachments with their parents, parent guides need to help these parent–child dyads repair their relationships using the principles of reflective relationship-based guidance. Helping parents practice positive parenting, as described in the next chapter, is especially useful at this point.

Emotion Regulation, Attachment, and Socialization

The earlier example of Caitlin with her father illustrates the beginning of the socialization process of parental limit setting that will be discussed further in the next two chapters. Although Frank and Sharon were very responsive to Caitlin throughout this first year, as she became older they did not acquiesce to her every request or desire, but they set limits in ways that fostered the development of emotion regulation. In the earlier example, Frank acknowledged Caitlin's feelings when she wanted to remain outdoors and explained why they needed to go inside, but he did not give in to her demands. Instead, he brought her indoors, but then helped her to cope with her frustrated desire by distracting her with one of her favorite toys and staying with her until she was calm once again. In instances like this, Caitlin is learning to use engagement in an interesting activity (an emotion regulation strategy) to move out of a state of heightened tension and distress. By verbally acknowledging Caitlin's feelings, Frank both validated and labeled her feelings. By doing so, he was teaching Caitlin another valuable tool that she can use later on to regulate and cope with her emotions. Having words for one's emotions provides a way to stay in touch with and monitor one's feelings as well as to communicate them to others. This ability to monitor and evaluate one's emotional experiences is an important aspect of emotional regulation (Thompson & Calkins, 1996).

The security and confidence Caitlin feels in her relationships with her parents will help her deal with the inevitable conflicts that will arise in her second year as she strives to balance her desire for autonomy with her need to remain connected with her parents. Her secure attachments with her parents will make the socialization process go more smoothly for them, as well. Although there will be plenty of discord and tantrums, research has shown that children with secure attachments with their parents tend to comply more with parental demands than do children with insecure attachments (Londerville & Main, 1981); this association of attachment and compliance appears to be especially apparent in toddlers with temperaments judged to be relatively fearless (Kochanska, 1995). When the parent–child relationship is not on such solid ground, the toddler period can be even more challenging. In either event, there is plenty for parents to do—and for parent guides to facilitate—as they help toddlers address the developmental tasks of the second year.

7

Venturing Forth

12 to 18 Months

Fourteen-month-old Ashlin and her parents are visiting her grand-parents. As the adult family members sit on the patio visiting, Ashlin plays in and out of the house with her aunt's old teddy bear. After "in-troducing" the bear to the adults, she lays it on the floor in the family room that opens onto the patio. She then becomes interested in opening and closing the sliding screen door and walking in and out of the door. This process includes negotiating two steps and the door's track. Ashlin has been walking since age 10 months, so she quickly masters this task. She touches base with her parents several times, greeting them as she ar-rives on the patio. After a few trips, she spies a plastic squeeze bottle full of water. As she starts to pick it up, she looks to her grandmother for ap-proval, receives a smile and a nod, and begins to elaborate a play se-quence involving the bottle, the door, the steps, and the bear. The first time she tries to enter the house, she attempts to pull open the screen door with one hand while clutching the bottle against her chest with the other hand. After a couple of tries, she realizes that this does not work, so she sets the bottle down, opens the door using both hands, picks the bottle back up, and goes through the door. Then, she sets the bottle back down, carefully closes the door, picks up the bottle, and takes it to the bear where she murmurs something as she "feeds" the bear the bottle. Next, she retraces her steps and actions back outside, putting the bottle down again before shutting the door.

On one trip, when she leans over to put the bottle down on the patio, her momentum almost topples her. She looks up, startled, toward her father. He smiles reassuringly at her as she recovers her balance and continues her task. During this sequence, which she repeats at least 10 times, she is absorbed in her movements and her "drama" and is oblivious to the adult conversation going on around her. Nevertheless, on one occasion as she puts the bottle to the bear's mouth, her grandma says, "You're feeding teddy—mmm, teddy likes that!" At this comment, Ashlin turns and smiles briefly at her grandma then returns to her pretend play. During the many repetitions, her ease of mobility and the smoothness of this sequence of actions increase.

Parents of toddlers learn to appreciate those times when their children play quietly and happily as Ashlin did in the previous example, for this is a turbulent and challenging year for most children and their parents. At one moment, the child is running forth to explore the world; a little later he is climbing up on his father's lap to be cuddled. The same child who strongly asserts her own will in contradiction to her mother, at other times will cheerfully comply with her mother's wishes. Newly acquired walking and climbing skills send parents scurrying. New emotions are experienced, sometimes with great intensity and in rapid succession, creating emotional roller coaster rides for toddlers and their parents. There is the thrill of exploring on their own, the rage of not getting their way, and the despair and shame of provoking their parents' disapproval. The parent's role is to help their toddlers experience and handle this full range of emotions and to develop self-control while learning appropriate ways to assert their autonomy and to express their feelings.

A salient developmental task for the first half of this tumultuous year is the development of exploration and mastery skills (Lieberman & Pawl, 1990; Sroufe, 1996) as illustrated in the example of Ashlin's play. The urge to explore is countered by the need of toddlers to remain in touch with their attachment figures. The tension between these two desires gives this period a push-pull character that soon is reflected at the psychological level as a desire for both a sense of autonomy and a sense of connectedness (Lieberman, 1993). This push for autonomy and urge to explore inevitably creates the need for parents to set limits on their children's behavior, so the socialization process begins in earnest. The ways in which parents guide all of these developments have significant consequences for the child's overall emotional development.

A WHOLE NEW WORLD TO EXPLORE AND MASTER

One-year-olds' natural curiosity coupled with their increased mobility pro-pels them to explore their immediate environments and to attempt mas-tery of the challenges they encounter. The emotionally healthy toddler's exploration and experimentation is fueled by the energy of the heightened positive affect which characterizes many children as they round the corner into their second year. Margaret Mahler described the child during what she called the practicing period, as follows:

> During this precious six- to eight-month period, for the junior toddler (ten-twelve to sixteen-eighteen months) the world is his oyster... The child concentrates on practicing his mastery of his own skills and autonomous capacities. He is exhilarated by his own capacities, continually delighted with the discoveries he is making in his expanding world, quasi-enamored with the world and with his own omnipotence. (1980, p. 7)

In the previous example, Ashlin demonstrates the concentrated effort brought by 1-year-olds to the challenge of mastering new tasks. She had seen the adults go in and out of the sliding screen door and may have been intrigued by a door that opened and closed differently from the doors at home. Carrying things in and out of this door was an appealing chal-lenge; neither too easy nor too difficult. Typically, toddlers persist longer when dealing with tasks of moderate difficulty (Barrett, Morgan, & Maslin-Cole, 1993).

When entering this territory of exploration and mastery with their toddlers, parents will benefit from the support and guidance of someone they trust. Parent guides can help parents understand the importance of exploration to their children's development, especially when parents be-lieve their children are more interested in their surroundings than in them. If this topic has not already been addressed, many parents will appreciate information about *child-proofing* the house for the toddler's safety. Par-ents can also use feedback from parent guides highlighting times when they notice and appreciate their children's mastery efforts and accom-plishments as well as explorations and discoveries. For example, "You seem to know how to encourage her without interfering with what she is trying so hard to accomplish!"

This time can be a challenging one for parents, and guides will en-counter times when parents do not support their children's exploration and mastery. For example, some parents may curb their children's explo-rations either by saying "no!" every time their children reach for some-thing or by erecting barriers that unduly restrict their movements. Parent guides can raise parents' consciousness of their toddlers' need by provid-ing information about typical development through print or video media as a regular part of their time together. In this way, parents do not see in-formation and suggestions as critical of their behavior, and they are less likely to get defensive. Parent guides can ask parents to talk about what they think about their children now that they are getting around so much and learning how to do so many new things. This conversation provides an opportunity for parent guides to learn what the toddlers' behaviors mean to their parents and allows parent guides to offer other ways to frame those behaviors as needed.

If parents, however, allow their toddlers free reign of the house without providing adequate protection or supervision, it is important for parent guides to make observations or raise questions designed to help parents consider their toddlers' needs. For example, guides could talk through the child by saying, "You're really a climber; I'm afraid you'll fall from there." Likewise, they could say directly to parents, "You know her better then I do, but I worry about her in there by herself. Should we check on her?" or "Can he get down those stairs by himself without falling?" Questions such as these are reminders that require some response from parents and call for them to consider something they may not have considered without the question. (Of course, if the parent continues to let the child do something dangerous, the parent guide will need to be more direct with the parent.) Inquiry as intervention can also be used when parents cut short or punish their children's attempts at mastery. The parent guide may ask the parent what scared or bothered them about what the child was doing.

Parent guides may observe children who appear lackluster about exploring and mastery play. If it becomes apparent when talking with the mother that she is depressed, the parent guide may need to help the mother find supplemental care for the child from another family member or a child care program until her depression lessens. In this way, the child's need for encouragement and stimulation can be met while the parent receives treatment. Having a mother who is depressed can put a damper on both the toddler's persistence and pleasure when confronted with moderately challenging tasks (Redding, Harmon, & Morgan, 1990). There could be other reasons for the child's lack of exploratory and mastery play, such as mental retardation, illness, or childhood depression. The parent guide would need to learn more about the child's history as well as observe the child's interactions with the parents.

Mastering New Challenges

Not only do children at this age gain mobility, but their plane of vision changes so they can view things from a new vantage point that affords unexpected and changing perspectives, pleasures, challenges, and frustrations (Mahler, 1980). Toddlers inevitably encounter frustrations and hurdles as they explore and attempt new activities, just as Ashlin did when she tried to open the door while still clutching the water bottle. The ability learned during the first year to modulate and tolerate heightened arousal for longer periods of time prepares toddlers to stay organized in the face of these frustrations. This ability, in turn, enables them to engage in problem-solving either on their own, as Ashlin did, or with their parents' help. (The beginning of Chapter 2 offers an example of a child solving a problem with her mother's help—Caitlin trying to close the jack-in-the-box toy.) Staying organized emotionally long enough to successfully solve problems enhances toddlers' competence and hence their sense of self-efficacy. Feelings of self-efficacy are of utmost importance throughout life (Gowen, Nebrig, & Jodry, 1995) and need to be fostered in children right from the beginning. Parents' role is to allow their toddlers opportunities to resolve their own dilemmas, stepping in when needed with just enough support to help their toddlers succeed. By scaffolding toddlers' attempts to solve problems and to achieve goals, parents strengthen their mastery motivation and help them to become more competent (Maslin-Cole, Bretherton, & Morgan, 1993). Another way in which parents accomplish this feat is through following the child's lead during play, rather than attempting to direct and control their play, as Celeste helped Maureen do with Victor during floor time (see Chapter 3).

The extent to which children can exercise control over an object or event not only reinforces a sense of self-efficacy but also influences the extent to which the object or event seems threatening. In a study in which some of the 12-month-olds could control activation of a noisy mechanical monkey, those children who could control the monkey were less likely to be frightened of it and more apt to smile or laugh and approach and handle it than their age-mates who had no control over the toy (Parritz, Mangelsdorf, & Gunnar, 1992). Likewise, as discussed in Chapter 6, when toddlers perceive they have some control over the situation when approached by an unfamiliar person (i.e., when the person follows the child's lead), they are less apt to be fearful.

Professionals who seek to support parents during this stage of development should reinforce parents when they notice and appreciate their children's problem-solving attempts. For example, Juanita and her mother were in the pediatrician's office. The pediatrician let Juanita hold the instrument used for checking ears, whereupon Juanita tried to turn on the light as she saw the doctor do. Her mother commented, "There you go, honey, you've almost got it." The doctor reinforced her with, "Nice going, Mommy, you're encouraging her to figure things out for herself!" The pediatrician gave the parent an opportunity to encourage the child and then reinforced her ability to follow up with her child.

Parent guides may observe parents and toddlers for whom mastering new challenges is not a positive, exciting time but rather a time of disconnection and frustration. Parent guides can help by first learning as much as possible about what is behind what they are observing. For example, if parents jump in to solve all their children's problems for them, guides can ask questions such as, "What do you think would happen if he tried to get that ball (under the table) for himself?" With a positive relationship with parents, guides can provide direct guidance, for example, "I'm curious. Let's wait a moment and see if he can figure this out on his own." If the child is able to solve the problem, the guide can say to him, "That worked, didn't it? Nice going." With any of these responses, guides are vigilantly doing their own problem solving: What seems to be threatening to parents about this? She seems so overwhelmed by her child being upset; I wonder what it might mean to her. Careful inquiry and reflection will provide cues for parent guides about how to give parents the right amount of help in their problem solving, in parallel process to how they want parents to give the right amount of support to their children's problem-solving efforts.

Balancing Independence with Togetherness   During the second year, toddlers use their newly honed locomotor skills to venture forth into their environments. When they are the ones who initiate the separations from their parents, they will sometimes venture a substantial distance (Rheingold & Eckerman, 1971). For most children, though, there are limits to the distance they will go from their attachment figures—about 200 feet (Anderson, 1972). Even though they move away from their parents, toddlers still want them available as a secure base that they can turn to for help, comfort, and protection when needed—and sometimes just for emotional refueling. Securely attached toddlers will play comfortably on their own in these situations just as Ashlin did. They manifest a sense of security through a balance of interest, pleasure, curiosity, and exploration of the environment in the presence of their parents (Emde, Gaensbauer, & Harmon 1982).

By being allowed to move away and to return freely, toddlers are able to modulate their own arousal levels to some extent. This ability becomes an important strategy for self-regulation of emotions that permits learning of effective responses to the complex physical and social environments in which they live (Rosenblum, 1987). Some children make a game of separation and reunion with their attachment figures—a toddler version of Peekaboo. One day, Howie climbed up onto the couch and cuddled next to his mother, who hugged him and said, "Oh, I love you so much. I'll just never let you go." Howie smiled and cuddled closer for a moment and then broke loose and moved away laughing while his mother exclaimed, "Oh, you got away!" This soon became a game in which Howie expressed disappointment if his mother did not follow the rule of holding him close and then letting him escape only to recapture him when he came back to her. Alicia Lieberman (1993) described a similar game common with toddlers in which they run off again and again, only to squeal in delight on being pursued and scooped up by their mothers. "For a worn-out parent, this game may seem like an endless tease. For the toddler, it is a crucial reassurance that independence and togetherness can go hand in hand" (Lieberman, 1993, p. 15). The most important emotional accomplishment of the toddler years, according to Lieberman, is "reconciling the urge to become competent and self-reliant with the longing for parental love and protection" (1993, p. 2).

Parent guides can ask parents if their children ever engage in these kinds of separation/reunion games. If the parent says yes and comments on how irritating or tiring it is, a sensitive guide can acknowledge this reaction and then explain why kids this age love to play this game. They might offer to problem solve with parents about how to revise the game and also, if needed, how they can get some respite so they will have more energy for their active toddlers.

As parents and parent guides baby watch together, they will find examples of toddlers using their parents as secure bases. Parent guides can seize these opportunities to name what they observe and to comment on the importance of this behavior to toddlers. Sometimes, however, parent guides will observe parents who often are not physically or emotionally there for their toddlers to return to. In these instances, the guide might speak for the child to clue the mother into the child's need. If this does not work, the guide may wonder about what is interfering with the parent's responsiveness. She may do this wondering in her own mind or out loud with the parent as Helen does in the following example.

Lynette and her parent guide, Helen, were sitting on Lynette's back porch talking; Lynette had said a little earlier that she had a terrible headache. Fifteen-month-old Tina was going in and out of the house stopping now and then to ask her mother to do something or to show her something. Lynette acted as if she did not even know Tina was there. The second time this happened, Helen spoke for Tina, "Hey, Mom, look at this." Lynette glanced down at what she had without comment and went on talking with Helen. A little later, Tina came and leaned against her mother's knee, and again Lynette ignored her. Helen spoke for Tina a second time, "Tina, you're coming out here to touch base with your mom, aren't you?" Lynette gave her a half-

*hearted pat on her head. Because Lynette fairly often was distracted by
her own needs and thus unresponsive to the children, Helen responded,
"Lynette, it seems like you're just feeling so bad it's hard to give her the
kind of attention she's asking for." Lynette said, "I know, but I am
feeling terrible." Helen replied, "What can we do to help you feel better so you can be there for her, 'cause she really needs you?"*

In Lynette's case, she was stressed out over her relationship problems
and had a severe headache. With other parents, similar behaviors could
stem from other distractions. The parent guide's role is to first assume
that parents really want to respond well to their children and then to use
the strategies recommended throughout this book to explore with parents
how they can do that.

When children seem fearful of leaving their parents' sides, parent
guides need to do the detective work to find out why. Has the parent been
inconsistently available? Has the child experienced a recent separation,
such as starting child care or being in the hospital? Has there been a recent
trauma or loss in the family? Is the parent fearful of the child being separated from her? Finding answers to these and similar questions will guide
the intervention. When toddlers are fearful of leaving their parents' sides,
it is almost never helpful to start with putting them in child care or with a
substitute caregiver to help them learn to be away from their parents.

*Linda was abandoned by her mother when she was young and also
had her two older children removed from her care due to neglect stemming from her substance abuse. With her baby, Sheryl, who was born
after she was in recovery for her substance abuse, she was very anxious
and overprotective. By the time Sheryl was a toddler, she had difficulty
leaving her mother's side because, in a sense, she had not had permission from her mother to do so. The parent guide, Celeste, helped Linda
to deal with her anxious feelings and to understand the importance to
Sheryl of beginning the separation-individuation process. As Linda became more comfortable with this separation, she and Celeste encouraged Sheryl to venture away from Linda to play and explore. Initially,
Celeste, a familiar person to Sheryl, would sit on the floor some distance
from Linda and entice Sheryl to come play with some toys with her. On
subsequent visits, as Sheryl became engrossed in her play, Celeste would
gradually withdraw. Eventually, Sheryl was able to explore and play
more on her own, returning to her mother for refueling as any toddler
would do.*

Checking In   As they play, securely attached toddlers will check in with their parents occasionally by making eye contact, showing or sharing a toy (Rheingold et al., 1976), or saying something to them, as Ashlin did when playing at the patio door. They no longer require as much close proximity and physical contact as they needed at an earlier age; psychological contacts (e.g., showing, looking, smiling) at a distance generally suffice except in times of more intense distress. Sometimes a quick glance is sufficient. One study found that the average length of gaze of 12-month-olds directed at their mothers during play is only 1.33 seconds (Schore, 1994). Ashlin assured herself of her parents' ready availability by engaging them early on when she introduced her bear to them. She was subsequently reassured by her grandma's comment about feeding her bear and her father's smile of confidence when she almost lost her balance.

Usually, toddlers check in with their parents fairly frequently either from a distance (e.g., with glances, smiles, vocalizations, or through pointing at or showing the parent something) or by returning to the parent. There are many reasons why the toddler signals or returns to the parent when playing at a distance. Sometimes, it is just to share discoveries or other delights as Alan Sroufe illustrated with this example:

> A twelve-month-old infant sits playing with a variety of toys on the floor of a laboratory playroom. Her mother sits a short distance away. As the child examines various objects in front of her, a large puzzle piece (a brightly colored carrot) captures her attention. She grasps the carrot with widened eyes. Then, in a smooth motion, she turns and extends it toward the mother, smiling broadly and vocalizing. Mother returns her smile and comments about the carrot. (1996, p. 5)

Although 12-month-olds may show a toy to a stranger, they usually reserve the kind of affective sharing described in the above example (i.e., the showing of a toy accompanied by both smiling and vocalizing) for the special people in their lives (Sroufe, Cooper, & Marshall, 1988).

As noted in the previous chapter, toddlers also check in with their parents to discern their reactions in ambiguous situations; however, studies of this phenomenon, known as social referencing, reveal that the behavior of toddlers is not *always* governed by their parents' appraisals. They are quite capable of making up their own minds in certain situations. In one study, 12- and 13-month-olds were shown pleasant, ambiguous, or frightening toys (Gunnar & Stone, 1984). Their mothers were instructed to either smile or be neutral when the child was confronted with one of these toys. If the mother smiled, the children were more apt to play with the ambiguous toy than if her expression remained neutral. The mother's smile had no effect, however, on their tendency to play with the other two toys. Regardless of the mother's expression, they avoided the frightening toy and played with the pleasant one. Other studies have found gender and temperament differences in toddlers' tendencies to seek or heed their parents' appraisals. For instance, when mothers conveyed fearful appraisals of ambiguous toys, boys appeared less influenced by these maternal appraisals than did girls even though mothers' fearful messages to boys were more intense (Rosen, Adamson, & Bakeman, 1992). Other research has found that wary or inhibited children are somewhat more apt to check in with parents when faced with novelty than are less inhibited children (Parritz et al., 1992).

Parent guides can reinforce parents' awareness of, and helpful responses to, this behavior of toddlers by pointing out instances they observe of parents' appropriate responses to their toddler's checking in and commenting on the importance of this to their children's development. Some parents, however, have a tendency to ignore their children's *checking in* signals, as Samantha did when Katrina looked to her for reassurance as another child approached her in her playgroup (see Chapter 6), or the parent may give an inappropriate response to these signals such as being irritable with the child. Toddlers of such parents need someone to amplify their signals so that their parents can learn to read and respond appropriately. Parent guides can do this by speaking for the baby: "Hey, Daddy, look at what I'm doing!" or "I think I need some help with this, Mommy." They also could say to the parent, "It's interesting how kids want to know if you think everything's okay, like the way Jenni checked in with you just now."

Emotional Refueling and Retooling   Toddlers may also look to or return to their attachment figures for emotional refueling and retooling. Some toddlers return to their parents, lean against them for a few moments, gaze up at their parents' smiling faces, then return to their play reenergized or soothed and reassured depending on their needs at the moment (Brent & Resch, 1987; Lieberman, 1993). The parent's facial expressions act "as an amplifier of positive arousal, a generator of energy required for further physical explorations of the environment by the infant" (Schore, 1994, p. 102). These interactions also facilitate the growth and stabilization of pathways in the brain that function in the identification of the faces of familiar individuals, helping toddlers to form a mental link between their images of their parents' emotionally expressive faces and their own emotional responses (Schore, 1994). Whether the emotion prototypes that the toddlers form are positive or negative depends on the nature of the parent's expressions and the child's emotional responses.

Pseudo-Independence without Togetherness   Not all children, however, seek their parents for emotional refueling or even for comfort when distressed. For instance, during the Strange Situation procedure described in Chapter 2, infants classified as secure engaged in some form of direct communication with their mothers (i.e., eye contact, facial expression, vocalizations, showing and giving of toys) more often than infants classified as having *anxious/avoidant attachments* did. The avoidant infants who did communicate directly with their mothers did so only when they were feeling well. No secure infant stayed away from his or her mother when in a negative mood, but the avoidant infants tended not to seek comfort from their mothers when distressed. Sometimes children with *anxious/avoidant attachments* may appear to be very independent and not in need of contact with their mothers; however, physiological evidence indicates that they are actually feeling quite distressed in these situations (Spangler & Grossmann, 1993). This evidence suggests that their façade of independence is just a cover-up for their neediness. This interpretation is supported from evidence that many of these children manifest considerable dependency later on with their preschool teachers (Sroufe et al., 1983).

It is easy to see why infants who develop *anxious/avoidant attachments* behave in this way when the behaviors of their attachment figures are observed. During a play situation with their 12- and 18-month-olds, parents of infants classified as secure ignored only 4% of their children's signals whereas parents of avoidant infants ignored 18% of the signals addressed to them. Furthermore, in contrast to the parents of securely attached infants, the parents of the infants who had developed *anxious/ avoidant attachments* joined in when their children were already engrossed in their play but withdrew when their children showed evidence of negative feelings (Bretherton, 1987; Escher-Graeub & Grossmann, 1983). When parent guides observe this, they can help by speaking for the child, "This is frustrating—I don't know how to make it work." They also can speak directly by saying something like, "Looks like she's having trouble with that. What do you think will help?"

Attachment Disturbances and Disorders   Lack of comfort seeking when they are hurt, frightened, or ill may indicate that children have an attachment disturbance or disorder (Boris, Aoki, & Zeanah, 1999). Some other indicators include being exceedingly affectionate with relatively unfamiliar adults, excessive dependence on the parent, and fearful overcompliance with parent's instructions. When parent guides observe these behaviors and other behaviors that seem unusual for the child's age and situation, the guide will want to consider whether this is a pattern. They may want to ask the parent questions to determine whether the parent views this as typical for the child. When the child eagerly clambers up onto the guide's lap on their first visit, the guide might ask, "Wow, is he usually this friendly with people he's just met?" Likewise, when the child clings to her mother during a home visit instead of playing with her toys that are nearby, the guide might ask, "Does she usually like to stay right by your side when people visit?" The mother may laugh and say, "No, she's usually busy with her toys," and then go on to explain why that day is an exception. When asked these questions, the parents may also reveal some of their feelings about the child's behavior. For instance, the parent may be worried about the child's being clingy.

In some instances, the parent guide may intervene to see if the parent can help the child respond differently. Robin had stopped seeking help from his mother, Trisha, because he had learned through painful past experience that it was seldom forthcoming. The family's parent guide, Patti, tried to help Trisha tune into Robin's needs so that their relationship would at least be benign even if Trisha, due to her mental illness, could not be fully sensitive and responsive with Robin. Patti also worked with other attachment figures in Robin's life to sharpen their awareness of Robin's bids for help so that Robin would learn that they, at least, would be responsive.

Screening for attachment disturbances and disorders is aided when parent guides have opportunities to observe the child on different occasions and in different environments. Because attachment disturbances and disorders may occur only in the presence of one of the child's attachment figures, it is helpful to see if the behavior in question also occurs with the child's other attachment figures. Temperament factors need to be considered (Bagnato, Neisworth, Salvia, & Hunt, 1999; Zeanah & Boris, 2000). Does the child have a slow-to-warm-up temperament or disturbed attachment with inhibition? Is this a child with a risk-taking spirited temperament or a disordered attachment with self-endangerment? One clue is if the risk-taking is done or exaggerated only in the presence of one attachment figure. On the basis of careful observation and parent responses to questions about the observed behaviors, if the parent guide feels that the child's attachment with that parent may be disturbed, the guide should seek consultation from a clinician with training in this area.

A disturbance in the child's attachment with the parent typically means that the parent is not, or has not, interacted with the child in ways that nurture the child's feelings of being loved, understood, cared for, and protected by this parent. The parent guide's role is to try to understand what is interfering with the parent's ability to provide this kind of parenting (e.g., depression, substance abuse, childhood history of abuse, this child's temperament), and then to help the parent gain access to resources to address these factors. In addition, the parent guide will use the strategies described in Chapter 3 to improve the parent's relationship with the child that, in turn, can modify the nature of the child's attachment with the parent. To keep the child's development on course (or to get it back on course), the child may need quality supplemental care. When all of these measures are not sufficient or the observed child's behaviors indicate a severe disturbance, both the parents and the child should be referred for further evaluation and more intensive therapy (e.g., parent–child psychotherapy).

Separation Anxiety   The same 12-month-old who toddles happily away from his mother to play will sob when she starts to leave him and cling to her when she returns after a brief separation. This typical separation distress becomes apparent with most children by age 7–8 months and tends to peak during the middle of the second year (Crowell & Waters, 1990). Young toddlers do not yet have the ability to form well-developed memories of their parents to hold onto during their absence. Parents can help by leaving with the child tangible reminders of their love (e.g., photographs of them together, audiotapes of them reading a favorite story or singing a familiar song). Several techniques for helping parents ease separation anxiety are presented in the section on child care in Chapter 12.

LEARNING TO LIVE WITH OTHERS

Parents often delight in the enthusiasm with which their toddlers set forth to explore and master their small worlds. Nevertheless, this bundle of energy with a curiosity that knows no bounds and mobility that expands exponentially, presents many new challenges to parents who find themselves saying "no, no" and "don't" more and more. In one study, mothers of toddlers ages 12–15 months were observed issuing a prohibition on the average of once every 9 minutes (Power & Chapieski 1986)! What a change from a few months earlier when close to 90% of maternal physical and verbal behavior with their 10-month-olds consisted of affection, play, and caregiving with relatively few prohibitions (Tulkin & Kagan 1972). Childproofing the house can reduce the number of prohibitions somewhat but not completely—nor should it. Limit-setting is an important part of the parent's responsibility for socializing the child and furthering the child's development of emotion regulation. Whether and how it is done has profound consequences for the child.

Parenting Styles

Diane Baumrind (1967) described three basic styles of parenting: authoritative, authoritarian, and permissive. (Note: Because it is easy to confuse the terms *authoritative* and *authoritarian*, the authoritative style will be referred to as the positive style. This term was chosen because the authoritative style is more positive in tone and because research indicates that it yields more positive outcomes for children.) The *positive style* is warm and responsive, sets clear expectations, involves the child in decision making, and remains firm once limits are set. The *authoritarian style* values obedience as a virtue, favors punitive, forceful measures to curb self-will, and does not encourage the child's expression of wishes, believing that the child should accept a parent's word for what is right. The *permissive style* veers in another direction with inconsistent or lax discipline and few demands or expectations; for some parents this behavior stems from a belief that children have a natural tendency toward self-actualization if freed from restraint as much as is consistent with survival.

Baumrind studied the effects of each parenting style and found that preschoolers raised with a positive style tended to be energetic, friendly, and self-reliant whereas those raised with an authoritarian style were more apt to be irritable, conflict-ridden, withdrawn, and distrustful. Those raised with a permissive style tended to be more impulsive and aggressive and were the least self-reliant of all three groups. She continued to study these three groups throughout their childhood and found that the children of parents who practiced more positive (authoritative) parenting continued to fare better in various developmental domains than children raised with authoritarian and permissive styles. Other studies (e.g., Kuczynski & Kochanska, 1995) have found similar outcomes.

As Baumrind continued to study parenting styles and child outcomes, she identified another style of effective parenting. She observed that parents with what she calls the *harmonious style* almost never actually exercised control but appeared to have control in the sense that their children generally took pains to intuit and do what their parents wanted. "The atmosphere in these families was characterized by harmony, equanimity, and later rationality" (Baumrind, 1978, p. 265). Another parenting style, described by Maccoby and Martin (1983) as *indifferent-uninvolved*, is often associated with parental physical and emotional neglect. When children raised by emotionally unavailable (i.e., emotionally neglectful) mothers were observed at age 24 months in a problem-solving task with their mothers, they were angry, noncompliant, and easily frustrated, and they expressed very little positive affect. Later in preschool, they were noncompliant, negativistic, lacking in impulse control, highly dependent on their teachers for help and support, and tended to present many behavior problems (e.g., self-abusive behavior; Erickson, Egeland, & Pianta, 1989).

Positive Parenting   The positive (authoritative) style as described by Baumrind contains characteristics of caregiving associated in the first year of life with the development of secure attachment. That is, this parenting style is warm and affectionate as well as sensitive and responsive to the child's needs and wishes. Some of the additional elements deal primarily with the ways in which the positive style meets the developmental need that arises during toddlerhood for socialization.

Most parents begin to set limits on their toddlers' behaviors during the second year using one or some combination of these parenting styles. They do so in part to assure the safety of the child and in part for their own sanity. Thoughtful parents also begin socializing their toddlers with the goal of helping them learn to respect the rights and needs of others and to internalize a sense of right and wrong. Furthermore, they want to do so in ways that help their children develop responsible, considerate behavior; self-discipline; and the ability to solve problems and make good decisions for themselves. (Some suggestions for parents for limit setting are presented later in this chapter.)

Dealing with Toddler's Feelings   What does this mean for parenting of toddlers? The challenge for parents is how to honor their children's need to explore and develop autonomy and at the same time begin to develop inner controls on their behavior, self-regulation of their intense emotions, and recognition of the needs of others. For instance, in positive parenting, parents will tune into their toddlers' desires and feelings and try to find ways in which their children can act on them. When that is not possible, they will at least verbally acknowledge their children's feelings and let their children know in simple terms why the answer is no. This is what Caitlin's father did when he brought her in from outdoors against her wishes (as described at the end of the Chapter 6). Furthermore, he helped her to handle her feelings by getting her interested in playing once they were indoors.

Tantrums   Sometimes, even when their parents practice positive parenting, children's feelings spill over into full-blown tantrums. Toddlers are known for the intensity of their feelings—squeals of joyful excitement, outbursts of frustration and rage, and wails of anguish are not uncommon. Experiencing the heights and depths of emotion and learning that they can recover from them is part of the emotional learning that needs to occur during this period. When children tantrum, parents help this learning process by accepting their children's feelings while remaining firm on the issues that provoked these outbursts. For example, Freddy was drawing on a piece of paper with a crayon. When he began using the crayon on the sofa, however, his mother guided him back to the paper several times, and finally put the crayon out of reach, at which time Freddy began to yell and flail. His mother let him tantrum for a few moments, and when it began to subside, she pulled him close to her on the sofa and said, "I know you're angry, sweetie. Want to sit by me and look at this book?"

Win-Win Solutions   Parents can negotiate win-win outcomes with their toddlers through considering what the toddler wants and either finding a way to make it happen or by negotiating some sort of compromise. Parents can often avoid conflicts by offering their children attractive alternatives to what they want to have or want to do. This strategy helps their children learn that although a specific thing or activity might be prohibited, there are other ways in which their needs, interests, and desires can be met. Providing children some choices regarding what they wear, eat, and do, not only gives them healthy ways to feel that they have some control—some autonomy—but also helps them begin to develop some decision-making skills. By explaining in simple terms why they cannot do or have what they originally wanted and then negotiating a compromise with them, parents help their toddlers learn both that their needs and feelings count and that the needs and feelings of others are also of value and are to be respected. For example, 13-month-old Brennan wanted some of the grapes her 5-year-old sister was eating. Their mother said, holding up two other choices, "Sorry, honey, you could choke on those; here, do you want to chew on this apple or this banana?" When parents offer choices, they are beginning to teach their children skills in decision-making, problem-solving, and negotiation. These skills may seem too difficult for a little 1-year-old to learn, but the process of learning them can begin even at this early age.

Pediatrician T. Berry Brazelton (1992) views mealtime as a time when toddlers can pretty much do things their way, which generally means eating what they want from what is provided and doing so with their fingers. He assures parents that a "rounded diet" at every meal cannot be a goal for the second year as long as a healthy selection of food is provided. He points out that a toddler may eat almost exclusively one type of food for several days then switch to another so that by the time a month has passed, he has actually consumed a rounded diet. This information is something for parents to discuss with their pediatricians or public health nurses. The important thing for the promotion of healthy emotional development is that the highchair tray does not become a stage for feeding wars.

Sleeping is another area in which conflicts can arise. Brazelton (1992) noted that just before beginning to walk, many babies start waking up during the light sleep that usually occurs about once every 4 hours at night. He ascribes this phenomenon to the fledgling toddler's strong urge to walk. The recommendations given in the previous chapter (e.g., having regular bedtime routines, helping children sooth themselves back to sleep) are applicable when these night wakings occur.

Setting Limits   Although there are plenty of opportunities for parents to acquiesce to their toddlers' wishes or negotiate compromises, there are times when parents must step in and stop or prohibit what their toddlers want to do. When these prohibitions are presented in a kind yet firm manner and supported by reason, they are more apt to be accepted as in the following example. At age 15 months, Charisa and her mother visited her grandmother who told Charisa when she started to open the buffet door, "No, no, please don't open that—there are breakable things inside." A few days later, Charisa approached a similar looking cabinet in a hotel lobby. She reached toward it then looked at her grandma, shook her head, and said "no, no." Her grandma smiled and said, "That's right—that's a no, no." Charisa said "no, no" again and walked away.

Even when parents set limits firmly without being harsh, toddlers often protest and do so vehemently, as Freddy did—sometimes just to fulfil their need to assert their own will. Responses to limit-setting may vary in accordance with the child's temperament. For instance, protests of children with spirited temperaments will be loud and long, and children who are slow to adapt to changes will balk the most at having to stop an activity that they are into. Parent guides can help parents understand and make reasonable accommodations to the children's temperaments such as giving slow-to-adapt children advance warning that they will need to stop what they are doing.

Restricting the number of times when prohibitions are needed helps parents maintain their equilibrium while dealing with their children's resistance, which can make the job of parenting a toddler go more smoothly. It is often easier for a parent to be both firm and kind when not engaged in one battle after another. Then, they can speak with that tone of conviction that lets the toddler know that the parent's "no" is really a "no." Furthermore, issuing fewer don'ts and more dos (i.e., positive requests for constructive and prosocial behaviors) during the early years is associated with better compliance and fewer behavior problems both then and later at age 5 years (Kuczynski & Kochanska, 1995). One way in which the number of don'ts can be reduced is to childproof and block off an area of the house so that the child can explore and play safely and freely.

Another suggestion for positive parenting is to take the child's desires and wishes into account when feasible. Doing this fosters the important development of the toddler's sense of autonomy. As the toddler's cognitive and language abilities grow, learning to negotiate their desires and wishes with their parents helps them begin to learn valuable life-long skills. It also helps when parents are clear when something is not negotiable and when they expect their children to comply. Children respond better to a parent's calm confidence than to angry impatience. When parents provide simple and specific explanations for requests and prohibitions, toddlers can learn that there are reasons behind the things that people should and should not do or have. When setting limits, it is important that parents acknowledge, label, and accept the child's feelings even when (especially when) the child's actions cannot be accepted. Toddlers are known for the intensity of their feelings, the expression of which can be ferocious at times. The parent needs to be a secure base for the toddler's exploration of his feelings just as the parent is a secure base for exploration of the environment (Lieberman, 1993). With the parent's help, the toddler learns that he or she can experience deep feelings of anger, disappointment, and sadness and be okay. When parents also label these feelings for their toddlers, the children can begin to develop a vocabulary for feelings that will eventually help them to talk about their feelings (instead of just fussing, screaming, and sobbing) and to regulate their emotions because they have a way of symbolizing them for themselves. The following example illustrates the practice of some of the principles of positive parenting.

> *Brennan's household was brimming full of visiting relatives, so Brennan was wired, but her mother needed to get her to change her clothes so they could all go out to dinner. First, she set out all of the clothes Brennan needed to wear; then, she sat on the floor beside them and told Brennan to come change her clothes so they could go out to eat. Brennan took a couple of steps away and looked teasingly at her mother, but her mother just sat quietly and expectantly. In a this-is-the-way-it-is voice she repeated, "You need to get dressed now so we can go to dinner." Her quiet patience and confidence in Brennan's cooperation won out, and Brennan came to her and let her mother dress her.*

Some parents will have difficulty feeling, much less exuding, this air of calm confidence. All of the things parent guides do to help parents gain a sense of self-efficacy are interventions that help parents be more calm and confident with their children. These interventions include strategies discussed throughout this book, such as highlighting instances of positive parenting, acknowledging parents' feelings, helping them deal with various issues in their lives, and so forth.

Expression of Emotions

Ashlin "feeding" her toy bear is a typical behavior observed in children during their second year. In this episode, Ashlin not only enacted her developing internal model of the parent–child relationship as one of care and nurturance, but she also demonstrated an important new development, the ability to represent things and events. Brain developments around this time greatly enhance the child's ability to form mental representations (Schore, 1994), which in turn leads to the development of language and pretend play (Piaget, 1951). As these skills develop, they greatly expand toddlers' means for thinking about themselves and the world and for communicating with others (Lieberman, 1996).

Providing developmental guidance to heighten parents' appreciation of their children's pretend play at this age begins with observation and inquiry into what the parents have observed and do already. For example, watching 14-month-old Robin together with his mother, Trisha, Patti commented, "I notice he likes to feed his doll baby; that's so great that he's beginning to pretend. Does he like you to pretend with him?" Robin's mother told Patti how Robin liked it when she told him that he was being a good daddy. "And when I say, 'Love your baby,' he gives his doll a big hug—it's so cute!" Patti then gave Trisha positive feedback about the pretend play and how important it is to Robin's development.

As parent guides baby watch with parents, they can reinforce parents' awareness of the importance of pretend play to their children's development. When parent guides do not observe instances of pretend play, they can wonder aloud with the parents whether they have observed their children doing so. "You know, a lot of children this age like to do pretend things like pretend to feed their teddy bears or dolls, or pretend their toy car's a real car by making motor noises. Have you noticed (child's name) doing anything like that?" If the parent says yes and gives some examples, the parent guide can talk about the benefits of this activity to the child's development and how parents can facilitate this development by dipping into the child's play from time to time. If the parent says no, they have not observed this activity, the parent guide can explore with the parent why this might be. Perhaps the child does not have toys that encourage this type of play or perhaps no one engages the child in pretend play. After explaining the importance of pretense, the parent guide can suggest they try floor time and offer to coach the parent in engaging the child in this type of play. The child will need some appropriate toys (e.g., doll, toy trucks, toy animals), so the parent guide may need to offer to bring some to get started.

When children are beginning to develop pretend play, adults can enter their play and respond in ways that highlight or expand the play's pretense potential. For instance, Taisha pushes a toy truck across the floor, and her Mom says, "Brmm, brmm—here comes your truck. I'd better get out of the way!" Another example is when Jacob clutches a teddy bear, and the caregiver says, "Oooh, love that teddy! Do you think he's hungry?" When Jacob nods yes, she hands him a toy baby bottle and says "You're taking such good care of your teddy" as Jacob puts the baby bottle to the bear's mouth. By responding to children as though they are pretending, parents and other caregivers can nudge what may be just functional play into actual pretend play. (Additional suggestions for how parents and other caregivers facilitate pretend play are presented in Gowen, 1995.)

As pretend play develops throughout the second year, indicators of other major developments emerge. At first, children pretend at things they actually do such as pretending to sleep and to eat. Then, shortly before the middle of the second year, they begin to extend these activities to others and pretend to feed their mothers, bathe their teddy bears, and put their dolls to bed. By the second half of the second year, children typically pretend that their dolls and toy figures can carry out various actions (e.g., they pretend that their dolls can feed themselves and toy people can drive their toy cars). These developments represent children's emerging understanding of agency (i.e., being active agents who can make things happen) and correspond with their developing sense of self—especially their understanding that they can cause things to happen. This realization has important implications for their development of a sense of autonomy and their relationships with their attachment figures. The next chapter describes these developments and how parent guides can help parents to promote them.

8

Me, Myself, and I

18 to 24 Months

Sophia is getting dressed in anticipation of a visit from her new nursery school friend, Isabelle. Her mother, Heather, knowing that 22-month-old Sophia has very definite ideas about what she wants to wear, holds up two pairs of slacks, "Do you want to wear the blue ones or the green ones today?" Sophia takes the green ones, sits down, and starts putting both feet into the same pant leg. As Heather begins easing Sophia's right leg into the right pant leg, she starts talking with her about Isabelle's visit. "Aren't you excited that Isabelle's coming over? What's the first thing you want to do when she gets here?" As soon as her mother finishes dressing her, Sophia proudly pulls on her rain boots—something she insists on wearing as often as possible. Just then, the doorbell rings. Sophia jumps up and runs to greet her friend. Isabelle's mother says hi to Sophia and then asks Heather, "Does she like to be called Sophie or Sophia?" Sophia pipes up, "Pia." Isabelle's mother turns to Sophia, smiles and says, "Hi, So-pia." Sophia responds, "No, Pia." Heather explains, "She's decided that her name is Pia, and that's that." The two girls start getting some toys off the shelf. When Isabelle picks up an alphabet book, Sophia runs over and starts to grab it, "Mine, mine." Heather goes over and tells Sophia, "Remember, your friend is here, and we share with our friends." As she says this, she hands Sophia another book, opens it, and says, "Ohh, what's this a picture of?" Sophia replies, "Doggie." Heather says, "That's right," and then turns back to her conversation with the other mother. Sophia looks up as Isabelle drops the alphabet book but does not take it; instead, she picks up a wooden spoon, holds it like a telephone, and says, "Hi, Daddy." Heather notices this and says to Isabelle's mother, "She really misses her daddy. We all do. I'll be glad when we can join him." When Heather leaves the room, Sophia cries out, "Mommy, Mommy!" Heather sticks her head around the corner, "It's okay, honey, I'll be right back. I'm just getting some coffee for Isabelle's mommy. Why don't you show Isabelle and her mommy the toy that we got at the store yesterday?"

During the second half of the second year, toddlers develop a more clearly defined sense of self. They begin to realize that they are separate little beings who can do things on their own. This realization enhances their sense of autonomy and potency, but it also brings new anxieties and problems. The push-pull of moving away and being independent and then returning to feel reassured and reconnected is now enacted at an increasingly more psychological level. Parent guides can help parents and other caregivers recognize and understand the special issues of this new stage and how they can help their toddlers use these challenges to enhance their emotional development. Doing this often involves practicing *positive parenting* as described in Chapter 7.

THE DEVELOPING SENSE OF SELF

The toddler's sense of himself as a separate, independent person becomes more clearly articulated during this period. Parent guides can alert parents to the various signs of this development—for example, how it shows up in the child's language—and explain its importance. Toddlers at this stage begin to use more personal pronouns—"me," "mine," and "I" pop up in their language more frequently. They also begin to use more self-evaluative terms and self-descriptive terms. Sophia insisted on being called "Pia." When another toddler, Jackie, did something he felt proud of, he would say, "Big boy!" A 20-month-old was observed saying "turn" as he turned the lid on a container and "up" as he climbed onto a box (Kagan, 1981). Parents facilitate this language development by making simple comments on what the child is doing as he plays.

Toddlers' developing sense of self is also evident when they begin to recognize themselves in pictures and in mirrors. Young babies are often delighted when they see the baby in the mirror wave his or her arms as they wave theirs. Early in the second year, however, they may become more serious and subdued and stare intently at the image as though they realize that the baby in the mirror's movements are somehow related to their own. It is not until around the middle of the second year, though, that they show evidence that they are watching an image of themselves. This phenomenon was studied in a series of clever experiments in which the toddler after looking at himself in the mirror was distracted while a smudge of rouge was placed surreptitiously on his nose (or forehead) and then returned to the mirror. By around age 21 months, the toddlers after noticing the rouge on the babies in the mirror would touch their own noses (or foreheads). Before then, they might point at the rouge on the babies in the mirror but show no signs that they recognized themselves in the mirror (Lewis & Brooks-Gunn, 1979). Evidence that this self-recognition is connected with cognitive development is provided by a study of children with Down syndrome who did not show that they recognized themselves in the mirror until they had achieved the mental age of about 20 months (Sroufe, 1996).

Enchantment with the Body

Along with this budding sense of self comes an enchantment with the body and its parts and products. Toddlers love to run around naked and be admired. Getting dressed immediately after a bath was simply not acceptable for Gabriel. He insisted on first running around the house naked in what his parents termed his "after bath dash." Toddlers are fascinated and often proud of what their bodies can produce—feces, urine, mucus, gas—all are *their* accomplishments! Parents can foster a sense of pleasure and pride in their toddlers' physical selves while still helping them find socially acceptable ways of doing so. Charisa's parents helped her learn that she could talk about bodily functions and reveal body parts at home within the family but not in public. Toddlers soon discover and learn about gender differences and are often envious as well as intrigued by these differences. Howie was crushed when he learned that men cannot also give birth to babies. Although womb-envy among little boys has not received the attention that penis-envy among little girls has, it is also a part of toddlers' coming to terms with their gender identities.

It is a challenge for some parents to accept and be matter of fact about their children's interest in their body parts and products, so anticipatory guidance before they reach this age can be helpful. Parent guides can explain what to expect and why and then ask parents how they feel about this matter. This discussion can be followed by exploring with the parents how they plan to handle this normal part of their children's development. When children are already at this stage, parent guides may observe parents saying, as their toddler touches his or her private parts, "Stop that! That's naughty!" The parent guide might say something like, "Children at this age are so interested in *all* of the parts of their bodies. What are your ideas for helping (name the child) feel good about his body and yet learn when it is okay to explore his body and when it isn't the thing to do?" The parent may indicate that there is no time nor place where it is okay for the child to "play with himself." The parent guide can acknowledge the parent's feelings by pointing out that many people used to think that masturbation was harmful and should be prevented, but that we now know that it is just a typical way for children to calm themselves and to learn about their bodies. In discussing this subject with parents, guides can help them understand that many parents have found that the more fuss they make over their children's masturbation, the more frequently the children engage in the behavior. If it seems from a parent's or child care worker's description of the child's masturbation that it is excessive, the guide can explain that this may indicate that the child is experiencing too much tension and needs more down time. (Depending on the overall situation, the parent guide may need to get more information to determine if there are other indicators of possible sexual abuse.) Parent guides may want to follow Brazelton's advice:

> When parents worry about a child masturbating, the first advice I offer is: Don't emphasize the behavior. Don't show disapproval or try to inhibit it. If it is frequent, look for underlying reasons. Is the child very tense? Is he overstimulated? Has he other ways of self-comforting? (1992, p. 295)

"Me Do"—Striving for Autonomy

Toddlers at this stage become increasingly aware of the fact that they can make things happen. Their sense of self coupled with their ability to represent (re-present) the past and imagine the future help them experience connections between their acts and the consequences. They begin to set goals for themselves and often feel driven to accomplish them. At this age, Charisa insisted on putting on her own shirt—usually wrong side out. Her mother decided that allowing her this accomplishment was far more important than her appearance; she also found that putting shirts away right side out usually prevented this problem. After accomplishing some challenging task, toddlers will often display their sense of pride by calling their mothers' attention to their achievements (Stipek, Recchia, & McClintic, 1992). Younger children may smile when they have completed some task (e.g., fit chips into a shape sorter), but toddlers age 22 months or older appear more aware that these are *their* accomplishments. For instance, when 20-month-old Brennan made a song play by pressing a button on her toy, she quickly turned to her mother, smiled, and clapped her hands. Her mother shared in her delight by smiling and clapping in return. Experiencing accomplishments as Charisa and Brennan did builds the toddler's motivation to attempt to master further tasks in the future.

Parents strengthen their toddlers' mastery motivation by providing them opportunities to be challenged, assisting with tasks only as needed, and by acknowledging their achievements. Letting children do things on their own is time consuming and often requires some advance planning. Parent guides can ask parents if they have noticed that their toddlers want to do more things on their own. This question can open a discussion of both how important independence is for the child and how challenging it can be for parents. Together the guide and the parent can explore ways to meet the needs of both parent and child. The solution may include some structuring of the parent's activities—like leaving sufficient time for the child to get dressed before going somewhere—and structuring of tasks for the child. For instance, parents can sometimes find ways of assisting so that the child experiences the accomplishment of doing the last step, like pushing a button the rest of the way through the buttonhole. Of course, there are times when parents simply have to move things along, and parent guides can help them plan for these occasions as well. The strategy of redirecting the child's attention is often useful in these situations. Heather distracted Sophia by asking her questions so that she would be dressed before her friend, Adele, came. Then, Heather let Sophia do something on her own, put on her own boots, so that she could feel a sense of accomplishment.

Mastery motivation gets an additional boost when parents acknowledge their children's accomplishments. There is evidence that rewarding children frequently can actually diminish the intrinsic motivation that comes from meeting a challenge and achieving a self-determined goal (Kohn, 1993). Therefore, when appropriate, parent guides may suggest that parents recognize achievements with matter-of-fact descriptive comments ("You built a really tall tower.") rather than simple praise ("Oh, wow—that's really great!"). The first approach emphasizes what was accomplished and enhances language development (e.g., "tall tower"). Parents can also focus on the child's feelings of accomplishment with comments like, "Oh, aren't you *glad* that you put that red circle in the right place?" With some parents, however, any kind of positive acknowledgement of what the child has achieved is better than no comment at all and certainly better than negative comments like, "No, no—you're doing it all wrong."

Awareness of Failures   There is a flip side to toddlers' recognition of their own accomplishments—awareness of their failures. If they fail to accomplish some goal they have set for themselves, 18-month-olds may cry. This reaction is different from the 12-month-olds who may cry if their activity is interrupted but not just because they lacked the ability to accomplish the task (Kagan, 1981). Frustrations, disappointments, and failures are facts of life, and toddlers need to occasionally experience them, but they may at times need help in recouping and moving on. This fact is especially true for children with spirited temperaments who tend to feel and express their frustration very intensely. Although toddlers can regulate their own arousal levels some of the time using some of the strategies described in Chapter 2, their caregivers need to step in and help them when they are becoming overwhelmed (Sroufe, 1996). When Gabriel became very frustrated because the blocks he was stacking kept falling down, his Dad got down with him and said, "Umm, didn't work, did it? Let's see what's the problem." He then helped Gabriel to problem-solve until he could get the blocks to stack without falling.

Sometimes parents have a hard time discovering how to help in this way. They may give too much help or they may give no help and then chastise the child for getting upset. Samantha tended to respond to her daughter, Penny, in this way. She would ignore her when she was struggling with something and then, when Penny would get frustrated, yell at her for "losing it." One time, when Penny was 18 months old, she kept trying to eat peas with her spoon, but they kept falling out before she could get them into her mouth. Finally, in frustration, she banged her spoon on her tray. At this point, Samantha grabbed the spoon from her hand and yelled at her, "Stop that!" Samantha's parent guide, Katherine, spoke up for Penny saying, "What's up, Sammie?" To which Samantha said, "She shouldn't be banging her spoon." Katherine responded, "Wonder what she's trying to say with that? How 'bout we watch her for a moment?" This intervention helped Samantha back away from simply reacting; it walked her through the process of reflecting and attributing meaning to Penny's behavior. These tools then helped her to respond more helpfully in this situation and in many similar ones later on.

Desire to Do it All   The 1-year-old's desire to "do it all" creates challenges for caregivers especially when there is a need to accomplish the task quickly or when what the toddler wants to do is unsafe or would create an intolerable mess. Parents often comment on the battles that can ensue over getting their toddlers safely buckled into their car seats. Some toddlers insist that only the mother can buckle the belt. Others insist on doing it themselves, and some do not want to get into the car seat at all. A number of these parents report that it has been worth it to take the time, when possible, to think of what the child needs in these situations. For instance, one parent found that after her son tried a few times to fasten the belt, he was willing to let her do it. Another mother encouraged her daughter to climb into the car seat by having her pretend to put her baby doll into a car seat.

Sometimes caregivers need help finding creative ways to balance their toddlers' needs for mastery and autonomy with their own practical needs. The parent may complain, "She drives me crazy. I'm trying to get on the road, and we have this big battle because she won't get in the car seat (or she wants to put her own shoes on, or she wants to take a zillion toys with her)." The parent guide can problem-solve with the parent about ways in which, like the parents described previously, the parent might be able to give the child some leeway yet still accomplish the parent's goal. They can empathize with the parent, "Yes, it is frustrating at this age because they have such a strong need to try out some of their ways of doing things. Is there any way in which you can allow a little extra time for this when you need to go someplace?" The parent guide should also acknowledge that there are times when the parent needs to move quickly, and they should help the parent see how they can take charge quietly but firmly by practicing the principles of positive parenting described in Chapter 7 and recognizing that the child still may have a tantrum but will recover. The parent guide might add that when children have real opportunities for mastery at other times, they may be more tolerant of these necessary restrictions.

When parents make the effort to take into account their children's goals (i.e., their interests and desires) as well as their own, they can begin to develop "goal-corrected partnerships" with their children (Bowlby, 1982). "When the competing goals of parents and child can be accommodated or reconciled through negotiation, their relationship is characterized by flexible give-and-take, and it becomes a partnership where the parties work together to readjust their goals in order to arrive at a mutually agreeable course of action" (Lieberman, 1993, p. 42). Learning to do this can begin in simple ways during toddlerhood. Parents accomplish this by giving their children choices when possible and by being clear when something is not negotiable. Wearing something warm on a cold day is not negotiable, but the child can be given a choice about which sweater or jacket to wear.

Desire to Do it Their Way   Not only do toddlers want to do it all, but they also want to do it *their* way. Often they will insist on their way even when it is directly counter to what their parents want them to do. Sometimes, it seems as though they do so just for the sake of asserting themselves. For instance, a mother may say that it is time to leave and hold out her hand to the toddler who replies with a defiant "no" and then takes the mother's hand and cheerfully goes with her. The need of toddlers to establish their autonomy (their sense of self) often puts them in conflict with their parents. This conflict may be hard on the parent, but, if handled well, it is good for the child. Through these daily bouts of disagreements, resolutions, and reconciliations toddlers learn that they have "an autonomous will, that disagreements with loved ones are inevitable, and that anger can be experienced and survived" (Lieberman, 1993, p. 22).

Parent guides can help parents with this challenging developmental phase by helping them understand that these conflicts are a typical and important part of development; they can use anticipatory guidance earlier on and developmental guidance as they observe events happening or as parents tell them about these battles. Parent guides should also acknowledge how frustrating this process can be at times and offer to partner with parents to figure out ways to make things go as smoothly as possible. Sometimes this will mean engaging in reflective questioning with parents about what things seem to help, like allowing a little extra time when possible for transitions. They can also share that some parents have found that when they stay calm but firm in their expectations while giving their toddlers a few moments to do their thing that the child will come around (as Brennan did when her mother needed to dress her). Parent guides can explain, "Children seem to respond better when parents remain calm and stay the course than they do when parents get upset with them."

When 20-month-old Nell seemed set on doing something against her parents' wishes, they tended to alternate between impatience and abdication. For instance, one or both of them would yell, "Stop that!" or "Come here this moment!" and then go on and on about what, how, and why she should or should not do something. Then, when she did not comply, they would shrug and give up on the whole thing. Observing this, their parent guide, Helen, used the parents' expressed concern about Nell's language development as an opening to address this problem. She suggested that they tell Nell what they want her to do in just a few words (e.g., "Come here," "Bring it to me," "Put it back") and then wait and expect her to do it. She explained that giving brief, simple instructions would not only help Nell's language development but would also help her learn to comply more with their requests. She went on to explain that sometimes the child might need some physical guidance. For instance, when suggesting that when they want Nell to take the snack food back into the kitchen, they might first tell her, "Take the cheese puffs back to the kitchen." Then, if she does not do it after a few moments, go to her and offer to help her. Because Nell's parents expressed interest in trying this approach, their parent guide worked with them on this during several home visits.

When parents seem to have a hard time setting limits with their toddlers, parent guides will want to reflect on what might be causing this problem. Are the parents preoccupied with other things? Are they unsure of themselves? Some parents secretly admire a gutsy child and vicariously enjoy and identify with their acting out. Some parents, like Nell's mother and father, simply need to learn a more effective way to gain Nell's compliance.

Role of Attachment   Progress toward development of mastery motivation, problem-solving skills, and goal-directed behavior appears to go more smoothly in dyads where the toddlers have developed secure attachments with their caregivers. In a study in which 2-year-olds were confronted with problems of increasing difficulty, the securely attached toddlers effectively sought help as the problems became harder, and their caregivers provided clear and direct cues (Sroufe, 1996). These interactions resulted in greatly reduced negative affect, more positive problem solving, and a shared joy in the child's mastery. Children with *anxious/resistant attachments* tended to become more oppositional, frustrated, angry, and distressed as problems became more difficult. They sought more contact with their caregivers, but the contact became more negative and the quality of the caregiver assistance deteriorated as the pair became embroiled in conflict. Children with *anxious/avoidant attachments* tended to express their frustration and anger indirectly and to ignore their caregiver's direction. These partners often seemed emotionally uninvolved, even when the problems became too difficult for the child. The overall effectiveness of the mother–child pair in providing the child with a positive experience of mastery—"with capacities stretched but not strained" (Sroufe, 1996, p. 211)—was the best predictor of later self-regulation when these children became preschoolers.

The results of Sroufe's study underscore the importance of working with parent–child dyads during the first year of life to foster the development of secure infant–parent attachments. Parent guides, however, will sometimes find themselves working during the toddler years with dyads in which the children appear insecurely attached, that is, dyads similar to some of those in the Sroufe study. For the children whose needs are ignored by their parents, parent guides can speak for the child or direct the parent's attention to the child, as the parent guide did with Samantha for Katrina when she needed reassurance as a playmate approached her during playgroup (see Chapter 6).

Parent guides can assist parents and children in conflict to find more effective ways to problem-solve. For instance, Jeffrey tried unsuccessfully to put the wheels that he had taken off of his toy car back on. In frustration, he handed the car to his mother, Lynette, who said, angrily as she tried to put one of the wheels on, "I told you not to take those off." Jef-

frey grabbed the car back from her, and she scolded him, "Don't grab it."
Jeffrey then threw the car and the tires across the room. When a parent
guide observes an interaction like this one, he or she needs to reflect on
what he or she knows about this dyad and what else is going on at that
point of time in the parent's and child's lives, in addition to reflecting on
what he or she sees at the moment. What the parent guide decides to do,
then, will stem from these reflections. For instance, the guide may reframe
the situation by saying to the parent something like, "He really seems to
get mad when he tries to do something and can't." This is what Helen
(Lynette's parent guide) said, and it seemed to help Lynette view Jeffrey's
behavior differently and thus respond differently. Another way to reframe
the situation is to speak for the child, "You are really curious about how
things go together and come apart, aren't you?" or the guide may ask the
parent, "Is this the way it usually goes with you two?" This question can
open up a discussion in which the guide can find out if the parent is interested in trying anything different. In other situations, the parent guide
may not do anything at the moment but make a mental note that the
mother may need some help with her own frustration level or with stresses
in her life. If the interaction is videotaped, the guide and parent can watch
it and discuss it later when the parent is not in the midst of the event itself. When parents become more attentive and responsive and less apt to
be drawn into conflicts with their children, the children will be able to feel
more secure with their parents.

Self-Assertion versus Aggression   The goal is for toddlers to learn
to assert their will and, when suitable, negotiate compromises without resorting to aggression. Many parents, however, tend to promote a certain
amount of aggression especially in their sons (Zahn-Waxler, Cole, & Barrett, 1991). They punish aggression more often in boys than in girls, at
least in the moment, but they also encourage it in various ways. Because
boys are physically punished more than girls, they are more often exposed
to aggressive models. Parents also report a greater acceptance of anger in
boys than in girls. Even the toys typically given to boys tend to promote
aggressive play. Whereas girls are often given dolls and toy dishes that encourage nurturing behaviors, boys are often given vehicles, fighting char-
acters, and toy weapons that encourage more active, aggressive behaviors.

Lynette was concerned about Jeffrey's aggressive behavior, especially
toward her and his little sister. Lynette had perceived Jeffrey as being aggressive "like his father" while he was still a young infant. As he grew into
toddlerhood, aggressive behavior was promoted by the behavior of some
of the family members. For instance, Lynette and her partner, Hugh, noticed that Jeffrey seemed more aggressive after he had spent time at his
uncle's house with his uncle's rowdy friends. After discussing this situa-

tion with Helen, they decided to stop Jeffrey's visits to his uncle's house but to let him interact with his uncle at their home. Lynette was concerned about Hugh's spanking Jeffrey, especially spanking him for hitting his younger sister, so Helen talked with them about the message children are sent when grownups discipline them by hitting them. "I wonder what he's learning when he's told that he can't hit his little sister, yet people who are bigger and stronger hit him?" After talking about this and about some alternative discipline techniques, Hugh and Lynette agreed to try putting Jeffrey into time-out instead of spanking him when he misbehaved. They tried this technique and said Jeffrey's behavior improved.

When parents complain about their children's aggression, parent guides can first ask open-ended questions to learn more about the family's values regarding such things as how they want their children to stand up for themselves, what expressions of anger are acceptable, and so forth. These discussions often help parents become more aware of any conflicting feelings they may have about their children's aggression. Parents may not want their children to hit their siblings, yet may encourage them to fight back when hassled by other children. They may also be unaware of the contradiction between their hitting their children and telling their children not to hit younger children.

Biting   A typical toddler behavior that is especially upsetting to parents is biting, whether their child is the biter or the one bitten. Through anticipatory guidance, parent guides can let parents know that this is a typical behavior. They should expect it but also be reassured that there are things they can do to diminish its occurrence. When parents are upset over their children's biting, parent guides can empathize with their anger and their embarrassment when their child has bitten another child. They can then partner with the parent to find ways to stop this behavior. Parents can be led to understand that when toddlers bite, often it is because they are overloaded and out of control (Brazelton, 1992). When parents overreact and punish the child, it just makes the situation worse. Instead parents can calmly and firmly let their toddlers know: "You *cannot* bite other people. It hurts them." If the biting seemed to be in retaliation for something the other child did, then the parent can deal with that. "I know that you're mad because Jamie took your truck, but you can't bite him. Just tell him, 'Stop.'" Some parents have found that it helps to give the child something like a teether that they can bite when they feel the urge to do so.

Right and Wrong   "The process of acquiring a set of rules, values, and, ultimately, principles, as well as using such standards as guides for behavior, takes place over the entire course of childhood and adolescence" (Sroufe, 1996, p. 197). Most parents do not expect their children to begin obeying their rules until some time during the second year. This socialization process tends to go more smoothly when parents practice the principles of positive parenting (described in Chapter 7) and do so within the context of a secure and affectionate relationship developed during infancy. When one or both of these are missing (i.e., the child has an insecure attachment with the primary caregiver and/or the caregiver does not practice positive parenting), the process is compromised. For example, during Hal's first several months, he had very inconsistent parenting and was exposed to frequent episodes of family violence. By the time he went into foster care at age 13 months, he displayed serious oppositional behavior. Although the foster parent practiced positive caregiving, Hal was not responding well. This reaction was due in part to the number of children cared for by this foster parent and also to the fact that there was a need to place Hal in a new child care center. On a home visit, while the foster mother was talking with another worker, Helen took Hal, who was then nearly 2, outside to play for a few moments. Helen had a lot of difficulty getting Hal to go back inside but managed it by being consistently firm without getting angry with him. Helen was then able to empathize with the foster mother about how difficult and tiring it must be for her to care for Hal but how important it is to establish a consistently firm, caring relationship with him. Helen also emphasized the importance of expecting that Hal would comply eventually, knowing that foster parents can sometimes think that children are so troubled by the time they come to them that compliance will not develop. Helen and the foster mother discussed some ways that the foster parents could help Hal become more cooperative.

In addition to learning their parents' specific expectations, values, and prohibitions, toddlers during the second half of the second year begin to exhibit an understanding of the general notion of standards. Throughout the second year, toddlers encounter not only prohibitions but also their caregivers' evaluations and judgments of what's right and what's wrong, what's "good" and what's "bad." Soon, they adopt this judgmental approach and generalize it to various aspects of their experience. They develop a sense of the way things ought to be and become disturbed when things are not in keeping with these standards. When Sophia's grandmother started to put the dog biscuits on the washing machine, Sophia yelled, "No, no. Here!" and patted the dryer top where her mother always put them. For some toddlers, a missing button, chipped toy, or torn piece of clothing is a violation of such a standard (Kagan, 1981). These may seem rather inconsequential to parents, but for the toddlers they are one part of their awareness of standards and the notion of right versus wrong.

There is a lot for toddlers' minds to process: what is "good" and what is "bad," what will be prohibited and perhaps punished and what will be accepted and perhaps praised. Toddlers often check in visually with their caregivers when they are uncertain as to whether something is okay or not, just as Ashlin did when she picked up the water bottle and then looked at her grandmother while playing around the patio doorway. Although toddlers test the limits and assert their own wills, they also want to please their parents and to know what is okay and what is not.

Parents and other caregivers help their toddlers learn what is and is not acceptable behavior by being clear and consistent about their expectations and rules. Parent guides can help parents reflect on what they want the child to do in specific situations and what they are trying to teach their children. For example, when the child grabs something from the bookcase and the parent simply yells, "You know you're not supposed to have that," it is not clear to the child what he is supposed to do. The parent guide might say, "What do you want him to do?" If the parent responds, "I want him to put it back," the parent guide could then ask, "Do you think he will if you ask him to?" They can also talk about what the parent wants the child to learn. If the parent wants the child to leave things alone that are in a certain place, they can discuss how to be consistent about this, such as not putting any of the child's things there, always restricting the child's access to the place, putting some of the more tempting things in a different place out of reach, and so forth. By being reflective with parents, parent guides can help parents become more reflective and less reactive with their children.

Some parents need more than verbal reflection to help them be clear with their children about their expectations. Sometimes, as in the case with Nell's parents, they need instruction and coaching. As noted previously, Nell's parents were having difficulty gaining Nell's compliance with their reasonable expectations. Helen suggested that they put their heads together to find out what would work with Nell. When the parents indicated that they had no clue about what to do, Helen asked their permission to try something. "I don't know if it will work, but if it's okay with you, we can try something and see what happens." Helen had an idea that the following steps might work with Nell: 1) be clear and concise with instructions, 2) convey the expectation that the child will comply, 3) follow through with physical guidance if necessary, 4) reinforce the child's compliance, and 5) be consistent with this approach over time. With the parent's permission, she tried this approach both to get Nell to do something and to stop doing something; it worked in both instances. Then, she explained to the parents, in clear, concise terms, the steps she had followed. At the mother's request, she wrote down these steps, which the mother posted on her refrigerator and later said that she often referred to them. Helen's approach was different from simple modeling and giving the message, "I know what will work with your child, and this is it." Instead, it was done as an experiment—an exploration of what might work. This difference is subtle but important. In this example, Helen followed the principle of parallel process. She was clear and concise with the parents, conveyed a sense of confidence that the parents would try this approach, provided guidance (i.e., during another visit, coached them as they tried this approach with Nell), and was consistent in checking in with the parents regarding how it was working for them.

Cause and Effect   Then, there is the important question of causality. Toddlers are in the very early stages of understanding cause and effect and their reasoning about this concept is often faulty. It is up to caregivers to help them understand the connections between their actions and the consequences of those actions. "I know that you just wanted Kitty to stay here, but she doesn't like being held down. That's why she scratched you." As in this example, it is also useful sometimes to state the child's apparent motive (i.e., wanting the cat to stay put). Doing so acknowledges that the child's intention was okay even if the action on behalf of that intention was not (similar to recognizing that parents' behaviors are sometimes healthy strivings gone awry). Children who typically receive gentle control (e.g., guidance supported by reasons) are more apt to internalize their parents' values and rules than children who receive more negative and coercive control (Kochanska, 1997; Kochanska & Aksan, 1995).

During a late afternoon home visit, Helen observed Nell eating a bag of cheese puffs. Knowing of her parents' concern over Nell's eating habits and excessive weight, Helen said, "I notice she's eating cheese puffs. When's dinner?" Nell's mother replied, "As soon as you leave." Helen said, "Is it okay with you that she's eating cheese puffs just before dinner?" Nell's mother said, "No—after she does this she doesn't eat good." Helen paused then asked, "What would you like her to do when she goes for the cheese puffs?" Through continued reflective questioning, Helen helped Nell's mother build on their previous discussions about limit setting to develop a strategy for helping Nell understand when and where she could have occasional snacks and why she could not snack before meals. They discussed again the importance of keeping the instructions simple (to aid language development as well as compliance) and of being consistent ("It's confusing to her if sometimes it's permitted and sometimes it isn't").

Self-Control   Even in the best of circumstances, internalization of parental rules and prohibitions is a step-by-step process. The 1-year-old may say "no, no" and refrain from touching the forbidden object when the parent is present but pick it up when the parent is not there. It is probably not that this little guy is saying to himself, "Aha, Mom's gone so here's my chance." It may simply be that he is a recent graduate of the sensorimotor period during which time his behavior was pretty much governed by perceptual reality. The lure of the forbidden object sitting in front of him is stronger than some memory of a prohibition once the physical reminder of that prohibition (his parent) is not present. By the third year, though, many children do internalize their parents' rules and expectations and comply with them even when no adult is present. As noted, the extent to which they do so is largely a function of how they were taught. When prohibitions have been kept to a tolerable number and taught with a fair amount of clarity, consistency, and reason within the context of a warm and supportive relationship, then a reasonable degree of compliance can be expected. This is the parenting goal that Nell's parents, with Helen's support and guidance, are trying to achieve. Within this approach, toddlers still need plenty of opportunities to assert their own will and do some things their own way. One parent commented that sometimes it is a lot harder to do this, but she feels it is important to give her child choices and to take time to explain things to him.

A number of parents need help not only in recognizing the importance of this approach but in finding the time and emotional strength to do so. The role of the parent guide is to discern when information and encouragement are enough and when additional resources (e.g., counseling, assistance in finding child care, employment, housing, or transportation) are needed so that the parent has sufficient time and emotional strength for the demands of parenting. For example, when Tina was around 20 months of age, her mother, Lynette, was often ill. This combined with financial and relationship stresses made it difficult for Lynette to be positive, firm, and consistent in her parenting of Tina. In talking with Lynette about her difficulties in disciplining Tina, Helen acknowledged, "I know that all that's going on in your life makes it hard for you to do that. We need to figure out what will help in those areas so that you will have the energy to parent the way you want to." Seeking solutions to the life stresses Lynette was experiencing was addressed as a way to not only help her but also her children.

Keeping Connected

Although toddlers want to *do* things on their own, they don't want to *be* on their own. They feel a strong need to feel connected with their attachment figures. In fact, now that the thrill and novelty of venturing forth on their own two feet has subsided a bit, toddlers show renewed interest in being with and doing things with their parents. The parent becomes not just a secure base to go to and check in with, but is more and more desired as someone with whom the toddler can share new discoveries, interests, and accomplishments. Some parents may perceive this turn of events as their child regressing to being babyish, especially parents who are eager for their children to move on to become more independent. They may say, "She used to go over and play with things on her own, but now she keeps wanting my attention." Parent guides can help these parents understand that this is a typical part of development at this age. They can explain that by responding to these brief bids for attention they are reassuring their children that they are still there for them. "In the long run, this is what will help them be more self-confident and independent."

The toddlers' sense of themselves as separate individuals and their perception of what they can and cannot do heightens their awareness of their own separateness and relative helplessness (Mahler, Pine, & Bergman, 1975). They need the emotional support of their parents. Toddlers at this stage often become more demanding of their parent's attention for a few months. For instance, at age 18 months, Charisa did not want to share her mother's attention with the others in the parent–child creative movement class that her mother was teaching; this had not been a problem a few months earlier.

Separation anxiety tends to peak at around 18 months. One mother reported that her 20-month-old son awakened each night sobbing after she returned to full-time employment and was separated from him during the day. Another mother told how sick her son got when she tried taking him to a Mother's Morning Out program when he was 18 months old. She said she was relieved when she found out that other toddlers had problems with separations at this age. Some parents react with anger to this behavior whereas others respond by being overly solicitous. For example, Lynette immediately removed Jeffrey from child care when he had trouble with separation at this age, saying that he just could not be away from her. In addition to telling parents how typical this peak in separation anxiety is, parent guides can also help them ease the separation through doing some of the things suggested in the section on child care in Chapter 12. When possible, parents can be guided to begin out-of-home care either before or after this age of enhanced separation anxiety.

The Birth of Shame

Toddlers fear not only losing sight of their parents, but also fear losing their parents' love. They seek and need parental approval even though they often risk parental disapproval by asserting their will. Consider the toddler who joyfully demonstrates her climbing skills by scrambling onto the family's new couch. Suddenly, she encounters her father's disapproving look and stern prohibition. Her feelings of exhilaration and grandiosity are suddenly deflated. Physiologically there is an abrupt shift from sympathetic- to parasympathetic-dominant autonomic nervous system activity (Schore, 1994). There is a reduction of endorphins (feelings of pleasure) and an elevation of corticosteroid neurohormonal activity (feelings of distress). Typically children at this moment also experience feelings of shame. Their heads droop and their smiles disappear—they may start to cry. If handled correctly, these moderate feelings of shame can help children develop the ability to monitor and self-regulate their own behavior; these experiences influence the development of pathways in the brain that support this self-regulation of emotion and behavior (Schore, 1994). Of course, parents should not try to shame their children. Children will naturally feel shame in certain instances.

Repairing the Relationship   For the healthy development of emotion regulation to occur, however, the intensity and duration of the painful state of shame must be regulated by the parent. One-year-olds cannot yet effectively regulate their own distress states. Most toddlers seek to reestablish a loving relationship with the parent. They may look up at and reach toward the parent in an attempt to restore the ruptured relationship and to once more feel secure in the parent's affection. Parents need to respond by reassuring their toddlers of their love, letting them know that although the behavior that was prohibited is unacceptable, they are still loved and cherished. After being told to get off of the couch, the child may begin to cry. The father can take the child in his arms and tell her, "I know it's fun to bounce on things, but you can't bounce on the couch; the couch is for sitting." After comforting the child for a moment, the parent can then suggest some other activity—maybe bouncing around the room like a bunny rabbit or a quieter activity if the child seems to need that.

Through this act of interactive repair, the parent helps the dyad become psychobiologically reattuned and the child to return to a more positive affective state. Without it, the child may remain stuck for a period of time in a parasympathetic-dominant state of withdrawal (Schore, 1994). The process of reexperiencing positive affect following negative experience may help children learn that negativity can be endured and conquered (Malatesta-Magai, 1991). In this reparative process the child can develop an internal model of self as effective, of interactions as positive and reparable, and of the parent as reliable. If, however, "an attachment figure frequently rejects or ridicules the child's bids for comfort in stressful situations, the child may come to develop not only an internal working model of the parent as rejecting but also one of himself or herself as not worthy of help and comfort" (Bretherton, 1985, p. 12). Parent guides can use anticipatory guidance to inform parents about the importance of interactive repair during the early stages of the socialization process. In this way, they can help parents find ways to set limits while remaining emotionally available to their children.

When parents typically do not engage in this type of interactive repair after the child becomes upset, parent guides can begin addressing this through open inquiry into what the parent is feeling and experiencing and then proceed to mutual solution finding. For instance, the parent guide may observe the following interaction. The toddler is playing with the knobs on the stereo, the parent tells her to stop, and she keeps doing it. After a couple of rounds of this, the parent raises her voice and says very sternly, "I mean it. Stop playing with that!" moves the child, and walks away. The child bursts into tears, and the parent ignores her. The parent may be responding to her own anger or she may just be trying to remain stern and consistent and not give in to the child; however, in doing this the parent does not give the child an opportunity to recover—to repair their relationship—so the child is left comfortless.

When parent guides observe interactions like this, they first want to ask themselves whether this incident is isolated or seems to be a pattern. If the answer is the latter, the parent guide may wait until another visit or address it at the time and say something like, "You know, I was thinking about what happened . . ." or "When I see her get upset like that, I just feel for her. I feel like I want to go to her, put my arms around her, and let her know that even though what she did was wrong, people still like her. I wonder if you ever do that with her." This comment can open up the conversation. The parent may respond that she thinks that would be confusing—the child does something wrong and then, "If I go loving on her, she's not going to know that I mean business about this." The parent guide can say, "Well, I see what you mean, but how does she know that even when she does something wrong, you still love her? That she can come back to you even after she does something wrong?" The parent guide can work it through with the parent. Initially, parents may feel that by comforting their children they are "giving in" to them; they may need help understanding the distinction between not liking the child's behavior and still liking the child. The parent guide can also share information that this is a time in toddlers' lives when they do a lot of things that they get reprimanded for. They need to know that even though what they did was not acceptable, they are still loved.

Another parent might make up with the child after the child becomes upset but do so inappropriately. For instance, when the child dissolves into tears after the parent makes him stop playing, the parent might pick up the child, comfort him (so far, so good), but then say, "Well, I guess it's okay if you play a little while longer" and let him go back to doing whatever he had been doing. If the parent guide observes this, she might, depending on her relationship with the parent, simply make a mental note of it, wonder if it is a pattern, and, if it appears to be, address it at a later time. Some parents are so reluctant to upset their children that they try to avoid ever having their children feel that they have done something wrong. After exploring with these parents how they feel about upsetting their children, parent guides can help them understand the importance for the child's development of knowing when they have transgressed, which includes feeling upset about it, and then recovering from those feelings. It may be that these parents seldom experienced interactive repair, so they just remember their own intense feelings of shame, humiliation, and abandonment.

Schore (1994) distinguished between the child's feelings of shame (the child's response to parental disapproval) and feelings of humiliation (the child's response to parental contempt) and explained that the psychophysiological components of each are different. His discussion of the "terrifying eyes" of the enraged parent (Schore, 1994, p. 207) corresponds well with descriptions of frightening mothers whose children's attachment with them is disorganized and disoriented (Main & Hesse, 1990). Samantha was such a parent. When Penny did something that "pushed her buttons," she would turn on her with sudden rage. These outbursts appeared to be instances of emotional hi-jacking stemming from Samantha's childhood history of abuse. In addition to helping Samantha understand and address her children's developmental needs, her parent guide also taught her some calming techniques (e.g., deep breathing) and assisted her in finding psychotherapy.

Rapprochement

Margaret Mahler (1980) used the term *rapprochement* to describe the phase of development occurring in the second half of the second year. This term is defined by the dictionary as "an establishment of harmonious relations" (Oxford Universal Dictionary, 1955, p. 1657). This goal may seem overly idealistic for parents of tumultuous 1-year-olds, but the inevitable conflicts of this developmental period present important opportunities for the child, with their parents' help, to begin learning lessons that set the stage for a lifetime filled with many harmonious relationships. Toddlers can learn that although their wishes and needs are of value, they must, and can be, balanced with the needs and wishes of others. Twenty-month-old Brennan wanted to join in the game her grandmother was playing with her older sister, Ashlin. Because she was not old enough to do so without disrupting Ashlin's pleasure in playing the game, the grandmother restricted Brennan's access to the game but found a toy for her to play with and continued to interact with her while playing the game with Ashlin.

Negotiating skills begin to develop when parents listen to their toddlers and work with them to achieve compromises. For instance, when Ashlin was a toddler and had to wait in line with her parents to enter the restaurant, her father gave her two choices, "Do you want me to hold you or do you want to stand right next to me?" She decided to stand next to him, so he explained, "Okay, but you need to stay right with me." When parents give toddlers some choices, they not only grant the toddler a sense of independence but also start them on the road to responsible decision-making—especially when parents help them recognize the consequences of their choices. If after choosing to stand beside her father, Ashlin then "chose" to start running around, she would have learned that continuing to do so would result in her being held.

Even tantrums and *occasional* outbursts of parental anger can be of value. When parents let their toddlers have a tantrum and experience intense feelings of anger and shame but then help them recover, the toddlers learn that they can live through these moments of darkness and still be okay. Although parents sometimes frighten their toddlers with their anger, if they promptly recover, apologize, and reassure the toddler of their love, the toddler learns that anger is an inevitable but reparable breach in relationships (Lieberman, 1993). Parents find various ways of handling their own anger such as asking themselves, "Is this a battle worth fighting?" or putting both themselves and their toddler into time-out for a few minutes.

Sibling Relationships

The typical toddler push-pull relationship with their parents is further challenged when a new baby comes into the family. What a shock to suddenly see one's mother cuddling and cooing over another little child! The typical toddler fear of losing the parent's love is greatly heightened by this sight. Quite naturally the toddler feels displaced, especially if he or she has been the only child. Although this experience will be discomforting for their toddlers (and often for older children, as well), parents can take this opportunity to help their toddlers develop important relationship skills.

Ideally parent guides should be able to discuss this important event with parents both before and after the baby arrives. "As you no doubt know, children can feel pretty jealous when a new baby comes into the family. What are your ideas for how to help Jake handle his feelings when the baby arrives?" Their plans may include moving Jake into a "big boy's" bed if the baby is to sleep in his crib. This move is best done well in advance of the baby's arrival to diminish the feelings of being displaced. Although it is appropriate for parents to talk to their toddlers about the anticipated event, parents need to realize that the 1-year-old's ability to imagine the future is extremely limited. The new little brother or sister will not be a reality to the toddler until the baby is actually physically present. The toddler's reaction to this presence will differ depending, in part, on the toddler's temperament. The newcomer may be met with fierce anger or equally fierce "loving" as the toddler wants to constantly touch, hug, and kiss the baby—often with more than a hint of hostility. Some toddlers simply withdraw with a look of quiet sadness. Most toddlers will regress to babyish ways such as wanting to nurse or to use a bottle again. Parents can be guided to understand that this is typical and that it is okay to accommodate some of this while at the same time helping their toddlers feel good about the special things they can do that their baby sister or brother cannot do. By taking time to do things with their toddlers, parents can help them feel that they are still loved and cherished. This task may be a challenge for parents who are busy with other demands or distracted by other things. By keeping their focus on the big picture—the needs of all of the children and of the parents—parent guides can help parents meet this challenge. Entering toddlers into out-of-home care *at this time* as a way of gaining respite for their parents is, of course, not a good solution and hopefully can be avoided.

Parent guides may also want to explore with parents their feelings about now having two rather than just one child to love and care for. Some parents feel guilty over sensing that they do not love their two children "equally" (Brazelton, 1992). Parent guides can help them realize that they can love their two children differently, recognizing the unique characteristics of each child. Differences in parents' feelings for their children may be influenced by differences in the children's gender or temperament. Betsey acknowledged that her distress over the birth of a boy child stemmed from her history of abuse from men. Lynette viewed the spirited temperament of Jeffrey as indicative that he would be aggressive, "just like his father." When parents' feelings for their children are influenced by these "ghosts in the nursery," they will need help from their parent guides or from parent–infant therapists to separate their feelings for their babies from these influences.

EXPRESSING AND DEALING WITH FEELINGS

As toddlers enter their second year, they develop two new ways of expressing their needs and desires, their thoughts and their feelings—pretend play (creative symbolism) and language (conventional symbolism).

Through the creative symbolism of pretend play, toddlers can find safe ways to express a variety of feelings (Greenspan & Greenspan, 1989). Tony is feeling a little needy, so he crawls across the floor and rubs his head against his mother's leg, mewing like a kitten. Elaine expresses her anger as she rams her toy truck into her block structure, knocking it down. The warm, secure feelings of nurturance are represented by Keesha as she tenderly cradles and feeds her baby doll. Pretend play is a particularly useful way for very young children to express their feelings because their linguistic skills are still so limited.

Creative Symbolism—Pretend Play

By the end of the second year, most toddlers have developed a number of pretend play skills (Gowen, 1995). They can enact simple sequences—feed the doll, put him to bed, and say "nite, nite." Toy figures are made to carry out various actions—a horse gallops across the floor, a toy man hops into his car and drives away with a "brmm, brmm" motor sound. They rely less on representational toys (e.g., dolls, toy vehicles) and become more creative in their use of props for their pretend play (e.g., a wooden spoon becomes a telephone, imaginary coffee is poured into a cup). Through their pretend play, toddlers express their feelings, represent and "think" about their experiences, and try out behaviors they see others, especially their parents, exhibit. Sophia dealt with her feelings about her father's absence by pretending to talk with him on a pretend telephone.

As suggested in Chapter 7, parent guides should talk with parents about their children's pretend play—its importance and how it develops. If so indicated, they will also offer to help parents enrich their children's pretend play through floor time. First, they will want to determine how the parents feel about this type of play. Sometimes parents get upset with certain feelings their children express through their pretend play—especially feelings of aggression or dependency. Linda appreciated being reassured by Celeste that Sheryl's crashing toy cars together was a typical expression of anger or simply self-assertion and did not mean that she was going to be out of control like Sheryl's older sister was. When aggression dominates the child's play, however, it may signal a problem. One study found that the amount of aggression in the play of 3-year-olds predicted teachers' ratings of their aggression and hostility at age 5 (Gowen, 1984). Aggression was a predominant theme in Jeffrey's play; not surprising given the amount of aggression in his environment. As discussed previously, his mother's parent guide worked with her over a period of several months to diminish this problem.

Some parents react negatively to expressions of dependency in the child's pretend play. The child may rub up against the parent's leg and meow or pretend to be a baby. The parent may respond with irritation, "Quit acting silly." The parent guide should first ask about the parent's feelings evoked by the child's play. They may also wonder together about whether there is some reason that the child is in special need of reassurance from the parent at this time. Is there a new baby in the family? Has the parent been gone or distracted a lot recently? The parent guide can also point out that this is a typical part of pretend play and does not necessarily mean that there is some unmet need. The discussion may turn to reflection with the parent about what it was like for them as a child when they felt in need of special attention.

Conventional Symbolism—Language

During the second half of the second year, the toddler's expressive vocabulary expands quickly and two-word utterances start to crop up—"Daddy shoe," "more cookie," "Joey down." Labels for emotional states, both positive ("happy," "kiss," "love") and negative ("sad," "mad," "yuck"), are among those observed in 20-month-olds (Bretherton, McNew, & Beeghly-Smith, 1981). They, of course, understand much more than they can say, so it is important for caregivers to talk with them about feelings. Dunn and Brown (1991) found that themes of distress, pain, fatigue, and pleasure were the most commonly discussed topics of conversations about feeling states between children of 18 to 24 months and their mothers. By age 18 months, a number of the mothers were already discussing the causes of feelings with their toddlers.

Many parents and teachers of preschoolers are constantly reminding children to "use their words" to say what is upsetting them rather than resorting to whining, fussing, or physical attacks. To do this, children must be able to articulate their feelings. Toddlers who have been maltreated tend to be deficient in this ability (Beeghly & Cicchetti, 1994). Language processing problems and mental retardation may also be obstacles. Some other children who may have the ability to say what they feel do not do so because it has not been emphasized, modeled, or allowed by their parents. Occasionally, it may just seem like too much of a challenge to do so. Thirty-month-old Charisa, who had been urged by her mother many times over the past few weeks to say what she wanted instead of fussing, was quietly eating her lunch at the table with her mother and grandmother. Suddenly, she stopped eating and emphatically said, "I want to fuss and fuss and fuss!" After this expression of *her* feelings about this issue, she quietly continued her meal. Her message might have been, "I need to let you know how I *feel* about things as well as what I want."

When providing anticipatory guidance about the remarkable language development that occurs during the second year, parent guides can include a discussion of the importance of their children learning to express their feelings with words. Not only does this enable children to say their feelings rather than acting them out, but it gives them the tools to eventually be able to reflect on their feelings before acting—an extremely important step in the development of emotion regulation. This significant message will continue to be emphasized through developmental guidance as the child's language development proceeds. Parent guides will look for and highlight instances of parents' using simple language to talk with their children about their feelings. When they observe opportunities for parents to do this, the parent guide can wonder aloud what the child might be feeling. For example, the parent may just react by scolding the child who hit her younger brother when he took her toy. The parent guide can offer that labeling the child's feeling might help her learn to use her words instead of hitting. "What do you think she was feeling?" The parent might respond, "Well, I know she didn't like it when he took her toy, but she can't just haul off and smack him." The parent guide can say, "That's true—that's why she needs some other way to express how she felt when he took her toy. Maybe it would help if you say something like, 'I know it makes you mad when he takes your toys, but you can't hit him.' Maybe you could help her find a different toy. Then, she might not feel like she's always being taken advantage of."

Sometimes instead of not talking about what the child is feeling, parents go to the other extreme and talk beyond the child's ability to comprehend. "I know you're jealous of your baby sister. You used to be the only one, and now she's here, and you feel left out because we give her so much attention." So on and so forth! The parent guide can wonder with them how much of this they think the child understands. The guide should then encourage the parents to attend carefully to what feelings the child may be expressing with her behavior and then to label those feelings with simple terms.

In order for parents to be able to label their children's feelings, they need to be able to label their own. An important part of the relationship-based reflective model of parent guidance is helping parents talk about their feelings. Parent guides do this by attending carefully to parents' expressions of feelings and wondering aloud about what they observe. Helen did this when she reflected back to Lisa her feelings of sadness about being home alone with this baby and losing the camaraderie of her fellow workers. Parent guides will also use reflective questioning to encourage parents to label their feelings: "How did you feel when he said that? How do you feel when you have a hard time soothing your baby?" As children grow in their ability to understand language about feelings, parents can be encouraged to also verbalize their own feelings when interacting with their children: "I feel angry when you throw things." "I'm so proud of you when you put your toys away."

If, however, parents are not honest with their children about their own feelings, problems can arise. Children who are constantly reassured verbally that they are loved but are consistently rejected and treated harshly experience a mismatch between the words they hear and the behaviors they experience. Such a difference between experience as lived and as verbally represented may alter autobiographical memory in such a way that toddlers may become estranged from their own early experiences. As a result, children may develop multiple models of self (including a "false self") and of their attachment figures (e.g., the "good mother" *and* the "bad mother"; Emde & Buchsbaum, 1990).

New Fears and Anxieties

We have seen how toddlers' increased cognizance of cause and effect leads them to experience both pride in their accomplishments and shame or frustration over their failures. This awareness of causality can also generate anxiety when the child's causal reasoning goes awry. Lieberman described an 18-month-old who typically enjoyed playing in the water but suddenly developed a fear of the bathtub.

> On close observation it emerges that Cynthia eventually relaxes when she can hold on to her mother while in the bathtub, but screams and clings to the mother when the water bubbles down the drain at the end of the bath. Cynthia's mother suddenly remembers that a small toy animal went down the drain the week before. The child's fear then becomes clear: if her toy could disappear with the water, what would stop her from disappearing too? (1993, p. 35)

Parent guides can help parents appreciate that toddlers are trying to make sense of their world and to realize that sometimes their attempts to do so can lead to some bizarre conclusions. The guide might want to relate to parents the story about Cynthia and ask if that story sounds familiar to them—have they noticed their children being fearful in ways that do not make sense to an adult? If so, the guide can offer to be a detective with the parent and together they can search for clues to solve the mystery of why the child might be fearful in that situation. By doing this, the guide is communicating to the parent that what seems to the adult to be an unreasonable and incomprehensible fear may make perfect sense to the child—just as the fear of being washed down the drain did to Cynthia.

They are also sending the message that the role of parents is to refrain from simply dismissing or ridiculing children's fears but to try to understand their source. If parents are able to unravel the mystery behind the fears, they can then help their children straighten out their thinking about the situation, but even if they can't figure it out, they can acknowledge the children's feelings and try to reassure them. Parent guides can also offer this information as anticipatory guidance to individual parents or in a parent group. They can all smile together about the idiosyncrasies of 2-year-old logic.

TODDLERS AND TEMPERAMENT

Typical toddler behavior is colored by variations in the toddler's temperament. Parent guides can help parents understand how temperament characteristics of their children can interact with typical toddler behavior to create special parenting challenges. They can then ally with parents to find ways to accommodate their children's temperaments as they facilitate their development during this toddler stage.

Intensity of Reactions

The typical intensity of feelings of 1-year-olds is exaggerated in toddlers with spirited temperaments (Kurcinka, 1991). Whereas another child might simply whimper when she cannot have her way, the spirited toddler will let loose ear-splitting screams of protest. At this age, Charisa's reaction was immediate and intense if her mother tried to do anything for her that she wanted to do for herself. Frustration over failure to achieve some goal leads some of these children to bang their heads on the floor. Lieberman (1993) recommended that when this happens, the caregiver place the child in a crib and let the child know that she cannot let him hurt himself.

Activity Level

Average toddlers, thrilled by their ability to now venture forth and explore their environments, are energetic. This typical activity and energy level is multiplied many times over for spirited children. Caregivers must scramble and plan ahead to keep up with and protect these little bundles of energy who seem to be in perpetual motion. One spirited 18-month-old quickly clambered to the top of her new climbing gym and had to be rescued as she hung from the top rung. These toddlers need plenty of safe opportunities to practice their newly developing motor skills (Lieberman,

1993). Sitting still is not yet in their behavioral repertoire, so parents need to make sure these spirited children get sufficient rest before they become so wired they have difficulty calming down.

Approach/Withdrawal and Adaptability

Caregivers are especially challenged when high activity level is coupled with a propensity to approach and explore new objects and places. These are the toddler risk takers, the future sky divers and rock climbers who feel compelled to explore every nook and cranny regardless of the risk. Howie's mother was appalled to find him sitting in the new aquarium that had just been set on a table. Fortunately, it had not yet been filled with water and stocked with fish. Obviously, parents need to take special precautions to protect these energetic risk takers while providing opportunities for exercise and exploration. Parent guides can help parents find ways to engineer the environment so that they can minimize the number of restrictions and reprimands.

Toddlers who are slow to approach and adapt to novel situations offer other challenges to their caregivers. These shy, slow-to-warm-up children need understanding and help so they can experience and enjoy the types of exploration that are important for toddler development. When faced with a new situation or environment, they need time to adjust before they can explore. When Gabriel went with his mother to a toddler music class, it would take about the first half of the class before he would feel comfortable about joining in. It helps if the parent is close at hand, but, as discussed previously, these shy toddlers also need gentle encouragement to try new things, just as Gabriel's mother encouraged him. Even when they do venture forth, these toddlers may check in with their caregivers more frequently than other children do (Lieberman, 1993). Parent guides can ask parents about their children's response to new people and new places and then ally themselves with parents to find ways to encourage their children to try new things.

Some children with this temperament become anxious and fearful easily. These children often react with higher levels of fear and anxiety when punished by an angry parent than some other children do. The parent may complain, "She just goes all to pieces anytime I say no to her." The parent guide can explain that some children are just like this; it is their temperament. They can then help the parent find more positive, gentle ways to discipline. Parenting that de-emphasizes the use of power is especially important for these children (Kochanska, 1993).

Tantrums can be triggered when parents forget or do not have a chance to prepare the slow-to-adapt child for transitions to new activities, even when those activities are familiar ones such as bedtime or mealtime. Transition rituals, especially bedtime rituals, are sometimes helpful. Brennan has a sip of milk from a cup, brushes her teeth, kisses family members goodnight, takes a chosen stuffed animal, and walks off to bed. This bedtime routine occurs every night regardless of who is there. Sometimes children develop their own rituals that help them with separations. Jackie would climb onto the blue rocking horse at his nursery school to ease his separation anxiety each morning when his mother left him there.

Persistence

Combining the temperament trait of persistence with typical toddler assertiveness produces a stubbornness that can challenge the most understanding caregiver. Parent guides can help parents appreciate that persistence is a wonderful trait to be treasured and nurtured and how to deal with the challenges it can bring. It behooves parents to listen to their persistent toddlers' demands and try to find reasonable ways to accommodate them. By resisting the impulse to immediately say "no" and by looking for ways to say "yes" instead, parents can often avoid battles with their persistent toddlers. Childproofing the house—creating a "yes environment"—is especially important with these toddlers (Kurcinka, 1991, p. 100).

As with the slow-to-adapt child, parents find that their lives are easier when they prepare the persistent child for transitions. Charisa's mother tells her at breakfast what the plans for the morning are (e.g., we're going grocery shopping after breakfast), and then announces ahead of time each step that she needs to take, "When you finish eating, you need to change your clothes." After that, "Time to go to the bathroom." Then, "In 10 minutes we will get into the car." In child care and playgroup environments, storms can sometimes be avoided by notifying children ahead of time that the present activity needs to end shortly and then helping them shift their attention and interest to the next activity. For example, "We will put these toys away in a moment and then have snack."

Other Temperament Traits

Other temperament traits (e.g., rhythmicity/regularity, distractibility/perceptiveness, sensitivity/responsiveness, mood) may also interact with characteristics of toddlerhood to create special challenges for caregivers. Professionals can help parents deal with these challenges by observing the toddlers and by listening carefully to caregivers' descriptions of their toddlers' behaviors and considering how the toddlers' temperaments may be coloring their behaviors and their interactions with their parents and other caregivers. As noted in Chapter 2, consideration also needs to be given to how the toddler's temperament fits with the parent's temperament.

A SILVER LINING—
THE DEVELOPMENT OF PROSOCIAL BEHAVIOR

It is not all "storm and stress" with the toddler. There is a remarkable increase in prosocial behavior during the second half of the second year. In fact, prosocial behavior tends to peak around this time and declines somewhat by the time toddlers become preschoolers. By the time they are two, most toddlers display their sunny side in many ways. They share, help, and comfort others, engage in cooperative games, and empathize with another's distress (Brownell & Carriger, 1990; Hay, 1994).

Sharing

By age 18 months, most children spontaneously share food, toys, and other items with their parents, other children, and even the family dog. Some 1-year-olds will share toys with other toddlers when there are not enough toys to go around (Hay, Caplan, Castle, & Stimson, 1991), but parents and other caregivers cannot count on it! Not only do toddlers sometimes share (on their own terms!), they also take. The mere fact that another child is playing with a toy often makes it irresistible. Sometimes the toddler will reach for it even if they are holding one just like it (Caplan, Vespo, Pedersen, & Hay, 1991). Toddlers react differently in these situations. In child care, Gabriel would just look confused when another child would rip a toy out of his hands. Other toddlers scream in protest and some fight—and bite—back. Parents and other caregivers can help by encouraging and monitoring taking turns. Children can learn from this experience that sharing does not have to mean losing forever—they will get their turn.

Toddlers sometimes become more possessive when they are playing with other children in their own house with their own toys. For the entire 2-week visit of his 3-year-old cousin, Jackie would yell, "No way!" any time Veronica touched one of his toys, sat in his chair, drank from his glass, or in anyway invaded *his* territory. Possessiveness comes hand in hand with the toddler's burgeoning sense of self. Parent guides can explain this and then suggest that parents empathize with the child's desire to establish "I'm me and this is mine" by letting some things (a favorite chair, a favorite cup) be off limits to the other child. At the same time, parents should help their children take turns with the other child while playing with and using other things—everything cannot be off limits.

Parents ordinarily do not pay much attention to their toddler's sharing until it becomes an issue with their siblings or peers (Hay, Castle, Stimson, & Davies, 1995). A typical scene is when one child picks up a toy that another child has been playing with, the first child tries to grab it back, and both kids start screaming. The parent comes rushing in when the screaming starts. At this point, the parent might say, "Since you are fighting over this toy, I'm going to put it away for now. Let's find some other fun things to play with." She can then redirect each child's interest to another toy. Trying to affix blame for the incident is pointless. When parents complain about their children not sharing or when parent guides observe incidents such as the one just described, they can first ask parents what they've tried and whether that has helped. In exploring this with the parent, the guide can suggest that when it appears that a tussle over a toy is about the occur, the parent step in to teach turn-taking. The guide can add that learning to share is often a slow process—it takes a lot of patient teaching—so punishing children at this age for not sharing can just make matters worse. Some parents will benefit from their parent guides' suggesting some specific things they can do in teaching their children to share. With 1-year-olds it is often enough to simply redirect one or both children's attention to another toy. For example, when Adam tries to take a toy from Bruce, tell Bruce to say, "Stop"; then hand Adam another toy while telling him that he can have a turn in a minute. Keep it calm and keep it simple—a lengthy lecture on sharing will be completely lost on a 1-year-old. Avoid punishing one or both of the children. It is not "bad" for two children to want to play with the same toy; they just need to learn to take turns, and this process takes time. As children grow a little older, they can learn negotiating skills: "No, I'm playing with that," "Can I have a turn now?"

Empathy

Beginning early in the second year, toddlers will try to comfort others when they are upset, and their expressions of empathy and concern become more sophisticated as the year progresses (Dunn & Brown, 1991; Hay, 1994). A 14-month-old may hug or bring her teddy to her distressed mother, whereas a 24-month-old may ask his father who just stubbed his toe, "You be okay?" or advise him, "Be careful!" Parents report that toddlers will bring a bottle to a crying baby, help retrieve the baby's rattle, and even place a damp cloth on mother's forehead when she has a headache. It is not surprising, though, that the extent to which toddlers are empathic is associated with how empathic their mothers have been with them. Furthermore, toddlers tend to be more empathic if their mothers have tried to help them understand how their behavior affects other people (Zahn-Waxler et al., 1991).

By following the guiding principles introduced in Chapter 1, parent guides can use the strategies in Chapter 3 to help parents promote healthy emotional development at each stage. Many parents, however, are challenged by past and present situations that interfere with their parenting in ways that enhance the emotional development of their babies and toddlers. To help these parents, parent guides need to understand how certain circumstances (e.g., the parent's childhood experiences, substance abuse, domestic violence) can affect parenting and how to help parents address these issues. This is the topic of the four chapters in Section III.

III

Understanding the Caregiving Environment

9

Parents Are Babies Grown Up

How Parents' Early Emotional
Experiences Influence Caregiving

After leaving and returning several times, Linda's mother finally abandoned her when Linda was 7 years old. Maureen's mother frequently criticized her as she was growing up. As a child, Samantha experienced multiple caregivers, some of whom abused her physically and sexually. When these children grew up and became parents, they brought with them their legacies of these troubled childhoods.

Today's parents are yesteryear's babies and toddlers. Some were cared for in ways that fostered secure attachments with their parents and helped them develop the ability to experience and utilize a wide range of emotions in healthy ways. Although their relationships with their parents and other significant figures were certainly not perfect, they were nevertheless good enough for them to form reasonably positive internal working models of themselves and of relationships and to develop healthy emotion regulation. They bring these skills and feelings of confidence as well as models of caring and kindness into their role as parents. Others, such as Linda, Maureen, and Samantha, did not fare as well. The behaviors they developed to cope with rejection, hostility, indifference, loss, and sometimes severe abuse and neglect do not serve them well as adults and as parents. Although they want to be "good parents," they have major obstacles to overcome to achieve this goal. Then, there are variations of these two pathways. The early childhoods of some parents were troubled, but they were fortunate enough to form relationships with some caring adults along the way who helped them develop more positive models of close relationships. Still others whose early lives were benign suffer as adults because they did not receive sufficient support when in later childhood they experienced trauma (e.g., the death of a parent). Some parents and would-be parents have worked hard, sometimes in therapy, to confront and reflect on their pasts in ways that have healed old wounds and earned them the inner resources to parent well.

This chapter examines these links of the past to the present, along which parenting practices are passed from one generation to the next. By understanding this process, parent guides can better help parents modify these links in ways that help them replace undesirable caregiving behaviors with new ones that open up more emotionally healthy pathways for their young children. Although a number of these parents may need psychotherapy to make these changes, parent guides can assist this process through the use of the relationship-based reflective model of parent support and guidance.

FROM ONE GENERATION TO THE NEXT

The quality of caregiving that parents received as children often affects their ability to tune in to their babies' and toddlers' needs, to soothe them when they are distressed, and to know and do what is needed to keep them physically and psychologically safe. Parents who were themselves abused or neglected as young children may not have the memories, conscious or unconscious, of sensitive care on which to base their day-to-day behaviors with their babies and toddlers. They may also have developed maladaptive coping styles to protect themselves from reexperiencing painful childhood feelings evoked by their own children, as in the example in Chapter 3 of the mother who did not seem to hear her baby's cries. In addition, parents whose early experiences of being parented were inconsistent, neglectful, or harsh are likely to have developed emotionally laden internal working models of themselves as incapable and unlovable, of the world as an unsafe place, of people as untrustworthy, and of relationships as power driven and uncaring. Depending on the degree to which they bring these emotional processes to this new role and relationship, they will be creating a reality for themselves and their babies that reinforces those beliefs; the attachment process, which needs to be based on sensitive and responsive caregiving, will then be compromised.

The Ghosts in the Nursery

Selma Fraiberg (Fraiberg et al., 1975) called these lingering effects from the parent's past "the ghosts in the nursery." Their presence accounts, at least in part, for the fact that parents who were abused or neglected as children are more apt to abuse or neglect their own children than parents who were not maltreated as children (Kaufman & Zigler, 1987; Youngblade & Belsky, 1990). The form of the maltreatment may differ from one generation to the next. For instance, some mothers who were sexually abused as children then emotionally neglect their children (Lyons-Ruth & Block, 1996). Although parents may repeat specific parenting behaviors they experienced as children, it is the quality and meaning of attachment relationships that are carried forward from one generation to the next that are often the most potent influences on their parenting (Sroufe & Fleeson, 1986).

"Ghosts" who hover around cradles are most malevolent when the feelings of helplessness, despair, and rage associated with their childhood maltreatment have become buried in the basements of the parents' psyches. Many children who are maltreated repress these feelings because the pain of remembering (reexperiencing) them is too much to bear. As adults, they may report "the events of childhood abuse, tyranny, and desertion . . . in explicit and chilling detail" (Fraiberg et al., 1975, p. 419) but do so without a hint of the painful feelings that had accompanied those events. As long as feelings associated with childhood maltreatment remained locked away, parents seem condemned to reenact the maltreatment in some form with their own children, but when, in the safety of their relationships with their therapists, they are able to remember, reexperience, and work through these childhood feelings, they become "the protectors of their children against the repetition of their own conflicted past" (Fraiberg et al., 1975, p. 421).

Helping parents remember, reexperience, and deal with painful childhood feelings requires clinical training in therapeutic intervention. Parent guides who do not have this training, however, can be alert to signs that a parent may need therapy and encourage and support the parent in obtaining such therapy. Take, for example, Samantha. As a young child, Samantha experienced multiple caregivers because of her mother's tumultuous love life, and she was often cared for by her aunt who, perhaps due to the physical abuse she suffered as a child, allowed Samantha to be cared for by unstable adults who sexually abused her. Although Samantha talked with her parent guide on different occasions about these early experiences, she initially did so with very little affect; however, she was often irritable and impatient with people including members of her family, her children, and even the people who were trying to help her. As she continued to work with her guide and to tell more of her story, some of her feelings about her early abuse became apparent. It was about this time that she began therapy. With Samantha's permission, the therapist and guide collaborated in their work with Samantha. The parent guide used the relationship-based reflective model of support and guidance for Samantha's parenting, and her therapist worked with her on her deep-rooted psychological issues. Samantha and her partner were strongly committed to parenting their children well. After several months of intervention, Samantha became warmer and more responsive with her infant. She continued for some time to have difficulty relating warmly with her older child whose needs were partially met by her child care providers and by her father. Eventually, Samantha was able to relate more positively with her as well.

Even when parents remain conscious of some of the feelings associated with childhood trauma, the "ghosts" can cause problems for these parents. In these instances, parents often say that they want something better for their children than what they had, and they may be more open to professional help with their parenting (Fraiberg et al., 1975). With a tone of righteous indignation, Maureen complained to her parent guide, Celeste, that her mother had constantly put her down while she was growing up. "I couldn't do anything right as far as she was concerned." Knowing Maureen's sensitivity to criticism, Celeste was very careful about how she provided information to Maureen. She also highlighted whenever possible Maureen's competencies, especially as they related to her parenting. Although she might have benefited from it, Maureen did not receive psychotherapy; however, the work she did with Celeste and through the 12-step program in AA seemed sufficient in helping her become more comfortable and competent in parenting Victor and in life in general.

Links in the Chain

Whether or not a parent tends to recall certain childhood feelings, those feelings play a key role in how the parent feels and thinks about herself and others—that is, in the parent's internal working models of self, others, and relationships. Internal working models form one part of the chain that connects parents' childhood relationships and experiences with their attachment figures to the relationships and experiences their children have with them. Research during the 1990s demonstrated links between parents' representations of their feelings about and perceptions of their own childhoods (i.e., their internal working models) *and* their feelings about and perceptions of children and childrearing in general and of their own children in particular. All of these are linked with the quality of care they give their children which, in turn, affects the security of their children's attachments with them and the character of their children's internal working models.

Parent guides are better able to understand and guide parents when they are aware of how childhood experiences influence the development of internal working models (as described in Chapter 2) and how those models of self, others, and relationships are carried into adulthood and affect parents' perceptions of and behavior toward their children. The rest of this chapter presents results from research on five links of the chain that connects parents' childhood attachment experiences with those of their children: 1) parents' internal working models (i.e., their mental representations or views of self, others, and relationships), 2) adults' views of children and childrearing, 3) parents' views of their own children and childrearing, 4) parenting behaviors, and 5) infant–parent attachment. By following the principles of the reflective relationship-based model of intervention and using strategies presented in Chapter 3 and illustrated throughout this book, parent guides may be able to help parents banish the "ghosts from the nursery." Parent guides who are not clinically trained will need to support parents with more severe problems in obtaining infant–parent psychotherapy or other forms of treatment. There may also be a need for supplemental child care while parents are receiving needed treatments.

Parents' Internal Working Models   As a child, Maureen developed an internal model of herself as someone who could not do anything right. She told Celeste, "I couldn't please my mother no matter what I did— and I still can't!" When Celeste first started working with her, Maureen behaved as though she expected criticism and rejection from others—even from her baby. If Victor did not respond to her, she would say, "He doesn't like me." She tended to view relationships as controlling and judgmental; she felt that her mother was still trying to tell her how to live her life. In turn, Maureen was critical, judgmental, and controlling with others, especially her partner. Lisa's sense of inadequacy seemed to stem more from a feeling of insecurity in relationships, especially close relationships. She was not sure that she was lovable or that people were truly there for her. Relationships seemed tenuous and elusive and her attempts to grasp and hold onto them were characterized by an almost desperate neediness.

The quality and meaning of Maureen's and of Lisa's early attachment relationships are being carried forward into the next generation through their internal working models of self, others, and relationships. As described in Chapter 2, the process of developing these internal working models begins during infancy and continues throughout life, although changes in the models become more difficult with time. Internal working models are not simply internalized copies of attachment experiences like so many pages run through a copier. Rather, they go to the heart of those experiences to capture and hold their emotional essence. Internal working models are representations of the affective meanings that are abstracted and constructed from attachment experiences. These models or representations then guide thoughts, perceptions, and feelings as well as behavior and often shape and color memories (especially of relationships).

By developing sensitive, responsive, caring relationships with parents, guides provide the kind of corrective attachment experiences (Lieberman & Pawl, 1993) that may help parents modify their internal working models of relationships. Guides can influence parents' internal working models of themselves by intentionally finding opportunities to counter parents' negative images of themselves. For instance, Celeste highlighted for Maureen numerous instances of her doing things well to counter Maureen's internalized message from her mother that she could not do anything right.

Guides can challenge parents' negative views about relationships and other people by relating with the parents in ways that are contrary to those views. As discussed in Chapter 2, it can be difficult for parent guides to resist being pulled into the negative models of relationships that some parents have. For instance, if the parent's model of relationships is one of rejection then that parent may behave in ways (e.g., be hostile or demanding) that typically elicit rejection from others. The parent guide's role is to withstand being drawn into the parent's negative model while, at the same time, maintaining appropriate boundaries and limits. In this way, the parent guide is providing the parent a valuable corrective emotional experience.

Telling Their Stories   Asking parents to describe what it was like growing up with their parents or other caregivers can provide insight into the parents' internal working models. These stories help parent guides understand how early attachment experiences influence later parenting and other relationships. For instance, knowing that Linda had been abandoned as a child and hearing the sadness in her voice as she talked about this helped her parent guide to understand Linda's hesitation about leaving Sheryl with a babysitter. Samantha's account of how she had been abused shed light on her outbursts of rage toward her daughter. (Guidelines for facilitating parents' telling of their stories are presented in Chapter 3.)

Learning the parent's story is not a straightforward process. Much of the material—the feelings, memories of events, perceptions, and fantasies—underlying internal working models is held at an unconscious level (Bowlby, 1973). This fact is especially true when the material contains conflicting impressions (good mother versus bad mother) and painful feelings (Bretherton, 1987). Also, the initial foundation for internal working models was constructed from experiences prior to developing language with which to encode them. Therefore, asking adults to describe what it was like growing up with their parents or other caregivers may not yield accurate accounts of their early attachment experiences. Careful attention to *how* they talk about (or do not talk about) their early experiences, however, is very informative. Listening with a "third ear" to their nonverbal language is equally important (Trout, 1987b). By careful attention to the way in which the parents tell (both verbally and nonverbally) their stories, the parent guide can begin to understand the affective meanings held in their internal working models. These affective meanings influence how they perceive and behave toward their children.

The Adult Attachment Interview   Mary Main and her associates developed a procedure, the Adult Attachment Interview (AAI), for assessing these affective meanings—internal working models of attachment relationships (what Main refers to as the individual's state of mind regarding attachment; George, Kaplan & Main, 1985; Main & Goldwyn, 1989). Although a person trained to conduct clinical interviews could conduct this interview, coding the interview transcripts to reliably identify specific types of adult attachment requires extensive training. Nevertheless, knowing some of the questions to ask and the significance of different ways in which parents talk about their childhood experiences can help parent guides better understand the underlying affective meanings as they elicit and listen to parents' stories. This chapter presents some of what has been learned from the research about how parents' early attachment experiences affect their parenting both directly as well as indirectly through the kinds of caregiving environments they are able to provide. In this and other chapters, suggestions and examples are presented of ways in which parent guides can help parents tell their stories and then use what is learned to better understand the parents in order to support and guide their parenting efforts. The parents described in this book were not administered the AAI, so they cannot be reliably categorized as having a certain type of adult attachment. Nevertheless, the ways in which they described their childhood experiences and the nature of their interactions with their children are suggestive of the links among early experiences, adult attachments, and parenting behaviors.

The AAI is a powerful tool for researchers interested in studying this phenomenon. In this interview, individuals are asked about their childhood experiences with attachment figures, their feelings about them, and how they think these experiences influence them in the present. Near the beginning of this hour-long interview, they are asked to think of five adjectives that describe their relationship with each parent and to provide memories that support these general descriptions. The nature of these early relationships are then probed further with questions concerning memories of early separations, ways of seeking comfort (e.g., they are asked what they did when they were upset or hurt), feelings about which parent they felt closest to and why, and memories of being punished and of feeling rejected. Then, they are asked why they think their parents behaved as they did and, finally, how they think these early experiences have affected them as adults, including their relationships with their children, if they have any (Main, 1991; Slade & Aber, 1992).

When results of AAI interviews are analyzed, the *coherence* of the story is given as much or more attention than the actual content of the story. Coherence is defined in terms of the maxims of quality, quantity, relevance, and manner (Main, 1991). In a coherent story, parents provide evidence for what they say and avoid contradictions (quality), they are succinct and yet complete (quantity), they keep to the point (relevance), and they present the information in a clear and orderly way (manner). When analyzed in this way, four types of adult attachments can be identified: one secure type (autonomous) and three insecure types (dismissing, preoccupied, and unresolved; Main & Hesse, 1990). An additional insecure type "cannot classify" is sometimes identified (Hesse, 1996).

Adults who are rated as *secure/autonomous* in their adult attachments with their parents (or other attachment figures from childhood) tell their stories with ease. They tend to value attachment relationships and to feel that attachment experiences influence one's personality. Their stories are coherent with negative experiences well integrated into their overall view of attachment relationships. Many adults with *secure/autonomous attachments* recall favorable early experiences, but some of them describe unfavorable attachment-related experiences, particularly in the form of loss or rejection; however, they appear to have resolved feelings and thoughts about these negative early experiences in ways that allow them to be autonomous and secure relative to these attachments in the present. Often they have had "corrective experiences" with significant others (other relatives, a teacher or mentor, a therapist) which have helped them reformulate their internal working models of relationships. This type of secure adult attachment is often termed earned *secure/autonomous,* and security resulting from a favorable childhood is termed *continuous secure/ autonomous.*

Sonia is an example of a mother with features of an *earned secure/ autonomous* adult attachment. She grew up in an abusive family. Her father was physically and emotionally abusive to the children and his wife. Not only did her mother not protect her and the children from her father's wrath, but she was rejecting and emotionally abusive herself. For example, Sonia recalls her mother laughing at her when she got sand in her eyes at the beach. As she recalls this experience, her tone of voice and anguished expression convey some of the terror and distress she must have felt when this happened. Fortunately, Sonia's maternal grandmother, who came to visit regularly and with whom she spent her summers as a teenager, was very kind and loving. As an adult, Sonia married a gentle, caring man and together they provide sensitive, responsive caregiving to their young child.

Adults who are rated as *insecure/dismissing* may describe favorable early attachment relationships, but their stories differ from those of secure adults. When they do so, it is in global terms that are then contradicted by accounts of specific parental behaviors. For instance, a mother who described her relationship with her mother as being "just fine" later told how she would hide from her mother when she was hurt out of fear of angering her (Cassidy, 1994). This type of adult attachment is labeled "dismissing" because these adults appear to dismiss attachment relationships as being relatively unimportant. They have less to say about these relationships and tend to have difficulty recalling specific attachment experiences from their past. They tend to minimize attachment-related experiences. Mothers with dismissing attachments sometimes benefit from more distant interventions such as some gentle coaching while watching videotapes of their interactions with their babies (Bakermans-Kranenburg, Juffer, & van IJzendoorn, 1998) or being given written information. It is not known whether Susie's mother, Joan (see Chapter 4), would be classified as having a dismissing attachment, but she is an example of a mother who benefited from receiving information in this manner.

Adults who are rated as *insecure/preoccupied*, however, speak volumes about their attachment relationships, but do so in a rambling manner that lacks the coherence characteristic of stories given by respondents with *secure/autonomous* adult attachments. Often, as adults, they continue to be embroiled in angry relationships with their parents or they may make inordinate attempts to please them. Although they may talk about their parents and their childhood experiences with a lot of anger, they may not express the feelings that they had as children during those experiences (e.g., despair, fear, shame). Negative experiences from the past remain largely unresolved, keeping them from achieving a sense of autonomy and security regarding their attachment relationships. They tend to maximize attention to attachment.

As an adult, Maureen vacillated between trying to please her mother and complaining about her mother's continued criticism of her and intrusion into her life. She gestured quotation marks around the word "right" as she told Celeste, "I have tried to have the 'right' job, the 'right' partner, and a well-behaved kid, but nothing I do is ever really 'right' in her eyes." Although Maureen directly expressed her anger toward her mother for what she felt was unjust treatment, the feelings that she may have felt as a child (e.g., ineptness, shame) were expressed more indirectly in her behavior—for instance, the sense of inadequacy she expressed when she was not able to soothe Victor.

The third type of insecure adult attachment is labeled *insecure/ unresolved–disorganized* due to evidence of unresolved trauma involving an attachment figure (e.g. loss of a parent, abuse or neglect by an attachment figure; Main & Hesse, 1990). Their stories, especially the parts dealing with the trauma, seem confused, disorganized, and disoriented (Benoit & Parker, 1994). Some disorganization and disorientation may be present for many people in discussions during the first months following a trauma. When this continues past that point, however, it may indicate a failure to resolve the trauma. There may be continuing, striking lapses of reasoning in their discussions of the loss or abuse. For example, the individual may speak of a dead person as if that person were still alive (Main, 1996) or he or she may pay unusual attention to detail or use eulogistic speech (e.g., "she was dearly beloved by all who knew her and who witnessed her as she was torn from us"; Main & Hesse, 1990, p. 169). Some losses may not be experienced as trauma (i.e., as an experience of intense fear, terror, helplessness), but physical and sexual abuse, especially by a parent, are almost inevitably traumatic (Main & Hesse, 1990). The fact that Samantha's parent guide and other helpers had difficulty describing the manner in which Samantha relayed information about her childhood traumas indicates the disorganization and disorientation in her telling of her story. Samantha's frightening outbursts of temper with her daughter are characteristic of the behavior of many parents with *insecure/unresolved-disorganized* adult attachments.

A fourth insecure category, *cannot classify*, was later identified to distinguish those instances when the entire interview, rather than just the part dealing with the trauma, is disorganized and disoriented (Hesse, 1996). The individual may move abruptly from a dismissing to a preoccupied strategy or manifest two distinct states of mind with respect to two different individuals. This category has been found related to histories of psychiatric disorder, to marital and criminal violence, and to experiences of sexual abuse. In one study, 90% of the cannot classify individuals were raised in institutional care, compared with 45% of individuals in the remaining categories.

Views of Children and Childrearing   Even before they have children of their own, people form some pretty definite ideas about children and childrearing, and these ideas are linked with their perceptions and feelings about their own parents (i.e., with their adult attachments). College students who had not yet married and started a family were asked about their beliefs and desires about children and parenting. Their responses were then related to their attachment styles (Rholes, Simpson, Blakely, Lanigan, & Allen, 1997). Compared with those with more secure attachment styles, those with more *dismissing/avoidant* and *preoccupied/ambivalent* models of close relationships expressed more negative views of parenthood and parent–child relationships. They expected to be more easily aggravated by children, endorsed stricter disciplinary practices, and were less confident in their ability to relate to children. The students who were *dismissing/avoidant* in their attachment styles also expected to derive less satisfaction from parenting and, not surprisingly, expressed less interest in having children.

Parents' Views of Their Children   These more general views people have about children and childrearing become more focused as they approach parenthood, and parents often begin developing internal working models of their children during pregnancy. These representations of the unborn child may become modified somewhat after the child is born, influenced by characteristics of the child (e.g., temperament, gender, physical resemblance to others) as well as by changing circumstances in the parent's life. Nevertheless, they are usually heavily influenced by the parents' internal working models of their own early attachment figures.

Internal Working Model of the Child   The Working Model of the Child Interview (WMCI; Benoit, Zeanah, et al. 1997) assesses parents' representations of their babies. With some modification, this interview can also be used with expectant parents. Several expectant mothers were interviewed with the WMCI during their third trimester of pregnancy and again 1 year later, and their babies' attachments with them were assessed at age 12 months (Benoit, Parker, & Zeanah, 1997). Although some of the mothers changed their internal working models of their babies, 80% of them retained the same classification when their babies were almost a year old as they had before their babies were born. Furthermore, in 73% of the dyads, the 11-month WMCI agreed with the 12-month assessments of their infants' attachments with them. Using this assessment with mothers during pregnancy and tailoring interventions accordingly may ward off some problems after the babies are born.

Maternal Attributions   Parent guides need to pay very careful attention to how parents talk to and about their babies and toddlers. From the time Jeffrey was an infant, Lynette tended to attribute to him many characteristics, like aggression, that she perceived and objected to in his father. These attributions seemed to lead Lynette to attend to Jeffrey's aggressive behaviors (e.g., commenting on them in his presence, punishing him for them) and to ignore his more nurturing behaviors. Helen, her parent guide, responded by highlighting times when she observed Jeffrey doing things such as feeding his toy bear and reinforcing Lynette when she interacted with Jeffrey in ways that encouraged positive, cooperative behaviors.

It is largely through these attributions that the parent's internal representations of attachments take shape and influence their behavior with their babies. Alicia Lieberman (1997), who works with troubled infant–parent dyads, stated that parental attributions offer "an unedited view of fantasies and concrete perceptions" that guide the parent's behavior with the baby. She pointed out that all parents make attributions and some are essential for healthy development, but healthy attributions differ from unhealthy ones. Instead of reflecting parental self-esteem and pleasure in the child's positive characteristics, unhealthy attributions reflect the parents' fears, anger, or other suppressed or unacknowledged parts of themselves in relation to attachment. These attributions shape which baby behaviors the mother can become attuned to and which behaviors are ignored or misinterpreted, just as Lynette did when she viewed Jeffrey as being too aggressive. They can also influence the interactions so that the child eventually behaves in accordance with the caregiver's attributions. Zeanah, Finley-Belgrad, and Benoit (1997) provided the example of the mother who teased her 20-month-old until he was provoked into lashing back. She then took this as confirmation of her view of him as someone who abused and threatened her. In these various ways, the parent's interpretations and resulting ministrations "get woven into the very texture of how the baby experiences himself" (Lieberman, 1997, p. 284) and gradually shape the child's sense of who he is.

The significance of parental attributions of their children is highlighted by the results of a study of mothers of kindergarten children (George & Solomon, 1996). Their representations of their children and their caregiving role differed in ways that tended to match both their internal working models of attachment and the quality of their children's attachments with them. On the basis of their responses to questions about their perceptions of their children and their caregiving role, mothers were classified as secure, rejecting, uncertain, or helpless. These tended to match both their own attachment types and their children's attachments with them. For example, most mothers whose representations of their children and their childrearing role were considered rejecting had dismissing attachments with their own parents, and most of their children had *anxious/avoidant attachments* with them.

How the mothers in each group described their children and their childrearing roles reveals some of the connections among the various links in the chain that connects their early attachment experiences with the attachment of their children with them. Secure mothers were positive and realistic in their evaluations of their children and their caregiving roles, and they demonstrated strong commitment and belief in their ability to provide physical and psychological safety for their children. Rejecting mothers emphasized negative qualities and interactions. They portrayed themselves as undesirable or unwilling caregivers (e.g., strict, demanding, tough, impatient) and their children as undesirable and unwilling to respond to their care (e.g., he is a "pain," "monster," or "chore"). They emphasized their own perspectives and needs and seemed unwilling to acknowledge and therefore to integrate their children's attachment needs. During interviews, uncertain mothers were characterized by a striking inability to make decisions regarding their evaluations of self and child and by the opposing quality of their descriptions (good/bad, positive/negative). On the positive side, these mothers described both the child and caring for the child in glowing terms, but at some points during the interview, negative evaluations would suddenly emerge. It is easy to see why their children tend to have *anxious/resistant (ambivalent) attachments* with them. Finally, the mothers classified as helpless described themselves as lacking effective and appropriate resources to handle their children's behavior and to provide care. Their children were described as being out of control in one or two ways. Some were described as being wild or helpless and vulnerable and others as being precocious or powerful. These parent–child relationships appeared to be chaotic (i.e., out of control) or to involve role reversal where the children cared for themselves and/or cared for the parent.

By listening carefully to how parents talk about their children as well as how they interact with them, parent guides can tune into issues that need their sensitive and responsive attention. For instance, if the parent's portrayal of the child is primarily negative, the parent guide can highlight some of the child's positive characteristics and behaviors (but not in ways that directly contradict the parent's statements) and then observe how the parent responds to this. The guide can also wonder what is causing the parent to have such a negative view of this child, as Celeste did when Maureen referred to Victor as "a devil child." If there are other children, is the parent also negative about them? Does the child remind the parent of someone? What were the circumstances around the child's conception and birth? How was the parent treated by his or her parents?

Parenting Behavior   A number of studies have examined the relationship of the parents' adult attachments with the kind of caregiving they provide their children. In their work with families, parent guides may observe these various parenting behaviors. Sometimes, these parenting behaviors stem from current events in the parents' lives (e.g., domestic violence, depression), but often they arise from the parents' internal working models of self, others, and relationships. These studies can help parent guides reflect on what internal working models might be influencing the parents to parent in these ways, and how they can help these parents by providing corrective emotional experiences through the practice of relationship-based reflective interventions, in addition to helping parents address any life circumstances that are affecting their ability to parent their children well.

Parents who appear more secure and autonomous in their relationships with their parents tend to exhibit more desirable caregiving behaviors than do parents whose adult attachments are insecure. This has been demonstrated in studies of parents with their children at different ages. In caring for their infants, secure/autonomous mothers (including adolescent mothers) were more sensitive (Grossmann, Fremmer-Bombik, Rudolph, & Grossmann, 1988; Ward & Carlson, 1995), more accepting of their babies' individuality (Grossmann et al., 1988), and better attuned (Haft & Slade, 1989). Dismissing mothers tended not to attune to their babies' negative affect, whereas preoccupied mothers randomly attuned to both positive and negative affect. With their toddlers, mothers who valued attachments showed more understanding of developmental problems and of their children's individuality and reported more willingness to adjust family routines to the special needs of their 2-year-olds than did the mothers who did not value (i.e., dismissed) attachments (Grossmann et al., 1988). While assisting their preschoolers with various tasks, secure parents demonstrated more warmth, structure, and truly helpful behavior and did more to help their children learn and make discoveries on their own than did parents with detached adult attachments, who tended to be controlling and task-focused, or parents with preoccupied attachments who often presented instructions to their children in such a confusing manner that the children appeared overwhelmed (Crowell & Feldman, 1988).

Mothers' internal models of their relationships with their own parents are also associated with the ways in which they handle brief separations and reunions with their 2- to 4-year-olds (Crowell & Feldman, 1991). Secure mothers prepared their children well for the separation, left the room with little anxiety, and were affectionate with their children when they returned. The dismissing mothers left their children without difficulty, but did not prepare their children as well as the secure mothers did. When they returned, they remained physically distant from their children. The preoccupied mothers were very anxious, had difficulty leaving the room, and were the least helpful in preparing their children for the separation. Contrary to what one might expect, they did not approach their children when they returned.

In another study, the extent to which mothers were involved and responsive with their babies was associated with the severity of trauma (e.g., sexual abuse, physical abuse, witnessing violence) they had experienced growing up (Lyons-Ruth & Block, 1996), with severity of sexual abuse the strongest correlate of decreased maternal involvement. Maternal hostile-intrusive behavior was most strongly predicted by severity of physical abuse.

The behavior of parents of children who develop *anxious/disorganized-disoriented attachments* with them has been described as frightening or frightened (Main & Hesse, 1990). Some of the behaviors that have been reported by these authors and others include 1) suddenly moving an object or their own face very close to the baby's face, 2) unpredictable invasions of the baby's face (e.g., suddenly sliding their hands across the baby's face or throat, 3) teasing the baby in a scary way, 4) being extremely responsive to any indications of rejection on the part of the baby, and 5) indicating actual fear of the baby.

Infant–Parent Attachment   The quality of parents' adult attachments are very often mirrored in the security of the attachments their babies develop with them, as demonstrated by studies reviewed by van IJzendoorn and Bakermans-Kranenburg (1997). Caregivers with *secure/autonomous attachments* (whether earned or derived from favorable childhood experiences) tend to have children with secure attachments, and those with insecure adult attachments most often have children who during their second year are also classified as having insecure attachments (Benoit & Parker, 1994; Main, Kaplan, & Cassidy, 1985; Steele, Steele, & Fonagy, 1996; Ward & Carlson, 1995; Zeanah et al., 1993). These results have been the same whether the adult's attachment was assessed prenatally (Benoit & Parker, 1994; Steele, Steele & Fonagy, 1996; Ward & Carlson, 1995), concurrently (i.e., at ages 11–18 months; Benoit & Parker, 1994; Zeanah et al., 1993), or 4–5 years later (Grossmann et al., 1988; Main et al., 1985). Similar results have been found for low social economic status adolescent mothers (Ward & Carlson, 1995) and for fathers, although the association of fathers' adult attachment models and their babies' attachments with them is somewhat weaker than it is for mothers (Main et al., 1985; Steele et al., 1996).

Within the insecure classifications, the general tendency is for caregivers with dismissing adult attachments to have children with avoidant attachments (Zeanah et al., 1993), for those with preoccupied attachments to have children with resistant (ambivalent) attachments, and those with unresolved attachments to have children with *disorganized/disoriented attachments* with them. A sense of security or insecurity in attachments can even be transmitted across generations. One study found that the security of the mother's attachment with her parents was significantly related with both the security of her baby's attachment with her and the security of her mother's (the grandmother's) attachments with her parents (i.e., with the great grandparents; Benoit & Parker, 1994). However, such transmission is not inevitable.

When Links in the Chain Are Broken

History is not always destiny. Some people who experienced maltreatment as young children grow up to be caring, competent parents capable of raising children with secure infant–parent attachments and positive internal models of themselves, others, and relationships. These are the parents who are often classified in adult attachment research as having earned secure adult attachments. There are other parents who experienced fairly benign early childhoods but due to later misfortune develop problems that interfere with their ability to parent their children well.

Earned Security   Parents who were maltreated as children but have beaten the odds and manifest earned security in their adult attachments often parent just as well as parents who grew up in favorable circumstances. One study found that although parents (both mothers and fathers) of preschoolers with earned secure attachment classifications had higher rates of clinical depression than did parents with continuous secure attachments, the two groups did not differ from each other in warmth and support in interacting with their preschoolers during various structured and unstructured tasks. Both groups parented better than did the insecure parents (Pearson, Cohn, Cowan, & Cowan, 1994). In another study, the amount of daily stress parents experience was measured (Phelps, Belsky, & Crnic, 1998). Results indicated that among mothers experiencing high levels of stress, the earned secure mothers did not differ from the continuous secure mothers in positive parenting during interactions with their 27-month-old sons. Both of these groups manifest more positive parenting practices than the high stress insecure mothers did.

How do parents "earn" security? Some people whose attachment experiences with their parents were poor have had the good fortune to connect at some point in their lives with significant people who offer them different, more secure and caring relationships—a kindly grandparent or aunt who provides a safe and loving haven (like Sonia found), a preschool teacher who refuses to be put off by the child's acting out behavior, an elementary school teacher who notices and gets help for a socially rejected child, a mentor who provides support to a troubled teen—these are all experiences that help developing children modify their internal working models of self, others, and relationships in a positive direction. Even as adults, people who have negative internal working models can benefit from such corrective experiences with significant others as well as in their work with therapists and other parent guides (Lieberman & Pawl, 1993).

The ability and willingness to examine and reflect on one's life experiences also can help "earn" a sense of security as an adult in spite of adverse circumstances while growing up. One study found that a number of mothers whose infants demonstrated secure attachments with them tended to reflect more on attachment issues and to look for reasons for the behaviors of others, including their own parents (Grossmann et al., 1988).

From Secure to Insecure   Unfortunately, changes in security of attachment and concomitant internal working models can go in the other direction, that is, from secure to insecure. Various negative life events (e.g., loss of a parent, parental divorce, life-threatening illness of parent or child, parental psychiatric disorder or chemical dependency, physical or sexual abuse) can threaten the child's sense of security in attachment relationships. Whether these events cause a change in security of attachment depends on a number of conditions, such as the nature of the event (e.g., its severity, the relationship of the child with the perpetrator), and the support provided the child when and after the event occurred. For instance, when parents divorce, often it is high levels of parental conflict, rather than the divorce or family structural changes per se, that place children at risk. In any event, children who had secure relationships prior to the occurrence of trauma are in a better position to recover than those who did not.

Continuity   Although security of attachment can be earned, this is the exception rather than the rule. Studies of predominantly low-risk families that compared attachment security in infancy with attachment security as adolescents or young adults found that 72%–77% of the individuals retained the same attachment classification (secure or insecure; Hamilton, 2000; Waters, Merrick, Treboux, Crowell, & Albersheim, 2000). The adolescents and young adults who retained secure attachments grew up in families that experienced few stressful circumstances, whereas those with insecure attachments came from families characterized by various negative life events (e.g., loss of a parent, parental divorce, parental psychiatric disorder, abuse of the parent or child). Rather different results were found, however, in a study of young adults (ages 18–19) from high risk families (Weinfield, Sroufe, & Egeland, 2000). Only 35% of those who had been classified secure as infants retained that classification as adults, but 75% of those who had been classified as insecure as infants were still rated as insecure on the AAI as young adults. The authors suggest that the chaotic lives and negative experiences within their sample may account for these results.

One reason why continuity of attachment (security or insecurity) is often found may be the continuity of risk factors in the lives of so many people. Arnold Sameroff and his associates (Sameroff, Seifer, Baldwin, & Baldwin, 1993) examined the relationship of several risk factors with child outcomes when the children were age 4 years. They found that it was the sheer number of risk factors more than any individual risk factor that appeared to lead to poor outcomes for the children. Then, they revisited these families when the children were age 13 and learned that very little had changed. The families who experienced the most risk factors when their children were age 4 were still the ones at highest risk (i.e., with the most risk factors) 9 years later.

IMPLICATIONS FOR INTERVENTION

Chapter 2 describes how children's early caregiving experiences affect the development of the main ingredients of emotional development (i.e., their attachments with their parents; their internal models of self, others, and relationships; their development of emotion regulation). This chapter describes how these early attachment experiences can influence ways in which these children parent their own children when they grow up. Unfortunately, poor parenting practices are often passed from one generation to the next. As evidence cited in this chapter suggests, however, this need not be the case. The fact that corrective emotional experiences and self-reflection can help parents who began life with negative attachment relationships has immense significance for work with families of young children. It underscores the importance of practicing the principles of the relationship-based reflective model of parent support and guidance. The corrective emotional experiences parents have with parent guides and others who relate to them in sensitive, responsive ways and who help them reflect on their lives (as they tell their stories) facilitate modification of their internal representations of themselves and others in ways that free them to be more sensitive and responsive with their children. The strategies for nurturing parents described in Chapter 3 and illustrated throughout the book present ways in which parent guides can provide these corrective experiences.

In addition to being nurtured in these ways, many parents also need to learn different ways of interacting with their children. The parenting behaviors modeled for them when they were growing up may not be the best ones for promoting healthy emotional development in children. The strategies for enhancing parent–child interaction presented in Chapter 3 and illustrated throughout the book are ways in which parents can be guided to learn different ways to parent.

Strengthening the caregiving environment is the third focus for this model of early intervention; this focus was introduced in Chapter 3 and is discussed further in the next three chapters. Research results (e.g., Sameroff et al., 1993) suggest that without intervention, the number of risk factors experienced by a family do not tend to diminish over time. Some risk factors (e.g., depression, substance abuse, domestic violence) may stem from the effects of having had negative childhood experiences. These risk factors, in turn, make it difficult for the parent to parent well, thus contributing to the transmission of poor parenting from one generation to the next.

All of this—providing corrective emotional experiences, enhancing parent–child interaction, addressing risk factors—takes time, and babies cannot wait. Therefore, for some babies and toddlers, experience in quality substitute care for varying amounts of time is essential. In this way, they receive corrective emotional experiences, as well.

Parent guides who provide relationship-based reflective intervention can help break the cycle of poor parenting. As Maureen experienced Celeste's positive appreciation of her many competencies over time, she became more accepting and less critical of her child and more comfortable in her parenting role. In spite of her traumatic childhood, Samantha was able, with the guidance and support of her parent guide and the work she did with her therapist, to begin parenting in a different, more positive way. She became much more sensitive, responsive, and warm in her interactions with her baby. Although she still exploded at times with her older daughter, these incidents occurred less often, and she became more aware of what was happening and thus became more capable of bringing her reactions under control. These corrective emotional experiences with their parent guides (and for Samantha, also with her therapist) coupled with coaching in positive parenting practices and help with gaining access to resources to meet their families' various needs, helped break the cycle of negative parenting for these two families and for some others described in this book.

Not every story, though, is a success story for both parents and children. For example, Linda parented Sheryl much differently than she had her first two children, but her continued relapses into substance abuse resulted eventually in her losing custody of all three children; however, the positive parenting that Sheryl received during her first 3 years from her mother and later from her adoptive parents appear to have fostered healthy emotional development.

When parent guides and other professionals appreciate the ways in which the legacies of troubled childhoods can affect parents, they are better able to understand why some parents seem hostile or unmotivated, why they have made certain choices in their lives, and why they parent in the ways that they do. As pointed out previously, all interactions with parents can be interventions. To a parent who feels insecure beneath her tough exterior, a chance remark by some professional can be a stab in the heart or, if the remark highlights some positive feature of the mother's parenting, it can make her day. With enhanced understanding and the empathy it brings, chance remarks and other interventions, both large and small, can be better attuned to the psychological needs of the parents.

The results of having had negative emotional experiences while growing up can influence parenting in two major ways. As described in this chapter, the development of insecure attachments with their own parents and negative internal working models of selves, others, and relationships can have a direct negative effect on the quality of parents' interactions with their own children. These developments can also influence parents' lives in ways that in turn affect their abilities to parent well. They may become depressed or turn to alcohol and other drugs to self-medicate their psychic pain. Their negative models of others and relationships may result in poor choices for mates; inadequate relationship skills can interfere not only with their relationships with their children, but with their other relationships in the home and the workplace.

Numerous factors, both positive and negative, can influence caregiving. Not all of them stem from the parent's childhood experiences, but all of them deserve to be recognized and addressed in order to help parents enhance the emotional development of their children. Positive factors such as a supportive family, intelligence, and mental well-being are strengths to be nurtured and built on. Other factors such as poverty, drug addiction, spousal abuse, and depression need to be eliminated when possible. The next two chapters describe ways in which characteristics of parents and of their immediate environments can influence caregiving. These two chapters also discuss how parent guides can support and guide parents in their parenting while helping them obtain resources needed to address these difficulties.

10

What Parents Bring

How Parent Characteristics Influence Caregiving

"We were pretty messed up, so they came and took our kids." Tears well up in Linda's eyes as she tells her parent guide, Celeste, about losing custody of her two children almost 2 years earlier. She and her current husband, Robert, were drinking heavily when someone reported them to CPS for severe neglect of their children, 8-year-old Jane and 1-year-old Ben. Jane, who exhibited severe emotional and behavioral problems, was placed in a residential treatment program, and Ben was placed with a foster family. As part of their service agreement with CPS, Linda and Robert entered an inpatient alcohol rehabilitation center.

Celeste is talking with Linda and Robert to see if they want to receive regular home visits to support them as they parent their 3-month-old baby girl, Sheryl. A year after entering the treatment program, they had decided to have another child. "It's going to be different this time," Robert tells Celeste. The couple agree that they want regular home visits to help them with their parenting. Their goal is not only to do things differently with Sheryl but also to win back custody of Ben (Robert and Linda's child) and Jane (Linda's child by a former partner). Both Robert and Linda are in recovery and determined to maintain their sobriety.

Linda's story unfolded during her early visits with Celeste. Both of her parents were alcoholics, and her mother was mentally ill. When Linda was quite young, her mother simply disappeared for periods of several weeks. Finally, when Linda was 7 years old, her mother took her and her three siblings and left her husband for good—only to abandon the children after 2 months. Linda says that she has no memory of her mother from those early years. After their mother abandoned them, the children were raised by their father and his mother. Linda has fond memories of her grandmother; "I was the apple of her eye," she tells Celeste. Linda and her siblings were reunited with their mother when Linda was a teenager, but this was not a happy time for Linda. "I spent most of my spare time babysitting Mom's new kids," she says. After about a year, she moved back to her father's for a brief period and then left home altogether when she turned 17. After her relationship with Jane's father, she met Robert, who also came from a troubled background. For several years, they lived what Linda described as a hippie lifestyle. They hit bottom when the two children were taken away from them.

Like most parents, Linda and Robert were very sincere in their desire to parent their children well, but like many parents seen by parent guides, they experienced major challenges. This chapter discusses characteristics of parents (e.g., mental health, age, intelligence) that affect their caregiving; the next chapter addresses additional factors in the caregiving environment (e.g., financial resources, social support, domestic violence) that influence the way parents are able to care for their babies and toddlers. Some factors such as strong social support and good physical and mental well-being support parents' caregiving efforts. Other factors such as drug addiction, poverty, and abusive relationships make it difficult to parent well. In "real life" these factors interact in a dynamic fashion with the day-to-day circumstances of the families' lives.

Giving sensitive, responsive, and responsible care to a young child day after day (and night after night) is a challenge even under the best of circumstances. It often requires the parent, most often the mother, to put the baby's needs first. In the early months, for example, when the baby wakes up at night just after the parent has achieved a deep sleep, the parent is asked to put the baby's need for comfort and food before his or her own need for rest, and later, when their babies reach toddlerhood, parents are challenged by the push-pull nature of their toddlers' desire for independence (often expressed loudly in tantrums) coupled with the need for continued closeness. Getting through these periods goes more smoothly for many due to their strong bonds with their children; support from people close to them; and their emotional, mental, and physical strength. Parents whose emotional strength is compromised by their relationship histories; negative internal models of self, others, and relationships; poor emotion regulation; and inadequate coping mechanisms will have difficulty providing sensitive and responsive care for their babies and toddlers on a consistent basis. Linda's history of abandonment made it difficult for her to separate from Sheryl. When Linda finally did leave Sheryl with a babysitter so that she could attend an AA meeting, Sheryl acted out her mother's issues (as babies sometimes do) by crying inconsolably the entire time her mother was gone.

Parents may also have a diminished ability to learn from and about their young children due to cognitive limitations, immaturity, mental illness, or chemical dependency, and so they cannot meet their children's needs. Poverty, lack of social support, and domestic and community violence can also hinder adequate and appropriate parenting. Parents with these needs must be provided information, support, and sometimes treatment so that they can care for their children in ways that will promote their emotional development. Above all, parents need opportunities to experience positive, supportive, health-inducing relationships. This fact is especially true for parents whose ability to relate well with others, including their children, has been compromised by troubled relationships with their own parents during childhood.

Conditions that place babies, toddlers, and their parents at risk are often interrelated so that one risk factor seems to bring others in tow. For instance, parents' internal working models of self, others, and relationships spawned by early attachment experiences can affect choices of partners and the quality of those relationships as well as relationships with friends, co-workers, employers, and service providers. This condition in turn can affect employability, availability of social support, and the quality of intimate relationships. Psychoactive drugs may be used to ward off painful feelings arising from negative perceptions of one's self. Girls who had been sexually abused are at heightened risk for early sexual activity (Polit, White, & Morton, 1990) and hence for adolescent pregnancy (Roosa, Tein, Reinholtz, & Angelini, 1997). Furthermore, early and prolonged childhood sexual abuse is often a precursor of borderline personality disorder (Zanarini, 1997). Poor internal representations of self can lead to the development of clinical depression (Blatt & Homann, 1992) but so can struggling with poverty or living in a violent neighborhood or household, and, as if all of these problems were not enough, newborns of mothers who were depressed during pregnancy are more apt than babies of nondepressed mothers to be irritable and to have poor motor control, which then makes them more challenging to care for (Field, 1997).

Professionals cannot change families' pasts, but, as was discussed in Chapter 9, they can address the ways in which parents' childhood histories affect their interactions now and in the future, especially as their histories influence their relationships with their children. Professionals can and must identify other risk and protective factors that affect parents' abilities to provide adequate caregiving. They do this by helping families build on their strengths and mobilize resources to ameliorate those conditions that put them and their children at risk.

Helping families deal with multiple problems and crises can easily overwhelm parent guides, whose primary job is to provide support and guidance regarding parenting (e.g., parent guides in a Healthy Families program; Campbell, Earley, & Gray 1999). The challenge for parent guides in these situations is to remain focused on enhancing the parent–child relationship while being sensitive and responsive to parents' needs but not getting so caught up in the families' crises that the baby's needs are overlooked. Often this means helping families gain access to other community resources (e.g., substance abuse treatment, informal social support) and supporting them as they utilize these resources but keeping the main focus on fostering healthy parent–child relationships. In the example of Lisa and Ethan, Lisa was referred for psychotherapy and medication for her depression, helped to obtain other needed community supports, and supported in her efforts to mobilize and utilize these resources. While these things were happening, her parent guide, Helen, focused on observing, asking questions, and offering guidance in order to help Lisa provide Ethan with responsive, consistent caregiving. Parent guides can also contribute to the welfare of the families they serve by advocating for needed resources within the community and for better coordination of the resources that already exist. An unmet need identified in many communities, for example, is access to respite child care for parents who are overwhelmed by the unrelenting challenge of parenting, or who are confronted with crises and do not have reliable substitute caregivers available to them.

The goal of this chapter is to briefly describe some of the characteristics of parents that can interfere with effective parenting and to suggest actions that parent guides might take when they encounter these situations. It is well beyond the scope of this book to furnish a comprehensive picture of each of these characteristics; this chapter simply presents some information regarding them as they affect parenting of young children. In many cases, it is also beyond the work scope of professionals who provide parental guidance to address conditions that may be hindering parents' caregiving efforts (e.g., mental illness, substance abuse, poverty) beyond helping parents obtain resources needed to meet their needs; however, by understanding how some of these conditions can influence parenting, parent guides are in a better position to assist parents and their babies and toddlers while the parents are addressing their problems.

CHARACTERISTICS OF CAREGIVERS

When characteristics of the parents are presented as explanations for their parenting difficulties, some view this as "blaming the victim"—especially if the parent is a victim of spousal abuse or is poor and considered a victim of society. For instance, McLoyd and Wilson maintained that, "Ultimately, it is poverty itself that creates suboptimal conditions for maternal psychological functioning, child rearing, and child development" (1991, p. 128).

Two major issues underlie these controversies over identification of the causes of parenting difficulties. One is the issue of where to direct efforts to alleviate these difficulties. If, for instance, poverty (or spousal abuse) is seen as the major cause, then it makes sense to help the parent escape poverty (or spousal abuse); however, the parent may also benefit from additional resources such as mental health or substance abuse treatment, help in strengthening his or her social support network, and support and guidance for parenting. Through practicing parallel process, parent guides will be sensitive and responsive to parents' cues of needs in *all* areas of their lives that may be affecting their abilities to parent as well as they would like to. This chapter describes many of these needs and ways to help parents deal with them.

Another concern is that parents will feel blamed and deficient if they are diagnosed as having mental health problems or are treated as "victims" (Clark, 1995–1996). Parents who have lived through hard times (e.g., childhood or spousal abuse, chemical dependency, poverty) are rightly considered "survivors" rather than "victims." The relationship-based reflective model of providing parent guidance stresses the importance of respecting each individual and his or her life experiences. The practice of constantly identifying and building on each parent's unique strengths and providing opportunities for success counters feelings of inadequacy and builds self-esteem and self-efficacy in realistic ways. It also helps parent guides' perception of parents' abilities to grow.

Mental Health

The ways in which particular mental disorders of parents affect their relationships with their children and, in turn, the emotional development of their children are complex and relate to many other factors discussed in this chapter. For instance, depression may stem, at least in part, from such conditions as poverty and spousal abuse, and a borderline personality may be the result of a history of sexual abuse. Parents may try to self-medicate their condition through the use of alcohol and street drugs. By using the integrated services approach described in Chapter 12, professionals encountering mental disorders in parents will work in a coordinated fashion with other resource providers to ensure that all relevant factors associated with the disorder are addressed and that the child's healthy development is supported during the process.

As Constantino points out, the ways in which particular mental disorders are expressed in parent–child relationships may differ.

> A depressed mother may be acutely aware of her baby's developmental needs, but may not have the energy to maintain an active and stimulating interaction with him or her. A psychotic father may recognize his children's need for structure but may not be able to maintain consistent limits in dealing with their behavior. A personality disordered parent may be very invested in a child but may have difficulty distinguishing his or her own needs from those of the child. A parent with an anxiety disorder may be too internally focused to be emotionally available to his or her children. (1993, p. 4)

Even parents who share the same diagnosis of depression may manifest this disorder in different ways, as in the case examples presented later in this section.

Several factors affect the outcomes for children whose parents have mental illnesses. These children tend to fare better when they have another parent who does not have a mental illness and when they live in families that maintain warm and active interrelationships (Fisher, Kokes, Cole, Perkins, & Wynne, 1987). They do not do as well if the mentally ill parent has a conduct disorder, is hostile, or exhibits long-standing impairment of personality (Rutter, 1966; Rutter & Quinton, 1984). Studies of children of mothers with and without schizophrenia have found that how the mother parents (Goodman & Brumley, 1990) and the number of other risk factors present (Sameroff, Seifer, & Bartko, 1997) are more important to the children's outcomes than what the mother's diagnosis is per se. Through both initial and ongoing assessments and monitoring of parent–child interactions as described elsewhere in this book, parent guides can identify and address these problems with these parents. When necessary, they can help parents to obtain treatment for themselves and good supplemental care for their children.

Maternal Depression   Maternal depression deserves particular attention in a discussion of effects of parental mental illness on the caregiving context because of its prevalence. For instance, in a 1992 survey, about 40% of new mothers experienced mild postpartum depression and about

10% had major depression (O'Hara, 1995). Maternal depression does not necessarily lead to poor mothering, but it can make it more difficult for the mother to care for, nurture, regulate, and teach her young child (Goodman, Radke-Yarrow, & Teti, 1993). Although some depressed mothers are able to transcend their feelings of depression and provide warm, sensitive, responsive care of their babies, other have considerable difficulty doing so.

Relationship-based reflective intervention helps some mothers move out of their depression, especially postpartum depression (Cooper & Murray, 1997). Lisa is an example of such a mother. Before her first appointment with a therapist and doctor, her postpartum depression had begun to lift. Helen, her parent guide, acknowledged both Lisa's sad feelings and the possibility of her caring for her baby; she intentionally provided opportunities for Lisa to experience this possibility. With this support, Lisa moved toward hope that she could feel better. In her case, therapy including medication helped her to move along faster.

Effects of Maternal Depression on Young Children   Mothers who are depressed during pregnancy may be faced with a double whammy when their babies are born. Tiffany Field (1997) found that newborns born to mothers who were depressed during pregnancy were more fussy, less consolable, and had less developed motor tone than babies of nondepressed women. These conditions of a baby can exacerbate the difficulties depressed mothers typically experience in relating with their babies. These mothers are in special need of support and understanding as they deal with these challenges.

When considering the impact of maternal depression or other emotional disturbances on young children, it is important to remember that severity of the disturbance and whether it is transitory or chronic are key variables determining the long-range effect it will have on the child. A study conducted of infants of untreated depressed mothers found that these babies developed a depressed mood style as early as age 3 months (Field, 1992). This mood generalized to interactions with nondepressed women (nursery school teachers) and persisted over the first year if the mother's depression persisted. If mother's depression lifted by age 6 months, however, their babies no longer looked depressed and were developing typically by age 12 months. The compelling message of these findings, which are supported by others in the field (e.g., NICHD Early Child Care Research Network, 1999), is that it is important for mothers with depression to get treatment as early as possible in order to ameliorate the long-term effects on their babies.

Given the adverse effects of maternal depression on young children, parent guides need to encourage depressed mothers to get therapy. For instance, Connie's parent guide was able to appeal to her desire to feel less depressed so that she could better deal with the needs of her baby, Larry, who had developmental disabilities. Parent guides may help parents feel less hesitant about seeking therapy by saying, "You know, being a parent these days is pretty challenging, and you deserve all the help you can get. I've found that a lot of parents find it useful to get some counseling to help them feel better and deal with things." Whether receiving formal therapy and medication or not, most depressed mothers benefit from attention to all three of the intervention foci named in Chapter 3: nurturing parents, enhancing parent–child interaction, and strengthening the caregiving environment.

Nurturing Parents   By being aware of the different types of depression, parent guides can nurture depressed parents in ways that address their specific needs. Linda fits the profile of an individual with dependent depression (Blatt & Homann, 1992). This type is characterized by an intense reliance on others to provide and maintain a sense of well-being, considerable difficulty with separation and loss, and difficulty expressing anger for fear of destroying whatever need gratification others provide. For years, Linda remained in hostile-dependent relationships despite the fact that both she and her partners were diminished by these relationships. Her deep longing to be loved, cared for, nurtured, and protected—so characteristic of this type of depression—made it difficult for her to leave or confront her situation. Linda's depression had been chronic and resistant to treatment, and she had used alcohol for years to self-medicate her feelings of loneliness, helplessness, and weakness that are also typical of this type of depression.

When Linda's youngest child, Sheryl, was 3 months old, Celeste began to make weekly home visits. By listening, highlighting strengths, providing developmental guidance that was responsive to Linda's goals, speaking for her baby when Linda could not "hear" her, and being very dependable and available as needed, Celeste contributed to Linda's ability to stay sober, use therapy, and help Sheryl form a secure attachment with her. Celeste represented a person on whom Linda could (appropriately) depend, then later use as a secure base from which to try new ways of being with others, including her baby.

Another type of depression is characterized more by self-criticism and feelings of unworthiness, inferiority, failure, and guilt, and a striving for excessive achievement and perfection (Blatt & Homann, 1992). These individuals typically experience a chronic fear of disapproval, criticism, and loss of the acceptance and love of significant others. Both Maureen and Lisa, who were introduced earlier, could be described as mothers with this type of depression.

Maureen perceived her early years as a time of never being good enough for her mother, and she demonstrated with her own baby the belief that she could neither understand him nor meet his needs. Her need to gain approval was painfully disguised at times by her being critical of others' expectations and actions. Early in her relationship with Celeste, Maureen discounted or seemed not to hear comments that affirmed her or her efforts. It was through Celeste's being sensitively responsive in a consistent way over time that Maureen became able to view herself and her relational environment in more positive, realistic ways. Lisa displayed her feelings of inadequacy as she sadly described Ethan's crying during bath time and his falling asleep during feeding. Her words and her body language both spoke of her feeling of inadequacy in this new role of motherhood. In addition to highlighting for Lisa some of her many strengths, Helen, without minimizing her feelings, helped Lisa understand that her feelings of uncertainty in this new role were not uncommon.

Infant massage, as described in Chapter 3, is particularly beneficial for depressed mothers as well as for their babies. Depressed mothers who massaged their babies twice a week for 4 weeks were significantly less depressed, and physiological measures indicated less anxiety and stress as compared with mothers who practiced relaxation exercises for the same amount of time (Field, 1997). Their babies demonstrated decreased stress and increased calmness from massage, as well. With benefits to both mother and baby, infant massage should be considered whenever a depressed mother of an infant is referred for treatment. Caution must be exercised, though, if the mother or baby have been sexually abused.

Enhancing Parent–Child Interaction   Some depressed mothers are withdrawn and emotionally unavailable to their babies. They are generally unresponsive to their babies' cues and do little to stimulate and support their babies' activities. Other depressed mothers are intrusive and irritable with their babies. They often handle them roughly and actively interfere with their activities (Field, 1992, 1998; Tronick & Weinberg, 1997). Some mothers vacillate between these two ways of being with their babies. Research has demonstrated that babies of depressed mothers who are often withdrawn and emotionally unavailable tend to develop *anxious/ avoidant attachments,* whereas babies of more intrusive and irritable depressed mothers tend to develop *anxious/resistant (ambivalent) attachments* (Rosenblum, Mazet, & Benony, 1997).

The strategies for enhancing parent–child interaction described in Chapter 3 can be used to good effect with depressed mothers. Anticipatory guidance can prompt the withdrawn mother to notice more about her baby's development and can help the intrusive, irritable mother understand her baby's behaviors in ways that may lessen her irritability.

Speaking for or through the baby can increase the withdrawn mother's awareness of her baby's cues and help the intrusive mother notice her baby's responses to her intrusive behavior. Floor time is designed to help parents observe their baby's cues and draw them into playful interactions with their young children in nonintrusive ways. For instance, Celeste helped Maureen be less intrusive with Victor by guiding her in the use of floor time. The use of videotapes of parent–child interactions increases opportunities for parent guides to use various strategies (e.g., speaking for/through the baby and reflective questioning) to help both withdrawn and intrusive, irritable mothers.

While suffering from postpartum depression, Lisa often seemed withdrawn and unaware of what was happening with Ethan. Although Lisa complained that Ethan would fall back asleep after eating just a little bit and then wake up fussing a short time later, she did not seem to be aware that it was not a good time to feed him when he was half asleep. Her parent guide, Helen, acknowledged how frustrating this situation must be and then said, "You know, people who study babies have been learning some really interesting things. One of them is that babies need to be fully awake before they are able to take the amount of milk that they need, so maybe we can think about some ways that you can be sure that he's fully awake before you feed him. Then, he might eat more. For example, when he starts to wake up, you might wait a few moments to see if he falls back asleep. If he doesn't, try picking him up and changing his diaper or talking to him until he seems more fully awake before feeding him. If you try this, let me know how it works." By framing this suggestion in this way (i.e., by referring to what people who study babies have discovered), the information is presented to the mother, not as something that perhaps she should have known, but rather as an interesting discovery that is being shared with her.

Strengthening the Caregiving Environment   Strengthening the caregiving environment for the child may include improving the environment for the mother or finding supplemental care for the child or both. When parent guides learn or suspect that a parent is depressed, they may wonder to themselves or with the parent about situations that may be causing or contributing to the depression. For instance, Lila lived with her two small children in a trailer out in the country. As Helen, her parent guide, listened to Lila's sadness about feeling so isolated and lonely, she wondered if these factors might be contributing to Lila's depression and inhibiting the effects of her therapy and medication. Because Lila indicated that she wanted to move closer to town, Helen helped her problem-solve ways to do so and supported her in these efforts. As soon as they started down this path, Lila's depression began to lessen.

Sometimes the cause and effect relationship of an environmental factor such as lack of social support or employment may be more a result of the parent's depression than the cause of it. Lynette's physical and mental health problems seemed to sap her energy so much that she felt unable to do things that she said she wanted to do for herself and her children. Some parents, like Linda, try to self-medicate their depression and end up being dependent on alcohol or other drugs. When parent guides become aware of parents' depression, they need to look at the big picture as well as doing what they can to help the parent obtain treatment. Depression often co-exists with such caregiving environment conditions as poor marital relationships (O'Hara, 1997), spousal abuse (Gondolf, 1998), inadequate social supports (Brown & Harris, 1978; O'Hara, 1997), economic strains (Belle, 1982), an accumulation of stressful life events (O'Hara, 1997; Paykel, 1974;), and homelessness (Goodman, Saxe, & Harvey, 1991).

Some alternate quality care for the baby, when such care is not available in the home, is also needed when the mother has depression, so baby's development can proceed in a healthy way while the mother is getting better. Cohn, Campbell, & Ross (1991) found that for infants of depressed mothers, the number of hours of nonmaternal care were positively related to later secure attachment. Even very young babies can develop depressed moods that tend to elicit less positive responses from their caregivers (Field, 1992), so providers of alternate care need to be aware of this fact and adjust their responses accordingly.

Other Mental Health Disorders

When mental illness is suspected in the parent of a baby or toddler, obtaining an accurate diagnosis is important. A parent who may seem to be depressed may actually have another mental illness, such as borderline personality disorder or schizo-affective disorder, instead of or in addition to the depression. Treatment for these disorders is necessary, so parent guides need to make referrals for these conditions and also ensure that the children receive appropriate supplementary or substitute care and nurturing until their parents are able to provide such care.

There are times when a parent guide or another professional may observe that something is affecting a parent's caregiving behavior and suspect that a mental illness is the cause. For example, the parent may be grossly misreading the baby's hunger cues, responding instead to her own feelings of hunger or lack of it. A parent may also show no bonding behaviors with her newborn baby, referring to him as "it" and ignoring his cries. In instances such as these, the baby's life may depend on immediate and effective referral to parent–infant psychotherapy or therapy for the

parent combined with a parenting program, as was done with LaMont
and his family.

> *LaMont was referred by the health department to an infant-
> toddler program when he was 7 months old due to concerns about the
> mother–infant relationship. Patti, LaMont's parent guide, observed a
> number of troubling mother–baby interactions. Sometimes his mother,
> Shawndra, would appear distracted and not really psychologically
> there for LaMont as she held him or performed such basic care tasks as
> diapering. At other times, she was more "present" but in a disturbed
> and disturbing way. For instance, she would say things like, "You are
> evil" and "You're the Devil." These remarks seemed not to be in re-
> sponse to anything LaMont did. LaMont responded by doing what he
> could to move away from his mother. If she was holding him, he would
> arch his back; if he was sitting on the floor, he would try to scoot away.
> Patti felt that Shawndra's behaviors might indicate a mental disorder.
> She successfully encouraged her to seek mental health counseling by
> responding to Shawndra's complaints about her conflicts with her
> boyfriend and her mother and her difficulty sleeping. She suggested to
> Shawndra that she might want to see someone who could help her feel
> better and who might help her get medication. With this support,
> Shawndra was able to seek therapy for herself.

Joan and Jodie are examples of parents who were already receiving
mental health treatment when they came into a parent guidance program.
Joan was referred to an infant-toddler program when Susie was 4 weeks
old because her therapist noticed that Joan did not seem to engage with
Susie; she almost always held Susie facing away from her and referred to
her as "it." Eighteen-year-old Jodie, whose diagnoses included bipolar
disorder, personality disorder, and chemical dependency, was referred
during her pregnancy by the program that had treated her during adolescence for her violent and assaultive behavior. It is important to note that
these prompt referrals to a parent guidance program probably occurred
because mental health professionals along with others working with families of small children in their community had increased awareness of the
need to refer patients with young children to a parent guidance program.
This awareness stemmed from their participation in a series of seminars on
infant mental health that presented information on early emotional development and the importance of helping parents nurture this development
(Gowen & Nebrig, 1997).

Joan's schizoaffective disorder and depression were reflected in her interactions with Susie and with others, including Susie's first pediatrician. When Susie was 5 months old, Joan told her parent guide, Dianne, that she was going to switch her from formula to whole milk to save money. Dianne knew that Joan had an appointment with her pediatrician in a few days, so she encouraged her to mention this to him and ask his advice. She added, "You know, I've heard some things about the importance of keeping babies on formula for a year, and if you'd like, I can try to get some information for you about this." Dianne brought this up the following week, and Joan said the pediatrician had told her to put the baby back on formula, which she did, but she added, "He was mean, so I'm not going back to him again." Dianne listened empathetically to Joan's expression of her feelings and then told her that she had the information if Joan still wanted it, which she did. Dianne knew both from her observations of Joan and from her basic understanding of schizoaffective disorder that Joan had difficulty in relating with people and especially in taking direct advice from people. Her tendency to be on guard and to misinterpret the affective content in person-to-person communications often interfered with her ability to correctly understand what was being communicated. Conveying information and suggestions indirectly through written and videotaped materials seemed to make it easier for Joan to "own" and use the information.

Shortly after Jodie's son, Derek, was born, Patti began home visits to support this family that also included Derek's father. When Derek was about a year old, he was anemic and underweight. Patti was aware that Jodie ate very irregularly, so she began to wonder if Derek was being fed regularly. Jodie's response was vague to Patti's question about what Derek had eaten that day, so Patti asked, "What have you had to eat?" Jodie said, "Oh, nothing. I wasn't hungry." It became evident that Jodie only fed Derek when she herself was hungry, so Patti suggested that they figure out a way to keep track of how much Derek was eating. Together they decided that Jodie would write down the time of day and amount consumed each time Derek ate. Patti also provided information about what a baby Derek's age might need so Jodie could see if he was eating what he should. Jodie's problem in feeding Derek reflected her general tendency to interact with her baby in accordance with her own immediate needs and interests rather than in *response to Derek's behaviors. This tendency was exacerbated when Jodie went off her medication. Patti monitored Jodie's interactions with Derek for indications of this and, in cooperation with Jodie's therapist, did what she could to encourage Jodie to remain compliant with her treatment. In addition, she continued to use developmental guidance to increase Jodie's ability to hear and respond to Derek and, because Jodie's disability was so severe, to make sure that there was ample supplemental care for Derek. Derek spent a great deal of time with his paternal grandmother, who was a warm and caring attachment figure for him.*

By having permission and the opportunity to communicate as needed with Joan's and Jodie's therapists, Dianne and Patti were able to use an understanding of the mental illnesses of these two mothers to guide their work with them. In doing initial assessments and taking family histories, parent guides will often learn whether a parent has been or is receiving mental health treatment. Then, after a trusting relationship begins to form, the parent can be asked to sign a release form so that information can be shared between the therapist and parent guide. Parent guides can explain to parents, "You know, if I can talk with your therapist, then the two of us can work together to help you help your baby develop well."

Substance Abuse

Imagine being the baby of a parent who is very nurturing, warm, and engaging at one moment, and then, as the successive effects of being high, in withdrawal, and in need of another infusion of drugs are felt, she interacts with you in inconsistent, sometimes alarming ways. Sometimes she smiles when you smile at her, and sometimes she shows you a "still face" that causes you to become distressed and disorganized (i.e., emotionally dysregulated). Sometimes, when she is obsessed by how to get her next fix, she does not even hear you cry. Babies with this kind of inconsistent care cannot develop emotion regulation nor can they develop internal working models of their parents as trustworthy and of themselves as worthy of care. One mother in a family resource program who had just completed an intensive alcohol treatment program said to her parent guide, "This is the first time I have been able to really feel love for Anna" (her 9-month-old daughter). As is the case with mental health disorders, substance abuse by mothers (or other primary caregivers) often has a direct effect on their ability to build involved, nurturing relationships with their babies (Mayes & Bornstein, 1997; Zuckerman & Brown, 1993).

Enhancing Parent–Child Interaction   Linda sadly described some of the ways her earlier substance abuse affected her parenting. Due to the lack of consistency in parenting and the family's chaotic lifestyle, her older child, Jane, did not develop adequate emotion regulation and her behavior was often out of control. Linda was unable to help her, and when Jane's behavior got to him, her father would explode and punish Jane severely. By the time Jane was removed from the home by social services at the age of 8, she had developed severe emotional and behavioral problems. Ben, who was 7 years younger, experienced inconsistency and neglect for the first year of his life.

Parents who abuse alcohol and drugs often make poor decisions and arrangements for their children. Lois lost custody of her baby, Daniel, because she had allowed an active alcoholic to move in with them whose behavior was so rowdy that the police had been called. Paula had already lost two children due to neglect stemming both from her substance abuse and her codependency that led her to make poor decisions. She was devastated when her third child was taken from her because it was discovered that she had left him with a drug-abusing friend when she went to jail for shoplifting. A neighbor called CPS, who determined that Daniel was in an environment injurious to his health and safety.

Often when parents are clean and sober, they experience strong feelings of guilt over the ways in which they parented their children in the past, including concerns over the possible effects on their children of their use during pregnancy, and indeed, some of these children do develop problems due to their mothers' use of drugs during pregnancy or the rocky care they experienced before their parents went into recovery. Making amends is an important step in the 12-step program. Parent guides can support parents' making amends to their children by acknowledging their feelings of guilt but then focusing on the positive things they are doing now and by helping them understand and get services (including respite care) for their children's special needs. Another major way in which these parents make amends to their children is to do what they need to do in order to stay in recovery, and staying in recovery means more than just abstaining from using alcohol and other drugs. It also involves addressing the reasons they abused these substances.

Once they are fully in recovery, parents, with support from parent guides, can often do quite well. Linda's and Robert's parenting of Sheryl while they were in recovery was different from what it had been with Jane and Ben. The primary goal, then, for parent guides who work with parents who are substance abusers is to encourage them to seek treatment and to help them obtain supplemental child care until they are better able to care for their children themselves. Doing so can be a challenge; the parent has to first acknowledge the problem and then be willing to seek treatment.

Nurturing Parents   Often it is only after their children are taken away from them that parents "hit bottom" hard enough to quit abusing substances and go into treatment. This pattern was the case for Lois, Paula, Linda, and Robert. At least in this situation, the parent guide may know about the history of substance abuse and can therefore work with the parents to support their recovery. The parent guide may be a part of the treatment program or have permission from the parents to communicate with their treatment counselor or simply learn of their history directly from the parents.

In other situations, a parent guide may suspect that a parent is abusing substances but have no direct evidence of it. As one parent guide said, "People get pretty good at hiding it, and they certainly don't like to be accused." Because a parent guide's main concern is how well the children are being cared for, they will focus on this. If they observe signs that are troubling but do not amount to reportable abuse or neglect, they can wonder with the parent if something is bothering them. "I know how much you care for Susie, so I am wondering if something is troubling you because it doesn't seem like you to (then name the observation)." Because the guide has already established him- or herself as being there to help the parent achieve her parenting goals, this gives the parent an opportunity to share what is interfering with her parenting at the moment. Some women report that their primary motive for stopping drug use, entering treatment, or "cutting down" on drug use is concern for their children (Levy & Rutter, 1992).

Kim Insoo Berg recommended that after a good working relationship has been established with the parent, the parent guide can approach the situation of suspected substance abuse by saying something like:

> I can see that your life is very stressful. You have many serious problems to put up with. And I know that many people in your situation use drugs or drinking to cope with life's difficulties. What do you do that helps you from using too much drugs or alcohol? (1994, p. 210)

This approach reveals that the parent guide assumes that the parent may be using drugs or alcohol and that the question is simply how much or how little is used. It opens the way for a discussion of the issue.

One way to set the stage for parents to reveal substance abuse is to use a checklist to assess families' concerns, as recommended in Chapter 3. This opportunity allows parents to let their guides know of concerns they may have about substance abuse by themselves or other household members. When they develop sufficient trust in their parent guide, they may reveal their substance abuse and ask for help. It is more likely, however, that if anything is revealed, it will be the partner's substance abuse. This was the case with Clara who, after several weeks of home visits, complained to her parent guide, Dianne, about Hank's alcohol and drug abuse.

A mother may talk about her partner's substance abuse but not admit her own. This still gives the parent guide an opening to talk about how substance abuse can affect a person's behavior in ways that interfere with good parenting and to provide information about how they can help (and have helped) parents obtain treatment so that they can take better care of their children. This may be a first step to the mother seeking treatment for herself. Information about the effects of substance abuse and the availability of treatment can also be given in a nonthreatening manner in a group that discusses a number of different issues that parents might face, including substance abuse.

Parents may "tell" their parent guides of their substance abuse in other ways—drug paraphernalia on the coffee table, empty beer bottles everywhere, a heavy smell of alcohol on their breath at 11 A.M. The parent guide who has developed a relationship with the parent can say, "You know, I think you're telling me this for a reason. I think you're really concerned about your child and are wondering if this situation is good for him." The parent may deny or minimize the drug or alcohol use, blame it on someone else, or even get angry with the parent guide, but the guide must continue to focus on the parent's love for the child and the guide's expectation that the parent really does want what is best for the child. The guide will let parents know just how important they are to their children getting their needs met. Guides can also help parents envision what they want their children to say to them or about them when they are grown. It was this kind of persistent support and guidance that helped Lois go into and stay in recovery. The parent guide may also encounter a parent who admits to abuse of alcohol or other drugs but resists going into treatment. Even though Paula was told that she could keep her baby if she entered and did well in a new residential treatment program, one in which she could have her baby with her, it took several days before she was willing to make the leap.

Paula was lucky to have a residential program available in which she could be with her baby while in treatment. Unfortunately, many communities lack appropriate treatment programs to meet the needs of mothers and their children (Levy & Rutter, 1992; Zuckerman & Brown, 1993). Traditionally, treatment programs were designed by men to treat male alcoholics and addicts. Because these men were often alone, treatment focused on the individuals and not on the significant others in their lives. Fortunately, some communities are developing special treatment programs for women, and some are specifically for mothers and include services for their children (Mayes & Bornstein, 1996; Minuchin, 1999; Welle, Falkin, & Jainchill, 1998). Because the main variable that contributes to positive treatment outcomes is length of time in treatment, the issue of adequate child care is an important factor in helping mothers concentrate on their treatment. When services are provided for children, adults remain in treatment longer and participate more consistently (Mayes & Bornstein, 1996).

Even when women find treatment programs that respond to their unique needs, there are other reasons for not entering treatment: they may not have reliable transportation and child care, their partner may forbid it (this appears to be the case especially when partners are codefendants in criminal cases; Welle et al., 1998), or they may fear that their children will be taken away. If their guide has helped them find a solution to things like lack of transportation or child care, and they are still not going to treatment, then the guide can wonder about that with them. "You told me child care was a problem, and we've worked that out, and you're still not able to go into treatment. It seems like you're telling me that it feels really hard to do this." Pause. "Or is something else getting in the way?" At this point, the parent has an opportunity to talk about why she is hesitating. Often mothers fear that if they admit their addiction, their children will be taken away, and, depending on the community and the situation, this may be a realistic fear. Parent guides need to be well informed about practices in their community. They also need to advocate for approaches that are the least disruptive for children such as opportunities for parents to maintain contact with their children as long as they adhere to their treatment plans. Treatment and visitation plans need to provide for the fact that relapses are likely to occur. Maintaining the parent–child relationship as well as keeping the child safe must be considered in service planning.

Supporting Parents Who Are in Recovery   Once in recovery, parents need a lot of support to stay in recovery. Parent guides provide this support in many ways. Building on a foundation of a strong, caring relationship with the parents, guides use the strategies described in Chapter 3 to nurture the parents as they do the hard work of recovery. They listen as parents tell their stories and help them deal with their feelings of guilt and anguish over past treatment of their children. They highlight their strengths, provide concrete assistance (e.g., help arrange child care and transportation so they can attend AA or Narcotics Anonymous [NA] meetings), and encourage them to seek support from their AA or NA sponsors. Some communities have relapse prevention programs such as the one Lois attended three nights a week after completing the treatment program. The group selects different topics to discuss, often with speakers, including the topic of how substance abuse affects parenting. Participants have goals that they agree to work on.

Limit-setting can be a challenge when working with parents who have chemical dependency. Substance abusers often have long histories of being deceptive and manipulative, so it is not always easy to determine when a helping behavior is truly supportive or is just enabling the person to remain stuck in their addiction. Furthermore, relapses are a fact of life for people who are early into their recovery from addiction and alcoholism, and professionals working with parents who relapse may not agree on how to balance the needs of the children with those of the parents. For example, the staff of a drug rehabilitation program wanted to stop a mother's visits with her child as a consequence for her noncompliant behavior in the program, which was in opposition to the foster care staff who wanted to protect the child's contact with her mother (Minuchin, 1999). When children are in CPS custody, plans for how the parent should act if relapse occurs can be incorporated into the treatment plan. For instance, plans might state that if parents relapse and do not tell someone and get help, the chances are great that they will lose their children, but if they relapse and then take appropriate action, they still have a chance for reunification.

Dual Diagnosis For many people, alcoholism and other drug addictions coexist with psychiatric disorders (Luthar, Cushing, & McMahon, 1997), and they have a dual diagnosis of mental illness and chemical dependency. They may have used alcohol and other drugs to self-medicate for the effects of their emotional problems. These people are sometimes caught in the middle of the controversy among professionals who would prescribe medications for their disorders versus professionals who advocate for their abstaining from taking any kind of drugs. One mother who was dependent on alcohol, which she said she used to cope with her severe depression, complained because her substance abuse counselor and physician would not prescribe antidepressants because of her alcohol use. She asked her parent guide, "How do they expect me to stop drinking without help for my depression?" Because alcohol can interfere with the effectiveness and even the safety of many prescription drugs, the position of her therapist and physician was reasonable; the dilemma, however, remained for this mother. Resolution of situations such as this one need to be negotiated with the parent by the physician and perhaps the substance abuse counselor, and when feasible conditions under which medication can be prescribed should be established. Some mental health/substance abuse programs have an early morning program in which individuals can get a drug screen, if ordered, and have their treatment adjusted based on the results.

Strengthening the Caregiving Environment The lives of parents who have been strung out on drugs and alcohol for a while are often in shambles. They may be homeless and unemployed; bridges with family members may have been burned, leaving them bereft of a healthy social support system. They are in need of a lot of concrete assistance to turn their lives around. Parent guides can help them obtain community resources to meet these multiple needs while continually supporting and nurturing them in their parenting role. In AA or NA, they'll be counseled to find "new playmates and new playgrounds." Family resource centers that have parent support groups and child playgroups and are also available for parents to just drop in and chat with other parents and staff while watching their children play, provide an opportunity for parents to establish new friends and to have a safe and supportive place to hang out. It helps when centers intentionally provide this opportunity and connect themselves with substance abuse treatment programs.

Parents whose drug use and related activities resulted in convictions for crimes face additional hurdles. One father had gone into recovery and was full of hope for turning his life around and becoming a sober, responsible parent and provider. However, after months of having his prior conviction for dealing drugs stand in his way of getting a job, he relapsed and eventually left his wife and baby. Some communities have programs that work with both the ex-convicts and businesses to encourage the hiring of people with criminal records, and some even have businesses that are run by ex-convicts. Where such opportunities exist, parent guides may be able to help parents utilize them. Parent guides can also help parents who want to rush to make up in a manner of months the years they lost to drugs by reminding them that recovery of their lives as well as their sobriety should be taken "one step at a time."

Quality child care is especially important for babies and toddlers of parents who are struggling to overcome their addictions and put their lives together. When parents relapse, their children need a safety net. When Lois was involved in recovery efforts, she was able to put Daniel's needs before hers; when she relapsed, she was not able to do that. Because Daniel was still in foster care, he had consistent care even during those times. Parents whose children live with them need to arrange some supplemental care for their children, especially during the early stages of recovery. Because relapses are typically traumatic times for a family, it is not the time to introduce alternate care. Therefore, parent guides can help parents realize up front that it is important for them to have respite while they do the hard work of recovery and for their children to have a safe, familiar place to go should they relapse.

Substance Abuse by Other Household Members   Some babies and toddlers are living with a parent, either a father or mother, who is not using drugs but is buffeted about by the effects of the substance abuse of other household members. This was the case for some of the parents described in this book. When their partners are abusing alcohol and/or other drugs, these parents can become so confused and upset about their partner's addiction, dishonesty, and mood swings that it seriously interferes with their ability to parent their children well. Environmental circumstances related to a household members' substance abuse (e.g., involvement with law enforcement, incarceration, lack of money for rent and food, violence in the home, erratic schedules) can have a serious impact on both the nonalcoholic parent and the children. One study found that mothers whose husbands were heavy drinkers had higher rates of depression and lower marital satisfaction, and their children were twice as likely as children of fathers who were light drinkers to have insecure attachments with them (Eiden & Leonard, 1996).

When the substance abuse is by the parent's partner, the parent guide can express concern for what it must be like for the parent—the confusion, the worrying about the partner, the desire to protect the children but not to abandon their partner. Clara expressed to her parent guide, Dianne, her concern about Hank's buddies who often hung out at their house, drunk or high, and engaged in loud, aggressive behavior in front of their children. Because Hank did not follow through with treatment for himself, Dianne helped Clara use her concern about substance abuse plus her other concerns about Hank's abusive behavior toward her as motivation for moving into a place of her own.

Ideally, parents who have alcoholism or another addiction should receive treatment for their chemical dependency. How to help this happen is a major challenge for parent guides. The starting point is the parent's commitment to the children. As Dianne did with Clara, the parent guide can highlight for the mother the effects of the father's substance abuse on her and the children and then support the mother's efforts to appeal to the father's concern for his children as a way to encourage him to seek treatment. Additional support for nonalcoholic parents can come from their joining a group like Al-Anon. If the substance abusing parent has developed a relationship with the parent guide, there may be an opportunity for the parent guide to also appeal to that parent's concern for the children. If the substance abusing parent does not seek treatment or stop abusing alcohol and other drugs, then the parent guide can work with the nonabusing parent to determine if the situation warrants their taking the children and leaving, then developing a plan for making the move. Even when parents know it is in the best interest of their children, they may feel conflicted about leaving their partners. "I love him. I can't just abandon him—he needs me." It may help them to realize that the most loving thing they can do is to leave because by staying they are just enabling the other person to stay stuck in their addiction. If they leave, it may be the wake-up call that is needed to propel their partner into treatment. In Clara's case, she also felt she needed Hank, especially for child care, so Dianne helped her find other ways to meet this need.

Advocacy For Better Policies and Programs   Parent guides can play an important role as advocates for better policies and programs for pregnant women and parents who suffer from the disease of alcoholism and other chemical dependencies. Although the fear that all "crack babies" are doomed has abated as research has discovered that those earlier fears appear exaggerated (Day & Richardson, 1993), there remains an urgent need for improved services and policies to promote better prenatal care combined with substance abuse treatment for pregnant women addicted to cocaine, alcohol, or other drugs. Unfortunately there is a lack of such services. For instance, a survey of major hospitals in the United States found approximately 60% reported that they had no referral resources for pregnant addicts (Mayes & Bornstein, 1996). The criminalization of drug abuse by pregnant women has discouraged many women from seeking prenatal care, especially from public health clinics (Kasinsky, 1993). In addition, as described earlier, there is a need for more treatment programs that are specifically designed for women with their children.

Intelligence Level

Like many parents with mental retardation, Janice was affectionate and caring in her interactions with her children but had difficulty figuring out how to meet their needs. When Sally and Amanda were ages 1 and 3, social services removed them from the home because the unsafe and unsanitary environment put their health at risk. Janice's intellectual limitation impeded her ability to understand the effects of the environment on her children's health and her ability to organize her days so that she could manage household responsibilities. This is in keeping with results reported by Dowdney and Skuse (1993), who found that parenting was less likely to be competent when the parent's IQ score was less than 55–60, as in Janice's case. Above that, variations in IQ score did not appear to be of much influence. Janice's husband, Ken, whose IQ score is slightly higher than Janice's, had demonstrated more capability in caring for the children than Janice had, but he was at work during the day.

A few months after Sally and Amanda were placed in foster care, Janice gave birth to Kenny, who was soon placed in foster care with the other children. To help Janice learn how to care for Kenny, Sally, and Amanda, social services in conjunction with infant-toddler services developed a program that capitalized on two of Janice's strengths, her ability to read and her strong motivation to be a "good parent." Because research has demonstrated that parent training for people with mental retardation needs to be very concrete (Tymchuk & Feldman, 1991), a checklist was designed that listed basic care requirements, such as changing diapers as needed, washing hands before and after snacks, and keeping such things as medicine, cigarette butts, and small objects out of reach. General caregiving tasks, such as supervision, were broken into their elements (e.g., having the 1-year-old within view, being sure the children were not able to reach dangerous items, checking immediately if one of the children started to cry). Janice had biweekly supervised visits with her children either in her home or at the family resource center. During these visits, her parent guide, Wanda, initially modeled and gave direct instruction regarding the items on the checklist (e.g., diaper changing as needed, medicines out of reach, gates up) and later monitored Janice's ability to do these things without any cues. In addition to giving Janice lots of verbal feedback regarding her caregiving successes, the parent guide also provided visual feedback in the form of a bar graph. This graph not only helped Janice see where she was doing well, but also allowed her to see the areas in which she needed improvement. In addition, the bar graph provided objective information for CPS to determine if and when Janice was ready for reunification with her children. Wanda used developmental guidance to instruct Janice on the changing needs of the children, often spoke for the children, and highlighted specific things Janice did successfully in order to reinforce these responses.

Parents with mental retardation are often stumped when their initial efforts to accomplish something with their child (e.g., to soothe a distressed baby) do not work. Janice needed her parent guide to think out loud with her, asking questions to help Janice problem-solve. Wanda asked questions such as, "What might happen if Sally puts that in her mouth?" Pause. "What does she need you to do right now?" and "What if Amanda goes toward the open gate at the top of the porch steps?"

Pause. "How can you keep her from doing that?" Their cognitive limitations may also hinder their ability to anticipate next developmental steps and to facilitate their babies' growth in that direction. As her children's needs changed, anticipatory guidance was provided by adding new items to the checklist regarding developmentally appropriate activities. These were spelled out, instructed, modeled, and then monitored. For example, as Kenny began to crawl around, Wanda named the things that could hurt him, then she and Janice checked her house for dangerous objects. Wanda modeled distracting Kenny when he pulled up and reached for something they had put out of reach. These precautions were added to Janice's checklist, and monitored by the parent guides, with immediate feedback given to Janice regularly.

Tymchuk and Feldman (1991) concluded from their review of the literature that parent training with people with mental retardation also needs to include strategies to promote generalization and maintenance. Many, many opportunities were made available to Janice for her to practice, "overlearn," and thus maintain her new learning and new behaviors. Furthermore, Wanda and resource center staff helped her generalize behaviors she learned at home to the resource center and vice versa. Because Wanda worked with Janice in both environments, she could help other staff intentionally set up similar routines and use similar cues to those she used with Janice in her home. With concrete, experiential guidance and support, Janice began to acquire the basic caregiving skills she needed.

Maturity Level—Teen Parents

Rene and Samantha exemplify many of the problems faced by teenage mothers. Rene was 14 when Charlene was born. She and Charlene bounced back and forth between living with Robbie, Charlene's 19-year-old father, and living at home with her mother, her 16-year-old cousin, and her cousin's child, who was a few months older than Charlene. Samantha already had two children by the time she was 17 years old: Penny, her 18-month-old, and Katrina, her 1-month-old. The legacy of a very troubled childhood combined with her immaturity made raising these children an overwhelming task for Samantha.

One in eight children is born to a teenage mother (Children's Defense Fund, 2001). When these mothers have adequate social support and financial and personal resources, they often can parent their babies and toddlers appropriately. Unfortunately, many of them, like Samantha and Rene, come from poor and often troubled families (Breakwell, 1993; Hetherington, 1997). Like Samantha, several teenage mothers (61% in one large sample; Gershenson et al., 1989) have also been sexually abused either as children or adolescents.

Some of the parenting behaviors and caregiving issues of adolescent mothers who are depressed, have substance abuse problems, or are in abusive relationships resemble those of adult mothers who experience similar problems (e.g., Massat, 1995). These parenting difficulties are discussed in other sections of this chapter. This section focuses on how issues in adolescent development influence parenting and how best to guide and support teen parents. Because some adult parents first became parents when they were teens and they and others may still be somewhat immature, many of the suggestions presented in this section are applicable to them as well.

Psychological Neediness   Many adolescents who become pregnant exhibit "profound psychological neediness, the legacy of severe and often protracted emotional deprivation, beginning early and continuing through the adolescent years" (Musick, 1993, p. 100). Their unmet dependency and affiliative needs can influence their behavior in a number of ways. For some, the desire for a baby stems from a deep longing to have someone to love and to be loved by. Some teen mothers (and some adult mothers as well) use their babies to fulfill an unmet need to feel competent and special (Anderson, 1991). One mother wrote the following in her journal: "Dear Kimmie, I lov you. You make me feel special and needed. With out you my life was boring and almost meaningless" (Musick, 1993, p. 110).

When typical adolescent craving for heterosexual relationships is coupled with deep psychological neediness, teenage girls can become especially vulnerable to the sexual advances of their partners, leading to early pregnancies. (This topic will be returned to shortly.) Another way in which unmet needs influence adolescent pregnancies is when girls become pregnant as a way to gain recognition and nurturance from their mothers, if not directly, at least through their babies. It is not at all uncommon for a pregnant teenager to openly discuss her hope that the pregnancy will cause her mother to have a change of heart. By focusing attention on her plight, she can elicit the maternal care she was previously denied (Musick, 1993). When a teenager does this, the parent guide can first validate her feelings for her and let her know that her wish is not uncommon. Then, the guide can invite her to talk about how it has been for her with her mother. In doing this, the guide is listening to her story and being supportive in a way that perhaps she has not experienced before. Together they can explore whether she can expect these things to change once the baby is born. At a later time, the parent guide can talk with her about how she wants things to be different between her and her baby. Parent guides can be aware that although some other young mothers may have this as a hidden wish within their hearts, they may not be able to articulate it, but indications may show up in their behavior. Guides can help this desire come to light by asking the teen how her mother is responding to the pregnancy or to the baby.

For adolescents, psychological neediness is compounded by such adolescent development issues as the need to separate from their parents while maintaining their attachments with them, the search for their own identities, and their budding interest in heterosexual relationships. For interventions to be effective in helping these young mothers and their adolescent partners, they must address the psychological realities of their lives as well as their educational, vocational, and parenting needs. One way the relationship-based reflective model of intervention addresses this is through its strategies for nurturing the parent. These strategies are especially important for teen parents who may need "to be emotionally 're-fueled' through meaningful supportive relationships in order to have the capacity to provide the necessary emotional support and guidance to their infants" (Osofsky & Eberhart-Wright, 1988, p. 23).

Nurturing Parents   Samantha's story of her abusive childhood first emerged when she and her parent guide, Katherine, talked about conflicts Samantha was having with Jacob, the father of her children. Samantha explained, "Jacob thinks I should let Katrina cry sometimes instead of picking her up every time. But I'm doing it because no one was there for me when I was little and I cried." Katherine listened with empathy as Samantha told her story over their next several sessions together. Samantha spoke poignantly of the often sadistic physical and emotional abuse she had suffered at the hands of her mother and others, including her aunt. Her mother had had numerous sexual partners, at least one of whom had abused her sexually when she was a very young child. She was angry with her mother, both for abusing her and for not protecting her from abuse from others.

An important part of nurturing parents who have had troubled pasts is to 1) listen to their stories, 2) reflect on how their early experiences may have both shaped their internal working models of self and relationships and account for behaviors observed in the present, and 3) provide corrective emotional experiences and opportunities to connect the past with the present. This is especially true for adolescent parents for whom this process is complicated by their developmental issues. Giving a teen parent permission (and safe space) to tell her story is a powerful intervention. "As secrets (from herself, as well as others) surface, unspoken words lose their power, and her history loosens its grip on her life" (Musick, 1993,

p. 229). For many teen parents, telling their story can be the first step away from victimhood. As one teen put it, "I am happy . . . because I found out things in my life that I have hidden from myself" (Musick, 1993, p. 229).

Samantha's buried rage over her upbringing was demonstrated in her relationships with her children, especially with Penny, and with adults including professionals who were providing services to the family. She was very angry and controlling with Penny and equally angry and demanding with staff. As Katherine soon learned, Samantha was also hard on herself. She hated herself for getting so tense and upset with Penny. She told Katherine, "I don't want to treat her the way I was treated." Katherine asked Samantha if she would like help in figuring out some ways to calm herself when she began to get upset with the children. She said she would like help, so Katherine suggested some things such as hugging herself, taking deep breaths, or walking away for a few moments and encouraged Samantha to choose something that she thought would work for her. During subsequent visits, Katherine asked Samantha if she had tried any of these things and whether they had helped. In addition, if Katherine noticed that Samantha seemed to be getting tense or irritated with one of the children, she would offer herself as Samantha's inner voice: "This seems to be getting to you—which of those calming techniques do you want to try?" Samantha would then try one of the calming techniques, and they would talk about whether it was helpful, which it often was.

The importance of implementing a calming technique as soon as she began feeling tense was demonstrated in an incident that occurred when Samantha was at the playground with her two children and Katherine. Katherine held Katrina while Samantha put Penny into one of the toddler swings. Penny started wiggling around as Samantha was adjusting the swing. Suddenly, Samantha screamed at Penny, "Stop that!" Penny burst into tears, and Samantha caught Katherine's eye, shook her head, and asked, "Why did I do that?" Shortly before, she was talking with Katherine about the calming techniques she was learning to use and was disappointed in herself for not relying on them in this situation; however, it will take time and a lot of practice and emotional support for Samantha to overcome "emotional hijacking" stemming from her early experiences.

Establishing an Identity   Many children wonder, "What am I going to be when I grow up?" Developing a sense of identity is a major task for adolescents (Erikson, 1968). To evolve identities separate from their parents, they must achieve a certain degree of independence from their parents without sacrificing their attachments with them. Becoming mothers is one way of achieving these goals for some girls. They establish separate identities as mothers of their own babies while staying connected with their mothers by following in their footsteps (Musick, 1993) just as Rene did when she became pregnant with her first child at age 14, the same age her mother, Sarah, was when she gave birth to Rene.

Identity options related to future careers may seem unattainable or even threatening. Staff of programs for adolescent mothers are often perplexed when young mothers become pregnant again on the eve of moving into promising educational or occupational opportunities (Musick, 1993). Careful analyses of these situations have revealed that many of these young mothers feel (and often are made to feel) that they will cut themselves off from their families and friends by bettering themselves. Comments like, "I suppose you think you're better than us" strike home. Having another baby keeps them connected.

Because many teen mothers, especially young teenagers, live with their mothers and grandmothers, parent guides can try working with the entire family to facilitate support for the teen mothers' continuing their education and vocational training. In this way, they can establish identities as productive adults in addition to their identities as parents. This has worked well for Tamara, a teenage mother who lives with her mother, Lucia, and her son, Keith. Support for this family has come from Jan, a nurse who started visiting Tamara and Lucia during Tamara's pregnancy, and Wanda, the facilitator of a teen parents program. With the support of her mother as well as that from Jan and Wanda, Tamara has remained in school and is an active participant in the teen Lunch Bunch group. This program brings teen parents together for lunch once a week to discuss a topic that the teens choose.

Teen Parent Groups   When the teenagers' families are not receptive to intervention, or in addition to family intervention, teens can be encouraged to participate in special programs for teenage parents. For some teenagers, these groups can serve as surrogate families; for all participants the programs can enhance certain family functions.

> The best interventions fulfill key family functions for adolescents at risk. Like good families, these interventions have well-articulated expectations that they help teens internalize by consistent support and guidance. They set high standards and reinforce positive values . . . [. They] do what more advantaged families do naturally—they link expectations and goals with the tangible means to achieve them, providing real and realistic opportunities to grow. And, like healthy families, they protect, nurture, motivate, structure, mediate, teach, and enable, acting as a psychological safety net so that adolescents can falter without falling. (Musick, 1993, p. 227)

Group programs are especially beneficial for teens for a number of reasons. Peer relationships are especially important during adolescence. Being in a group can satisfy some of the teens' social needs and give them a chance to develop a new social support group with similar experiences and hopefully similar positive aspirations.

As a group, teenage parents can be encouraged and facilitated in gaining vocational and other educational skills in addition to parenting skills. Moving into the adult world of work and parenthood can seem overwhelming to teen parents. Parent guides, whether in a group or individual environment, can help teenagers break major tasks into their elements and assist them with the parts of the tasks that are initially beyond their capacity. For example, when Rene wanted to return to school, she and her parent guide, Marie, mapped out what needed to be done. Then, Marie offered to locate child care and go with her to talk with the principal; she also helped her talk through her fears about anticipated reactions of classmates. Marie's scaffolding provided Rene the assistance she needed to achieve her goal.

Chicago's Ounce of Prevention has programs that provide field trips for teenagers with and without their children so that they can gain knowledge of the wider world beyond what they see on television (Musick, 1993). These trips are not merely for entertainment but to inspire and equip the teens to move into this wider world. Communicating high expectations coupled with appropriate scaffolding gives the message, "We know you can make it, and we're here to help you." The program also provides formalized rites of passage such as award ceremonies, graduations, certificates, and other rituals that recognize and validate accomplishments and important transitions in the lives of their teenagers. In some communities, programs for teenagers have special celebrations on Mother's Day and Father's Day. These are important ways in which group programs for teens can help young parents feel pride in their achievements and mark their transitions into adulthood.

Enhancing Parent–Child Interaction   The typical challenges of parenting babies and toddlers are compounded by several of the developmental tasks of adolescence. Typically, adolescence is the time when children develop the ability to think hypothetically (i.e., formal operations; Furth, 1969; Piaget, 1973). When this ability is not fully developed, it may be difficult to think of possibilities, and that, in turn, can affect teenage parents' tendencies to anticipate the needs of their babies and toddlers. Annette found that when Jeremy was a baby, he would usually stop fussing when she put a pacifier in his mouth, so she continued doing this as he grew older. During a home visit, Jeremy, now 11 months old, was cruising along the edge of the coffee table when he reached toward a toy sitting on the table and began fussing when he could not reach it. Annette reached over and popped his pacifier into his mouth. Fortunately,

Jeremy spit it back out, giving Alice, the parent guide, the opportunity to speak through him, saying, "Sometimes that pacifier is just what you're wanting, but this time you're wanting something else, aren't you?" Pause. "What could it be?" Jeremy looked at Alice and then at his mother again. Alice responded, "Do you want Mommy to help you get that toy?" At this point, Annette handed Jeremy the toy, and he went happily on his way.

Physical changes and emotional ups and downs can make adolescents self-centered as they try to deal with these challenges of growing into adulthood. This egocentrism is at odds with the demands of parenthood to be more focused on fostering the development of another (Musick, 1993). Teen mothers tend to be less attuned to their babies' feeling states than adult mothers (Osofsky & Eberhart-Wright, 1988) and their play with their babies often appears more mother-focused than child-focused (Musick, 1993). Their egocentrism also leads some teenage mothers to confuse their needs and feeling states with those of their babies. As described in a previous section, it appeared that Derek's mother, Jodie, only fed Derek when she herself was hungry. Although Jodie's problem may have stemmed as much from her mental illness as from her age, similar behaviors (e.g., not putting a jacket on the child because the mother was not cold) have been observed with other teenage mothers.

Because adolescence is an era distinguished by the reemergence and reworking of attachment-separation issues, the teen mother's earlier losses or abandonments may be recapitulated with her child (Musick, 1993). If the teen mother became pregnant in the hopes that her baby would compensate for these losses and make life better for her, she may later harbor anger toward her baby when this fantasy is not fulfilled. Joy Osofsky and her associates (1988) suggested that this may be why they have observed more teasing and pinching of their babies by teenage mothers than by adult mothers. Underdeveloped emotion regulation stemming both from immaturity and troubled backgrounds cause many teen parents to be less in control of their impulses and emotions. This fact may explain why they are more inclined to use physical punishment with their babies and toddlers, especially when their children fail to meet these mothers' developmental expectations (DeLissovoy, 1973). Katherine noticed that during snack time in the playgroup, Samantha had unrealistic expectations for Penny, who was then 18 months old. She expected her to wait patiently in high chair while she opened a can of fruit cocktail and then not to make any mess eating it. When Penny took pieces of fruit from the bowl and put them on the tray, Samantha scolded her. Katherine commented on behalf of Penny, "She's at the age when babies love to take things in and out of places, isn't she?"

How a parent guide responds in a situation like this will depend on what she knows about a particular parent and the situation. For instance, in a similar situation she may have a pretty good idea that the mother knows that this is age-appropriate behavior for her child but that this mother just cannot stand messes and needs a way to deal with her tension. So, instead of simply naming the child's behavior as typical, the parent guide might validate the mother's feelings: "I know that this just drives you nuts. What could be a compromise here so she can do ordinary toddler stuff and you won't be irritated by it?" Then, the guide and the parent can problem-solve together. With yet another mother, the parent guide may know that the mother usually lets her child mess with things at home so she guesses that the mother may be feeling under the gun to make her child "behave" because there are other parents and professionals around. Because this mother is already feeling self-conscious about doing the "right" thing, the parent guide probably should not say anything at the moment but should take other opportunities with her and this group of parents to encourage them to find ways to allow age-appropriate experimentation. When she observes this mother letting her child explore and experiment at home, she can make a point of commenting on how helpful to her child this is.

As previously noted, teenage mothers are also more apt than older mothers to display hostile and childlike behaviors such as teasing and pinching. Often in the teen group, mothers could be seen playing games with their babies that had a hostile feel to them such as playfully slapping at the child's hand or grabbing a toy from the child and saying in a teasing way, "Oh, that's mine!" During one playgroup, Samantha started a tug-of-war game with a bright-colored scarf with Penny. At first, Penny seemed to enjoy the interaction, expecting Samantha to give the scarf right back. When she did not, Penny's expression turned to distress. Samantha seemed not to notice and kept the scarf. A staff member spoke to Penny, so that she could help Samantha read and respond to Penny's cries: "Ooh, you don't look too happy—are you not enjoying this game any more?" She then waited for Samantha to notice and change the game, which she did by letting Penny have the scarf back. Penny promptly put the scarf on her head, and Samantha responded, "Oh, you want to play Peekaboo now." This interaction occurred in the context of a teen group session in which the teenage mothers were using activities and discussion topics to expand their capacity to read and respond to their babies.

Teenage mothers also tend to know less about child development (Buchholtz & Korn-Bursztyn, 1993) and appropriate child care, as demonstrated in a study of expectant mothers aged 14–19 years and adult mothers who viewed photos of infants and children in a variety of potentially hazardous situations (McClure-Martinez & Cohn, 1996). The teen mothers were significantly less likely than the adult mothers to report that they would intervene in potentially dangerous situations such as a young child riding in a car without child restraints, sitting in a bath unattended, or being unattended in a crib with the railing down. It is important to note that in this study, if the teenager had had previous child care training and experience, she was more likely to indicate that she would intervene.

A great deal of information about child development and child care can be introduced to teenage parents in group situations. One activity that teens in a playgroup enjoyed was imitating their babies' sounds and doing so in an animated way. They were encouraged to notice how their babies responded to this and how their babies signaled to them that they were ready for a little break. The teen parents then discussed what they had observed, and the facilitator talked with them about how this activity helps their babies' brains develop.

Snack and play times in teen parent–child groups provide excellent opportunities for facilitators to provide guidance to teenage parents as they interact with their young children. The group can discuss in advance how these activities provide opportunities to watch their babies and toddlers and try to decipher their cues. Often teens can hear advice more easily when it is presented to a group rather than to them individually. Although this can be true for adult parents as well, the developmental press for autonomy makes some teen mothers especially resistant to receiving parenting advice from adults. The "speaking for (or through) the baby" technique either in group environments or individual visits can be especially effective in guiding teenage mothers (Carter et al., 1991). In a group environment, this can be used both during informal parent–child interactions, as in the above example of Samantha's tug-of-war game with Penny, and as a group activity in which the parents view a videotape of parent–child interaction and practice speaking for that baby and then try the technique with their own babies. They can also speak for each other's babies as long as they only make positive comments.

Programs that begin when teens become pregnant can be especially attractive as the expectant parents can feel that they are in a program that is special for them rather than being singled out later for parent "training" offered because they are "not doing well." Wanda, the leader of a teen program, has noted that when they enter the program during pregnancy, "they are more eager, interested, and have more positive attitudes."

Strengthening the Caregiving Environment   Rene, like many teenage mothers (especially younger ones), lived at least part of the time with her mother, Sarah, during Charlene's first 2 years. In some situations, this arrangement works well—the young mother feels supported emotionally and financially, and the baby is well cared for. In other families, though, co-residence and co-parenting by teen parents and their mothers are problematic (Tatum, Moseley, Boyd-Franklin, & Herzog, 1995). Although the teen mother's dream of an enhanced relationship with her mother may be partially fulfilled, at least temporarily, the mere presence of a baby in the house typically does not mend these mother–daughter relationships. In fact new issues arise, such as conflicts over who is the baby's primary caregiver—and who is the better caregiver.

In addition to Rene and Charlene, Sarah's household included 16-year-old cousin Nicole who had a child a few months older than Charlene. Sarah, Rene, and Nicole all had their own and differing ideas about such child-rearing issues as whether to wake babies to feed them, use a pacifier, and let babies cry. A number of community helpers were involved with this family—an early interventionist/care coordinator for Rene's child, Rene and Robbie's couple's therapist, as well as four different service providers for Sarah and for Nicole and her child. The effectiveness of this community effort was diminished at first by the lack of coordination and the sheer number of service professionals assigned to the family, so that the disorganized family system was mirrored by the disorganized helping system; both were often characterized by competition and disagreements. In recognition of this problem, the key players began meeting to coordinate their services, and the number of helpers were reduced, thus creating a more effective helping system.

Teen mothers, like all parents, need to feel competent in their parenting role. Too often, their parents (especially their mothers) interact with them and their babies in ways that diminish their self-esteem and feelings of parenting efficacy (Buchholtz & Korn-Bursztyn, 1993). This fact may be why studies often find that teen mothers (especially older ones) display better parenting when not living with their mothers (Black & Nitz, 1996; Spieker & Bensley, 1994). In spite of these problems, many teenage mothers tend to look more to their parents than to their partners for support (Lamb, 1998) and when they do not receive it (i.e., perceive rejection), they become depressed (McKenry, Browne, Kotch, & Symons, 1990). Seventeen-year-old Naomi felt dejected by her mother's inconsistent willingness to babysit her two children so that she could have some time for herself. Her mother would sometimes promise to care for them and then at the last minute change her mind or would be irritable when Naomi would ask for help. Her parent guide helped her find more reliable child care and also validated Naomi's feelings: "Naomi, don't think it's because you're bad or don't deserve help. Don't we wish your mother *could* be there for you!"

When parents can help their children who are teen parents gain both feelings of competence along with actual competence, then co-residence and co-parenting can work reasonably well, but often it is a challenge due both to troubled parent–teen relationships and to problematic parenting by the teen mothers. Teen mothers may express the typical adolescent push for independence by insisting on making all of the caregiving decisions about their babies, and their parents may think that some of these decisions are not in the best interest of the baby, sometimes for good reason. Sixteen-year-old Cynthia wanted to give her son cereal in a bottle at age 1 month so that he would sleep longer at night. Her mother, Irene, with whom she lived, agreed with the worker from the Special Supplemental Nutrition Program for Women, Infants, and Children (WIC) and the pediatrician that this was too early to introduce cereal. Irene's parent guide problem-solved with her how she might approach this with Cynthia without Cynthia reacting defensively. Irene decided to offer to go with Cynthia to her baby's 6-week checkup at the health department and ask the nurse an open-ended question about feeding. Irene practiced with her parent guide how to say this without criticizing Cynthia: "I know that things have changed since my children were little, so I'm wondering what parents are being told these days about when to start their babies on different kinds of food?" Irene was encouraged to use this problem-solving/practicing approach in other situations in which she differed in childrearing beliefs with Cynthia.

Relationships with Men   Two childhood conditions that are more common among pregnant adolescents than their nonpregnant peers are father absence and sexual abuse (Musick, 1993). Both conditions characterized Samantha's childhood. An understanding of how these childhood conditions can influence the behavior of adolescent girls—especially their relationships with men—can inform interventions to help these young mothers establish more healthy environments for themselves and their children and to prevent further pregnancies. Teenagers with histories of sexual abuse are often observed to have difficulty with perceptions of reality. Because of early betrayal by caregivers, Samantha tended to be distrustful of expressions of caring by her boyfriend, Jacob, and by helpers from early intervention. She often read negative motives and goals into their behaviors. Being aware of the likely origin of such perceptions, the helpers persisted in being responsive and consistent in their caring, and they helped Jacob be persistent, as well.

Both of these childhood conditions tend to make teenage girls more vulnerable in their relationships with men (Wekerle & Wolfe, 1998). A longing for the fathers they lost or never knew propels some girls into relationships with older men who, due to their feelings of inadequacy, seek relationships with girls they feel they can control. When the adolescent's longing is fueled by emotional neediness stemming from lack of maternal nurturance, she may hang onto abusive relationships or go from one male relationship to another in desperate attempts to fill this void. Often, in their efforts to please their partners, these girls not only give into their sexual advances but also put themselves (and their babies) at risk in various ways. When she was 5 years old, Annette's parents divorced after a heated custody battle in which her mother received custody of her and her father received custody of her older sister. She has had very little contact with her father and sister since then. As a teenager, Annette bore three children by different men, the first two of whom abused her.

A history of sexual abuse is a major risk factor for both initial and repeated adolescent pregnancies. Sexual victimization of girls by their stepfathers or current partners of their mothers (as happened to Samantha) is not at all uncommon (Finkelhor, 1984; Russell, 1986). Even when fathers are present, some may physically or sexually abuse their daughters or fail to protect them from abuse by others. From these early experiences of abuse, girls may learn patterns of passivity and helplessness in relation to men that make them highly prone to repeated victimization (Russell, 1986) or sexual precocity. Adolescents who have been sexually abused are more likely to have consensual sex at an earlier age than those who have not been abused (Polit et al., 1990). Their views on sexual relations become distorted; power rather than love becomes the dominant theme. As children, they may have learned to dissociate to lessen the psychic and physical pain of what was happening to them. In many severe cases, dissociative identity disorders (formerly known as multiple personality disorders) develop. These outcomes of early sexual abuse influence not only a tendency toward early pregnancies, but also the conditions in which these mothers and their young children live. Often they stay stuck in abusive relationships or do as Annette did and move from one such relationship to another, placing them and their children at risk. Furthermore, for both teen and adult mothers, a history of sexual abuse is often associated with reduced maternal responsiveness, and a history of physical abuse, with hostile-intrusive behavior with their children (Lyons-Ruth & Block, 1996).

Adolescent parents need accurate knowledge about what is and what is not appropriate sexual behavior. As one girl in Chicago's Ounce of Prevention Program said:

> If I hadn't been in [the program] . . . I would be ignorant. If something happens and you don't know, it's just like "O.k. I'm not going to say nothing." It's gonna stay like that . . . . and now you know you have to do something about it. You know what to do, what to say. (Musick, 1993, p. 231).

There are a variety of reasons why an adolescent might not know what is appropriate sexual behavior. For instance, if an adolescent girl had been sexually abused earlier in her life, her view of what is and is not appropriate becomes distorted. Sexuality as a general topic can be a subject for group discussion, but discussion of individual experiences of sexual abuse is best done one-on-one at this age.

Teen Fathers   Although a number of teen mothers become pregnant by men who are older (Lamb, 1998; Rhein et al., 1997) and/or abusive, this is not always the case. Some of the fathers are also in their teens and want to be involved in the care and upbringing of their children (Lamb, 1998; Miller, 1997). Rene's partner, Robbie, was committed to helping Rene parent their child, and they began living together shortly after Charlene's birth. Their relationship was quite rocky for a while, beset by typical adolescent issues such as jealousy over real or suspected interest by each partner in other people. Marie, their parent guide, supported their efforts to make a go of their relationship and helped them obtain couple's therapy. Shortly after Charlene's first birthday, they got married. Keeping these young fathers in the picture often benefits both the young mothers and their babies. When teen fathers have been a part of the decision-making regarding pregnancy and birth, they tend to be more involved later with their children (Miller, 1997), and teen mothers with support from the babies' fathers exhibit more responsiveness to their babies (Caldwell & Antonucci, 1997).

Marriage is not as common as it was in the previous generation of adolescent parents, but it does occur. The divorce rate is high for teenage marriages (Lamb, 1998; Osofsky & Eberhart-Wright, 1988), but the children of mothers who married (especially older teen mothers) tend to fare better than those of mothers who stayed single (Caldwell & Antonucci, 1997). Even when teenage parents do not marry, some fathers are involved in the care of their young children, at least in the beginning. Some other fathers want to be involved but face obstacles for doing so.

Many teen mothers live with their parents, and some of these parents (and the teen mothers, as well) blame the fathers for the pregnancies and are so angry that they ban the fathers from any contact with their babies (Miller, 1997). In some families, the mothers, grandmothers, and great-grandmothers harbor intense anger at men that is projected onto the babies' fathers (Tatum et al., 1995). Often the teenage fathers are in school and unemployed and are unable to support the mothers and their babies. They feel guilty because they cannot fulfill the role of breadwinners for their fledgling families (Caldwell & Antonucci, 1997). Their ability to deal with these stressors is complicated by the fact that they too are dealing with the developmental issues of adolescence (e.g., the search for identity). Marie was consistently available to Charlene's dad, Robbie, just as she was for Rene. She met with the two of them together when possible but mainly was available to Robbie by telephone. He did not hesitate to call Marie when he had questions or concerns about Charlene or about his relationship with Rene. Rene's and Robbie's commitment to each other and to Charlene combined with their many strengths (e.g., Rene's persistence in finishing school), and Marie's guidance and support enabled them to build a strong family together.

Life Skills

Parents differ in the extent to which they possess a variety of skills that can make their lives, and consequently their children's lives, run more smoothly. Money management skills (e.g., the ability to budget and to shop wisely) are important for any family and especially so when income is low. A number of communities are offering workshops on job-related skills (e.g., how to prepare resumes, interview, dress appropriately, be responsible on the job) to help parents move from welfare to work. The extent to which parents possess good social skills affects the ability to garner social support as well as to get and hold jobs. In communities across the country, life skills courses (e.g., Survival Skills for Women; Thurston, 1982) are being offered in a variety of environments—programs for teenage parents, family resource centers, homeless shelters, drug treatment programs, language and culture classes for new citizens, and reentry programs for individuals coming out of prison.

Parent guides can help parents strengthen their life skills in both direct and indirect ways. Social skills often evolve as parents experience countless interactions with their guides that are thoughtful, sensitive, and responsive. Within these caring relationships, guides and parents can reflect on parents' personal aspirations and identify together what might be impeding the parents from realizing them. Then, guides can provide some direct assistance (e.g., helping them problem-solve and be more reflective, connecting them with services in the community) to help parents develop the skills needed to meet their personal goals.

When Lynette left Hugh and moved with Jeffrey and Tina into her own apartment, Helen reviewed with her the needs and goals she had earlier set forth in her individualized family support plan and asked, "Now that you have your own place, I was wondering if you have some other sorts of needs and goals that you would like to work on." Lynette replied that she had bought a car and that between having to pay rent and car payments she now lacked enough money to keep Jeffrey in child care. She told Helen, "I need help with money management, and I'd like to attend a parenting class." Helen reinforced Lynette's desire to strengthen her skills in these areas and told her about a parent education program that offered money management counsel-

ing. When Lynette expressed interest in this, Helen gave her the telephone number of the program's facilitator and agreed to contact this person and let her know that Lynette would be calling her. Then, Helen followed up at the next visit to see how it had worked out for Lynette.

This chapter addressed some of the ways parent guides nurture parents and enhance parent–child interaction while helping parents obtain resources to deal with such challenges as substance abuse and mental retardation. The next chapter addresses other circumstances within the caregiving environment that challenge parents' abilities to parent well and what the role of parent guides is when working with families in these circumstances.

11

Families Matter

How Family Circumstances Influence Caregiving

When, at the beginning of one of their home visits, Helen asked Joanne how her baby Chrissy was doing, Joanne sadly responded, "Things aren't going too well." With Helen's encouragement, Joanne told Helen about her latest episode with her husband: "He's at it again. Last week he pushed me so hard I fell against the door. I went to the ER—I thought my nose was broken." She went on to explain that fortunately her nose was not broken and that, as battered women so often do, she had made up a story to the emergency room physician about how she was injured. She then sighed and said, "I'm not sure how much more I can take."

Domestic violence is just one of the environmental circumstances that makes life difficult for parents and their children. Inadequate housing, community violence, poverty, and lack of social support are all circumstances that strain parents' abilities to parent their babies and toddlers well. A combination of any of these adverse environmental circumstances with some inadequacy of personal resources (e.g., depression) constitutes a major obstacle to parenting; however, favorable environmental circumstances such as adequate financial resources and a supportive social network can be a boon to parents of young children and can help them in their efforts to address any lack of personal resources they might experience. This chapter examines some of the ways in which certain environmental circumstances have an impact on families and their children and presents some ways in which parent guides can support and assist families experiencing these circumstances.

In addition to environmental circumstances such as the adequacy of material resources and social support, there are numerous other, often related, stressors that can chip away at parents' time, energy, and emotional resources for parenting (e.g., number of other people in their care, loss of employment, family crises, illness of a family member). Although all families can be expected to encounter these or similar stressors from time to time, sometimes stressors can be too great for parents' personal or social supports to manage in ways that avoid their seriously compromising the quality of their caregiving. In supporting parents, their guides need to carefully assess both the family's stressors and their strengths, including social supports, that can reduce the effects of these stressors on the parent–child relationship.

Environmental circumstances for babies and toddlers also include the type of care they receive from caregivers other than their parents. An increasing number of babies and toddlers receive regular supplemental care in child care centers, family child care, and homes of relatives and family friends. Some babies and toddlers experience longer-term separations from their parents when they are hospitalized or placed in foster care or when their parents are hospitalized, incarcerated, or divorced. These environmental circumstances and how parent guides can help with them are addressed in Chapter 12.

SOCIAL SUPPORT

Parent guides who have ongoing contact with parents typically become important sources of social support for these parents. This circumstance is especially true for guides who visit parents regularly in their homes. As parents develop trust in their guides and as guides provide emotional support and concrete assistance to the parents, it is natural for parents to develop some dependency on their guides. This is to be expected and, for some parents, can be a significant opportunity for them to learn that there are people who are dependable and trustworthy. The task for guides, however, is to help parents strengthen their social support systems and gradually lessen their dependency on them. Guides do this by helping parents:

- Map and evaluate their social support networks

- Strengthen and, if needed, expand or change these networks

- Enhance their social skills

In addition, parent guides can help enhance the support parents can receive from their communities.

Map and Evaluate Social Support Networks

Social support comes from many sources, both informal (e.g., family members, friends, neighbors, fellow employees) and more formal (e.g., nurses, ministers, rabbis, parent guides, social workers, therapists). Combined, these sources of support form the parent's social support network.

Parents' social support networks may differ in a variety of ways. They may be large or small, stable or fluid, and members of a network may be close at hand or widely dispersed. There may be a lot of give and take or the network relationships may lack reciprocity. Members may support and nurture one another, frequently denigrate or argue with each other or exhibit some combination of these two styles. Recipients of support differ in how they perceive the helpfulness and the availability of various sources of support. Social support for one person in the family may have a negative effect on other family members. For instance, a grandmother may feel in competition with her daughter's and granddaughter's parent guide.

Parents, especially mothers, may feel socially isolated for a number of reasons. They may lack access to their sources of support because they have no telephone or transportation, or they have a controlling partner who does not permit access. They may live in a depressed neighborhood where they can gain social contact but very little useful support from neighbors who are just as stressed as they are. For many parents, family members are their preferred and most stable sources of support, but for some this support is limited by geographical distance. Sometimes kin or other members of a social network make more demands and create more stress than they provide useful and valued support.

Functions of Social Support   Members of social networks, both formal and informal, provide many types of support:

- Emotional sustenance (e.g., sympathy, pep talks, reinforcement of instances of positive parenting)

- Counseling, advice, guidance, and information (e.g., how to get a spot out of the carpet, how to help your toddler sleep through the night, who is a good auto mechanic, where to get substance abuse counseling)

- Material resources and assistance (e.g., financial assistance, help with moving, a ride to the health clinic)

- Skill acquisition (e.g., car maintenance skills, parenting skills)

Some functions, such as social monitoring and social control (e.g., noting and reporting child abuse), may be exercised by members of the informal social network but fall more often to members of the formal network (Thompson, 1995). Other functions (e.g., recreation, romance) are more often carried out by members of the informal network although there may be recreational activities at a family resource center. Spiritual sustenance may come from both formal and informal sources of support within an individual's faith community.

All of these aspects of social support need to be considered when helping parents assess, enhance, and utilize their social support networks (Dunst et al., 1988; Thompson, 1995). As part of the initial assessment process, parent guides can ask parents about their social support network (Project AIMS, 1990). They may preface this assessment by saying, "Taking care of little ones is a big job. Most parents find they need lots of support from others—someone to go to when they need help with things or answers to questions, a shoulder to cry on or simply someone to relax and have a good time with. One way in which I can help you help (name child) is to know more about what kind of support you have and what more you might want and need. All parents deserve to have support for the important job of parenting their little ones."

What people are available for various types of support? If certain classes of people are not mentioned (e.g., friends, kin, neighbors), parent guides can ask about them. What kinds of support might these people offer? Do they currently or have they in the past provided this type of support? How helpful are they? How does the parent feel about accepting support from these people? Is there sufficient give and take in the relationship, and, if not, how can that be improved? As a parent guide and parent reflect together about the parent's social network, the parent guide can look for and reinforce the parent's strengths in this area, such as the parent contacting people in her social network appropriately as needed and offering to be a resource to others. Parent guides may also note (either mentally or out loud) issues that may need to be addressed. For instance, the parent may say that when she seeks help from a certain family member, they provide the help but belittle her in the process, or the parent may not seek help from a friend or neighbor due to shyness or depression. Parents' partners may forbid them from having contact with certain people who could be helpful. Lack of a telephone, transportation, or social skills are other obstacles to receiving social support. From this initial assessment and ongoing assessments as needs for support arise, the parent may discover areas in which their support network needs strengthening.

Strengthening Parents' Social Support Networks   After parent guides review the parents' social support networks with them, they can discuss with parents ways to strengthen their networks so they and their children can receive the support they need.

> *Lila confided to her parent guide that she felt very lonely and cut off from everyone. She and her 13-month-old daughter, Becky, had recently moved to a new state with her boyfriend, who then left them living in a trailer down a lonely road in the mountains. Not only did Lila feel isolated and lonely, but she had an extreme fear that she would have an asthma attack in the middle of the night and that no one would be there to care for Becky. Because she felt anxious and depressed, she went to the mental health center seeking medication. In addition to receiving therapy and medication, she was referred to a home visiting program for parents. Her parent guide helped her reach her goal of moving into town, and through one of her new neighbors, she connected with a church for social support.*

How parent guides help parents strengthen their social support networks will depend on the personal resources and circumstances of the parents as well as on available community resources. For some parents, as for Lila, linkage with a church of their choice can be a good beginning. As parents move into new jobs or educational opportunities, they can be encouraged and supported in forming new friendships. Family resource centers and support groups (e.g., a teen parent group, a battered women's group, AA, NA, Al-Anon, Parents Anonymous) are other options.

Many people are intimidated by the idea of just walking in cold to a new group of people. A parent guide can ease the way by first inviting the parent to go with her to a small parent's group or playgroup that she facilitates where the parent can meet other parents. The parent may then feel comfortable attending some other functions with the parents she has met. Parent guides will want to suggest groups and functions that they think would be a good match for this parent. To do this effectively, the parent guide needs to know the parent's preferences, abilities, interests, and needs for support and also to be familiar with characteristics of the support option (for example, its expectations, warmth, level of acceptance, hours of operation, availability of transportation) in order to maximize the possibility that the parent can indeed benefit from and enjoy the experience. An Hispanic mother of two young children with special needs told her early interventionist that she was very concerned about her husband's drinking. Her parent guide connected her with a facilitated support group of mostly Spanish-speaking women with similar concerns (i.e., husbands or partners who were substance abusers or were abusive toward them). Not only did the mother receive support for her concerns about her husband, but when her medically fragile child died several months later, the group was a source of support for her during her grief.

Even when parents recognize that they want and need to improve their social support networks, there may be barriers to their doing so: lack of transportation, telephone, child care, or awareness of opportunities; a controlling partner; shyness or depression; language barriers; support that is a "mixed blessing" (e.g., family helps them but also puts them down or is unreliable); "burned bridges" with kin and supportive friends; or attachments to kin, partners, or friends who are detriments to good parenting (e.g., substance abusers). Parents guides can reflect with parents about what seems to stand in the way of their gaining the kind of support they want and how they might overcome these barriers.

To overcome some of these barriers, parent guides may need to help parents draw on their existing support system or on community resources to obtain such things as transportation and child care. When language is an obstacle, the parent guide can seek an interpreter or, as Helen did with Angela (see Chapter 1), help her learn to ask in English for a given service. Some hurdles are more complex and require reflection and ongoing support from the parent guide to overcome.

Sometimes parents are receiving a particular kind of support, but the quality of that support is not to their liking. In these situations, parent guides can help parents sort out whether they should try to improve the way the support is being provided or if they should (and can) obtain the support from some other source. Even though she did not like the way Hugh interacted with the children (especially Jeffrey), Lynette continued to sometimes ask him to take care of them when she had something she had to do, like go to a therapy session, because she did not perceive that she had anyone else to ask. When efforts to help Hugh change his ways were unsuccessful, Lynette was encouraged to seek child care from other sources. Lynette's mother was willing to help her with child care (and in other ways) if she would leave Hugh. She also wanted to help Lynette manage her money more wisely so she would not have to be financially dependent on Hugh and his family. Lynette gradually came to the realization that she did want to leave Hugh, but she resisted the idea of letting her mother help her manage her money. Her parent guide reminded her that she had said more than once that she wanted help with managing her money. She helped Lynette feel okay about letting her mother help her in addition to taking a money management class. The next time the parent guide visited Lynette, she had left Hugh, and the children were being cared for by her mother.

Family members are a favored source of social support for many parents, but sometimes parents feel that this support is a mixed blessing. Joanne sometimes took her three children and moved in with her parents when she felt she had to leave her abusive husband. She also felt abused by her parents, however, because they were so critical of her, so she would return to her husband. Her parent guide proposed the option of moving to the battered women's shelter, but this change was too big a move for Joanne to contemplate at the time. So, the parent guide discussed with Joanne what she thought it would take for her parents to be less critical of her. When parents are open to it, parent guides can sometimes engage the grandparents as part of the team for the grandchildren and, by working with the extended family, help them resolve issues that interfere with the "team's" effectiveness.

Sometimes, the social support parents are receiving conflicts with what they and their parent guides are identifying as most helpful for them and their children. Friends and kin may offer advice that is contrary to good parenting practices (e.g., it's okay to put chocolate milk in the baby's bottle, to prop the bottle, to spank tiny babies, to let them just cry it out night after night). In these situations, parent guides can ask the parents questions such as: What do you think about it? What does your doctor or nurse or WIC worker say? The guide can explain that what others are suggesting may have been common practice at one time but that now we have learned that this is really not the best thing for babies and explain why. In these ways, parent guides can support parents in making their own choices without putting down the friends and relatives who are giving well-meaning but erroneous advice.

In these circumstances, parent guides may suggest to parents that family members and friends be included in one or more home or office visits where parent guides can have respectful discussions of these issues with all involved. As part of their effort to enhance mothers' informal support systems, the Elmira Early Infancy Project encouraged mothers' husbands or partners, close friends, and relatives to participate in the home visits and to provide other sources of support (Olds & Henderson, 1989). The Pride in Parenting Program strives to include key members of the kinship network in visits with parents and their children. It is, of course, up to the parents to decide if they want to do this and who they want to include.

Family ties may interfere with parents' forming new sources of support. As noted in the earlier discussion of teenage parents, a young mother may feel conflicted by her aspirations to achieve a better life for herself and her baby and her desire to not alienate her kin and lose that source of support by seeming "uppity" to them. Finding ways to maintain their relationships with family members while building other sources of support for their aspirations can be a daunting task for young mothers, one that parent guides can help them with. Suggestions for doing so are presented in the section on teen parents in Chapter 10.

Some parents have burned their bridges to important sources of support, such as their families. This behavior is especially true for parents caught up in substance abuse or abusive relationships. Joanne's parents eventually withdrew their support because their daughter kept returning with the children to her abusive partner. Lois, like many substance abusers, eventually became disconnected from her family due not only to her substance abuse and its accompanying lifestyle, but also because of the deep shame she felt about her life. It is often easier for people in Joanne's situation to regain their parents' support because their parents may view them as victims and be willing to help them if they are willing to leave their abusers. Substance abusing parents like Lois, whom we met in Chapter 10, may need to demonstrate a prolonged period of being clean and sober with significant changes in lifestyle before their families are willing to be supportive. Making amends, as directed in 12-step programs, may also help. Parent guides can encourage them to fully participate in a 12-step program (e.g., attend meetings, get a sponsor, work through the steps) by relating this to the welfare of their children.

Intimate relationships are a significant aspect of the social support networks of parents. Often, it is difficult for parents to relinquish these attachments even when they agree that these relationships are detrimental to them and their children. Mothers like Joanne often find it difficult to leave their abusive partners. (More about this topic will be discussed later in this chapter.) Parents in recovery from chemical dependencies may hang onto relationships with substance-abusing partners. This situation was the case for Lois, who continued to remain emotionally dependent on her boyfriend. Her recovery counselor noted that this constituted the biggest risk of relapse for her and made sure that this issue was addressed in Lois's treatment program. Her parent guide provided additional support and guidance by helping Lois identify other adults who could be supportive and by reinforcing the work being done in her individual therapy and her 12-step program. She highlighted for Lois ways in which her recovery work was benefiting her and her child.

An often overlooked feature of social support for a family is how the social support (and social supporters) for one person have an impact on other family members. For instance, a father may derive emotional support from his drinking buddies, leaving his wife feeling isolated and neglected. This situation was the case with the wife of an Hispanic farm worker. Back in their native country, she would have had other women nearby with whom she could socialize while her husband was with his friends, but she did not have any friends in her new country. To meet this need, her parent guide helped her connect with a group of other Hispanic mothers in similar situations who met at a nearby community center.

Some parent guides may want to consider providing a program specifically designed to help parents strengthen their support systems and mobilize needed resources. Results from such a program found that not only were the social support networks of the participating parents improved (i.e., more members and more supportive members), but also that these parents exhibited improved parenting when compared with a control group (Gaudin, Wodarski, Arkinson, & Avery, 1990–1991). Initial assessments of the parents' social networks, psychosocial skills, and barriers to development of their networks helped parents and program staff identify and set goals for the interventions. Interventions included personal networking with existing or potential network members to enhance supportive relationships, development of parent groups (e.g., for mutual problem sharing and solving), involvement of volunteers as well as neighbors who were already known in the community as informal helpers, and social skills training. Parent guides can incorporate many of the elements of the Gaudin et al. (1990–1991) program either directly or through linkages with other resources (e.g., parent groups, family resource centers).

Enhancing Parents' Social Skills   Parent guides assist parents in developing their social skills both indirectly through their relationships with them, and directly by helping them resolve relationship issues and by referring them for relationship counseling. By practicing the parallel process—that is, by being with parents as they would want them to be with others—parent guides can promote social skills in parents. In so doing, they not only model appropriate social behavior but they may also help parents modify their internal working models of what relationships are like. As parents experience trustworthiness, support, and caring from their guides, they may be able to emerge from their shells and soften their defensiveness so that they can both give and receive social support more effectively, as Maureen did in her work with a support group (see Chapter 1).

Help with Relationship Issues   Opportunities to help parents enhance their social skills arise when parents share with their guides problems they are having with friends, neighbors, or family members. Eric's mother, Ellen, complained to her parent guide that her parents felt that she was not able to parent Eric well due to her mental illness. Her guide helped her learn to be less reactive with her parents and to develop less confrontational ways of responding. As Ellen became less defensive, her guide helped her to see the ways in which her family was being supportive of her and Eric.

Sometimes social support relationships become lopsided—one person does most of the taking while the other does most of the giving. When this occurs, the provision of support may foster feelings of dependency or indebtedness on the part of the recipient and feelings of being used and burned out on the part of the giver. When this happens, parent guides can help the receiver find ways to give back (e.g., make and take to their helper their favorite dessert) thus making the relationship more reciprocal. In doing this, the parent guide is also highlighting for the parent that they have strengths—they have something to give. Parent guides can help parents who are "givers" (i.e., who feel overwhelmed by demands made of them) set better boundaries.

Participation by the parent in a program with which the parent guide is affiliated can provide opportunities for social skills development. When parents interact in this controlled and familiar environment, program staff can assist those interactions and model acceptance and responsiveness for the parents gathered there. Parents can gain skills and confidence in the more sheltered environment that they can then use in other informal social support situations. After each group attended, the parent and parent guide can talk about what it was like.

Janice and her 18-month-old, Sally, went with their parent guide, Wanda, to a parent–child playgroup. At one point, Sally started to enter an area where she should not have gone. Because her mother did not get her, another mother did. When Wanda later asked Janice how the group was for her, she said she did not like it that the other parent made Sally leave this area. Wanda played out the event with Janice until Janice was less angry at the other mother and felt that she could have some power if she were ever in a similar situation again. Janice needed to be in the "calm water" of her own home to sort out what had happened and how she might respond differently next time. While in the "white water"—the turbulence—of the infant-toddler playgroup, Janice would not have been able to do this. Some parents need this one-to-one time with their parent guides in calm waters in order to reflect on what has happened, think about alternatives, and sometimes even practice (e.g., role play) these alternatives. In this way, they can build social skills that will enable them to enjoy and more effectively utilize these opportunities for social support. Without this help, some parents may not go back to the group.

Enhance Community Support   All families draw on a number of community resources to support their childrearing efforts (e.g., treatment programs, social services, recreational opportunities, child care, faith community). When the number of resources needed is great and the ability to obtain them is limited (e.g., lack of telephone, transportation and child care, low energy due to depression), the task of mobilizing needed resources can be especially challenging. Even when these obstacles are over-come, others may be present such as the shear number of different places to go, redundant forms to complete, long periods in waiting rooms, and sometimes surly treatment by staff. Josephine, a volunteer social worker at a child care center, took a couple of children from the center to a com-munity agency, where she was treated with gruffness and condescension until the receptionist realized she was a social worker and not the mother of the children. Without pointing a finger at any one person or agency, parent guides can advocate for family-friendly, relationship-based prac-tices within the community.

The previous section explored some ways in which parent guides sup-port and assist parents to obtain social support both from formal and in-formal sources. This section presents some of the ways in which parent guides can help community resource providers be more supportive of the parents with whom the guides work. Guidelines for improving integration of services and resources are presented in Chapter 12.

Effective community efforts to support families in the crucial respon-sibility of promoting the early development of their children include the following characteristics:

- Supports are comprehensive and integrated within the community (see Chapter 12).

- They invite family participation in planning support services.

- They draw on families' informal sources of support as well as more formal community resources to meet families' needs.

- They are accessible to families.

Parent guides can facilitate this whole process through both their for-mal contacts (e.g., interagency meetings) and informal contacts (e.g., oc-casional lunches and coffee breaks) with members of other programs.

Family Participation   In a state preschool interagency planning meet-ing, Dianne, a parent guide, successfully advocated that state guidelines for local preschool interagency councils require inclusion of parents in in-teragency meetings to plan services for their children with disabilities, thus following the principle, "nothing about us without us." Once parents are invited to meetings, the next challenge is to determine how to effectively include them. The first obstacle is scheduling. Professionals, especially those with families, often do not want to take time away from their fami-lies to attend meetings in the evenings or weekends, but many parents work weekdays, so they cannot attend meetings during the professionals' regular work hours. Often programs find that they can accommodate parents' schedules by having meetings in the early morning, evening, or on Saturdays and then adjust the schedules of staff as needed. For instance, one family resource program scheduled each staff member to be at their family resource center one Saturday a month and to take off another day during that week.

Although it is essential that parents attend meetings in which their children are discussed, other meetings, such as those for community planning, can involve parents in other ways. Parents who cannot attend (or do not feel comfortable attending) these meetings, can give their input by proxy—that is, via their parent guides. In order to provide opportunities for a number of parents to provide input to a task force on family support, one community had a series of family forums on the topic, asking such questions as: What does family support mean to you? What would be some resources that would be useful? Are there barriers to obtaining existing resources? In addition to input from parents who participated in these focus groups, parent guides solicited responses from other parents and reported their responses to the groups.

Professionals are accustomed to participating in meetings, but often parents are not. If professionals want to involve parents at the table, they need to help them be effective voices at the table. One county contracts with a mediation center for one of their staff to serve as a facilitator of the meetings, thus providing a disinterested third party who is trained and skilled in helping people talk about difficult issues. Several communities provide leadership training for parents who wish to serve on community committees. Another strategy is to identify someone in the group (committee, task force, board) who pairs with a parent as a mentor. Sometimes, parents choose an advocate or mentor to come with them to meetings during which placement for their children will be discussed. Underlining this process has to be the belief that parents want to do what is right for their children and that parents have something important to contribute to discussions about their children and about community services for families. Professionals are not the only ones with expertise!

In some communities, *action teams* responsible for planning for children in the child protection system now include family members and other informal support resources. People around the table commit to the support activities that the family and the team identify as needed for meeting the needs of this family's children. Parent guides can help parents identify those people that they think could provide such support and invite them to the team. This often includes clergy, neighbors, and kin. If parents are not able to identify informal support resources, it is the responsibility of the service community to be aware of community volunteers that could be introduced to these families. It really does take a village to raise a child.

Meeting Families' Needs for Support   Parent guides can work with others to both plan ways to strengthen their communities' ability to meet families' needs as well as to meet the needs of the specific families with whom they work. Many communities now realize the need for comprehensive strategic planning regarding resources for children and families. Communities That Care is a promising model for such planning. In this model, community stakeholders and leaders with political or statutory power and consumers engage in a thorough assessment process that identifies community needs for prevention and for intervention services across a broad spectrum of resources. Based on that assessment, funding is targeted and integrated to achieve sustainable services available to families for the future.

To both strengthen community resources and to meet specific needs of families, representatives from a wide variety of programs for young children can meet on a regular basis to increase integration of services and to identify gaps in community services. They can staff individual families whose needs are not being met by current services, and together they can problem-solve how those needs might be met. Sometimes the solutions come from helping families to more effectively obtain an informal social network such as the time one such community group helped a young mother obtain respite care from some women in a group member's church.

Community services are more effective when they are relationship-based and the platinum rule is practiced in all contexts, not only with parents but also among resource providers. In her influential book about effective community programs and how they can be successfully replicated, Lisbeth Schorr stated, "Successful programs operate in environments that encourage practitioners to build strong relationships based on mutual trust and respect. It is the quality of these relationships that most profoundly differentiates effective from ineffective programs and institutions" (1997, p. 10). Parent guides assist this by modeling the platinum rule— by doing unto other resources providers as they would have them do unto parents. The most potent thing parent guides can do in this regard is to listen nonjudgmentally to other resources providers to hear what their hopes and fears for a family or families are. Then, as they would want providers to do with parents, they would ask reflective questions to help them discover ways in which they could act that would help families move toward these hoped-for outcomes. For example, a parent guide worked with a child protection worker who was resisting the idea that 1-year-old Tim needed to be reunited with his mother who had complied with her service plan. First, through listening and asking reflective questions, the parent guide helped the worker articulate her fears about the mother's limitations. Then, they were able to devise a very specific set of observable behaviors that could be monitored in the home and provide the data needed for future decision-making regarding this family.

Parent guides can also directly advocate for the relationship-based reflective approach. Even when directly advocating, however, they need to keep the parallel process in mind. For example, a parent guide hopes that a Guardian ad Litem (GAL), who has great power in the local courtroom, will acknowledge the positive attributes of a mother, though they both know that in the past she had not been able to protect her baby from abuse by her boyfriend. The parent guide first asked about and listened respectfully to the concerns for the baby's safety that were paramount in the GAL's mind. Only then, after joining him in those concerns, could the parent guide describe the progress she had observed in the mother and ask for a more nonjudgmental look at the mother.

To be truly supportive of families, services and resources must be readily accessible. Parent guides can help with this by maintaining awareness of any difficulties that the families they serve encounter in their efforts to obtain services and resources for their children and themselves. Guides can then advocate for the needed changes (e.g., in schedules and locations of services) while in the meantime helping families find ways to overcome these barriers. Accessibility includes how receptive and approachable help providers are. Parent guides, who often have a more complete understanding of a family, can help other providers appreciate some of the family's strengths just as Lynette and Hugh's parent guide did for them.

Faith Community   Parent guides can use any discussion of social support as an opportunity to inquire about past, present or desired connection with a faith community. Lynette told her parent guide, Helen, that she was reluctant to leave Hugh because she did not have anyone else to support and help her. (This was before she reconnected with her mother.) Helen asked her if in the past, or presently, she was involved with a church and if a church was a place that could be a source of social support for her. Lynette said that she used to attend a church but was not doing so now. She added that a member of a church that she had gone to for some material assistance had visited her recently, so she had decided to try that church. When Helen inquired about this church on subsequent home visits, she learned that Lynette and her children were attending the new church and that the members of the congregation were supportive of her and the children. A little later, she told Helen that she was to be baptized the next Sunday. When Lynette told Helen that going to this church was helping, Helen asked, "Can you tell me how is it helping?" One of the things Lynette said was, "I feel that God loves me." The church was more than just a social support system for Lynette; it put her in touch with feeling beloved by God, as she understood God.

Involvement in a faith community can be a strong positive influence on the caregiving environment of infants and toddlers in several ways. As an informal support system, religious organizations can provide emotional support in the form of other parents who are experiencing parenting as a new role and experienced adults who may offer validation and a listening ear. Concrete support in the form of "parents' night out," parenting classes, "mother's morning out," marriage enrichment groups, and crisis help are often available in faith communities. At least as important as the social supports offered by faith communities is the spiritual nurturance that adults and children may receive there. One mother, who as a child had been cared for by various family members due to her mother's illness, credited the perception of being cared for and protected by a loving God that she encountered in a church as a major way that she coped with the uncertainty of the caregiving she received.

Patricia mentioned to her Parents as Teachers parent guide, Melanie, that she was looking for some occasional child care. Melanie told her about the "mother's morning out" program at a local church, and Patricia started taking her child there. When the church offered a 4-week parenting series, she went to it. She met people there who were in the Sunday school class, so she started attending that class, as well. When she learned that the church had trained lay counselors, she requested to meet with one of them. She later became involved in a church program that paired older adults with families, like foster grandparents. When Melanie first started visiting Patricia, she was extremely shy and anxious. With the multiple sources of support she experienced through her faith community, she grew into a confident and competent young woman and parent—confident enough to speak out at a public meeting about the need for child care.

Involvement with a church or other religious organization, however, is not always a supportive experience for families. Churches can sometimes be places where people feel underdressed or hear, as one mother did, such comments as, "If you'd just be nicer to your husband, he wouldn't beat you." A parent guide heard her pastor say to another parishioner, "If you pray earnestly, then the devil that made you mentally ill will go away."

Spousal Support   Although social support from any source can be very helpful, spousal support is especially beneficial and can moderate adverse effects of stress (Crnic, Greenberg, Ragozin, Robinson, & Basham,

1983). (Note: To avoid cumbersome wording, the term *spouse* will be used to refer to both an intimate partner as well as an actual spouse.) The quality of spousal support, of course, depends largely on the quality of the spousal relationship. One study found that even when there were differences in individual psychological adjustment, mothers were warmer and more sensitive with their 3-month-olds, and fathers held more positive attitudes toward their babies and their roles as parents, when they were in close and confiding marriages as assessed prenatally (Cox, Owen, Lewis, & Henderson, 1989). In general, mothers with low social support and unhappy marriages tend to behave less optimally with their babies than do mothers with good support networks and happy marriages (Teti & Gelfand, 1997).

Having a supportive spouse can be especially beneficial when one of the parents has a mental illness. In a study of 77 children of parents who were hospitalized for mental disorders, the subgroup of children who were functioning well tended to reside in families that maintained warm and active interrelationships among its members (Fisher et al., 1987). The presence of supportive others in the caregiving system is important both directly, by offering the baby a positive experience of warm and sensitive caregiving, and indirectly by supporting the parent who is struggling with a mental illness or some other challenge (e.g., a chronic health problem). Fay experienced bouts of severe depression throughout her adulthood, but the strong support she felt from her husband as well as other family members and friends, enabled them to raise two healthy children.

Fathers can provide many types of support to the women who are the mothers of their small children, including assistance with child care and housework along with emotional and economic support. Although fathers of young children tend to emphasize breadwinning and socialization as their major responsibilities, many say they would prefer to spend more time with their children and worry because they do not (Russell & Radojevic, 1992). These researchers also found that fathers tended to be more involved with child care when they were included in decision making prior to the birth of the child, attended the birth, had opportunities to learn about child development and parenting skills, and were encouraged by the mothers to share child care. They noted that some mothers who overtly sought the fathers' involvement covertly viewed it as encroachment on their domain of perceived power and expertise.

Sometimes mothers, especially ones who feel a bit shaky in their parenting role, need help in feeling okay about sharing this role with the fathers. They may get jealous when their babies and toddlers pay attention to their fathers. For example, Maureen became annoyed with Victor when, at age 9 months, he loudly protested his father's leaving for work. Celeste, who was there at the time, wondered aloud: "I'm wondering what makes that crying so hard to take today." Maureen responded that it really irritated her that Victor would "prefer" his father when "I take care of him all the time and try to keep him happy, and his father hardly pays any attention to him." Celeste responded, "It feels like he doesn't appreciate how much you're trying to help him, huh?" In this way, Celeste normalized the situation and avoided taking sides with either parent. Some mothers feel especially threatened when they perceive someone else—even their baby's father—as being a better parent. By being sensitive to this, parent guides can help these mothers feel more confident in their parenting role so that they can accept the important contributions of the fathers. Both fathers and mothers can benefit from knowing that fathers can play a special and beneficial role in the lives of their babies and toddlers (Pruett, 1997).

Unfortunately, in some families the men who are or could be in the father role are a potential threat to the welfare of the children due to their abusive behavior, substance abuse, or other problematic behavior. In these situations, when attempts to involve the fathers in treatment are unsuccessful, parent guides often end up supporting the mothers in leaving these men for the welfare of both the mothers and their children. Of course, if the situation poses an immediate threat to the children, CPS should be contacted if the mother does not remove the children from the situation.

In a number of other families with whom parent guides work, there is no male presence in the household. If the mothers so desire, parent guides can work with them to help them identify appropriate males in their family or community who might serve as male role models for their children (Pruett, 1997). In doing so, parent guides will want to be sensitive to feelings these mothers may have about men based on past experiences they have had with males.

Many parents are single and do not have any spousal support during at least some of the child-rearing years. One out of two children in the United States will live in a single-parent family at some point in their childhood; one in three are born to unmarried parents; and one in four lives with only one parent (Children's Defense Fund, 2001). These parents, who are most often mothers, are in special need of strong social support networks.

There are also parents with spouses who are less supportive than they wish they would be. They may complain to their parent guides that their partners are overly critical or emotionally unavailable, or that there seems to be a lot of tension between them. Kate's parents, Julia and Jackson, talked at first individually and then together with Helen about their conflicts. The problem that emerged from these discussions was that Julia would get upset with Jackson but she would not tell him, so he would keep on doing whatever it was that was bothering her. She would then become more withdrawn and depressed and get sharp with him. He could not understand what was going on, so he would get angry with her over these behaviors. The fight would escalate. Helen, their parent guide, listened to their complaints and helped them get couples counseling. She also reminded them of the tremendous strain they had been under dealing with the aftermath of abuse of Julia's first child by an ex-boyfriend. By normalizing their need for extra support, she helped them cooperate in marital therapy and benefit from it.

Spousal Abuse

Instead of receiving support from their spouses or partners, some mothers are subjected to abuse of various forms (physical, sexual, emotional) from their partners. This had been the case at one time or another for a number of the mothers described in this book. An estimated one in three American wives are physically abused by their husbands at some point during their marriages (Straus & Gelles, 1986) and such abuse is the single major cause of injury to women, more common than muggings, auto accidents, and cancer deaths combined (Committee on the Judiciary, U.S. Senate, 1992).[1]

People often wonder why women choose—and stay with—partners who are critical, domineering, or abusive. Parent guides can work more effectively with women caught in abusive relationships when they appreciate some of these reasons. An understanding of the influence of internal working models of self, others, and relationships can shed some light on this question. For instance, women who at a deep level view relationships as being power-oriented and view themselves as unworthy of care are particularly susceptible to joining with partners who fit these models. Such partners will be demanding, controlling, and have expectations of their spouses that they do not have for themselves. Often, beneath their bravado these men are very insecure and needy, which hooks into the strong desire some women have to feel needed. As Carol, who after several years left her abusive husband, explained, "Their neediness can be quite a turn on—our relationship was very passionate." Some additional reasons that women remain stuck in abusive relationships include the belief (and assurances from their partners) that the man will change, the feel-

---

[1]Because in many cases the victim is the woman and because virtually all of the research and clinical literature pertains to male perpetrators of abuse against women, this discussion will center on abuse of women by their male partners and will be referred to as spousal abuse whether the couple is married or not. The authors are aware that spousal abuse by women sometimes occurs and recommend that parent guides address any effects this may have on the welfare of the children by focusing the parents' attention on the needs of their children and by encouraging the couple to seek counseling.

ing that their children need a father, fear that if they leave their abuser will kill them or that they will lose their children, and real or perceived lack of economic resources to live on their own. Furthermore, as one woman who left her abuser after a period of years explained, "They do such a psychological number on you that you begin to believe you're not worth anything and that you can't make it on your own."

Strengthening the Caregiving Environment   When parent guides learn of—or suspect—spousal abuse, the first step is to let the mother know that they are concerned for her safety and the safety of her children and explore with her what she wants to do about it.

Helen nodded sympathetically as Joanne told her about going to the emergency room after being hit by her husband. After a brief pause, Helen then asked where their three children had been while this was happening. She asked this question to help Joanne keep in mind that she was not the only one adversely affected by her husband's abusive behavior. Often it is concern for the children that motivates mothers to finally leave abusive situations. After learning that the younger children were outside playing in the yard with their older sister, Helen said, "We've talked before about how hard this is for you." Joanne responded, "Yeah, I know. He's so mean." Helen said, "If you decide to leave him, is there a friend or someone in your family you could stay with?" Joanne replied, "Yeah, my mama, but she's so mad at me for going back to him last time that she might not let me come there again." Helen asked, "Is there anyone else?" Joanne shook her head, "No, not really." When Helen then asked her if she wanted her to check out the women's shelter, Joanne just sighed and said, "I don't know. I'll think about it." Helen replied, "You know I don't want you to be hurt, and I don't want the children to get hurt either." Joanne said, "Oh, but he won't hurt the kids." On this and other occasions, Helen continued to explore with Joanne her feelings about her situation and how it had an impact on her and her children and to let her know about her options.

When some mixture of the many reasons why women stay with abusive partners combines with deep depression, as was the case with Joanne (and many other battered women), leaving the abusive relationship can seem too difficult. The unknown may feel more scary than the life they are accustomed to. Parent guides can explore with mothers their reasons for not leaving and then problem-solve with them ways to overcome these barriers. Sometimes, as for Joanne, they are not yet ready to seriously contemplate leaving, but parent guides can express their concern and willingness to help as well as plant seeds for thought such as the effects of the abuser's behavior on their children and the fact that there are resources available to them should they decide to leave. Over time, these efforts combined with ongoing nurturing may help these mothers find the strength to move out—and stay away. It took several separations and returns before Joanne became strong enough to be on her own with her children.

This vacillation is not unusual for women living with abusive partners. Another mother, Carol, said that she not only had seesawed between living with and leaving her husband but had actually divorced and then remarried him before finally leaving him for good. The fact that these women sometimes feel that they continue to love their abusive partners should not be overlooked. Carol said that it was very helpful to her when staff at the women's shelter acknowledged her feelings and then explained to her that it was more loving of her to leave him than to stay and let him continue to engage in behavior that was destructive for him as well as for her and the children. "Viewing it this way," she later explained, "helped me not feel so guilty about leaving him."

While domestic violence knows no economic boundaries, women who are poor often have fewer resources for escaping the violence. In order to help mothers who want to leave violent households, parent guides need to become informed about the options available in their communities. If the mother leaves with her children, where can they stay? For how long? What opportunities are there for employment and for child care while she seeks a job and then while she works? How realistic are her fears that she will lose her children because she does not have stable housing and income? What kind of threats has her partner made if she should leave? Does he have a gun? How can she protect herself and her children from reprisals from him? Helpful information can be obtained about local options from the community's battered women's program.

Parent guides can also advise mothers to gather together the things they will need to take with them should they decide to leave with the children, such as an extra set of keys, spare cash, change for phone calls (avoid credit cards, which can be traced), extra clothes, identification cards, driver's license, car registration, personal pictures and other special items, jewelry and other valuables, children's favorite toys and blankets, and important documents (e.g., birth certificates, social security cards, school and vaccination records, work permits, green card, passports, divorce papers, medical records, insurance papers). Gondolf (1998) suggested that as many of these things as is feasible be stored at a friend's house or in a prepacked bag that can be grabbed quickly. Such a bag, however, would need to be inconspicuous.

Sometimes parent guides do not hear directly from mothers about spousal abuse, but observe things that make them suspect that it is occurring. They may observe bruises and other injuries that are explained in unconvincing ways, or the mothers may say that their partners will not let them attend the playgroup or other events or appointments. This kind of controlling behavior is often an indicator of abuse that is either occurring or likely to occur in the future. When parent guides observe signs of injuries, they can ask caring questions about what happened and let the mother know they are concerned about her welfare and the welfare of the children. If the mother is vague (or her answer does not seem reasonable) and she has previously alluded to abuse by her spouse, the guide can refer to these previous comments about her spouse's behavior and add, "How can I help you and the children be safe?" She can continue to express her concern through such questions as, "What do you want to do now?" "Did you go to the emergency room or to the doctor?" "What did you tell them?" When it appears that the mother's spouse is being controlling, the parent guide and the mother can explore the mother's feelings about this. They can then problem-solve ways to respond.

Without direct and careful questioning about their spousal relationships within a supportive atmosphere, many abused women will not disclose what is happening for a number of reasons. They may fear reprisals against them or their children, they may feel ashamed, or they may be accustomed to being disbelieved or blamed. A study of women in a psychiatric outpatient clinic found that nearly 70% of the women had experienced major physical or sexual assaults, but nearly three-fourths had never disclosed this to a clinician despite in-depth social history interviews (Jacobson, 1989). Gondolf (1998) suggested that clinicians in such environments use "funnel questioning," that is, begin with a general open-ended question (e.g., how is your relationship going?) and move stepwise to more specific questions.

The Perpetrators   The needs of the men who abuse their partners should also be addressed, but they are often very resistant to receiving any kind of treatment because they do not think they need it. Most tend to deny or minimize and justify the abuse (Gondolf, 1998). They may claim that their wives or girlfriends deserved it or they may blame their behavior on their tempers, drinking, stress, an abusive childhood, or a really bad day. A high percentage of batterers appear to have psychopathology, and many of them were abused during childhood, leaving them susceptible to emotional hijacking and its out-of-control behavior. Although these men need and deserve treatment for their psychiatric disorders, that treatment in itself is usually not sufficient to stop their abusive behavior (Gondolf, 1998). This behavior as well as the constellation of controlling behaviors must be directly confronted and stopped, which can be done in a positive, supportive, and encouraging (albeit confrontational) way that helps expose the problem, establish that it can be changed, and engage the man in the change process. While some batterers are helped by such efforts, many are not. Between 30% and 60% of men who enter batterer programs drop out in 3 months, and about 20%–40% who complete the programs reoffend within 6 months to a year after the program (Gondolf, 1998). Wives and partners of batterers need to realize this fact and beware of false hopes that may put them back into harm's way.

Nurturing Parents   Women who are physically abused by their partners are usually emotionally abused as well. Although it is important to help all parents identify and build on their strengths, this fact is especially true for mothers who have been subjected to abuse (Browne, 1998).

Arely's husband often interacted with her with criticism, put-downs, derogatory descriptions of her as a wife and mother, and demeaning behaviors. One such behavior was so humiliating that she said she thought of it every day of her life and how totally degraded it had made her feel. During a home visit when Arely described how all of the members of her own family, except her grandmother, had also been very abusive of her, Helen asked her what had helped when people were mean to her. With a wistful look in her eye, Arely described how her grandmother would comfort her by stroking her head while telling her how much she loved her. Helen encouraged Arely when she was upset to visualize being with her grandmother, feeling her hand stroking her hair, and hearing her loving voice say, "My dear one." Arely tried this and later told Helen that not only was it helping her, but also was helping in her interactions with her 18-month-old, Noah. She described how this memory of her grandmother had helped calm her so that she could soothe Noah when, late one night, he had screamed and carried on because he was overly tired and could not get to sleep.

Sometimes helping mothers live with their abusive situations is about the best that their parent guides can do for them. For instance, one mother had been brought to this country from Central America by her husband who is an American citizen. Although he was very abusive of her, her options as an illegal alien were, at that time, very limited. She could have applied for citizenship as the wife of a citizen, but her husband did not allow her to have the papers that documented their marriage. If she had gone to a battered women's shelter, she feared that she would lose her children, and because she did not have a way of living on her own in this country, she may have been right. (Note: Parent guides who work with immigrants can obtain information about their rights by contacting

Immigration and Naturalization Services; their telephone numbers are presented on their web site, www.ins.usdoj.gov.)

As described earlier, even those women who do have more options for leaving their abusers do not find it at all easy to do so. They have a strong need to be nurtured and to have their strengths highlighted and enhanced. Often, they also need direct help in overcoming the effects of the criticisms and put downs that they have heard so often and have internalized. There is often a tendency for women who are abused to blame themselves for the actions of the perpetrators, an unfortunate opinion that sometimes is reinforced by others. Women in abusive and controlling relationships may also focus all of their attention on what their partner wants, says, and does.

> *Nineteen-year-old Vanessa is married to an abusive man almost 10 years her senior whom she both fears and admires. She left him once but is now back with him and expecting their first child. "Her conversation focuses almost entirely on what Patrick said about this, and what Patrick said about that, and what he wants to do," explains Sean, her cousin who wants to be a support person for her, someone she can turn to if and when she's ready to leave Patrick. Sean listens and then gently steers the conversation back to her, expressing interest in her ideas, her preferences, and her plans for the baby.*

It is often from these nurturing experiences that women can build the strength and confidence to move out and make lives of their own. Over time, the nurturance and support Clara received from her parent guide, Dianne, and her therapist, Litanya, helped her finally leave her abusive partner. Although she would leave and return and leave again, each time she left she seemed a bit stronger. As she grew in strength and confidence, her parents became more hopeful and helpful, thus increasing her social support system.

Spousal Abuse and Mental Health Disorders   Many women who are experiencing spousal abuse exhibit various symptoms of mental disorders including depression, dissociative disorder, anxiety disorders, and personality disorders (Gondolf, 1998). Nurturing these mothers includes helping them obtain the resources they need, which may include mental health treatment. Some battered women's advocates, however, feel that these symptoms are simply the result of the abuse and will disappear once the woman is out of the abusive situation. They express concern that a mental health diagnosis ignores the effects of the abuse and unnecessarily stigmatizes these women. This view contrasts with that of many mental health professionals who maintain that some battered women do have longstanding psychiatric disorders (e.g., borderline personality disorder) that must be recognized and treated. A growing number of both mental health clinicians and battered women's advocates are encouraging the diagnosis of posttraumatic stress disorder (PTSD) for battered women as the best available diagnostic option (Browne, 1993), recognizing that not all battered women suffer from PTSD or any other mental disorder (Gondolf, 1998). The principal challenge for all professionals is to interpret symptoms in the context of abuse and battering (Gondolf, 1998) and to ensure that these women have support for obtaining safety and resources (including mental health treatment when needed) for themselves and their children.

When mothers decide to take their children and leave their abusers, they will need support, counseling and assistance in establishing independent lives (e.g., housing, employment, financial assistance). They may also need support in navigating the court system to obtain restraining orders on their abusers and to protect custody of their children. If the mother is in a battered women's shelter or homeless shelter, her parent guide can collaborate with shelter staff in providing this assistance. If the mother moves in with a relative or friend, the parent guide may be able to enlist the shelter's staff's aid in supporting and protecting the mother and the children. In many communities, even if the mother is not living in the battered women's shelter, she can still attend their groups.

Enhancing Parent–Child Interactions

Spousal abuse victimizes not only the mothers but also their children, both directly as witnesses and sometimes victims of the abuse (O'Keefe, 1995), and indirectly as a result of the effects of the abuse on mothers' parenting behaviors. In homes where domestic violence occurs, children are physically abused and neglected at a rate 15 times higher than the national average (Osofsky, 1998). Physical abuse of the mother can result in injuries that interfere with her parenting and may involve separation from her children if the injuries require hospitalization. Seeing or hearing abuse is stressful and often frightening to even the youngest witnesses. Child witnesses to violence are especially at risk for PTSD if they have a close relationship to the victim or perpetrator (Zeanah & Scheeringa, 1996). Symptoms associated with PTSD have been documented in children as young as 20 months (Groves, 1996). Sometimes mothers minimize the adverse effects that witnessing spousal abuse might have on their children, thinking (or hoping) that if the children themselves are not being abused, then it is not harming them.

When Clara would describe Hank's abusive behavior of her (e.g., yelling at her and calling her obscene names and sometimes pushing or hitting her), her parent guide, Dianne, would ask, "And where was Dee Dee while this was happening?" Clara would reply in a dismissive tone, "Oh, she was in the next room," or, if the altercation had occurred in the yard, "She was in the car." On one occasion, while she was describing an incident like this, Dianne responded as she usually did by saying, "You know, it's hard for me to imagine that she couldn't have seen it, heard it, and been affected by it." Clara's shoulders sagged, and she looked down for a moment before replying sadly, "Yeah, I know. The other day, Hank was yelling at me, and Dee Dee ran in from the other room yelling, 'Don't you hit my mommy!' " Dianne said softly, "She's having to protect her mommy at age 3. She's being robbed of her childhood." Clara sighed, "Yeah, she shouldn't feel like she has to take care of her mommy." Dianne replied, "No, she shouldn't."

Chronic spousal abuse leads to various psychological conditions (e.g., depression, dissociation, agitation, anxiety) that impair mothers' abilities to be sensitive and responsive with their babies and toddlers. The mother may become so preoccupied with safety and survival that she is unable to fully assess her children's needs or mental states, or she may become numb or desensitized to the violence in her life to the point that she minimizes its impact on her children, just as Clara did (Zuckerman, 1998).

The sense of powerlessness and despair engendered by their partners' abuse can also lead mothers to feel inept and overwhelmed in their attempts to parent their children. Arely's behaviors with Noah, her 18-month-old, reflected her lack of feelings of self-efficacy and self-worth that were related to the abuse she experienced from her husband and from her parents many years earlier. She was stymied by Noah's budding independence, and she was frustrated by her inability to get him to comply. She also was so depleted that she had little to give him in the way of nurturance. Helen, who visited her weekly or more often when needed, was intentional about noticing and highlighting instances of Arely's positive parenting, for example, when she responded positively to Noah's wanting to sit on her lap and when, in another situation, she followed through firmly after saying "no" appropriately. Helen made sure Arely knew how important such parenting behaviors are for Noah's development. She encouraged Arely to continue doing those things during the week and promised that they would talk about her experience at their next visit. This provided yet another opportunity for Arely to receive positive feedback for her actions and to feel cherished. Arely became able to note for herself those interactions with Noah that were nurturing and appropriately authoritative, and the parent guide began to see more and more instances of helpful interactions that she could highlight. Such feedback was given in the larger context of the parent guide's validating Arely's perceptions of her husband's treatment of her and assuring her that she did not deserve this treatment. Helen also reminded her of her options.

Results of a recent 15-year follow-up study of more than 300 mothers and their children underscore the importance of addressing domestic violence for the sake of the children as well as for the welfare of the mothers. Families who had received regular home visitation during pregnancy and infancy had significantly fewer child maltreatment reports than families who did not receive home visitation; however, this beneficial effect of home visitation decreased as the level of domestic violence increased. This intervention did not significantly reduce child maltreatment among mothers reporting more than 28 incidents of domestic violence during the 15-year period since the birth of the child (Eckenrode et al., 2000).

Strengthening Community Resources

Parent guides can play an important role in disseminating information about spousal abuse and in advocating for enhanced community resources. For instance, parent guides who facilitate parenting groups can inform all of the parents about spousal abuse. These parents can then serve as informal resources to women, both within and outside the group, who may be suffering abuse. Some tips that may be useful for these informal helpers are

- Do not say the batterer is bad, doesn't deserve her, and so forth. Keep him out of the discussion as much as possible. Focus on her, her safety and your concern for her.

- Do not agree to keep a confidence when a child's safety is at stake.

- Tell her what information you have and that you believe she is being hurt and controlled. Let her know you care about her and that her safety is very important to you.

- Tell her there are ways to keep safe, and that together you and she will get the help that she needs. It is important for her to understand that she has options.

- Learn about domestic violence so you will understand about why she is confused.

- If she is 18 or older, let her know that you know she is an adult, and she is the one who must decide on what action to take and when. Let her know that when she is ready, you will be there to help her stop the violence.

- Be supportive of her, but not of the abusive relationship. Do not loan her money that will enable her to stay in the violent situation (even for children's clothes, doctor bills, and so forth). Let her know that you will support her as much as you can when she is not in the violent relationship.

- Warn her not to leave information about resources for battered women where the abuser might find it.

Parent guides can also draw on what is being developed in other communities to advocate for improved services for battered women within their communities. Across the country, communities are strengthening their services in a variety of ways. In at least one community, child development and mental health services are collaborating to provide training to police and 24-hour crisis services to victims and witnesses of domestic and community violence (Osofsky, 1998). Mental health practitioners are screening for spousal abuse and cooperating with battered women program staff in attending to the special needs of women who have been abused (Gondolf, 1998). Legal services help women obtain restraining orders against their batterers. Programs for battered women work with other community services and businesses to inform the public, including potential victims, about the problem of domestic violence and specifically how victims can obtain safety for themselves and their children (e.g., placing brochures in health clinics and doctor's offices, posting hot line numbers in women's bathrooms).

In spite of its prevalence, the problem of spousal abuse is often overlooked. Several studies have found gross underreporting of spousal abuse by clinicians in psychiatric facilities, emergency rooms, and other clinical environments (Gondolf, 1998). Very few if any direct questions about abuse were asked, and when women volunteered such information there was often inadequate follow-up questioning. When the abuse was noted, it was often recorded simply as "marital discord." Not only do these experiences deny women opportunities to obtain the help they need, but they also belittle the importance of their suffering and can lead to a deepening of feelings of despair, guilt, and self-blame. Parent guides can check with the battered women with whom they work about their experiences in these environments and offset any negative perceptions arising from unsupportive encounters. They can also advocate for training of people like emergency room staff and police officers about the needs of victims of domestic and community violence.

Economic Resources

Raising children in poverty is a daunting task—one faced by far too many parents. The statistics are appalling: 1 child out of every 5 in the United States of America is born into poverty, and 1 of every 3 will be poor at some point in his or her childhood. *Poor* means living below the federal poverty line ($13,290 for a family of three) and 26% of poor children live at less than half that level (Children's Defense Fund, 2001). In 1999, unemployment was down and more parents were working, but many were still poor. As they moved from welfare to work, many entered jobs that paid below-poverty wages; 78% of poor children live in working families who do not make enough money to escape poverty (Children's Defense Fund, 2001). Furthermore, employee fringe benefits such as health insurance are fewer or nonexistent for people on the bottom rung of the economic ladder. The lack of living-wage jobs can lead to long-term poverty that is especially detrimental to these families. Mothers who are either unmarried or gave birth in their teens and who are poorly educated have children who are especially at risk for long-term poverty (Furstenberg, Brooks-Gunn, & Morgan, 1987). However, as Furstenberg and colleagues state, based on their longitudinal study of children born to poor, adolescent mothers, "It is never too late for effective intervention" (1987, p. 128).

Esperanza is a single mom who came from Mexico with her husband, who then left her pregnant and with another child. Fortunately, Esperanza has strong inner resources (e.g., self-confidence, initiative, good problem-solving skills) and the appropriate paperwork to get a green card. Because her child was premature, she received early intervention services. Through her child service coordinator, Esperanza learned about computer classes for Spanish speakers. She completed these classes and found employment as a data processor. Her son was well cared for in a child care environment in which he also received special instruction to help him "catch up," as he had been born prematurely. After 2 years of these supports, Esperanza was able to provide for her child and herself and to also provide emotional support for other Hispanic parents.

Joanne and her children did not fare as well for quite a while. She continued to return to her abusive husband largely because she did not have a job and saw no way to house and feed her children on her own. Her perception that she could not obtain sufficient economic resources interacted with her long-standing depression, making it very difficult for her to develop and carry out a plan as Esperanza had.

Families living in poverty face many challenges. It often takes Herculean efforts to just provide the basics: housing, health care, child care, even food. Surveys conducted in 1997 and 1999 in 13 states found that although conditions had improved somewhat over that time, food concerns were still common. Half of the poor children lived in families that either worried about or had difficulties paying for food (Zedlewski, 2000). Often the only affordable housing is in unsafe neighborhoods where the elements that hold a community together and sustain its residents have long since disintegrated (Halpern, 1993). "Together, the correlates of poverty preoccupy parents in ways that undermine their preoccupation with their infants. These correlates sap parents' physical energy, try their patience, undermine their sense of competence, and reduce their sense of control over their lives." (Halpern, 1993, p. 78). Whether unemployed or working, parents experiencing stresses correlated with poverty can benefit from psychological and social support from their parent guides as well as concrete assistance in meeting their needs.

Nurturing Parents   The stress of dealing with the conditions of poverty can undermine a parent's sense of competency even when, like Esperanza, they have strong personal resources of mental and physical health and the ability to relate well with others (suggesting the presence of positive internal working models). They need the encouragement of parent guides who can highlight for them the strengths they have as people and as parents, and who can help them set realistic goals and achieve them as Esperanza's parent guide did with her.

When in addition to the day-by-day stress of trying to make ends meet, parents experience other difficulties (e.g., the legacy of a troubled childhood, substance abuse, social isolation), their ability to parent well can be severely compromised and their need for nurturance is heightened. This was the case with Joanne who, in addition to being poor, was depressed and in an abusive relationship. Her parent guide nurtured her by looking for and highlighting Joanne's positive behaviors, such as sending the younger children outside with their older sister if she saw things heating up between her and her husband so the children would not experience and witness conflict and violence. The parent guide also nurtured her by not being judgmental when she kept returning to her husband and by always taking a problem-solving approach with her. Her guide acknowledged how difficult her situation was while reminding her of her options and highlighting the needs of her children.

Parent guides also nurture parents who experience poverty by helping them identify barriers to their obtaining informal and formal support to meet both their emotional and instrumental needs. Helen did this when she helped Lynette overcome barriers to receiving support from her mother and assisted her in receiving support from a parenting program and Head Start.

Strengthening the Caregiving Environment   Child care plays a critical role in providing both psychological and social support to infants and toddlers *and* their parents, especially when parents must work at less than living-wage jobs. Parents who are working while parenting young children need child care providers to share with them the responsibility of nurturing their children, who are, after all, the community's children as well. Parent guides can help parents locate the best child care that is available and affordable as well as work with child care providers to strengthen their ability to nurture both the children *and* the parents.

Advocacy for more and better affordable child care is needed. A large national study found that families living in poverty tended to use informal child care (e.g., care by relatives, family-care homes) and that this care was often of poor quality. The children living in poverty who were cared for in child care centers, however, often received care of higher quality than that obtained by moderate-income families due to the availability in some communities of subsidized center-based care for poor families (NICHD Early Child Care Research Network, 1997b).

In addition to helping parents find quality child care, parent guides can help parents living in poverty to strengthen the environments in which they care for their children by accessing community resources to gain and maintain employment. Many communities offer training not only in specific vocational skills but also in job-related skills such as interviewing, resume writing, and appropriate on-the-job behavior. Developing these job-related skills in the computer classes helped Esperanza gain employment. Parent guides can inform parents of these and other community resources, such as the continued availability of food stamps for some people even after they have gone off of welfare, money management counseling that can help them stretch their limited financial resources, and ways to obtain affordable safe housing. They can also help them cut through the red tape that often ensnarls access to services, as well as advocate for more user-friendly policies and procedures in their communities.

Enhancing Parent–Child Interaction   Halpern (1993) asserted that the sense of powerlessness so often engendered by grinding poverty can have an adverse effect on parenting in various ways (e.g., failure to recognize children's achievements and encourage their mastery efforts). Parent guides can counter these feelings by acknowledging the challenges of dealing with poverty and by consistently highlighting for parents the positive things they are doing to improve their situation and to take care of their families. They can also engage in solution-finding with parents to seek ways in which the parents can carve out little pockets of time for their children, establish routines, and take care of themselves so that they have more emotional and physical energy for their parenting.

Culture

An environmental circumstance that is important for professionals working with young families to appreciate is the caregiver's culture. Culture is defined as the body of beliefs, values, and behavior patterns that identifies a particular group of people. Beliefs, values, and behaviors related to child rearing constitute a central aspect of culture. Diana Baumrind, in her discussion of differing child rearing practices reminds us that "what is 'normal' or 'expectable' in one culture frequently is anathema in another" (1993, p. 1301). Thus, in a family with roots in Guatemala, for example, the old adage (American interpretation), "Children should be seen and not heard," is counter to the preschool teacher's belief that the family should encourage the child to talk more. In some cultures, looking someone directly in the eye is a sign of disrespect; families from these cultures would resist the amount of eye contact other cultures find important. In some cultural groups, loud talking is an acceptable way to interact; yelling at a child in such a family does not necessarily carry with it the same sense of anger that it would in a family of a different culture. There is evidence of cultural differences in the manner in which physical punishment is used with children (Baumrind, 1972, 1978; Deater-Deckard & Dodge, 1997; Deater-Deckard, Dodge, Bates, & Pettit, 1996; Kelley, Power, & Wimbush, 1992). In a number of cultural groups that live in the United States, seeking help outside the family has a certain amount of shame associated with it; reluctance to come to a program or a clinic should not be interpreted as "resistance" or lack of motivation.

Professionals who wish to be helpful to families from cultures different from theirs should respectfully learn as much as they can about how to interpret behaviors and communicate nonjudgmentally with these families, perhaps through consultation with someone else from that culture. They should furthermore keep in mind that there are individual differences even within a given culture and should listen and watch carefully and openly in order to learn more about how it is with this particular family and its cultural beliefs.

Community Violence

Far too many parents face the constant stress and challenge of trying to keep themselves and their children safe while living in communities characterized by frequent and unpredictable violence. Efforts to cope with the ongoing threat of violence often entail behaviors that limit opportunities for both parents and children. For instance, both parents and children may keep to themselves, thus missing social support that families in less threatening environments can enjoy, and children who must be kept indoors are deprived of outdoor play. Even when family members themselves are safe, the exposure to violence committed against others is very stressful. In a study of children in a low-income, high-violence neighborhood in New Orleans, 91% of fifth graders had witnessed some type of violence (Osofsky, 1998). Another study found that every child living in a public housing project in Chicago had had firsthand encounters with a shooting by age 5 years (Garbarino, Kostelny, & Barry, 1998).

In some communities, parent guides and other help-providers have initiated programs that coordinate efforts of social services agencies and the police department (Marens, 1994; Osofsky, 1998). For instance, in New Orleans child development and mental health services provide educational programs for police trainees and officers on the effects of violence on children, and these programs are integrated with a 24-hour mental health crisis referral and consultation service (Osofsky, 1998). Police officers report feeling more comfortable and supported when intervening when they have more education about such matters as children's responses to exposure to violence, conflict resolution, and referral services.

It is a testament to the strength, commitment, and ingenuity of some parents that they are able to raise well-adapted children in neighborhoods characterized by violence, disarray, and drug dealing (Kozol, 1995). A study of first and second graders raised in violent neighborhoods in Washington, D.C., found that 67% of those raised in stable, internally safe homes were doing well both academically and socioemotionally, whereas none of the children from unstable, unsafe homes were doing well in these two areas of development (Richters & Martinez, 1993).

Intervention Community violence is one of the aspects of family safety and well-being that parent guides and parents deal with in their work together. As parent guides assess family needs early in their work with parents, neighborhood safety is one of the topics that would be addressed. If parents are concerned, parent guides can assist them to set and work toward the goal of relocating, offering whatever concrete assistance is appropriate and possible. As with other areas of change, however, parents are in different places in their ability to do what might be in their children's best interest. Some parents may need help moving from contemplation of the problem of safety to actually making a move. They may need someone to "speak for the baby" by asking questions about safety issues and then supporting them in making changes that are indicated. For example, it appeared to nudge Clara another step toward moving away from a violent home environment when Dianne and her therapist helped her to stop minimizing the effects of Hank's behavior on her child. Other parents are more ready for action; their need is for help finding a solution and moving toward it. Concrete assistance, like making telephone calls, may be needed. Still other parents, who may not have the choice of leaving a violent neighborhood, may need ongoing support and reinforcement for their efforts to provide stable and internally safe homes where they are—homes in which their children can experience sensitive and consistent care.

Homelessness

About one third of the homeless population are members of homeless families, and homeless children comprise the fastest growing segment of the homeless population (Lindsey, 1998). Family homelessness is expected to increase even further with the reduction of public assistance, especially as families meet their limits on assistance or when the economy takes a downward turn. Approximately 80%–85% of homeless families are headed by single women. The causes of their homelessness are varied—some people escaped from abusive relationships, others lost their jobs or did not earn enough to maintain their housing. Failure of some absentee fathers to pay child support contributes to the problem.

The structure and rules of homeless shelters originally designed for single men and women are not well suited to the needs of families. For instance, many shelters require that residents, regardless of the weather and the age of the children, must leave the shelter in the early morning and not return until dinnertime. Furthermore, some shelters require that the residents look for work during this time period, a difficult task when there is no available child care. Most shelters forbid the use of corporal punishment, which is difficult for some mothers unless shelter staff help them learn other ways to discipline their children.

The recent trend toward provision of transitional housing for homeless families is an effort to address some of these problems (Dunlap & Fogel, 1998; Fogel, 1997). Transitional housing programs provide longer-term housing along with various social services, both directly as a part of the housing program (e.g., parent support groups, life skills training, money management classes, conflict resolution training) and in collaboration with community programs (e.g., substance abuse treatment, vocational training). Often plans with personalized goals are developed with each resident when they enter the program. These programs serve as a bridge between emergency shelters and permanent housing.

Interventions   Staff of homeless shelters are in an excellent position to provide guidance and support to parents. Parents in shelters need the same interventions that are needed by parents in their own homes: sensitive and responsive relationships and supportive policies, people, and environments. Shelter staff and others in their communities need to advocate for resources so that this kind of parental support and guidance is available in shelters that house parents and their children. Optimally, in order for shelter policies and practices to support families, they should:

- Develop individual goals and action plans for gaining the skills (e.g., money-management, job readiness) and resources (e.g., employment) necessary to obtain and maintain permanent housing. Support and monitor implementation of these plans.

- Allow parents of infants and toddlers to stay in the shelter during the day when necessary (e.g., when they or their children are ill), caring for their own children and providing respite for each other with supportive supervision.

- Provide or help parents obtain quality child care so that their children are well cared for while they look for work or participate in treatment and training programs.

- Provide parent support groups and opportunities to learn positive parenting.

- Grant parents as much authority and control as possible regarding daily care of their children (e.g., bedtimes, bath times, eating arrangements).

- Train staff in basic child care practices and in relationship-based intervention so that in their day-to-day work they can interact with both the parents and their children in ways that enhance parents' ability to parent well. For example, they can model nonviolent discipline, highlight instances of nurturance and appropriate limit setting, and build supportive relationships with parents (Zeifert & Brown, 1991).

- Teach parents conflict management and problem-solving skills in their day-to-day interactions with staff and through opportunities such as community meetings and support groups in the shelter (Fogel, 1997).

- Provide opportunities, as needed, to learn other life skills (e.g., money management, job-readiness skills, GED classes), to receive mental health and substance abuse treatment, and to obtain legal services.

- Provide parents counseling and support to help them resolve their emotional crises. This will help the children as well as the parents. It is difficult for parents to calm their children as long as they are upset and scared and worried.

Conclusion

The tremendous difficulties faced by some parents—mental illness, drug addiction, spousal abuse, homelessness—challenge the professionals working with these families as well as the parents themselves. The relationship histories of some parents make it difficult for them to trust and accept help from others. They may act hostile or apathetic, be demanding or seem indifferent, leaving parent guides feeling that cultivating caring, trustworthy relationships is nearly impossible. Parent guides can become so overwhelmed by the constant crises that plague some families that efforts to help the parents enhance their interactions with their babies and toddlers gets lost in the maelstrom. Some parent guides must deal with CPS, the court system, the child care system, and other community agencies whose practices and policies are sometimes at odds with what the parent guides hope to accomplish with the families. Tough decisions must be made. Are the resources that are in place sufficient to assure the child's psychological and physical well-being so the child can remain with the parent and thus preserve the child's attachment to that parent? Is a contemplated helping behavior going to be truly supportive or will it just enable the parent to remain stuck in self-defeating behavior? Parent guidance can be emotionally and intellectually demanding; the task can seem overwhelming and the parent guide's own sense of self-efficacy can feel threatened (Halpern, 1995).

REFLECTIVE SUPERVISION

Parent guides need and deserve support and supervision that helps them handle their own feelings as well as develop the special helping skills that their work requires. This support comes, and these special skills are taught and honed, in the context of reflective supervision, a process that parallels and supports the reflective intervention of parent guides with parents.

Lynette's parent guide, Helen, found herself overwhelmed by the litany of problems Lynette presented at each home visit; she found herself being engulfed in Lynette's whirlwind of anger, blaming, and frustra-

tion with members of her family. She wanted to facilitate positive change in the environment in which Jeffrey and Tina were growing, but she felt a bit like Sisyphus in the Greek myth—as soon as she pushed a particular rock to the top of the mountain, it and she came tumbling down under the force of yet another crisis or change of focus on Lynette's part.

Helen's supervisor used a reflective model of supervision. First, she asked nonjudgmental and open-ended questions that allowed Helen to step back and examine her own thoughts and feelings about what she was observing and doing with Lynette and her family. "What are your goals for Lynette and Jeffrey? Do you know what Lynette's goals for herself are? Are your expectations of Lynette realistic?" Then they collaborated, with the supervisor highlighting Helen's strengths as they worked through her concerns. "You have been very respectful of Lynette. She knows that you care about her and her family, and that you are there for them. I wonder if it's time to encourage Lynette toward more independence and accountability?" Her supervisor provided support so that together they could deal with the emotional and intellectual challenges of the work. "It sounds like you're feeling like all your hard work is not paying off. Let's look at where Lynette has come from, instead of how far she still has to go."

In this collaborative effort, Helen's supervisor supported her in making difficult decisions when needed. "Yes, I agree that it's time to let Lynette know there are consequences for her not being home for visits more than twice in a row. It does seem time to talk with her also about keeping Jeffrey in child care regularly. Let's talk about how you might say these things, still showing respect for her efforts." They also discussed ways to strengthen Helen's efforts to utilize community resources to address this family's needs so that Helen could have more time and energy to focus on the parent–child relationships and how well the children's needs were being addressed.

Even in the midst of program constraints, this type of reflective supervision on a regular basis was protected, as a vital part of a parent guide program that sought to address the obstacles to nurturant parenting that Lynette and others that Helen visited were facing. Through the parallel process, Helen was able to maintain the same working relationship with Lynette that her supervisor had with her; one of reflection, collaboration, and regularity, the three main elements of effective supervision (Fenichel, 1992).

For supervisors and supervisees not trained in a mental health field, some of the skills involved in relationship-based reflective supervision are unfamiliar and may even seem contrary to what they learned in their own professional training (Bertacchi & Norman-Murch, 1999). Supervisors may be accustomed to being responsible for setting the agenda for supervisory sessions; they may understand supervision primarily as a response to something wrong or below expectations; or they and their staff may have experienced supervisors as people who are there to judge their work. One of the authors had the experience several years ago of a new staff person who confessed after a few weeks, "When you said we would have scheduled supervision, I got really anxious; for me that meant someone coming into my classroom, watching me, then telling me what I was doing wrong." Both supervisors and supervisees may have to learn a new paradigm when doing relationship-based reflective practice. The best guiding principle for supervisors in this situation is to practice parallel process (Pawl, 1994–1995) and to follow the platinum rule as it fits the supervision process: Do unto parent guides as you would have them do unto parents.

Regularly scheduled meetings for both individual and team supervision are essential. Although impromptu meetings to address crises may also be needed, if these are the only times supervision occurs then it becomes entirely reactive rather than proactive. In proactive supervision, staff can build understanding and skills in a particular area or follow a particularly complex family situation. For instance, in one peer supervision session, staff in a home visiting program came prepared to discuss a particular professional journal article and how it related to their work with families. At other times, the staff of this same program shared and supported each other as they dealt with such things as client deaths and babies with serious disabilities and other serious injuries. Together, they faced their emotional pain and experienced support to move forward.

Clarification of what each party can expect from supervisory meetings is a necessary first step, especially for parent guides who have not experienced this type of supervision before. Supervisors can make it clear that during their meetings they expect to hear how things are going with the families served by their staff and that they will all work together to problem-solve solutions to difficulties and to celebrate the accomplishments of families and staff. Staff members who are unfamiliar with this type of supervision may restrict their discussions to paperwork and billing issues. Although these issues may need to be addressed at times, staff can be gently reminded of the importance of discussing what is going on with their families during both individual and team meetings. Some staff may be uncomfortable talking about their work with their supervisor, fearing that they will be judged and criticized. This parallels the experience some parents have, especially initially, with their guides. In both situations, care is taken to establish relationships in which the supervisees—and parents—can feel safe in talking about what is happening and in expressing their fears, hopes, and concerns. Establishing a sense of trust, safety, and mutual respect between supervisor and supervisee is just as important as doing so between a parent guide and parent.

The strategies of reflective questioning and wondering that are used with parents (as described in Chapter 3) are also used in supervision to prompt reflection (e.g., about underlying issues or transference issues) and to help staff discover solutions to difficulties they and the families they serve might face. A parent guide came to her supervisor with concerns about a mother's anger toward her 2-year-old. To help the parent guide reflect on her reaction to the mother's anger, the supervisor asked, "What might happen if you asked Joey's mother what she finds upsetting in his behavior?" The parent guide answered, "I think she find's it upsetting because . . ." The supervisor said, "But what might happen if you asked *her* that question?" The parent guide responded, "Maybe I could learn more about how I could help her." The supervisor said, "Why don't you try it and see." (This conversation is presented in an abbreviated form—usually such an interchange would take about 10 minutes). Such dialogues can help parent guides develop a clearer vision of their work with families. "The supervisor or mentor offers an enlarged perspective, another pair of eyes, a mirror" (Fenichel, 1992).

Staff are also encouraged to discuss their own reactions to experiences they have with families. As discussed previously, countertransference issues occur in all human relationships and need to be managed so that they do not disrupt the important work parent guides do with families. This concept was illustrated by the earlier example of Janet, the parent guide who came to supervision almost in tears because the mother she was to visit that day had just been hostile and blaming on the telephone.

Supervisors can ask questions designed to help staff become more aware of their own assumptions, values, and reactions to a family or child. This should always be done from a position of support and collaboration, so that the staff person does not feel ashamed of their reactions or interpretations, but rather helped to grow in their ability to do their work. If, for example, the supervisor gently "wonders" aloud to the worker about the meaning of an event or a behavior, she establishes a relationship of mutual inquiry rather than critical judgment (Bertacchi & Norman-Murch, 1999).

Supervisors must balance the function of mentoring with that of monitoring the performance of the staff they supervise. An important way of integrating these two functions is to maintain a steady focus on the mutual commitment and responsibility to their work with families (Bertacchi & Norman-Murch, 1999). This approach works best when practiced consistently rather than waiting for formal performance evaluations. So, for example, staff are expected to bring to scheduled supervision a list of families and/or issues that they want to talk about in supervision. At times, the supervisor would ask, "For next time, let's discuss that family in more depth; I'll look over the record so I'm up-to-date, and I'd like you to think about particular issues you'd like to talk about."

Responsibility for monitoring staff performance also means that supervisors sometimes must confront staff. Setting limits with staff is similar to the need for them to set limits with families (see Chapter 3). If a parent guide has lost perspective about a family or another agency and this affects the quality of her work, the supervisor should help her look at this in terms of her goals for families and her role. As with other situations, the supervisor's goal is to guide, not to criticize. "How do you think saying it that way (to a CPS worker) will help you work with this family?" or "How do you think the mother understands your giving her your home telephone number?" She might also suggest that next time they discuss a family who had not been reviewed recently.

When Reflective Supervision Is Not Available

When reflective supervision, as described above, is not available, parent guides will need to seek support and guidance from other sources. These sources can include their colleagues and supervision from professionals in their field. In one program, the parent guides who were particularly interested in helping parents enhance emotional development met biweekly to share readings about infant mental health and to discuss and support one another in their work with families. In another community, parent guides from different programs (early intervention, health department, social services, child care centers) came together once a month for a similar purpose. Support and guidance for this work can also be obtained from the annual conferences of ZERO TO THREE: National Center for Infants, Toddlers, and Families and training sessions provided by the Infant Parent Institute in Champaign, Illinois, and The Reginald S. Lourie Center in Rockville, Maryland. A resource for supervisors who wish to provide reflective supervision is *Learning through supervision and mentorship to support the development of infants and toddlers and their families: A source book* by Emily Fenichel (1992), published by ZERO TO THREE.

In addition to needing support and guidance themselves in order to do the challenging work of supporting and guiding parents, parent guides often must collaborate with others in the community to meet the needs of families. How effectively a community nourishes its families often depends on how well various community helpers work together. The next chapter discusses ways in which parent guides can support efforts within their communities to provide a well-knit safety net for families, including child care for children.

12

Weaving a Safety Net

How Communities Support Caregiving

Lynette's and Hugh's efforts to parent their children well were challenged in may ways. Their relationship was tumultuous; they disagreed about almost everything. Although they both were very committed to their children, some of their strongest disagreements were over how to parent their children. Hugh's hot temper often got him into trouble, and Lynette had been diagnosed with depression and personality disorder, for which she had received treatment from a psychiatrist intermittently. The pregnancy with Jeffrey had been difficult, and he was born a month before his due date. He was hospitalized at age 2 weeks because of a respiratory infection and was in the neonatal intensive care unit (NICU) for 4 weeks. Around this time, Hugh had to be away for a few months, so Lynette had the challenge of caring for a sick baby by herself.

When Jeffrey was 10 months old, Lynette came to the mental health center to get medicine for what she called her "agitation." The intake therapist immediately called the infant-toddler services of the same agency, and Helen, an infant-toddler specialist, quickly joined them. Helen and the therapist made arrangements with Lynette for the first home visit, knowing from past history that after Lynette's present crisis, she would be hard to find again. Less than a year after home visiting began, Lynette and Hugh had a second child, Tina, who was also born prematurely and required a stay in the NICU. Lynette and her family illustrate the need of some families for collaboration and persistence by a number of community helpers if the caregiving environment is to support the emotional development of their children.

INTEGRATED SERVICES AND RESOURCES

Parent guides' efforts to promote positive parent–child interactions and to nurture parents may be insufficient in the face of factors in the caregiving environment that threaten parents' efforts to care for their young children. Poverty, mental illness, drug addiction, spousal abuse, lack of social support, and mental retardation are conditions that challenge many parents. Furthermore, some parents will need more than parent guides can offer them to overcome the negative internal models developed during their troubled childhoods that interfere with their efforts to parent well. In order for parent guides to be effective in helping parents meet these challenges and strengthen the caregiving environments for their children, they need a network of support and resources within their communities.

To be effective, the threads of a safety net must be tightly interwoven with no gaps for families to fall through. The people who came together to form a safety net for Lynette, Hugh, and their children were intentional in their efforts to weave a network of formal and informal support for them. The goal was to establish "a viable mother–child unit, embedded within an extended family and community and able to use available resources for continuing growth" (Minuchin, 1999, p. 25). Work toward this goal began with the first contact when the intake therapist was joined by Helen, who would become the family's parent guide.

Throughout their time working together, Helen, Lynette, her therapist, and her psychiatrist shared information about her progress and regression, adjusting their interventions as they received information from one another. Helen, as the parent guide, became the hub of formal and informal supports that were added and subtracted as the family's needs changed over time. For example, when Lynette, through her own work in therapy, became strong enough emotionally to make plans to leave Hugh, Helen helped her gain access to the agency network to get help with housing. She and Lynette's therapist worked closely together to support Lynette's tenuous efforts during this time. This process required regular contacts among Helen, the therapist, and the psychiatrist; it also entailed occasional sessions of all three together with Lynette. These sessions helped Lynette to experience the team that was both supporting her and holding her accountable. Because the home visiting program was part of the community mental health program, confidentiality was not an issue and collaboration was facilitated. Responding to Jeffrey's need for more consistent caregiving while his mother was in her own transition, Helen helped Lynette arrange for child care, planning with the director to ensure a smooth transition. Lynette also wanted the help and support of her parents, from whom she had been somewhat estranged during the past 2 years. Because her mother was unwilling to support her unless she agreed to leave Hugh, Lynette asked Helen to contact her mother and back up her statement that she was, in fact, making moves in this direction. Helen did this, and Lynette's mother was invited to participate in the support network growing around Lynette and her children.

The pediatric specialists, the parenting guide who made home visits, Lynette's therapist and psychiatrist, the social services agency, the child care provider, and Lynette's extended family could not have accomplished separately what they were able to accomplish when services and supports were integrated. The presence of one person who serves as the "hub" or resource coordinator for the family is often crucial to the success of efforts to provide the family the assistance they want and need. Helen served this function for Lynette and her family.

Some communities have found ways to truly integrate services and resources so that families are not faced with the loosely stitched patchwork of services that sometimes allows them to fall through the cracks or encounter conflicting expectations from different agencies. This integration can be a daunting task for an overburdened system that must handle complex situations quickly, but it can be done, as more and more communities are demonstrating, with beneficial results for children and their families. In one community, representatives from various programs and agencies come together monthly to search for "threads" to strengthen the safety net both for families of young children and the community as a whole. At one meeting, the group came up with a creative solution for a 16-year-old mother who had no family support or other access to respite care. One member of the group offered to see if any of the older women in her church "who love to babysit" would be willing to help, which they were. The group also noted the need to develop more resources for respite care in the community.

Creating Integrated Services

Minuchin (1999) listed five concepts that can guide the creation of integrated services for people in need: 1) the facilitation of connections and relationships, 2) a focus on strengths, 3) the recognition and resolution of conflict, 4) the balance between collaboration and boundaries, and 5) the handling of transition periods. (These concepts are illustrated next.) Children and families benefit when parent guides work to put these concepts into practice both within families and within their communities. The goal is to weave together all of the needed resources, both formal and informal, into a strong supportive fabric rather than simply moving family members from service to service like figures on a children's board game.

Facilitation of Connections and Relationships   The parent guide for Lynette and her family did several things to promote positive, supportive relationships at all levels—among Lynette and her children, Lynette and her mother, the family and service providers, and service providers. While Hugh and Lynette were still living together, Helen intentionally included him in her discussions with Lynette about the children, something they both seemed to appreciate. For instance, during one visit, when Hugh jumped up to attend to the children, Helen suggested that they could both go and settle the children and then both return to their discussion, which they did.

The challenge for parent guides is to maintain awareness of the importance of relationships at all levels and all times and to do what they can to promote these connections and relationships. Is there communication and joint planning among all of the people involved with the family? Are efforts made to strengthen the family's informal support system? Is the mother left out of the loop while her child is in foster care, or is she also in communication with her child's doctor, child care provider, and foster family? Do service providers get together sometimes for joint training sessions or for informal opportunities to talk over lunch or coffee?

In a research and demonstration project to study the effects of early intervention on the development of mother–infant attachment, monthly seminars on infant mental health were offered to a wide range of community providers working with families of infants, including child care center directors, public health nurses, CPS workers, and others (Gowen & Nebrig, 1997). These seminars both fostered the development of relationships within the help-giving community and developed a more common appreciation of the mental health needs of young children and their families. Furthermore, the intervention staff intentionally practiced parallel process as they built relationships with other professionals in the community and modeled and reinforced best practices in their interactions with these professionals. Everyone benefits when turfism is relinquished and help-givers nurture one another.

Focus on Strengths   The importance of focusing on the strengths of the family and its members when providing parent guidance was discussed previously. Parent guides can also help others who may not know the family as well as they do to appreciate the family's special strengths and positive attributes. Others tended to view Lynette as a very dependent woman and were concerned that she might abuse prescription drugs, and they saw Hugh as an emotionally abusive partner. They did not see any of their strengths. Helen, because she was a regular visitor in their home *and* because she deliberately looked for their strengths, was able to share what she learned with other providers. For instance, Helen observed how caring Lynette was of Hugh's grandparents, with whom they had lived for a time, and how Hugh was willing to overcome his pride and go to a therapist. Helen was aware of the many ways in which they demonstrated their commitment to their children. When Helen helped them see that Jeffrey became more aggressive after visits at his uncle's house where he was exposed to some rough friends of his uncle, they limited his visits with his uncle to get-togethers at their own home. Helen shared information about these specific strengths and efforts with some of the other professionals involved with this family, thus broadening their view of them.

Parent guides will find that their work with other service providers will go more smoothly when they intentionally look for and highlight their strengths, as well. These strengths can include, in addition to the person's area of expertise, such things as a sense of humor, an ability to cut to the chase in discussions of thorny issues, creativity in problem-solving, and knowledge of the community. Work on behalf of the family needs to be built on the strengths of all the players just as work within the family is built on the strengths of family members, and professionals appreciate having their strengths recognized just as much as parents do! When one member of Lynette's team became discouraged by lack of progress, it helped when others could reinforce what that team member brought to the family.

Recognition and Resolution of Conflict   Areas of professional expertise can sometimes act as blinders, narrowing the person's perspective in ways that shut out other aspects of a family's needs. Minuchin (1999) gives the example of the staff of the mother's drug rehab program who wanted to stop the mother's visits with her child as a consequence for her noncompliant behavior in the program, while the foster care staff wanted to protect the child's contacts with this mother. Minuchin explained, "Staff members on both sides were more concerned with the rightness of their views than the necessity to resolve the conflict on behalf of their clients" (p. 25).

Parent guides who are regular home visitors are often in a good position to help others step out of the box of their own professional concerns and perspectives to see the bigger picture of a family's overall needs. To do this, they need to recognize the mandates and constraints under which others are working, and understand each other's core beliefs and values about children and families. When conflicts arise, they will listen first to feelings and then to facts; they can then search together to find common ground. Regular interagency team conferences are needed to do this effectively.

Parent guides can also play a role at times in helping parents resolve conflicts within their informal social networks so that they can benefit from this source of support. The only informal social support that Clara had was from Hank's sister, Carolyn. They exchanged child care, and Carolyn often gave Clara a ride into town when she had a therapy or doctor's appointment. Clara felt that most of Hank's family did not care about her and her children and that they were critical of her parenting. "They think I should whip Dee Dee, but they whipped Hank, and I see how much good that did!" Whenever Clara perceived any indication that Carolyn might be siding with the rest of her family against her, Clara would get upset and not have anything to do with her, thus cutting off her one source of support. To Clara, it was a black or white situation—you're either for me or against me. Dianne helped Clara understand Carolyn's position as both her friend *and* a member of Hank's family; Clara was better able then to maintain her mutually supportive relationship with Carolyn.

Balance Between Collaboration and Boundaries   When community helpers collaborate with one another and with family members, they need to respect each other's areas of expertise, avoid encroaching on each other's turf, and respect the confidentiality rights of families. Although at least three services were being provided to Lynette and her family from the mental health center and two from other providers in the community, the distinct roles and responsibilities of each were clear. The home visits focused on the effects on the children of the mother's physical and mental illnesses and the parents' conflicts; issues about working out these conflicts and managing this illness were addressed by the therapist, the psychiatrist, and Lynette's physician. Health care for Jeffrey and Tina was managed by their pediatrician, and Jeffrey's day-by-day development was nurtured by his child care providers as well as by his parents. Other service providers (e.g., the housing agency) entered the picture as needed; much-needed family support was gained when Lynette reestablished her relationship with her mother. Efforts to work collaboratively as a team were balanced by recognizing and respecting each player's strengths and areas of expertise and clarifying each person's role and responsibilities. Although information was shared to some extent among the team members, care was taken to protect the family's confidentiality. The parent guide played a key role as the "hub" for these collaborative efforts.

The multiple needs and perpetual crises of some families can easily overwhelm professionals who are their parent guides (Campbell, Earley,

& Gray, 1999). Two conditions can help these parent guides protect themselves against these "forces of risk." First of all, parent guides need to be well connected with a strong, integrated network of community resources, both formal and informal, that they can help families access. Second, when fostering the healthy development of young children is their primary responsibility, parent guides need to be very clear with themselves, with the families, and with others in the community about their role. While they nurture the parents and help them strengthen their caregiving environments, they do so *in the service of the children*. Guides maintain this focus by keeping their eyes on the babies so they will not get lost in the deluge of family troubles. One enterprising supervisor hung a sign over her desk that read: "THE BABY! WHAT DID THE BABY DO?" (Campbell et al., 1999).

In these situations, parent guides often need to help parents keep *their* eyes on their babies as well. With parents who focus almost exclusively on their own issues (e.g., ongoing relationship problems), parent guides should acknowledge and deal with their concerns but also encourage the parent to consider how these problems are affecting their children. Parent guides need to keep in mind that the three foci of their work are 1) enhancing parent–child interactions and relationships, 2) nurturing parents so that they are able to interact and relate well with their children, and 3) helping parents strengthen their caregiving environments so that they have sufficient resources to parent well. It is a balancing act.

Handling of Transition Periods   The birth of a baby, the removal of a child to foster care, entry into a drug rehab program, transition to a new therapist for the parent or a new child care class for the child—all transitions, whether positive or not, are to some extent stressful. The stress can be lessened when community programs work together to provide support and to make transitions as seamless as possible. The first step is to acknowledge and facilitate the expression of feelings that accompany transitions— grief over losses, anxiety about change, expectations of benefits. Several ways in which children's anxiety over separation from parents can be eased are presented later in this chapter.

The feelings of parents and of professionals need to be addressed, as well. When Lisa stopped working when Ethan was born, she grieved the loss of both the companionship and support of fellow workers and the sense of self-efficacy she gained from doing her job well. Helen, her parent guide, allowed Lisa's expression of grief and then helped her find new sources of social support and to develop feelings of competence as a parent. When families move on to other programs, parent guides can experience the loss of the relationships they had developed with these parents and their children. Sometimes, parent guides continue to feel concerned about a family and wonder whether their needs will be met by the new program. In these situations, supervisors can help parent guides acknowledge and deal with these losses so that they can "let go" and not inadvertently sabotage the family's new relationships.

Transitions from one program or place to another go more smoothly when everyone involved begins early to prepare for the change and can remain connected for a period of time after the transition. For instance, in North Carolina, children eligible for early intervention services transfer from one agency to another at age 3 years. Formal preparation for this transition begins when the parents and staff from both agencies sit down together when the child is 30 months old. The group begins to address the following issues: What will this child need? What further assessments will be helpful? How will the desired services be provided? Can they be provided? The group then has 6 months to work on these issues and to resolve conflicts that arise, such as when parents want more than what the agency feels they can offer.

Conclusion

No matter how skillfully parent guides work collaboratively with other community helpers to nurture parents and to help parents strengthen their caregiving environments and nurture their children, it takes time for changes in parenting behavior to occur. In the meantime, the children continue to grow and develop. Strengthening the caregiving environment for babies and toddlers sometimes means giving them good supplemental care to ensure their healthy emotional development while their parents deal with their personal and family issues or go to work to support their families.

CHILD CARE WITHIN THE COMMUNITY

Many infants and toddlers spend time each week in some form of regular supplemental care—a child care center, family child care, in the home of a relative, or in their own home with a baby sitter. A large national study found that 81% of infants experienced regular nonmaternal child care during the first 12 months, with most starting prior to age 4 months (NICHD Early Child Care Research Network, 1997a). With the welfare-to-work initiative, an increasing number of parents must work; they, too, require child care. Sprinkled throughout this book are recommendations to provide children with quality supplemental care when parents, for a variety of reasons (e.g., depression, recovery from chemical dependency) are not able at that time to provide care that nourishes healthy emotional development. Quality child care, however, is in short supply in many communities. It is estimated that positive caregiving, whether in care centers or other environments, is either "somewhat uncharacteristic" or "very uncharacteristic" for almost two thirds of the children ages 1 to 3 years in this country (NICHD Early Child Care Research Network, in press). When quality child care *is* available, many families cannot afford it.

When parent guides inform themselves about the availability, affordability, and quality of infant-toddler child care in their communities, they can share this information with parents. When what is available and affordable is not good enough, they can perform a valuable service for families by advocating for more and better child care and by helping to educate child care workers about ways to meet the developmental needs of infants and toddlers. As part of a research and demonstration project, the authors presented monthly seminars on topics related to infant mental health that were attended by a variety of community help-givers, including child care workers (Gowen, 1993b). Information provided throughout this book about caring for infants and toddlers in ways that nourish healthy emotional development can be presented to child care providers as well as parents.

Care that is sensitive and responsive to their needs and interests is important to babies and toddlers regardless of who is providing the care. For instance, researchers found that the quality of supplemental care babies and toddlers had received was an important predictor of social-emotional behavior at ages 2–3 years, although the quality of maternal care was the most important predictor (NICHD Early Child Care Research Network, 1998). These and similar results from other studies suggest that quality child care is especially important when parents are unable for a variety of reasons to provide the type of care that fosters healthy social and emotional development.

Characteristics of Good Group Care for Infants and Toddlers

In addition to sensitive and responsive care from caregivers, characteristics of quality infant-toddler care in groups include the following, adapted from *Caring for Infants and Toddlers in Groups* (Lally et al., 1995):

- Small groups with high caregiver–child ratios are needed so that each child can receive the individual attention he or she needs. Recommended maximum group sizes and caregiver–child ratios: babies who are not yet mobile, six babies with two caregivers; up to age 18 months, nine children with three caregivers; 18 months to 3 years, 12 children with three caregivers; and for mixed-age groups, no more than two children under age 2 years per group.

- Continuity of care is needed so that the caregiver can learn to read the cues of the babies and toddlers in their care and how to respond to their needs. When each child is assigned a primary caregiver, then that caregiver and child can get to know one another and the parents also have one key person with whom they can interact regarding their child's development. Ideally, this caregiver will remain with the child from time of entry until the child is 3 years old. If this is not feasible, the primary caregiver should stay with the child for at least 1 year. At one time, some child care providers and parents feared that attachment to a child care provider might weaken babies' attachments to their parents; however, under the right circumstances, babies can become comfortably attached to more than one or two people. For these attachments to be secure, they not only need to be warm, caring, sensitive, and responsive but also to have some degree of consistency. For this reason, child care experts now advise child care centers to have one person who is the primary caregiver for each baby rather than interchangeable multiple caregivers (Howes, 1998).

- Meeting individual needs within the group context requires, among other things, an appreciation by staff of individual differences, including differences in temperament and how to respond to those differences. (See section on temperament in Chapter 2.) Flexible scheduling is also important, especially for babies so they can sleep when they are sleepy, eat when they are hungry, and play when they are ready to play.

- By establishing positive, respectful relationships and frequent open communication with parents, child care providers are better able to understand the needs of each child and to provide consistency of care. Efforts to understand and accommodate elements of the parents' culture and language will benefit the child and family. Support from the child care staff can be especially meaningful to parents who are struggling with issues such as those described in this book.

- A physical environment that is safe, healthy, and age-appropriate is also important for nourishing the emotional development of babies and toddlers. "The physical environment—indoors and out—can promote or impede intimate, satisfying relationships" (Lally et al., 1995, p. 41).

A national study of children in center care examined the association between meeting recommended standards for child–staff ratios, group sizes, caregiver training, and caregiver education and children's development at ages 24 and 36 months. The study found that children in groups that met more of these standards had better scores on school readiness and language comprehension as well as fewer behavior problems at age 36 months than did children in groups that met fewer standards (NICHD Early Child Care Research Network, 1999).

Separation from Their Parents

Whether the parent leaves the child at home with a babysitter or leaves the child in someone else's care, the separation from the parent is distressful for the child, at least until the child becomes familiar and comfortable with the new person and environment. As previously noted, separation anxiety typically emerges around age 7–8 months and peaks at about age 18 months. Parent guides can share with parents the following practices for lessening the anxiety of separation, whether parents are simply leaving the child for an hour or for a somewhat longer period of time, at home with a babysitter or in a child care environment (Brazelton, 1992; Lieberman 1993):

- If the child has never been left before, leave the child for just 15 minutes. Tell the child that you will return and then when you do, remind him that you said you would return.

- Make sure the child is familiar and comfortable with the caregiver and with the place in which he will be staying.

- Help the caregiver become familiar with the child's personal style, likes and dislikes, specific worries and fears, and daily routine.

- Encourage the caregiver to speak to the child about you during the separation, to let him know that it is all right for him to miss you when he becomes distressed and calls for you, and to reassure him that you will return.

- Send with the child a beloved toy (e.g., a stuffed animal) that can serve as a transitional object. Having something familiar to see and smell is especially important for young babies. Some parents bring the bumper pads from their babies' cribs to the child care center so their babies will have something familiar to see, smell, and touch.

- Let the caregiver know about your baby's usual routines (e.g., when you usually feed her, how she likes to be held, what often works to comfort her when she is upset).

- Stress what you and the child will do when you are reunited; be specific and realistic so that there can be follow through.

For a major separation such as the beginning of a child-care arrangement, tell your toddler what will be happening at least a few days before it actually takes place. Choose language that is simple and straightforward, and use a positive tone of voice. Give your child room to ask questions and express misgivings. Tell him what he will be doing while you are apart. Reassure him that you will be thinking of him and teach him that he can think about you during the separation. These preparations work particularly well with older, more verbal toddlers, but younger toddlers can understand simpler explanations and a reassuring, loving tone of voice. (Lieberman, 1993, pp. 151–152)

Careful handling of the parent's reunion with the toddler is also important for helping the toddler adjust to separations. Toddlers who had been holding it together during their parents' absence can break down and cry on reunion or even express anger toward their parents for leaving them. This reaction can be a crushing blow to a parent who is expecting a joyful reunion with a kiss and a hug. Parents can help their toddlers by acknowledging and accepting their feelings and letting them know that they are glad to see them. Parents can learn from the substitute caregivers some of the things their children did in their absence. Talking about this with their children can let them know that they care about them even when not with them.

Toddlers are also upset when separated from familiar caregivers and friends and moved to a different class in their child care center or nursery school (Field, Vega-Lahr, & Jagadish, 1984). Often they become fussy and have trouble napping. Two-year-olds even manifest these problems in anticipation of the move as well as afterwards. The transition is less troublesome, however, if a friend moves with them.

When babies and toddlers enter child care, the separations are often difficult for the parents as well as for the children. Sometimes parents feel that if their children need supplemental care it means that they have failed as parents. Guides can help parents realize that everyone needs a break now and then from caring for their children, especially when they are dealing with whatever issues the parents are confronting. One parent guide needed to assure the mother that she was being a "good mom" by letting her child go to child care and play with other children. She helped the mother see that she could have more time and energy for her child when he came home if she had had a break during the day. Parent guides can also support parents in dealing with any anxiety they might feel about leaving their children in the care of others. Their children will feel more secure in their child care environments when their parents are not worried about leaving them there.

Providing Support and Consultation for Child Care Staff

Although all children deserve supplemental care that meets the standards for quality presented previously, children who are living in troubled homes are especially in need of high quality care that is tailored to fit their needs. Parent guides are often in a good position to offer providers of supplemental care support and consultation as to how to meet the needs of these children.

Parent guides may want to get permission from parents to talk with their children's care providers about how the child care staff can best help their children. The guides can then serve as a liaison between the child care staff and the family as well as supporting parents in their contacts with the staff. When parent guides talk with child care providers, they can help child care staff understand any special needs of the children; they do not need to reveal any confidences of the families to do this. They can simply let the staff know that they are working with the child in the home (if that is the case) and that both they and the parents want them to see how the child is doing in child care. They can ask staff what they have noticed about the child (both strengths and concerns), what things they are trying, and what is working well for them and the child. Using the staff's responses to these questions, parent guides can then talk about what they have observed in the home and what they and the parents have tried that has worked well. In this way, they can provide guidance to the staff about ways to meet the particular developmental needs of the children and to enhance consistency of care between home and center. As parents become more confident, parent guides can facilitate their assuming this role for themselves.

If the supplemental care is fulfilling its purpose of helping children get back on course with their development, then improvements should gradually become apparent. Guides can assist child care staff in monitoring and supporting children's development by 1) informing them of the specific relational and caregiving needs of the individual children, 2) identifying some things to look for in the children's play behaviors and their interactions with other children and adults, and 3) discussing ways to build their relationship with the children to facilitate their development through their play and social interactions. Monitoring and guiding children's emotional development, as described throughout this book, is especially important.

Guides can also help substitute caregivers see their role as not only helping the child but also supporting the family. Sometimes caregivers want to "rescue" the child from parents whom they view as inadequate or worse. The guide can acknowledge caregivers' concerns for these children while helping them see that it is in the children's best interest for them to be supportive of the parents. Parent guides can counter negative attitudes and hopefully ward off competition between caregivers by sharing their appreciation of family strengths and the challenges faced by families (without breaching a family's confidentiality).

In addition to providing consultation and support to caregivers (including members of the family's informal network who provide care), parent guides can be helpful to families by becoming informed about the options for supplemental care that exist in the community. This includes knowing what types of care are available (family child care, child care centers, crisis nurseries, drop-in child care), how accessible the care is (cost and transportation), and the quality of the care.

LONG-TERM SEPARATIONS OF BABIES AND TODDLERS FROM THEIR PARENTS

Young children are separated either permanently or for extended periods of time from one or both of their parents for a variety of reasons: hospitalization of the child; death, hospitalization, or incarceration of a parent; divorce; or removal of the child from the parent's custody due to abuse or neglect. These separations can have profound effects on emotional development, given the importance of the establishment of children's attachments with their primary caregivers. Efforts to promote continued attachments of young children with their parents is essential if it is anticipated that the children will be reunited with their parents at a later date. As discussed throughout this book, attachments, emotion regulation, and internal working models are being formed by infants and toddlers during their early years. These developments occur within the child's relationships with a few significant caregivers. Therefore, abrupt and long-term separations from those caregivers (usually the parents) need to be taken very seriously and handled very carefully. Infants and toddlers notice and have strong feelings about what is happening to them even if they do not have words to talk about it. This phenomenon is poignantly illustrated in the video *Multiple Transitions: A Young Child's View of Foster Care and Adoption* produced by Michael Trout (1997).

When separations from parents must happen to young children, those who are making decisions will need to be very cognizant of these effects in order to help the children survive the experience with the least amount of disruption in the process of emotional development as possible. General considerations include having a familiar person as substitute caregiver whenever feasible; maintaining familiar routines and surrounding the child with familiar things as much as possible (clothes, food, blankets, and so forth); and having the adults work with each other, sharing as much information as needed to minimize the amount and the rate of change for the child. Many of the previously presented recommendations for helping children deal with short-term separations will also be helpful when children must deal with longer-term separations.

Although babies below the age of 7–9 months may not experience as much anxiety over being separated from their parents as older babies and toddlers do, they may be distressed by being in an unfamiliar environment and treated in unfamiliar ways. The baby's sense of security can be enhanced by making minimal changes in routines such as feeding (e.g., same formula, favorite finger foods and other solids, same time of day) and sleeping (e.g., being rocked, music box, crib size). Having familiar playthings, like a favorite stuffed animal, and even familiar odors can help (e.g., use of the bumper pad from the baby's crib, use of the same detergent to launder crib sheets). With toddlers, it is also helpful to have pictures of their parents and people who will talk positively with them about their parents. Robin's mother, Trisha, was in a psychiatric hospital for several weeks. The family's parent guide, Patti, arranged and facilitated weekly visits for Robin at the hospital, and looked at pictures of Trisha with Robin between visits. Robin could point to his mother in the picture when asked, "Where's Mommy?"

The negative effects of long separations are being addressed in some situations by allowing babies to be with their mothers when the mothers must be out of their homes. A few residential treatment programs for mothers with chemical dependency have arranged for babies to be admitted with their mothers, and at least one prison in the United States allows approved mothers to keep their babies with them until age 12–18 months (Harris, 1992–1993). More programs like these are needed to avoid the negative effects of long separations during this stage of development and to support the developing attachment of babies to their mothers and the mothers' continued relationships with their babies.

Children Placed Out of Home Due to Maltreatment

Sadly, parent guides occasionally encounter situations in which it is apparent that a parent is neglecting or abusing his or her child. In these situations, parent guides have no legal or ethical choice but to make a report to CPS. If there is reason to believe that dealing directly with the parent would put the parent guide at risk, then the guide needs to make the report to CPS. When feasible, however, the report needs to be done within the context of the parent guide's relationship with the parent. The guide may say something such as, "Like you, I want what's best for (child's name). I'm really concerned that . . ."

- "You're desperate enough to let (person who's an active alcoholic) take care of her."
- "You're not able to continue in recovery."
- "You aren't able to stop the violence around him."
- "There continue to be dangerous things within his reach."
- "You can't protect her from being physically abused."

The guide then says that she knows that the condition named is threatening the child's physical and emotional safety, and adds, "The work we're doing together doesn't seem to be enough to keep (child's name) safe. Because of that *and* because I'm obligated by law, this needs to be reported as suspected abuse (neglect). The best way to do it would be for you to call or go to child protective services. If you'd like, I will go (call) with you." If the parent disagrees with the idea that this is reportable or indicates inability to report it directly, the parent guide would say, "As I said before, I'm obligated to report suspected abuse (neglect), so I really don't have a choice. I'm hoping that child protective services will be able to offer services that will feel helpful to you." The parent guide could then name services that might be made available such as child care, housing assistance, or transportation for medical care. In many cases, especially when a parent guide is involved, CPS can provide further intervention so that the children can safely remain in their homes. In other instances, children are removed, in which case another set of challenges face the parent, the parent guide, and, most especially, the child.

It is an almost incomprehensible challenge when a toddler is separated from his or her parent and placed in foster care. At age 16 months, Freddy was removed from his mother's custody after his father had abused his younger sister. His foster parents reported that during the first week, Freddy cried much of the night and was angry and oppositional during the day. He was unmanageable when he had supervised visits with Marisa, his mother, refusing any requests and sobbing uncontrollably when separating at the end of the visit.

Thinking about abuse and neglect as factors in the caregiving context of a young child, we can identify two major ways in which the developing child is affected. First, of course, is the trauma of the maltreatment itself, a trauma which may be repeated many times before someone intervenes. Second, is the effect of separation from the parent and the familiar environment that becomes necessary in order to protect the child from further maltreatment. As discussed in Chapter 2, children form attachments, however disturbed, with their primary caregivers. When separated from their primary caregivers, young children are confronted with the challenge of trusting another caregiver, sometimes a series of caregivers, and the cost of this to the developing child, added to the initial abuse, is enormous. In addition to any treatment indicated by the nature of the child's experience in the home, there are three phases of care for the child: 1) the initial separation from the parents, 2) care during the separation, and 3) reunification or termination of parental rights.

The Initial Separation   For the reasons cited previously, abrupt separations of infants and toddlers from their parents under traumatic conditions should be avoided if at all possible. When feasible, the child should be allowed to stay with a nonoffending parent with appropriate provisions to assure the child's safety and welfare. In some situations (e.g., in some neglect cases), the child may be able to remain with the parent—the attachment figure—while efforts are put into place to address conditions that are detrimental to the child's welfare. When abrupt separations are absolutely necessary for the safety of the child, every effort needs to be made to minimize the trauma. Letting the child be taken by a responsible, familiar adult with whom the child has a positive relationship is highly desirable. The procedures described previously in this chapter for easing the trauma of the separation need to be followed.

Care During the Separation   When children do have to be taken from their parents, parent guides can work with foster parents to continue to put into place the procedures described previously for lessening the distress for babies and toddlers of being taken away from familiar people and surroundings. Changes (e.g., a new child care center or new pediatrician) should be avoided as much as possible. Regular, frequent visits with the child's parent(s) in emotionally and physically safe conditions should be arranged if reunification with the parent(s) remains a realistic part of the service plan, and, in some situations, even if parental rights are to be terminated. For instance, a mother may fail to demonstrate that she can maintain a safe and healthy environment for her child, yet she may have a warm and caring relationship with the child. To protect the child from losing this relationship, ongoing contact with the mother in a safe situation can become part of the child's adoption plan. This was the case for Marisa and Freddy.

In CPS cases, it is often necessary to have trained parent guides present to assist and supervise parents during these visits. Babies' needs and behaviors change quickly during the first year, and parents are under stress during these separations as well as their babies. Therefore, parents will need support and perhaps coaching in order for the visits to contribute to their babies' continued emotional development. During Marisa's supervised visits with Freddy, their parent guide provided support and information to Marisa to help her contain Freddy's anger. She coached Marisa during their visits to balance soothing touch and voice with familiar limit-setting to help Freddy feel safe. By holding visits at the foster parents' home and having the mother and foster parent sharing information about how care was being provided, Freddy was better able to regulate his strong emotions and to accept nurturing from both sets of parents.

Some children may appear traumatized by the parent's visits; this was the case for 9-month-old Katie. The parent guide coached the foster parent to hold Katie, once she was relaxed, on her lap, leaning against her and facing her mother. In this position, the foster parent could sense when Katie began to become tense. At that point, the foster parent would turn Katie around, cuddle her for a few moments, then return her to her lap. The birth mother was also coached in how to interact with Katie in nonthreatening ways. With this process, Katie gradually experienced fewer and briefer episodes of stress and eventually was able to be held by, and respond positively to, her mother.

In recent years, there has been more emphasis on training foster parents about working with the birth parents to maintain their relationship with their children. For this to be effective, foster parents need to understand that their foster parenting is a service to the family and not just a service to the child that they are "rescuing" from the family. This realization is not easy because it is often hard for foster parents to get past the fact that this child was taken from the parents due to neglect and/or abuse. They may need help in understanding that working in a positive manner with the birth parents is in the best interest of the child, especially when the child might be reunified with the parents. Even if parental rights are to be terminated, it is still important to do this because many adopted children search for their birth parents when they reach adulthood. For these children, their relationships with their birth parents remain important.

During training, foster parents can be helped to change their perceptions of birth parents by seeing them as "babies grown up"—babies who often were themselves victims of maltreatment but who did not receive the kind of loving care these foster parents are prepared to give the babies they are taking in. This view can be presented not as an excuse but as an explanation for these parents' behaviors. In this way, foster parents can view them as parents who still remain responsible for their behavior, but who are in need of help to heal the psychic wounds from their childhood so that they can hopefully move on to becoming better parents in the future.

Whenever possible, babies and toddlers should not be moved precipitously from one foster home to another, disrupting any attachments that they are forming and making it difficult for them to form secure attachments with anyone. Tiffany was placed in a foster home when she was born because her mother was in prison. After one month, she was moved to another foster home, and at age 10 months she was placed in still another home. As a result, Tiffany did not experience reasonable consistency in caregiving. Each parent smelled different, sounded different, came to her when she cried at a different pace, and responded to her cues differently. By age 15 months, Tiffany was described as being "very clingy" with her foster mother and cried whenever she was out of sight. Many babies who are placed in foster care were taken from their parents due to inadequate care; this history plus the trauma of multiple placements leaves them at high risk for attachment disorders.

In some communities, support for foster parents and adoptive parents is gained through a program called One Church One Child. In this program, the congregation of a faith community agrees to provide support to members of the congregation who adopt or give foster care to children. The support could include respite care, meals, transportation, financial support, and so forth.

Support for Birth Parents During the Separation   Birth parents need support and guidance in their efforts to regain custody of their children. This process starts with the development of appropriate plans for reunification that 1) identify what happened that caused the need for removing the child, 2) state as measurable behavioral outcomes what the parent needs to do differently related to this initial concern, and 3) list resources and activities parents can utilize to make the necessary changes in their behaviors and situations. For example, Daniel was removed from Lois's care because she had placed him in an unsafe situation when she allowed a substance abusing friend to move in and have rowdy parties at her place. The "measurable behavioral outcome" related to this action that became part of her plan was that she make safe choices of people to be around her child. In order for her to make these safe choices, she needed to be clean and sober. This requirement became part of her plan as it related to the original concern over her unsafe child care arrangements. Because her relationship with her boyfriend interfered with her maintaining sobriety, this issue also needed to be addressed—again as it related to the original concern. The resources and activities which Lois could utilize to make these changes included a 28-day residential treatment followed by intensive out-patient treatment, individual therapy regarding her relationship with her boyfriend and her parenting goals (e.g., how she would make plans for what she would do if faced with various contingencies), an NA group, and a parenting group for support and guidance. The parent guide's role was to maintain Lois's motivation and commitment to her plan. She did this by helping Lois make the necessary arrangements (e.g., transportation) to carry out her plan and by keeping their focus on the goal of being reunified with, and meeting the needs of, her child. Like most parents in this situation, Lois felt sad and angry over having her child removed from her care. Her parent guide needed to help Lois deal with these feelings in a nurturing way.

The decision to return children to their parents' custody needs to be made on the basis of the changes in their behavior and situation (Step 2 of the plan) rather than on how many of the recommended resources and activities they used. For instance, it is not how many parenting classes parents attend, but how their parenting has changed that matters. When this is not done, the parent may fulfill requirements like attending parenting classes and think they should therefore get their children back, but social services may have the feeling—and realistically so—that things have not really changed sufficiently, so they up the ante, and parents feel cheated.

Reunification   Removal of children from foster care to reunify them with one or both parents constitutes another separation for the child. The same procedures for easing the distress of separations need to be in place at this time as were recommended for the initial separation from the parents. Because the separation from the foster parents usually does not need to be as abrupt, some preparation of the child for the move can be made. This preparation is especially important when for some reason the child has not been able to maintain regular contact with the parents during separation from them. This was the case for Jonathan, whose parents had moved to another state while he was in foster care. When the court was satisfied, through their contacts with social services in the parents' new home state, that it was safe for Jonathan to return to them, plans for reunification were made. The parent guide, who had been visiting Jonathan in his foster home, worked with both families to make this transition go as smoothly as possible. The birth mother came several days before Jonathan was to go with her. She visited with him in the foster parents' home and in the friend's home where she was staying. The foster parent shared information with her about Jonathan's recent development, interests, likes, and dislikes. His favorite toys were sent with him, and he was able to maintain contact for a while with the foster parents by telephone after the move. In addition, the foster parents were provided grief counseling to help them deal with the loss of this child. When the birth parents and foster parents live in the same town, the foster parents may offer to remain available for babysitting, at least for a while, so the children do not lose relationships that have become important to them.

Termination of Parental Rights Two-year-old Joseph sat between his foster mother—soon to become his adoptive mother—and his birth mother; he put a hand on the knee of each and said, "My two mommies." Joseph was lucky. Even though his parents' parental rights had been terminated, his foster parents, with help from their parent guide, facilitated his maintaining a positive and safe relationship with his mother. Typically, this arrangement is just made for the nonoffending parent in cases of physical or sexual abuse.

When the child's father is no longer in the home and the mother is charged with abuse or neglect, the system has the responsibility of trying to contact the father to determine if he would be an appropriate person to take custody of the child. In some cases, the grandparents (maternal or paternal) will be the ones to provide foster care and, if parental rights are terminated, will adopt the child. When Yvonne and Brad separated and social services decided to terminate parental rights for Yvonne due to her neglect, Brad was offered the opportunity to have custody of the children. When he declined, custody was awarded to Yvonne's mother, and Yvonne maintained contact with her children through supervised visits at her mother's house.

Kin Care More and more, children are being placed with their relatives, especially with their grandparents. An estimated 4 million American children are now being raised by their grandparents; this is an increase of 50% in the 1990s (Clemetson, 2000). More kinship placements are being made partly because it is better for the children as long as their relatives have the personal and financial resources to provide good care. These placements are also being made to save the government money. In most states, kin providing care do not receive the financial assistance that foster parents do, even though they are performing the same benefit to society. Eighteen states have subsidized guardianship programs that provide financial and legal support for kinship care, but most of these programs require children to become wards of the state before assistance is given (Clemetson, 2000). Many grandparents object to this measure.

In addition to the financial burden created by assuming the responsibility of raising their grandchildren, grandparents face other hardships. Often their guardianship is informal because gaining legal custody requires suing their own children, "a step too heartbreaking for many families to take" (Clemetson, 2000, p. 61). Simple tasks such as enrolling children in school and getting medical care can become nightmares. Some states (e.g., Kentucky and Indiana) are remedying this situation by enacting de facto custodial laws giving long-term grandparent caregivers the same status as parents. When grandparents are raising their grandchildren because their children cannot due to alcoholism, drug addiction, incarceration, or abandonment, they may have the added burden of an ongoing sense of grief and failure that their child cannot parent these children.

In many communities, grandparents raising grandkids are organizing to provide support for one another and to advocate for better policies and programs. The American Association of Retired Persons (AARP) Grandparent Information Center lists close to 700 such groups; this center also provides helpful information to grandparents who are raising their grandchildren. Parent guides can inform grandparents of the AARP resource and of any groups that may exist in their community. Many grandparents, however, are swimming as fast as they can to keep up with what may be a sudden new responsibility, and they do not feel that they have time and energy to attend a support group. These grandparents may appreciate having their parent guide give them the names and telephone numbers of other grandparents who are willing to provide telephone support as well as sharing with them what the guide is learning from the experience of other grandparents who are in similar situations.

Incarcerated Parents

When fathers are incarcerated, the children are usually cared for by their mothers; however, when mothers are the ones who are sent to prison, the children are cared for in a variety of ways—by grandparents, other relatives, and sometimes the fathers (Snyder-Joy & Carlo, 1998). For this reason, perhaps, most of the research and clinical literature on incarcerated parents have addressed the characteristics and needs of incarcerated mothers and their children. Nevertheless, some fathers who are incarcerated may need many of the same kinds of support to maintain relationships with their children that incarcerated mothers do.

> *Erica said that her two children ages 18 months and 4 years were being cared for by the female friend with whom she and her children had been living before she was arrested. At first, she indicated that she felt good about this arrangement, saying, "She cares for them as if they were her own." A little later, however, she expressed concern that her friend might try to take her children away from her. Erica was talking with Kristen, a law student who was helping her identify and address some of her needs. Erica went on to explain that her friend was no longer keeping in touch with her.*

The number of women in state and federal prisons almost doubled in a little less than a decade from 44,065 in 1990 to 87,199 by June 30, 1999 (Beck, 2000)—an increase fueled primarily by changes in sentencing laws for drug-related charges (Clark, 1995–1996). The majority of these women (70%–80%) are mothers, and most were the primary caregivers of their children at the time of arrest. Being separated from their children is felt by most to be the worst part of their incarceration. As one mother puts it, "I can do time alone OK. But it's not knowing what's happening to my son that hurts most" (Baunach, 1985, p. 121). For the child, the separation is likely to have long-lasting effects.

Interventions to support incarcerated mothers and their young children, and to prepare for their reunification, should include the following: 1) maintenance of the mother–child relationship through visitation and other means, 2) interventions to address the mothers' problems (e.g., substance abuse, mental illness, lack of education), and 3) appropriate care for the children from time of arrest until their lives are stabilized following their mothers' release (or termination of parental rights, if that occurs). In most cases, there are barriers to implementing one or more of these interventions.

Maintaining the Mother–Child Relationship: The Family's Role   The negative view of mothers who have been convicted of crimes militates against efforts to support maintaining the mother–child relationship (Coll, Surrey, Buccio-Notaro, & Molla, 1998; Snyder-Joy & Carlo, 1998). "If she were a good mother, she wouldn't have gotten into trouble" is the view often held by members of the mothers' families as well as by the general public and the criminal justice system. Husbands, boyfriends, and family members often refuse to bring children to visit their mothers, citing a number of reasons for this refusal (e.g., transportation, time demands, not wanting to expose the children to the prison environment; Coll et al., 1998). Some families do not want the children to know that their mothers are in prison (Snyder-Joy & Carlo, 1998). Some mothers also do not want their children to see them in prison or even know that they are there. Sheila started crying when the law student, Kristen, started talking with her about her 3-year-old daughter. She said that she missed her terribly but did not want her to see her in jail. She added, "Besides, if she comes here to see me, it'll just be too hard for my sister to pull her away when it's time to go." Her tears told how hard the separations would be for her, as well.

All too often, mothers in prison lose touch not only with their children but, as in Erica's case, they even lose contact with the people who are caring for their children. Another mother, Rebecca, said that her 4-year-old son was being cared for by his godmother and visited on weekends by his father who worked out of town during the week. She had lost all contact with both of them. She explained that she received no responses to the letters she sent to the father and that the godmother had moved, and she did not have her new address.

It is understandable that some family members are angry with a mother for ending up in prison. Nevertheless, they can be encouraged to think of the child's welfare and when reunification is likely, this means maintaining the mother–child relationship. There are various ways in which professionals working with these families can help them do this. The process is best begun with healing relationships within the family. Most mothers who are in prison feel a great deal of shame and guilt for having let their children down in this way (Clark, 1995–1996). Their families do not need to exacerbate these feelings. Neither should they excuse the mother's wrongful behavior but instead try to support her in making necessary changes in her life. When given hope and opportunities to change and make amends, a mother's desire to do better by her child can be a strong motivation for turning her life around. Mothers who are reluctant to have their children visit them in prison or know that they are there can be encouraged to realize that for a very young child, not being in contact is more upsetting than seeing mommy in what to them is simply a strange environment. Parent guides can help both the mothers and their family members plan how to talk with the children about their mothers' incarceration and how to prepare them for visits.

Taneesha, another law student, listened as Chantelle fretted about how she was going to get a present for her 3-year-old whose birthday was coming up in a few days. "And Christmas gifts—how am I going to get all of them Christmas gifts?" Several mothers expressed similar concerns to the law students who visited them. On one hand, not being able to go out and buy presents for their children is a consequence of the behaviors that landed Chantelle and the other mothers in jail and prison. On the other hand, being able to recognize these important events in their children's lives is an important part of maintaining their relationships.

Some families do attempt to keep the children and mothers involved with one another through visitations, telephone calls, photos, and correspondence between the mothers and both their children and the children's caregivers. In this case, there are still barriers such as the distance between the children's homes and the prisons. In some instances, families have been successful in getting their incarcerated family member moved to a prison closer to them, which facilitates their visiting them. Other obstacles to keeping in touch include lack of transportation, inability to go to the prison at the visitation times, and the cost of collect calls from the prisons to the families. In some areas, major communication companies are gouging prisoners with exorbitant calling rates often six times the typical long-distance charge (Goldberg & Evans, 1999). Families may gain support and information from the organizations for families of inmates that exist in some communities and states. (See web sites: www.fcnetwork. org and www.prisonactivist.org.)

Decision-Making Authority   A major issue for incarcerated mothers, one that is central to the maintenance of their relationships with their children, is how to handle decision-making regarding the children. There are several ways in which this can be handled, each with its own set of advantages and disadvantages, according to Alexander Scherr, director of a law school clinic (personal communication, June 28, 2000). Often mothers simply have informal oral agreements with the surrogate parents. This arrangement depends on the existence of trusting, reasonably positive relationships and clear, frequent communication among the parties. Surrogate parents in this situation, however, can run into problems when, for instance, they seek medical attention for the child.

Two types of agreements that are more formal are contracts with the surrogate parents for care of the child and the granting of power of attorney to the surrogate parents. Both of these options give parents an opportunity to specify in writing the parameters of the decision-making authority they are granting. Sheila was concerned that Heather might have a hearing problem, so Kristen helped Sheila draw up a power of attorney for Sheila's sister that enabled the sister to authorize medical evaluation and treatment for Heather.

Even these agreements are not always honored by such third parties as doctors and school officials. This problem is resolved if a fourth option, the naming of the surrogate parents as legal guardians of the child, is chosen. Under this arrangement, though, the mother loses all decision-making rights regarding her child while the guardianship remains in effect. Guardianships can be permanent or temporary; when they are temporary they typically can be revoked by the mothers when no longer needed. Taneesha, another law student, helped Julia arrange for her mother to have temporary guardianship of her child.

With legal advice and assistance, parent guides can help incarcerated mothers explore the various options available in their state for assuring appropriate decision-making for their children and choose the one that best fits their situation. In some instances, however, the mother's parental rights are terminated by the court. Incarcerated mothers are usually in a poor position to fight such action when it is initiated.

Maintaining the Mother–Child Relationship: The System's Role   In general, the criminal justice system is interested only in punishing people convicted of crimes, and issues such as the effects on children and their mothers of the mothers' incarceration are of little or no concern to them (Coll et al., 1998). Often having visitation rights is a reward for the mother for good behavior, not an inherent right of her motherhood nor even of her children. There are, however, a few programs scattered throughout the country that do attempt to support mother–child relationships.

Most babies born to incarcerated mothers are either separated from their mothers at birth or, if allowed to remain with their mothers, do so for no longer than 1 or 2 weeks. In Bedford Hills Correctional Facility in New York, however, babies of approved mothers may stay until they are 12 months of age (or 18 months if the mother is to be released by that time; Harris, 1992–1993). The baby sleeps in a crib in the mother's cell usually until age 6 weeks, at which time the mother returns to her classes and the baby goes into the prison infant child care center. Women must apply before the birth to keep their babies at the prison. Those who are deemed physically or emotionally unable to care for their children are denied. For instance, anyone convicted of serious abuse of her other children is denied. Correctional facilities vary greatly in the extent to which they recognize and support children's need for an ongoing relationship with their mothers (Coll et al., 1998). Professionals serving babies and toddlers whose mothers are incarcerated need to become familiar with and, when possible, to influence the approaches taken by the facilities in which these mothers are housed.

Interventions to Address the Mother's Problems   The majority of mothers who are incarcerated are poor, undereducated, use drugs and/or alcohol, and report histories of physical and sexual abuse as children or adults (Clark, 1995–1996). These issues need to be addressed if these mothers are to succeed in caring for their children after being released from prison. Some programs for women who face drug-related criminal charges recognize that "drug use remains, for many women, a consequence of and ineffective coping response to severe and extensive childhood physical or sexual abuse and the emotional or mental health consequences of such abuse" (Welle et al., 1998, p. 162). Some of these programs offer incest and domestic violence survivor groups, assign therapeutic rather than punitive sanctions, and train corrections staff to support treatment goals. The Neil J. Houston House addresses many of these problems in a coordinated and gender-specific way. It is a minimum security, community-based prerelease facility for pregnant women with histories of substance-abuse (Coll et al., 1998). The women in this program receive pre- and postnatal care, substance abuse treatment, and life-skills education. Parent guides can advocate for similar programs in their states.

Before mothers are released from prison, plans need to be developed for resources and services to support their reentry into society. The mothers with whom Kristen, Taneesha, and the other law students met asked a lot of questions about resources they could draw on after their release to help them get their lives together. They wanted information about such things as how to get housing, employment, job training, drug treatment, counseling, and their driver's licenses reinstated; often they asked about how they could retain or regain custody of their children. When one mother was informed of a new substance abuse treatment program for women in the community, she said that no one had ever told her about *any* kind of treatment or even AA meetings before. Another mother who had been in prison before said that after her last release she had trouble establishing herself and that this time she would like to have a "postrelease sponsor." For all mothers, their postrelease plans should include support for their assuming (or reassuming) the role of primary caregivers of their young children.

Caring for the Children   Care for children of incarcerated mothers occurs primarily in the same three phases described above in the section regarding children who are removed from their homes due to maltreatment (i.e., dealing with the initial separation from the mother, maintaining the relationship with the mother over time, and preparing for and handling the reunification with the mother or termination of parental rights, if that occurs). One difference is that the separation from the mother may be for a much longer period of time than may occur when children are removed from their parents by social services. Reunification, then, means another major separation for the child, this time from the family who has provided care in the mother's absence. Therefore, it is important that the child be able to maintain contact with the surrogate parents for a period of time. Another difference is that when mothers are arrested and incarcerated, social services may not be involved. These children may not receive the support and services that children removed by social services do. Parent guides may want to advocate for provision of support and services by appropriate programs to families caring for children of incarcerated mothers.

Parents in Hospitals or Other Residential Treatment Facilities

In Great Britain, special mother–baby units have been developed to care for new mothers who require hospitalization for depression or other psychiatric disorder after delivery so their babies can stay with them (O'Hara, 1997). In most circumstances, however, babies and toddlers require alternate care when their parents are hospitalized or are in some type of residential treatment facility (e.g., residential drug treatment programs).

The procedures described above for helping young children deal with such separations are applicable in these situations, as well. Robin and his mother, Trisha, whom we have met previously, were separated when Robin was a toddler and Trisha had to be hospitalized for a serious psychiatric crisis. During the hospitalization, their parent guide took Robin to visit his mother, helped them have phone conversations, and used pictures of the two of them together to help Robin have continuity of the existence of his mother even when separated.

Hospitalization of the Child

Hospitalization of a child is a frightening experience for both the child and parents, but there are ways to lessen the stress. Parent guides can help parents take the first step, which is to prepare themselves. "Before you can help your child, you must handle your own anxiety about the separation and the coming event" (Brazelton, 1992, p. 299). Parents can also be advised to ask their doctor or the hospital staff about the procedures to which their children will be exposed. They can then arrange to be with their children at critical times, such as the day of admission, the day of an operation, or at the time of any painful procedures. It is important that the parent spend nights with the child throughout the stay for toddlers and for at least the first night for older children. "Even if you have to fight with the hospital to arrange this, I would advise it" (Brazelton, 1992, p. 299).

Children respond to their parents' attitudes and anxieties so it is important for parents to maintain a positive attitude and communicate reassurance. Toddlers will benefit from their parents giving them simple, honest explanations of what to expect and how the various procedures will help them get better. Babies will not understand verbal messages, but they will respond to their parents talking to them in calm, soothing tones. When at all possible, a parent should be with a child when frightening procedures are performed, and they should reassure the child that it is okay to cry. Some children feel that getting sick is punishment for having done something bad; parents can reassure them that this is not the case. The security of a child's attachment with the parent can be strengthened by the parent's ability to comfort the child during the crises of a serious illness or injury resulting in hospitalization and treatments that are often traumatic for the child.

Parent guides may want to explore with parents their feelings about their children's illnesses and injuries, feelings that may arise from their childhood experiences of serious illnesses and injuries and how their parents responded to them at those times. A few parents blame their children for the accidents that resulted in injuries or even for their illness. With reflective questioning, parent guides can help defuse these feelings before they are laid on the child. They may find that the blaming stems from the parent's sense of guilt—their feeling that they did not take proper care of their child. A few other parents seem almost too eager to seek medical treatment for their children and, in rare cases, this may be an indication of a serious disorder known as factitious disorder by proxy (formerly known as Munchhausen by proxy). In this disorder, there is an "intentional production or feigning of physical or psychological signs or symptoms in another person who is under the individual's care for the purpose of indirectly assuming the sick role" (American Psychiatric Association, 1994, p. 228). For example, a caregiver may greatly exaggerate the child's symptoms and do so in visits to multiple doctors so that the child ends up becoming ill because she is overmedicated, or a caregiver may induce symptoms in her child through medication or other means. Parents with this disorder are apparently trying to fulfill a psychological need for attention by doctors. When parent guides observe children with medical problems that seem unusually persistent and whose parents seem focused on the child's medical condition to the degree that it feels that something is amiss, the parent guide should seek a consult with the child's physician. The physician is then the one who will report the child to CPS if he or she decides that the parent's behavior is resulting in child abuse.

Pediatric nurses play a critical role when a child is in the hospital, serving, in effect, as surrogate parents during the parents' absence. The previously presented suggestions for helping infants and toddlers deal with separations can be used by nurses as they bridge the chasm between hospitalized infants and toddlers and their parents.

Conclusion

A comprehensive, integrated community network of resources, both formal and informal, is needed to serve families and children who have multiple needs. How these services and resources are tailored to fit the needs of a particular family and child is determined by the nature and number of these needs as well as by the strengths and resources of the family, child, and community.

TAILORING GUIDANCE TO THE NEEDS OF FAMILIES

There is no "one size fits all" in providing parent guidance. The level of intensity of the intervention will vary as a function of the level of need across families and within families across time. Families differ in the *types* of services and resources needed, as well. The rule of thumb is to begin with careful, respectful assessment and provide the least intensive, least intrusive response indicated. Ongoing assessment informs the level of intensity and types of services needed at any point in time: What do the parents indicate they want or need? Is there evidence of some disturbance or limitation in the family that puts the child's development at risk? Does this parent need more or different help in order to provide more sensitive, responsive care for this child? Are things getting better or worse or staying the same? Do the parents need less involvement as they move toward more competence and confidence and as they develop appropriate community supports?

Research on intervention programs for families with greater and more intense needs suggest that their interventions need to be greater and more intense as well (Egeland et al., 2000). It is not surprising that short-term, didactic parenting classes are often not successful, especially when they are the only intervention available to parents whose children have been removed due to maltreatment.

Some parents may need nothing more than a parent support group or some information about promoting child development and available community resources (Barnard et al., 1988). One study even found that just providing soft baby-carriers to new mothers resulted in a significant difference between the experimental and control groups in percentage of 13-month-olds who exhibited secure attachments with their mothers (Anisfeld, Casper, Nozyce, & Cunningham, 1990). New parents may appreciate a few home visits to help them get started on the journey of parenthood. Other parents may demonstrate or express a particular need that indicates the presence of factors in the parent, the child, or their living circumstances that may be obstacles to provision of "good enough" parenting. These parents may benefit from preventive intervention such as participation in a support group for teen parents or assistance in finding adequate child care and financial resources. When serious problems are discovered with parents, their babies, their interactions, or their living circumstances, prompt referral to intensive services such as psychotherapy, substance abuse treatment, or a battered women's program, in collaboration with parent–infant psychotherapy or some other parent–child work is needed. Table 12.1 lists some of the indicators of need for these three intensity levels (i.e., promotion/prevention, preventive intervention, and therapeutic intervention), some of the services that address needs at these three levels, and some of the environments in which these services are provided. Often parents at the second and third levels of need can benefit from services listed at the lower levels of need, as well.

Table 12.1. Levels of support and guidance

Level	Indicator	Services[a]	Settings[a]
Promotion/ prevention	Interest in child development and parenting	Print materials, videos, parent education/support, home visits	Doctor's offices, child care centers for children or families, churches, families' homes
Preventive intervention	Some limitation in parent, child, their relationship, or environment	Supportive case management, support groups, community services[b]	Early intervention programs, family resource centers, community programs, high schools, families' homes
Therapeutic intervention	A disturbance in parent, child, their relationship, or environment	Mental health treatment, community services, infant–parent psychotherapy[b]	Mental health clinics, therapists' offices, families' homes

[a]These are samples of the possible services and settings.
[b]In addition to services in previous levels.

Promotion/Prevention

Many parents, especially first-time parents, are eager to learn ways to promote healthy physical, emotional, and cognitive development of their young children. There are a number of good print materials and programs (e.g., Parents as Teachers [PAT]) that can help these parents, either on their own or with a parent guide. Provision of these materials and programs are usually sufficient when there are no apparent inadequacies or disturbances in the parent–child relationship or factors in the parent, child, or caregiving environment that place the child's development at risk.

At all three levels of promotion/intervention, care must be taken in providing advice and information to parents on how to promote the development of their children. Parents who feel insecure and inadequate may interpret this as criticism of them and their parenting ability. A teen mom who was living in a residential program for teenage mothers angrily confided to one of the authors: "I'm sick and tired of their telling me how to take care of my baby. I know what my baby needs!" Far too often, parents who have been reported to CPS for neglect or abuse are sent to parenting classes in which a didactic approach leaves them feeling resentful and talked down to. As discussed throughout this book, there are better ways to provide developmental guidance. In providing print materials and programs, guides also need to be sensitive to how the information fits with the parents' cultural values. A review of the materials by a few people from the parent's culture can help in this respect.

Preventive Intervention

Even when well received, provision of print materials and parent education programs are seldom sufficient when parenting is challenged by such factors as poverty, inadequate child care, and lack of social support. In these circumstances, the parent guide will help the family find or develop the resources they need while continuing to support them in their parenting of the child. By highlighting specific instances of their positive parenting, parent guides can give these parents the additional boost they may need to overcome whatever obstacles they are facing. Helen was in Lynette's kitchen talking with her about some of the things that were stressing her when Helen noticed how Jeffrey, then 10 months old, was babbling on and on. Helen said to Lynette, "You must talk to him a lot. Babies do that when their parents talk to them a lot." Then, she said, "I'm just curious, what do you think is important for parents to do with children this age?" Lynette responded, "I have low self-esteem, so I think the most important thing is for parents to help babies get positive self-esteem." Helen nodded, "I agree—that's so important, and I can see that he just knows he's wonderful!" Lynette smiled, "Yeah, he does." Comments like this are like putting money into a parent's emotional bank—money she can draw on when she needs it. (Note: Although Lynette and her family needed the third level of intervention, therapeutic intervention, they also benefited from services and resources provided at the first and second levels.)

Preventive intervention is also needed when observations of parent–child interactions reveal some limitation that, although not indicative of a serious disturbance, may over time lessen the child's chances for optimal development if left unchecked. Katie, a teenage mother, was a warm and caring mother, but Melanie, her PAT parent guide, was concerned about the lack of playful interactions between Katie and her baby. Katie's easygoing, laid-back style was great for calming Krystal when she was upset but not as well suited for engaging her in interactive games. When Katie tried to play with Krystal, she did not notice Krystal's subtle responses, so she tended not to pursue the activity. When Melanie introduced some baby games during their 6-month visit, she noticed this again and commented: "It seems like it is hard to get her to play; does it seem that way to you?" Katie looked thoughtful for a moment and then replied: "Yes, it does." This comment combined with the PAT information about the importance of interactive games at this age seemed to be sufficient because when Melanie returned a month later, she noticed many instances of playful interactions between Katie and Krystal.

Therapeutic Intervention

During Celeste's early visits with Maureen and Victor, she noted Maureen's tension in handling Victor and heard Maureen's negative comments about her baby. Lisa expressed with her posture, tears, and words her deep feelings of depression and parenting inadequacy during Helen's first visit with her and her baby, Ethan. Lynette's history of mental illness, rebellion as a teenager, and involvement in traumatic relationships were all red flags to the therapist from whom she sought medication. All three of these families manifest indicators of need for intensive and prompt intervention of various sorts to address factors affecting the parent–child relationship and the parent's ability to parent well.

The presence of parent guides who can focus on the needs of the children and the dynamics of the parent–child interactions while other issues (e.g., substance abuse, spousal abuse) are being addressed is both essential for the welfare of the developing children and very challenging. Parent guides who have appropriate clinical training (e.g., in parent–infant psychotherapy) can work with these parents to address their psychological issues as they affect their parenting while coordinating their work with that of other service providers (e.g., substance abuse counselors) within a network of integrated services. Parent guides who do not have clinical training still have an important role to play by attending to the needs of the children and supporting the parents. They will help parents obtain good supplementary child care and other community resources as needed (e.g., psychotherapy), and will support and guide parents as they grow in their abilities to parent their children. Again, this works best when the parent guides can collaborate with providers of other services (e.g., the parent's therapist, social services workers) and members of the family's social support network.

Often paraprofessionals are recruited and trained to provide parent guidance and support as parent guides, and this works well in many situations. There is evidence, however, that suggests that families who manifest indicators of more serious disturbances may benefit from having more highly trained professionals as parent guides as well as receiving specialized treatment for their specific issues (Egeland et al., 2000; Olds & Kitzman, 1993). When results of three intervention studies were compared, the one project that relied solely on paraprofessionals to provide guidance and support to high-risk families did not obtain as favorable results for the babies in its sample as did the other two projects that primarily employed professionals (Gowen & Nebrig, 1997). This tentative conclusion needs to be tested in a more controlled manner, but it makes sense that more highly trained parent guides will be more effective with parents who have more complex needs. Although all parents can benefit from positive support, whether it comes from a family member, friend, paraprofessional, or professional, some parents, especially those who are haunted by "ghosts in the nursery," require more. It often takes special skills to help these parents change their internal working models of the parent–infant relationship, of themselves as parents, and of their infants. Parent–infant therapists are especially trained for this work (Lieberman & Pawl, 1993; Stern, 1995). Other parent guides, however, can facilitate this process by the ways in which they relate and interact with parents and their children, and by working in tandem with psychotherapists who can help the parents deal with their psychological issues.

OVERCOMING OBSTACLES

Time after time, parents overcome incredible obstacles in order to care and provide for their children. They do this by drawing on their own inner resources and by seeking support from others—their friends, family members, and various community resources—to address the various factors that are hindering effective parenting. When parent guides meet and travel with families in the midst of such obstacles, they have opportunities to assist and support them to discover the strengths, skills, and resources they need to deal with these challenges. To do this, parent guides have to believe that parents truly want what is best for their children.

Parent guides often face many challenges as well: heart-tugging emotional demands, too little time to accomplish all they want to do for and with families, insufficient resources, frustrating red tape, and family situations that seem just too confusing and difficult to handle. Parent guides also need support from co-workers, supervisors, friends, family, and their faith communities to realize their own strengths, skills, and resources for performing this valuable work. Like Kim Insoo Berg, they may find that what keeps them going is "blind faith."

> My faith is that all clients possess the resources to solve their problems; all clients know what is best for them; and all clients are doing the best they can right now under very difficult circumstances. I cannot expect anything more of anyone, including myself, but that we do the best we can right now and hope for the best in the future. (1994, p. 218)

References

Adamson, L.B., & Bakeman, R. (1985). Affect and attention: Infants observed with mothers and peers. *Child Development, 56,* 582–593.

Ainsworth, M.D., Blehar, M., Waters, E., & Wall, S. (1978). *Patterns of attachment: A psychological study of the strange situation.* Mahwah, NJ: Lawrence Erlbaum Associates.

Ainsworth, M.D.S., & Wittig, B.A. (1969). Attachment and exploratory behavior of one-year-olds in a strange situation. In B.M. Foss (Ed.), *Determinants of infant behavior* (Vol. 4; pp. 113–136). London: Methuen.

American Psychiatric Association (1994). *Desk reference to the diagnostic criteria from DSM-IV.* Washington, DC: Author.

Anderson, E. (1991). Neighborhood effects on teenage pregnancy. In C. Jencks & P.E. Peterson (Eds.), *The urban underclass* (pp. 375–398). Washington DC: The Brookings Institution Press.

Anderson, J.W. (1972). Attachment behaviour out of doors. In N. B. Jones (Ed.), *Ethological studies of child behaviour* (pp. 199–215). Cambridge: Cambridge University Press.

Anisfeld, E., Casper, V., Nozyce, M., & Cunningham, N. (1990). Does infant carrying promote attachment? An experimental study of the effects of increased physical contact on the development of attachment. *Child Development, 61,* 1617–1627.

Bagnato, S.J., Neisworth, J.T., Salvia, J., & Hunt, F.M. (1999). *Temperament and atypical behavior scale (TABS): Early childhood indicators of developmental dysfunction. Assessment tool.* Baltimore: Paul H. Brookes Publishing Co.

Bakeman, R., & Adamson, L.B. (1984). Coordinating attention to people and objects in mother–infant and peer–infant interactions. *Child Development, 55,* 1278–1289.

Bakermans-Kranenburg, M.J., Juffer, F., & van IJzendoorn, M.H. (1998). Interventions with video feedback and attachment discussions: Does type of maternal insecurity make a difference? *Infant Mental Health Journal, 19*(2), 202–219.

Balaban, M.T. (1995). Affective influences on startle in five-month-old infants: Reactions to facial expressions of emotion. *Child Development, 66,* 28–36.

Barnard, K.E., Magyary, D., Sumner, G., Booth, C.L., Mitchell, S.K., & Spieker, S. (1988). Prevention of parenting alterations for women with low social support. *Psychiatry, 51,* 248–254.

Barrett, K.C., Morgan, G.A., & Maslin-Cole, C. (1993). Three studies on the development of mastery motivation in infancy and toddlerhood. In D. Messer (Ed.), *Mastery motivation in early childhood: Development, measurement and social processes* (pp. 83–108). London: Routledge.

Baumrind, D. (1967). Child care practices anteceding three patterns of preschool behavior. *Genetic Psychology Monographs, 75,* 43–88.

Baumrind, D. (1972). An exploratory study of socialization effects on Black children: Some Black–White comparisons. *Child Development, 43,* 261–267.

Baumrind, D. (1978). Parental disciplinary patterns and social competence in children. *Youth and Society, 9,* 230–276.

Baumrind, D. (1993). The average expectable environment is not good enough: A response to Scarr. *Child Development, 64,* 1299–1317.

Baunach, P.J. (1985). *Mothers in prison.* New Brunswick, NJ: Transaction Books.

Beck, A.J. (2000, April). Prison and jail inmates at midyear 1999. *Bureau of Justice Statistics Bulletin.* Washington, D.C.: U.S. Department of Justice.

Beeghly, M., & Cicchetti, D. (1994). Child maltreatment, attachment, and the self system: Emergence of an internal state lexicon in toddlers at high social risk. *Development and Psychopathology, 6,* 5–30.

Belenky, M.F., Clinchy, B.M., Goldberger, N.R., & Tarule, J.M. (1997). *Women's ways of knowing: The development of self, voice, and the mind.* New York: Basic Books.

Bell, S.M., & Ainsworth, M.D.S. (1972). Infant crying and maternal responsiveness. *Child Development, 43,* 1171–1190.

Belle, D. (Ed.). (1982). *Lives in stress: Women and depression.* Thousand Oaks, CA: Sage Publications.

Benoit, D., & Parker, K.C.H. (1994). Stability and transmission of attachment across three generations. *Child Development, 65,* 1444–1456.

Benoit, D., Parker, K.C.H., & Zeanah, C.H. (1997). Mothers' representations of their infants assessed prenatally: Stability and association with infants' attachment classifications. *Journal of Child Psychology and Psychiatry and Allied Disciplines, 38,* 307–313.

Benoit, D., Zeanah, C.H., Parker, K.C.H., Nicholson, E., & Coolbear, J. (1997). "Working model of the child interview": Infant clinical status related to maternal perceptions. *Infant Mental Health Journal, 18,* 107–121.

Berg, I.K. (1994). *Family-based services: A solution-focused approach.* New York: W.W. Norton.

Bertacchi, J., & Norman-Murch, T. (1999). Implementing reflective supervision in non-clinical settings: Challenges to practice. *Zero to Three, 20*(1), 18–23.

Black, M.M., & Nitz, K. (1996). Grandmother co-residence, parenting, and child development among low income, urban teen mothers. *Journal of Adolescent Health, 18,* 218–226.

Blatt, S.J., & Homann, E. (1992). Parent–child interaction in the etiology of dependent and self-critical depression. *Clinical Psychology Review, 12,* 47–91.

Boris, N.W., Aoki, Y., & Zeanah, C.H. (1999). The development of infant–parent attachment: Considerations for assessment. *Infants and Young Children, 11,* 1–10.

Bowlby, J. (1973). *Attachment and loss: Vol. 2. Separation, anxiety, and anger.* New York: Basic Books.

Bowlby, J. (1980). *Attachment and loss: Vol. 3. Loss, sadness and depression.* New York: Basic Books.

Bowlby, J. (1982). *Attachment and loss: Vol. 1. Attachment* (2nd ed.). New York: Basic Books. (Original work published 1969)

Brazelton, T.B. (1992). *Touchpoints: Your child's emotional and behavioral development.* Reading, MA: Addison Wesley Longman.

Breakwell, G.M. (1993). Psychological and social characteristics of teenagers who have children. In A. Lawson & D.L. Rhode (Eds.), *The politics of pregnancy:*

Adolescent sexuality and public policy (pp. 159–173). New Haven, CT: Yale University Press.

Brent, L., & Resch, R.C. (1987). A paradigm of infant–mother reciprocity: A reexamination of "emotional refueling." *Psychoanalytic Psychology, 4,* 15–31.

Bretherton, I. (1985). Attachment theory: Retrospect and prospect. In I. Bretherton & E. Waters (Eds.), Growing points of attachment theory and research (pp. 3–35). *Monographs of the Society for Research in Child Development, 50* (1–2, Serial No. 209).

Bretherton, I. (1987). New perspectives on attachment relations: Security, communication, and internal working models. In J.D. Osofsky (Ed.), *Handbook of infant development* (2nd ed., pp. 1061–1100). New York: John Wiley & Sons.

Bretherton, I., McNew, S., & Beeghly-Smith, M. (1981). Early person knowledge as expressed in gestural and verbal communication: When do infants acquire a "theory of mind"? In M.E. Lamb & L.R. Sherrod (Eds.), *Infant social cognition: Empirical and theoretical considerations* (pp. 333–373). Mahwah, NJ: Lawrence Erlbaum Associates.

Brown, G.W., & Harris, T. (1978). *Social origins of depression: A study of psychiatric disorder in women.* New York: Free Press.

Browne, A. (1993). Violence against women by male partners: Prevalence, outcomes, and policy implications. *American Psychologist, 48,* 1077–1087.

Browne, A. (1998). Recognizing the strengths of battered women. In E.W. Gondolf, *Assessing woman battering in mental health services* (pp. 95–105). Thousand Oaks, CA: Sage Publications.

Brownell, C.A., & Carriger, M.S. (1990). Changes in cooperation and self-other differentiation during the second year. *Child Development, 61,* 1164–1174.

Buchholtz, E.S., & Korn-Bursztyn, C. (1993). Children of adolescent mothers: Are they at risk for abuse? *Adolescence, 28,* 361–382.

Bushnell, I.W.R., Sai, F., & Mullin, J.T. (1989). Neonatal recognition of the mother's face. *British Journal of Developmental Psychology, 7,* 3–15.

Caldwell, C.H., & Antonucci, T.C. (1997). Childbearing during adolescence: Mental health risks and opportunities. In J. Schulenberg, J.L. Maggs, & K. Hurrelmann (Eds.), *Health risks and developmental transitions during adolescence* (pp. 220–245). Cambridge: Cambridge University Press.

Calkins, S.D., & Fox, N.A. (1994). Individual differences in the biological aspects of temperament. In J.E. Bates & T.D. Wachs (Eds.), *Temperament: Individual differences at the interface of biology and behavior* (pp. 199–217). Washington, DC: American Psychological Association.

Campbell, S., Earley, N., & Gray, M. (1999). Fortifying programs against the "forces of risk." *Zero to Three, 19*(5), 27–33.

Camras, L.A., & Sachs, V.B. (1991). Social referencing and caretaker expressive behavior in a day care setting. *Infant Behavior and Development, 14,* 27–36.

Canfield, R.L., & Haith M.M. (1991). Young infants' visual expectations for symmetric and asymmetric stimulus sequences. *Developmental Psychology, 27,* 198–208.

Caplan, M., Vespo, J., Pedersen, J., & Hay, D.F. (1991). Conflict and its resolution in small groups of one- and two-year-olds. *Child Development, 62,* 1513–1524.

Carey, W.B., & McDevitt, S.C. (1995). *Coping with children's temperament.* New York: Basic Books.

Caron, A.J., Caron, R.F., Caldwell, R.C., & Weiss, S.S. (1973). Infant perception of the structural properties of the face. *Developmental Psychology, 9,* 385–399.

Carter, S.L., Osofsky, J.D., & Hann, D.M. (1991). Speaking for the baby: A therapeutic intervention with adolescent mothers and their infants. *Infant Mental Health Journal, 12,* 291–301.

Cassidy, J. (1994). Emotion regulation: Influences of attachment relationships. In N.A. Fox (Ed.), The development of emotion regulation: Biological and behavioral considerations (pp. 228–249). *Monographs of the Society for Research in Child Development, 59* (2–3, Serial No. 240).

Cassidy, J., & Berlin, L.J. (1994). The insecure/ambivalent pattern of attachment: Theory and practice. *Child Development, 65,* 971–991.

Chess, S., & Thomas, A. (1996). *Temperament: Theory and practice.* Philadelphia: Brunner/Mazel.

Children's Defense Fund. (2001). *The state of America's children yearbook.* Washington, DC: Author.

Chugani, H.T. (1994). Development of regional brain glucose metabolism in relation to behavior and plasticity. In G. Dawson & K.W. Fischer (Eds.), *Human behavior and the developing brain* (pp. 153–175). New York: The Guilford Press.

Clark, J. (1995–1996). Love them and leave them: Paradox, conflict, and ambivalence among incarcerated mothers. *Zero to Three, 16*(3), 29–35.

Clemetson, L. (2000, June 12). Grandma knows best. *Newsweek,* 60–61.

Cohn, J.F., Campbell, S.B., & Ross, S. (1991). Infant response in the still-face paradigm at 6 months predicts avoidant and secure attachment at 12 months. *Development and Psychopathology, 3,* 367–376.

Cohn, J.F., & Tronick, E.Z. (1989). Specificity of infants' response to mothers' affective behaviour. *Journal of the American Academy of Child and Adolescent Psychiatry, 28,* 242–248.

Coll, C.G., Surrey, J.L., Buccio-Notaro, P., & Molla, B. (1998). Incarcerated mothers: Crimes and punishments. In C.G. Coll, J.L. Surrey, & K. Weingarten (Eds.), *Mothering against the odds: Diverse voices of contemporary mothers* (pp. 255–274). New York: The Guilford Press.

Committee on the Judiciary, U.S. Senate 102nd Congress (October, 1992). *Violence against women: A week in the life of America.* Washington, DC: U.S. Government Printing Office.

Constantino, J.N. (1993). Parents, mental illness, and the primary health care of infants and young children. *Zero to Three, 13*(5), 1–10.

Cooper, P.J., & Murray, L. (1997). The impact of psychological treatments of postpartum depression on maternal mood and infant development. In L. Murray & P.J. Cooper (Eds.), *Postpartum depression and child development* (pp. 201–220). New York: The Guilford Press.

Cooper, R.P., & Aslin, R.N. (1989). The language environment of the young infant: Implications for early perceptual development. *Canadian Journal of Psychology, 43,* 247–265.

Cox, M.J., Owen, M.T., Henderson, V.K., & Margand, N.A. (1992). Prediction of infant–father and infant–mother attachment. *Developmental Psychology, 28*(3), 474–483.

Cox, M.J., Owen, M.T., Lewis, J.M., & Henderson, V.K. (1989). Marriage, adult adjustment, and early parenting. *Child Development, 60,* 1015–1024.

Cramer, B.B. (1987). Objective and subjective aspects of parent–infant relations: An attempt at correlation between infant studies and clinical work. In J.D. Osofsky (Ed.), *Handbook of infant development* (2nd ed., pp. 1037–1057). New York: John Wiley & Sons.

Crittenden, P.M. (1988). Relationships at risk. In J. Belsky & T. Nezworski (Eds.), *Clinical implications of attachment* (pp. 136–174). Mahwah, NJ: Lawrence Erlbaum Associates

Crittenden, P.M. (1993). Characteristics of neglectful parents: An information processing approach. *Criminal Justice and Behavior, 20,* 27–48.

Crnic, K.A., Greenberg, M.T., Ragozin, A.S., Robinson, N.M., & Basham, R.B. (1983). Effects of stress and social support on mothers and premature and full-term infants. *Child Development, 54,* 209–217.

Crowell, J.A., & Feldman, S.S. (1988). Mothers' internal models of relationships and children's behavioral and developmental status: A study of mother–child interaction. *Child Development, 59,* 1273–1285.

Crowell, J.A., & Feldman, S.S. (1991). Mothers' working models of attachment relationships and mother and child behavior during separation and reunion. *Developmental Psychology, 27,* 597–605.

Crowell, J.A., & Waters, E. (1990). Separation anxiety. In M. Lewis & S.M. Miller (Eds.), *Handbook of developmental psychopathology* (pp. 209–218). New York: Kluwer Academic/Plenum Publishers.

Dahl, R.E. (1996). The regulation of sleep and arousal: Development and psychopathology. *Development and Psychopathology, 8,* 3–27.

Dawson, G. (1994). Development of emotional expression and emotion regulation in infancy: Contributions of the frontal lobe. In G. Dawson & K.W. Fischer (Eds.), *Human behavior and the developing brain* (pp. 346–379). New York: The Guilford Press.

Day, N.L., & Richardson, G.A. (1993). Cocaine use and crack babies: Science, the media, and miscommunication. *Neurotoxicology and Teratology, 15,* 293–294.

De Wolff, M.S., & van IJzendoorn, M.H. (1997). Sensitivity and attachment: A meta-analysis on parental antecedents of infant attachment. *Child Development, 68,* 571–591.

Deater-Deckard, K., & Dodge, K.A. (1997). Externalizing behavior problems and discipline revisited: Nonlinear effects and variation by culture, context, and gender. *Psychological Inquiry, 8,* 161–175.

Deater-Deckard, K., Dodge, K.A., Bates, J.E., & Pettit, G.S. (1996). Physical discipline among African American and European American mothers: Links to children's externalizing behaviors. *Developmental Psychology, 32,* 1065–1072.

DeCasper, A.J., & Fifer, W.P. (1980). Of human bonding: Newborns prefer their mothers' voices. *Science, 208,* 1174–1176.

deHaan, M., & Nelson, C.A. (1997). Recognition of the mother's face by six-month-old infants: A neurobehavioral study. *Child Development, 68,* 187–210.

DeLissovoy, V. (1973). Child care by adolescent parents. *Children Today, 2*(4), 22–25.

Desrochers, S., Ricard, M., Decarie, T.G., & Allard, L. (1994). Developmental synchrony between social referencing and Piagetian sensorimotor causality. *Infant Behavior and Development, 17,* 303–309.

Dowdney, L., & Skuse, D. (1993). Parenting provided by adults with mental retardation. *Journal of Child Psychology and Psychiatry and Allied Disciplines, 34,* 25–47.

Dunlap, K.M., & Fogel, S.J. (1998). A preliminary analysis of research on recovery from homelessness. *Journal of Social Distress and the Homeless, 7,* 175–188.

Dunn, J., & Brown, J. (1991). Relationships, talk about feelings, and the development of affect regulation in early childhood. In J. Garber & K.A. Dodge

(Eds.), *The development of emotion regulation and dysregulation* (pp. 89–108). New York: Cambridge University Press.

Dunst, C., Trivette, C., & Deal, A. (1988). *Enabling and empowering families: Principles and guidelines for practice.* Cambridge, MA: Brookline Books.

Eckenrode, J., Ganzel, B., Henderson, C.R., Jr., Smith, E., Olds, D.L., Powers, J., Cole, R., Kitzman, H., & Sidora, K. (2000). Preventing child abuse and neglect with a program of nurse home visitation: The limiting effects of domestic violence. *Journal of American Medical Association, 284,* 1385–1391.

Egeland, B., & Erickson, M.F. (1990). Rising above the past: Strategies for helping new mothers break the pattern of abuse and neglect. *ZERO TO THREE, 11*(2), 29–35.

Egeland, B., Weinfield, N.S., Bosquet, M., & Cheng, V.K. (2000). Remembering, repeating, and working through: Lessons from attachment-based interventions. In J.D. Osofsky & H.E. Fitzgerald (Eds.), *WAIMH handbook of infant mental health: Vol. 4. Infant mental health in groups at high risk* (pp. 35–89). New York: John Wiley & Sons.

Eiden, R.D., & Leonard, K.E. (1996). Paternal alcohol use and the mother–infant relationship. *Development and Psychopathology, 8,* 307–323.

Emde, R.N. (1989). The infant's relationship experience: Developmental and affective aspects. In A.J. Sameroff & R.N. Emde (Eds.), *Relationship disturbances in early childhood* (pp. 33–51). New York: Basic Books.

Emde, R.N., & Buchsbaum, H.K. (1990). "Didn't you hear my mommy?" Autonomy with connectedness in moral self emergence. In D. Cicchetti & M. Beeghly (Eds.), *The self in transition* (pp. 35–60). Chicago: University of Chicago Press.

Emde, R.N., Gaensbauer, T., & Harmon, R.J. (1982). Using our emotions: Some principles for appraising emotional development and intervention. In M. Lewis & L.T. Taft (Eds.), *Developmental disabilities: Theory, assessment and intervention* (pp. 409–424). Jamaica, NY: SP Medical and Scientific Books.

Erickson, M.F., Egeland, B., & Pianta, R. (1989). The effects of maltreatment on the development of young children. In D. Cicchetti & V. Carlson (Eds.), *Child maltreatment: Theory and research on the causes and consequences of child abuse and neglect* (pp. 647–684). New York: Cambridge University Press.

Erickson, M.F., Korfmacher, J., & Egeland, B.R. (1992). Attachments past and present: Implications for therapeutic intervention with mother–infant dyads. *Development and Psychopathology, 4,* 495–507.

Erickson, M.F., Sroufe, L.A., & Egeland, B. (1985). The relationship between quality of attachment and behavior problems in preschool in a high-risk sample. In I. Bretherton & E. Waters (Eds.), Growing points of attachment theory and research (pp. 147–166). *Monographs of the Society for Research in Child Development, 50* (1–2, Serial No. 209).

Erikson, E.H. (1968). *Identity: Youth and crisis.* New York: W.W. Norton.

Escher-Graeub, D., & Grossmann, K.E. (1983). Bindungssicherheit im zweiten Lebensjahrdie Regensburger Querschnittuntersuchung [Attachment security in the second year of life: The Regensburg cross-sectional study] Research Report, University of Regensburg.

Feinman, S., & Lewis, M. (1983). Social referencing at ten months: A second-order effect on infants' responses to strangers. *Child Development, 54,* 878–887.

Fenichel, E. (1992). *Learning through supervision and mentorship to support the development of infants and toddlers and their families: A source book.* Arlington, VA: ZERO TO THREE.

Fernald, A. (1993). Approval and disapproval: Infant responsiveness to vocal affect in familiar and unfamiliar languages. *Child Development, 64,* 657–674.

Field, T. (1992). Infants of depressed mothers. *Development and Psychopathology, 4,* 49–66.

Field, T. (1997). The treatment of depressed mothers and their infants. In L. Murray & P.J. Cooper (Eds.), *Postpartum depression and child development* (pp. 221–236). New York: The Guilford Press.

Field, T. (1998). Maternal depression effects on infants and early interventions. *Preventive Medicine, 27,* 200–203.

Field, T.M., Cohen, D., Garcia, R., & Greenberg, R. (1984). Mother–stranger face discrimination by the newborn. *Infant Behavior and Development, 7,* 19–25.

Field, T.M., Schanberg, S.M., Scafidi, F., Bauer, C.R., Vega-Lahr, N., Garcia, R., Nystrom, J., & Kuhn, C.M. (1986). Tactile/kinesthetic stimulation effects on preterm neonates. *Pediatrics, 77*(5), 654–658.

Field, T.M., Vega-Lahr, N., & Jagadish, S. (1984). Separation stress of nursery school infants and toddlers graduating to new classes. *Infant Behavior and Development, 7,* 277–284.

Field, T.M., Woodson, R., Greenberg, R., & Cohen, D. (1982). Discrimination and imitation of facial expressions by neonates. *Science, 218,* 179–181.

Finkelhor, D. (1984). *Child sexual abuse: New theory and research.* New York: Free Press.

Fisher, L., Kokes, R.F., Cole, R.E., Perkins, P.M., & Wynne, L.C. (1987). Competent children at risk: A study of well functioning offspring of disturbed parents. In E.J. Anthony & B.J. Cohler (Eds.), *The invulnerable child* (pp. 211–228). New York: The Guilford Press.

Fogel, S.J. (1997). Moving along: An exploratory study of homeless women with children using a transitional housing program. *Journal of Sociology and Social Welfare, 24*(3), 113–133.

Foley, G.M. (1994). Parent–professional relationships: Finding an optimal distance. *Zero To Three, 14*(4), 19–22.

Fonagy, P., Steele, M., Steele, H., Moran, G.S., & Higgitt, A.C. (1991). The capacity for understanding mental states: The reflective self in parent and child and its significance for security of attachment. *Infant Mental Health Journal, 12,* 201–218.

Fox, N.A. (1994). Dynamic cerebral processes underlying emotion regulation. In N.A. Fox (Ed.), The development of emotion regulation: Biological and behavioral considerations (pp. 152–166). *Monographs of the Society for Research in Child Development, 59* (2–3, Serial No. 240).

Fraiberg, S., Adelson, E., & Shapiro, V. (1975). Ghosts in the nursery: A psychoanalytic approach to the problems of impaired infant–mother relationships. *Journal of the American Academy of Child Psychiatry, 14,* 387–421.

Frodi, A. (1985). When empathy fails: Aversive infant crying and child abuse. In B.M. Lester, & C.F.Z. Boukydis (Eds.), *Infant crying: Theoretical and research perspectives* (pp. 263–277). New York: Kluwer Academic/Plenum Publishers.

Frodi, A.M., & Lamb, M.E. (1980). Child abusers' responses to infant smiles and cries. *Child Development, 51,* 238–241.

Frodi, A.M., Lamb, M.E., Leavitt, L.A., Donovan, W.L., Neff, C., & Sherry, D. (1978). Fathers' and mothers' responses to the faces and cries of normal and premature infants. *Developmental Psychology, 14,* 490–498.

Furstenberg, F.F., Jr., Brooks-Gunn, J., & Morgan, S.P. (1987). *Adolescent mothers in later life.* Cambridge, England: Cambridge University Press.

Furth, H.G. (1969). *Piaget and knowledge: Theoretical foundations.* Upper Saddle River, NJ: Prentice-Hall.

Garbarino, J., Kostelny, K., & Barry, F. (1998). Neighborhood-based programs. In P.K. Trickett & C.J. Schellenbach (Eds.), *Violence against children in the family and the community* (pp. 287–314). Washington, DC: American Psychological Association.

Gaudin, J.M., Jr., Wodarski, J.S., Arkinson, M.K., & Avery, L.S. (1990–1991). Remedying child neglect: Effectiveness of social network interventions. *Journal of Applied Social Sciences, 15,* 97–123.

George, C., Kaplan, N., & Main, M. (1985). *The Berkeley adult attachment interview.* Unpublished protocol, University of California, Department of Psychology, Berkeley.

George, C., & Solomon, J. (1996). Representational models of relationships: Links between caregiving and attachment. *Infant Mental Health Journal, 17,* 198–216.

Gershenson, H.P., Musick, J.S., Ruch-Ross, H.S., Magee, V., Rubino, K.K., & Rosenberg, D. (1989). The prevalence of coercive sexual experience among teenage mothers. *Journal of Interpersonal Violence, 4,* 204–219.

Goldberg, E., & Evans, L. (June–July, 1999). The prison industrial complex and the global economy. *Nexus,* 17–22.

Goleman, D. (1995). *Emotional intelligence: Why it can matter more than IQ.* New York: Bantam Books.

Gondolf, E.W. (1998). *Assessing woman battering in mental health services.* Thousand Oaks, CA: Sage Publications.

Goodman, L., Saxe, L., & Harvey, M. (1991). Homelessness as psychological trauma. *American Psychologist, 46,* 1219–1225.

Goodman, S.H., & Brumley, H.E. (1990). Schizophrenic and depressed mothers: Relational deficits in parenting. *Developmental Psychology, 26,* 31–39.

Goodman, S.H., Radke-Yarrow, M., & Teti, D. (1993). Maternal depression as a context for child rearing. *Zero to Three, 13*(5).

Gowen, J.W. (1984, April). *Aggression in the play of three- and five-year-old SES children.* Paper presented at the Eighth Biennial Meeting of the Southeastern Conference on Human Development, Athens, GA.

Gowen, J.W. (1993a). *Effects of neglect on the early development of children.* Final report submitted to U.S. Department of Health and Human Services Administration for Children and Families, National Center on Child Abuse and Neglect (Grant No. 90-CA-1462).

Gowen, J.W. (1993b). A system of care for at-risk infants and their families. *Proceedings of the Sixth Annual Research Conference, A System of Care for Children's Mental Health,* 327–332.

Gowen, J.W. (1995). Research in review: The early development of symbolic play. *Young Children, 50*(3), 75–84.

Gowen, J.W., & Nebrig, J.B. (1997). Infant–mother attachment at risk: How early intervention can help. *Infants and Young Children, 9,* 62–78.

Gowen, J.W., Nebrig, J., & Jodry, W.L. (1995). Promoting parenting self-efficacy. *Network, 4*(3), 12–22. (Available from National Training Resource Center, Private Bag 4004, Kimberly Centre, Levin, New Zealand).

Greenspan, S.I., & Greenspan, N.T. (1989). *The essential partnership: How parents and children can meet the emotional challenges of infancy and childhood.* New York: Viking.

Greenstein, B. (1998). Engagement is everything. *ZERO TO THREE, 18*(4), 16.

Grolnick, W.S., Bridges, L.J., & Connell, J.P. (1996). Emotion regulation in two-year-olds: Strategies and emotional expression in four contexts. *Child Development, 67,* 928–941.

Grossmann, K., Fremmer-Bombik, E., Rudolph, J., & Grossmann, K.E. (1988). Maternal attachment representations as related to patterns of infant-mother attachment and maternal care during the first year. In R.A. Hinde & J. Stevenson-Hinde (Eds.), *Relationships within families: Mutual influences* (pp. 241–260). Oxford, England: Clarendon Press.

Grossmann, K.E., Grossmann, K., & Schwan, A. (1986). Capturing the wider view of attachment: A reanalysis of Ainsworth's Strange Situation. In C.E. Izard & P.B. Read (Eds.). *Measuring emotions in infants and children* (Vol. 2; pp. 124–171). Cambridge, England: Cambridge University Press.

Groves, B.M. (1996). Children without refuge: Young witnesses to domestic violence. In J.D. Osofsky & E. Fenichel (Eds.), *Islands of safety: Assessing and treating young victims of violence* (pp. 29–34). Washington, DC: ZERO TO THREE.

Gunnar, M.R. (1994). Psychoendocrine studies of temperament and stress in early childhood: Expanding current models. In J.E. Bates & T.D. Wachs (Eds.), *Temperament: Individual differences at the interface of biology and behavior* (pp. 175–198). Washington, DC: American Psychological Association.

Gunnar, M. (December, 1998). *The biology of emotional regulation.* Paper presented at the ZERO TO THREE Thirteenth National Training Institute, Washington, DC.

Gunnar, M.R., Brodersen, L., Nachmias, M., Buss, K., & Rigatuso, J. (1996). Stress reactivity and attachment security. *Developmental Psychobiology, 29,* 191–204.

Gunnar, M.R., & Stone, C. (1984). The effects of positive maternal affect on infant responses to pleasant, ambiguous, and fear-provoking toys. *Child Development, 55,* 1231–1236.

Haft, W., & Slade, A. (1989). Affect attunement and maternal attachment: A pilot study. *Infant Mental Health Journal, 10,* 157–172.

Halpern, R. (1993). Poverty and infant development. In C.H. Zeanah, Jr. (Ed.), *Handbook of infant mental health* (pp. 73–86). New York: The Guilford Press.

Halpern, R. (1995). Parent support and education programs: Their role in the continuum of child and family services. In I.M. Schwartz, & P. Au Claire (Eds.), *Home based services for troubled children* (pp. 99–100). Lincoln: University of Nebraska Press.

Hamilton, C. (2000). Continuity and discontinuity of attachment from infancy through adolescence. *Child Development, 71,* 690–694.

Hanna, S., Wilford, S., Benham, H., Carter, J., & Brodkin, A.M. (1990). *Floor time: Tuning in to each child (A professional development program guide).* New York: Scholastic.

Harris, J. (1992–1993). Babies in prison. *ZERO TO THREE, 13*(3), 17–21.

Haviland, J. M., & Lelwica, M. (1987). The induced affect response: 10-week-old infants' responses to three emotion expressions. *Developmental Psychology, 23,* 97–104.

Hay, D.F. (1994). Prosocial development. *Journal of Child Psychology and Psychiatry and Allied Disciplines, 35,* 29–71.

Hay, D.F., Caplan, M., Castle, J., & Stimson, C.A. (1991). Does sharing become increasingly "rational" in the second year of life? *Developmental Psychology, 27,* 987–993.

Hay, D.F., Castle, J., Stimson, C.A., & Davies, L. (1995). The social construction of character in toddlerhood. In M. Killen & D. Hart (Eds.), *Morality in every-*

day life: Developmental perspectives (pp. 23–51). New York: Cambridge University Press.

Heller, S.S., & Zeanah, C.H. (1999). Attachment disturbances in infants born subsequent to perinatal loss: A pilot study. *Infant Mental Health Journal, 20,* 188–199.

Hesse, E. (1996). Discourse, memory, and the adult attachment interview: A note with emphasis on the emerging cannot classify category. *Infant Mental Health Journal, 17,* 4–11.

Hetherington, E.M. (1997). Teenaged childbearing and divorce. In S.S. Luthar, J.A. Burack, D. Cicchetti, & J.R. Weisz (Eds.), *Developmental psychopathology: Perspectives on adjustment, risk, and disorder* (pp. 350–373). Cambridge, England: Cambridge University Press.

Hirshberg, L. (1990). When infants look to their parents: II. Twelve-month-olds' response to conflicting parental emotional signals. *Child Development, 61,* 1187–1191.

Hirshberg, L.M., & Svejda, M. (1990). When infants look to their parents: I. Infants' social referencing of mothers compared to fathers. *Child Development, 61,* 1175–1186.

Howes, C. (1998). Continuity of care: The importance of infant, toddler, parent relationships. *Zero to Three, 18*(6), 7–11.

Huttenlocher, P.R. (1994). Synaptogenesis in human cerebral cortex. In G. Dawson & K.W. Fischer (Eds.), *Human behavior and the developing brain* (pp. 137–152). New York: The Guilford Press.

Jacobson, A. (1989). Physical and sexual assault histories among psychiatric outpatients. *American Journal of Psychiatry, 146,* 755–758.

Jones, S.S. (1996). Imitation or exploration? Young infants' matching of adults' oral gestures. *Child Development, 67,* 1952–1969.

Kagan, J. (1981). *The second year: The emergence of self-awareness.* Cambridge, MA: Harvard University Press.

Kagan, J. (1994). *Galen's prophecy: Temperament in human nature.* New York: Basic Books.

Kagan, J. (1996). Temperamental contributions to the development of social behavior. In D. Magnusson (Ed.), *The lifespan development of individuals: Behavioral, neurobiological, and psychosocial perspectives* (pp. 376–393). Cambridge, England: Cambridge University Press.

Kasinsky, R.G. (1993). Criminalizing of pregnant women drug abusers. In C.C. Culliver (Ed.), *Female criminality: The state of the art* (pp. 483–501). New York: Garland Publishing.

Kaufman, G. (1989). *The psychology of shame.* New York: Springer-Verlag.

Kaufman, J., & Zigler, E. (1987). Do abused children become abusive parents? *American Journal of Orthopsychiatry, 57,* 186–192.

Kaye, K. (1982). *The mental and social life of babies.* Chicago: University of Chicago Press.

Kaye, K., & Fogel, A. (1980). The temporal structure of face-to-face communication between mothers and infants. *Developmental Psychology, 16,* 454–464.

Kelley, M.L., Power, T.G., & Wimbush, D.D. (1992). Determinants of disciplinary practices in low-income Black mothers. *Child Development, 63,* 573–582.

Klass, C.S. (1996). *Home visiting: Promoting healthy parent and child development.* Baltimore: Paul H. Brookes Publishing Co.

Klass, C.S. (1997). The home visitor–parent relationship: The linchpin of home visiting. *Zero To Three, 17*(4), 1, 3–9.

Kochanska, G. (1993). Toward a synthesis of parental socialization and child temperament in early development of conscience. *Child Development, 64,* 325–347.

Kochanska, G. (1995). Children's temperament, mothers' discipline, and security of attachment: Multiple pathways to emerging internalization. *Child Development, 66,* 597–615.

Kochanska, G. (1997). Mutually responsive orientation between mothers and their young children: Implications for early socialization. *Child Development, 68,* 94–112.

Kochanska, G., & Aksan, N. (1995). Mother–child mutually positive affect, the quality of child compliance to requests and prohibitions, and maternal control as correlates of early internalization. *Child Development, 66,* 236–254.

Kohn, A. (1993). *Punished by rewards: The trouble with gold stars, incentive plans, A's, praise, and other bribes.* Boston: Houghton Mifflin Co.

Kohnstamm, G.A., Bates, J.E., & Rothbart, M.K. (Eds.). (1989). *Temperament in childhood.* New York: John Wiley & Sons.

Kozol, J. (1995). *Amazing grace: The lives of children and the conscience of a nation.* New York: Crown.

Kuchuk, A., Vibbert, M., & Bornstein, M.H. (1986). The perception of smiling and its experiential correlates in three-month-old infants. *Child Development, 57,* 1054–1061.

Kuczynski, L., & Kochanska, G. (1995). Function and content of maternal demands: Developmental significance of early demands for competent action. *Child Development, 66,* 616–628.

Kugiumutzakis, G. (1986). *The origin, development and function of early infant imitation.* Unpublished doctoral dissertation, Department of Psychology, University of Uppsala, Sweden.

Kurcinka, M.S. (1991). *Raising your spirited child.* New York: HarperCollins.

Lally, J.R., Griffin, A., Fenichel, E., Segal, M., Szanton, E., & Weissbourd, B. (1995). *Caring for infants and toddlers in groups: Developmentally appropriate practice.* Arlington, VA: ZERO TO THREE.

Lamb, M.E. (1998). The ecology of adolescent pregnancy and parenthood. In A.R. Pence (Ed.), *Ecological research with children and families: From concepts to methodology.* New York: Teachers College Press.

Larson, M.C., Gunnar, M.R., & Hertsgaard, L. (1991). The effects of morning naps, car trips, and maternal separation on adrenocortical activity in human infants. *Child Development, 62,* 362–372.

Lederberg, A.R., & Mobley, C.E. (1990). The effect of hearing impairment on the quality of attachment and mother–toddler interaction. *Child Development, 61,* 1596–1604.

Lester, G.M., Boukydis, C.F.Z., Garcia-Coll, C.T., Hole, W., & Peucker, M. (1992). Infantile colic: Acoustic cry characteristics, maternal perception of cry and temperament. *Infant Behavior and Development, 15,* 15–26.

Levy, S.J., & Rutter, E. (1992). *Children of drug abusers.* Lanham, MD: Lexington Books.

Lewis, M., & Brooks-Gunn, J. (1979). *Social cognition and the acquisition of self.* New York: Kluwer Academic/Plenum Publishers.

Lieberman, A.F. (1993). *The emotional life of the toddler.* New York: Free Press.

Lieberman, A.F. (1996). Aggression and sexuality in relation to toddler attachment: Implications for the caregiving system. *Infant Mental Health Journal, 17,* 276–292.

Lieberman, A.F. (1997). Toddlers' internalization of maternal attributions as a factor in quality of attachment. In L. Atkinson & K.J. Zucker (Eds.), *Attachment and psychopathology* (pp. 277–291). New York: The Guilford Press.

Lieberman, A.F., & Pawl, J.H. (1990). Disorder of attachment and secure base behavior in the second year of life: Conceptual issues and clinical intervention. In M.T. Greenberg, D. Cicchetti, & E.M. Cummings (Eds.), *Attachment in the preschool years: Theory, research, and intervention* (pp. 375–397). Chicago: University of Chicago Press.

Lieberman, A.F., & Pawl, J.H. (1993). Infant–parent psychotherapy. In C.H. Zeanah, Jr. (Ed.), *Handbook of infant mental health* (pp. 427–442). New York: The Guilford Press.

Lindsey, E.W. (1998). The impact of homelessness and shelter life on family relationships. *Family Relations, 47,* 243–252.

Linehan, M. (1993). *Cognitive-behavioral treatment of borderline personality disorder.* New York: The Guilford Press.

Londerville, S., & Main, M. (1981). Security of attachment, compliance, and maternal training methods in the second year of life. *Developmental Psychology, 17,* 289–299.

Lounsbury, M.L., & Bates, J.E. (1982). The cries of infants of differing levels of perceived temperamental difficultness: Acoustic properties and effects on listeners. *Child Development, 53,* 677–686.

Luthar, S.S., Cushing, G., & McMahon, T.J. (1997). Interdisciplinary interface: Developmental principles brought to substance abuse research. In S.S. Luthar, J.A. Burack, D. Cicchetti, & J.R. Weisz (Eds.), *Developmental psychopathology: Perspectives on adjustment, risk, and disorder* (pp. 437–456). Cambridge, England: Cambridge University Press.

Lyons-Ruth, K., Alpern, L., & Repacholi, B. (1993). Disorganized infant attachment classification and maternal psychosocial problems as predictors of hostile-aggressive behavior in the preschool classroom. *Child Development, 64,* 572–585.

Lyons-Ruth, K., & Block, D. (1996). The disturbed caregiving system: Relations among childhood trauma, maternal caregiving, and infant affect and attachment. *Infant Mental Health Journal, 17,* 257–275.

Lyons-Ruth, K., Connell, D.B., Grunebaum, H.U., & Botein, S. (1990). Infants at social risk: Maternal depression and family support services as mediators of infant development and security of attachment. *Child Development, 61,* 85–98.

Maccoby, E.E., & Martin, J.A. (1983). Socialization in the context of the family: Parent–child interaction. In P.H. Mussen (Series Ed.) & E.M. Hetherington (Vol. Ed.), *Handbook of child psychology: Vol. 4, Socialization, personality, and social development* (4th ed., pp. 1–101). New York: John Wiley & Sons.

MacFarlane, A. (1977). *The psychology of childbirth.* Cambridge, MA: Harvard University Press.

Mahler, M.S. (1980). Rapprochement subphase of the separation-individuation process. In R.F. Lax, S. Bach, & J.A. Burland (Eds.), *Rapprochement: The critical subphase of separation-individuation* (pp. 3–19). Northvale, NJ: Jason Aronson.

Mahler, M.S., Pine, F., & Bergman, A. (1975). *The psychological birth of the human infant: Symbiosis and individuation.* New York: Basic Books.

Main, M. (1991). Metacognitive knowledge, metacognitive monitoring, and singular (coherent) vs. multiple (incoherent) model of attachment: Findings and directions for future research. In C.M. Parkes, J. Stevenson-Hinde, and P. Marris (Eds.), *Attachment across the life cycle* (pp. 127–159). New York: Tavistock/ Routledge.

Main, M. (1996) Introduction to the special section on attachment and psychopathology: 2. Overview of the field of attachment. *Journal of Consulting and Clinical Psychology, 64,* 237–243.

Main, M., & Goldwyn, R. (1989). *Adult attachment classification system.* Unpublished manual, University of California, Department of Psychology, Berkeley.

Main, M., & Hesse, E. (1990). Parents' unresolved traumatic experiences are related to infant disorganized attachment status: Is frightened and/or frightening parental behavior the linking mechanism? In Greenberg, M.T., Cicchetti, D., & Cummings, E.M. (Eds.), *Attachment in the preschool years* (pp. 161–182). Chicago: University of Chicago Press.

Main, M., Kaplan, N., & Cassidy, J. (1985). Security in infancy, childhood, and adulthood: A move to the level of representation. In I. Bretherton & E. Waters (Eds.), Growing points of attachment theory and research. *Monographs of the Society for Research in Child Development, 50* (1–2, Serial No. 209).

Main, M., & Solomon, J. (1986). Discovery of an insecure-disorganized/disoriented attachment pattern. In T.B. Brazelton & M.W. Yogman (Eds.), *Affective development in infancy* (pp. 95–124). Norwood, NJ: Ablex Publishing Corp.

Main, M., & Solomon, J. (1990). Procedures for identifying infants as disorganized/disoriented during the Ainsworth Strange Situation. In M. T. Greenberg, D. Cicchetti, & E. M. Cummings (Eds.), *Attachment in the preschool years* (pp. 121–160). Chicago: University of Chicago Press.

Main, M., & Weston, D.R. (1981). The quality of the toddler's relationship to mother and to father: Related to conflict behavior and readiness to establish new relationships. *Child Development, 52,* 932–940.

Malatesta, C.Z., Grigoryev, P., Lamb, C., Albin, M., & Culver, C. (1986). Emotion socialization and expressive development in preterm and full-term infants. *Child Development, 57,* 316–330.

Malatesta-Magai, C. (1991). Emotional socialization: Its role in personality and developmental psychopathology. In D. Cicchetti & S.L. Toth (Eds.), *Internalizing and externalizing expressions of dysfunction: Vol. 2. Rochester symposium on developmental psychopathology* (pp. 203–224). Mahwah, NJ: Lawrence Erlbaum Associates.

Marens, S. (1994). Community violence and children's development: Collaborative interventions. In C. Chiland & J.G. Young (Eds.), *Children and violence* (pp. 109–124). Northvale, NJ: Jason Aronson.

Maslin-Cole, C., Bretherton, I., & Morgan, G.A. (1993). Toddler mastery motivation and competence: Links with attachment security, maternal scaffolding and family climate. In D. Messer (Ed.), *Mastery motivation in early childhood: Development, measurement and social processes* (pp. 205–229). London: Routledge.

Massat, C.R. (1995). Is older better? Adolescent parenthood and maltreatment. *Child Welfare, 74,* 325–336.

Maurer, D., & Salapatek, P. (1976). Developmental changes in the scanning of faces by young infants. *Child Development, 47,* 523–527.

Mayes, L.C., & Bornstein, M.H. (1996). The context of development for young children from cocaine-abusing families. In P.M. Kato & T. Mann (Eds.), *Handbook of diversity issues in health psychology* (pp. 69–95). New York: Kluwer Academic/Plenum Publishers.

Mayes, L.C., & Bornstein, M.H. (1997). The development of children exposed to cocaine. In S.S. Luthar, J.A. Burack, D. Cicchetti, & J.R. Weisz (Eds.),

Developmental psychopathology: Perspective on adjustment, risk, and disorder (pp. 166–188). Cambridge, England: Cambridge University Press.

Mayes, L.C., Bornstein, M.H., Chawarska, K., Haynes, O.M., & Granger, R.H. (1996). Impaired regulation of arousal in 3-month-old infants exposed prenatally to cocaine and other drugs. *Development and Psychopathology, 8,* 29–42.

McClure-Martinez, K., & Cohn, L.D. (1996). Adolescent and adult mothers' perceptions of hazardous situations for their children. *Journal of Adolescent Health, 18,* 227–231.

McKenry, P.C., Browne, D.H., Kotch, J.B., & Symons, M.J. (1990). Mediators of depression among low-income, adolescent mothers of infants: A longitudinal perspective. *Journal of Youth and Adolescence, 19,* 327–347.

McLoyd, V.C., & Wilson, L. (1991). The strain of living poor: Parenting, social support, and child mental health. In A.C. Huston (Ed.), *Children in poverty: Child development and public policy* (pp. 105–135). Cambridge, England: Cambridge University Press.

Mehler, J., Bertoncini, J., Barriere, M., & Jassik-Gerschenfeld, D. (1978). Infant recognition of mother's voice. *Perception, 7,* 491–497.

Meisels, S.J. (2001). Fusing assessment and intervention: Changing parents' and providers' views of young children. *Zero to Three, 21*(4), 4–10.

Melmed, M.E., & Ciervo, L. (1997). A focus on fathers: Findings from parent research. *Zero to Three, 18*(1), 32–35.

Miller, D.B. (1997). Adolescent fathers: What we know and what we need to know. *Child and Adolescent Social Work Journal, 14,* 55–69.

Miller, S.A. (1995). Parents' attributions for their children's behavior. *Child Development, 66,* 1557–1584.

Minuchin, P. (1999). Agency networks: Creating integrated services for people in need. *Zero To Three, 20*(1), 24–29.

Moon, C., Cooper, R.P., & Fifer, W.P. (1993). Two-day-olds prefer their native language. *Infant Behavior and Development, 16,* 495–500.

Muir, E. (1992). Watching, waiting, and wondering: Applying psychoanalytic principals to mother–infant intervention. *Infant Mental Health Journal, 13,* 319–328.

Murray, A. (1985). Aversiveness is in the mind of the beholder: Perception of infant crying by adults. In B.M. Lester & C.F.Z. Boukydis (Eds.), *Infant crying: Theoretical and research perspectives* (pp. 217–239). New York: Kluwer Academic/Plenum Publishers.

Murray, L., & Trevarthen, C. (1985). Emotional regulation of interactions between two-month-olds and their mothers. In T. Field & N. Fox (Eds.), *Social perception in infants* (pp. 177–197). Norwood, NJ: Ablex Publishing Corp.

Musick, J.S. (1993). *Young, poor, and pregnant: The psychology of teenage motherhood.* New Haven, CT: Yale University Press.

National Institute of Child Health and Human Development (NICHD) Early Child Care Research Network (1997a). Child care in the first year of life. *Merrill-Palmer Quarterly, 43*(3), 340–360.

NICHD Early Child Care Research Network (1997b). Poverty and patterns of child care. In G.J. Duncan & J. Brooks-Gunn (Eds.), *Consequences of growing up poor* (pp. 100–131). New York: Russell Sage Foundation.

NICHD Early Child Care Research Network (1998). Early child care and self-control, compliance, and problem behavior at twenty-four and thirty-six months. *Child Development, 69*(4), 1145–1170.

NICHD Early Child Care Research Network (1999). Chronicity of maternal depressive symptoms, maternal sensitivity, and child functioning at 36 months. *Developmental Psychology, 35*(5), 1297–1310.

NICHD Early Child Care Research Network (in press). Characteristics and quality of child care for toddlers and preschoolers. *Journal of Applied Developmental Science.*

O'Hara, M.W. (1995). *Postpartum depression: Causes and consequences.* New York: Springer-Verlag.

O'Hara, M.W. (1997). The nature of postpartum depressive disorders. In L. Murray & P.J. Cooper (Eds.), *Postpartum depression and child development* (pp. 3–31). New York: The Guilford Press.

O'Keefe, M. (1995). Predictors of child abuse in maritally violent families. *Journal of Interpersonal Violence, 10,* 3–25.

Olds, D.L., & Henderson, C.R., Jr. (1989). The prevention of maltreatment. In D. Cicchetti & V. Carlson (Eds.), *Child maltreatment: Theory and research on the causes and consequences of child abuse and neglect* (pp. 722–763). Cambridge, England: Cambridge University Press.

Olds, D.L., & Kitzman, H. (1993). Review of research on home visiting for pregnant women and parents of young children. *The Future of Children, 3,* 53–92.

Osofsky, J.D. (1998). Children as invisible victims of domestic and community violence. In G.W. Holden, R. Geffner, & E.N. Jouriles (Eds.), *Children exposed to marital violence: Theory, research, and applied issues* (pp. 95–117). Washington, DC: American Psychological Association.

Osofsky, J.D., & Eberhart-Wright, A. (1988). Affective exchanges between high risk mothers and infants. *International Journal of Psycho-Analysis, 69,* 221–231.

The Oxford Universal Dictionary (3rd ed.). (1933/1955). Oxford, England: Clarendon Press.

Panneton, R.K., & DeCasper, A.J. (1986, April). *Newborns' postnatal preference for a prenatally experienced melody.* Poster presented at the Biennial International Conference on Infant Studies, Beverly Hills, CA.

Parke, R., & Sawin, D. (1975, April). *Infant characteristics and behavior as elicitors of maternal and paternal responsiveness in the newborn period.* Paper presented at the meeting of the Society for Research in Child Development, Denver, CO.

Parker, H., & Parker, S. (1986). Father–daughter sexual abuse: An emerging perspective. *American Journal of Orthopsychiatry, 56,* 531–549.

Parritz, R.H., Mangelsdorf, S., & Gunnar, M.R. (1992). Control, social referencing, and the infant's appraisal of threat. In S. Feinman (Ed.), *Social referencing and the social construction of reality in infancy* (pp. 209-228). New York: Kluwer Academic/Plenum Publishers.

Pawl, J.H. (1994–1995). On supervision. *Zero To Three, 15*(3), 21–29.

Pawl, J.H. (1995). The therapeutic relationship as human connectedness: Being held in another's mind. *Zero To Three, 15*(4), 1, 3–5.

Paykel, E.S. (1974). Recent life events and clinical depression. In E.K. Gunderson & R.H. Rahe (Eds.), *Life stress and illness* (pp. 134–163). Springfield, IL: Charles C Thomas.

Pearson, J.L., Cohn, D.A., Cowan, P.A., & Cowan, C.P. (1994). Earned- and continuous-security in adult attachment: Relation to depressive symptomatology and parenting style. *Development and Psychopathology, 6,* 359–373.

Perry, B.D. (1997). Incubated in terror: Neurodevelopmental factors in the "cycle of violence." In J.D. Osofsky (Ed.), *Children, youth and violence: The search for solutions* (pp. 124–148). New York: The Guilford Press.

Perry, B.D., Hogan, L., & Marlin, S.J. (2000). Curiosity, pleasure and play: A neurodevelopmental perspective. (Available at www.bcm.tmc.edu/cta/curiosity.htm)

Phelps, J.L., Belsky, J., & Crnic, K. (1998). Earned security, daily stress, and parenting: A comparison of five alternative models. *Development and Psychopathology, 10,* 21–38.

Piaget, J. (1951). *Play, dreams and imitation in childhood* (C. Gattegno & F.M. Hodgson, Trans.). New York: W.W. Norton. (Original work published 1946)

Piaget, J. (1952). *The origins of intelligence in children* (M. Cook, Trans.). New York: W.W. Norton. (Original work published 1936)

Piaget, J. (1973). *The psychology of intelligence* (M. Piercy & D.E. Berlyne, Trans.). Totowa, NJ: Littlefield, Adams & Co. (Original work published 1947)

Pipp-Siegel, S., Siegel, C.H., & Dean, J. (1999). Neurological aspects of the disorganized/disoriented attachment classification system: Differentiating quality of the attachment relationship from neurological impairment. In J.I. Vondra & D. Barnett (Eds.), Atypical attachment in infancy and early childhood among children at developmental risk. *Monographs of the Society for Research in Child Development, 64* (3, Serial No. 258), 25–44.

Polit, D.F., White, C.M., & Morton, T.D. (1990). Child sexual abuse and premarital intercourse among high-risk adolescents. *Journal of Adolescent Health Care, 11,* 231–234.

Power, T.G., & Chapieski, M.L. (1986). Childrearing and impulse control in toddlers: A naturalistic investigation. *Developmental Psychology, 22,* 271–275.

Project AIMS (1990). *Developmental indicators of emotional health: A brief assessment system of practice for use with children from birth through five years and their families (users' manual).* Portland, ME: Project AIMS, Human Services Development Institute, University of Southern Maine.

Pruett, K.D. (1997). How men and children affect each other's development. *Zero to Three, 18*(1), 3–11.

Redding, R.E., Harmon, R.J., & Morgan, G.A. (1990). Maternal depression and infants' mastery behavior. *Infant Behavior and Development, 13,* 391–396.

Reddy, V., Hay, D., Murray, L., & Trevarthen, C. (1997) Communication in infancy: Mutual regulation of affect and attention. In G. Bremner, A. Slater, & G. Butterworth (Eds.), *Infant development: Recent advances* (pp. 247–273). Philadelphia: Psychology Press.

Restak, R.M. (1995). *Brainscapes.* New York: Hyperion.

Rhein, L.M., Ginsburg, K.R., Schwartz, D.F., Pinto-Martin, J.A., Zhao, H., Morgan, A.P., & Slap, G.B. (1997). Teen father participation in child rearing: Family perspectives. *Journal of Adolescent Health, 21,* 244–252.

Rheingold, H.L., & Eckerman, C.O. (1971). Departures from the mother. In H.R. Schaffer (Ed.), *The origins of human social relations* (pp. 73–82). San Diego: Academic Press.

Rheingold, H.L., Hay, D.F., & West, M.J. (1976). Sharing in the second year of life. *Child Development, 47,* 1148–1158.

Rholes, W.S., Simpson, J.A., Blakely, B.S., Lanigan, L., & Allen, E.A. (1997). Adult attachment styles, the desire to have children, and working models of parenthood. *Journal of Personality, 65,* 357–385.

Richters, J., & Martinez, P. (1993). Violent communities, family choices, and children's chances: An algorithm for improving the odds. *Development and Psychopathology, 5,* 609–627.

Roosa, M.W., Tein, J., Reinholtz, C., & Angelini, P.J. (1997). Relationship of childhood sexual abuse to teenage pregnancy. *Journal of Marriage and the Family, 59,* 119–130.

Rosen, W.D., Adamson, L.B., & Bakeman, R. (1992). An experimental investigation of infant social referencing: Mothers' messages and gender differences. *Developmental Psychology, 28,* 1172–1178.

Rosenblum, L.A. (1987). Influences of environmental demand on maternal behavior and infant development. In N.A. Krasnegor, E.M. Blass, M.A. Hofer, & W.P. Smotherman (Eds.), *Perinatal development: A psychobiological perspective* (pp. 377–395). San Diego: Academic Press.

Rosenblum, O., Mazet, P., & Benony, H. (1997). Mother and infant affective involvement states and maternal depression. *Infant Mental Health Journal, 18,* 350–363.

Rothbart, M.K., Derryberry, D., & Posner, M.I. (1994). A psychobiological approach to the development of temperament. In J.E. Bates & T.D. Wachs (Eds.), *Temperament: Individual differences at the interface of biology and behavior* (pp. 83–116). Washington, DC: American Psychological Association.

Ruff, H.A., Saltarelli, L.M., Capozzoli, M., & Dubiner, K (1992). The differentiation of activity in infants' exploration of objects. *Developmental Psychology, 28,* 851–861.

Russell, D.E.H. (1986). *The secret trauma: Incest in the lives of girls and women.* New York: Basic Books.

Russell, G., & Radojevic, M. (1992). The changing role of fathers? Current understandings and future directions for research and practice. *Infant Mental Health Journal, 13,* 296–311.

Rutter, M. (1966). Children of sick parents: An environmental and psychiatric study. *Institute of Psychiatry Maudsley Monographs, 16.* London: Oxford University Press.

Rutter, M. (1997). Clinical implications of attachment concepts: Retrospect and prospect. In L. Atkinson & K.J. Zucker (Eds.), *Attachment and psychopathology* (pp. 17–46). New York: The Guilford Press.

Rutter, M., & Quinton, D. (1984). Parental psychiatric disorder: Effects on children. *Psychological Medicine, 14,* 853–880.

Sameroff, A.J., Seifer, R., Baldwin, A., & Baldwin, C. (1993). Stability of intelligence from preschool to adolescence: The influence of social and family risk factors. *Child Development, 64,* 80–97.

Sameroff, A.J., Seifer, R., & Bartko, W.T. (1997). Environmental perspectives on adaptation during childhood and adolescence. In S.S. Luthar, J.A. Burack, D. Cicchetti, & J.R. Weisz (Eds.), *Developmental psychopathology: Perspectives on adjustment, risk, and disorder* (pp. 507–526). Cambridge, England: Cambridge University Press.

Sander, L.W. (1975). Infant and caretaking environment. In E.J. Anthony (Ed.), *Explorations in child psychiatry* (pp. 129-166). New York: Kluwer Academic/Plenum Publishers.

Schaffer, H.R. (1984). *The child's entry into a social world.* San Diego: Academic Press.

Schore, A.N. (1994). *Affect regulation and the origin of the self: The neurobiology of emotional development.* Mahwah, NJ: Lawrence Erlbaum Associates.

Schorr, L.B. (1997). *Common purpose: Strengthening families and neighborhoods to rebuild America.* New York: Anchor Books/Doubleday.

Schwartz, A., Campos, J., & Baisel, E. (1973). The visual cliff: Cardiac and behavioral correlates on the deep and shallow sides at five and nine months of age. *Journal of Experimental Child Psychology, 15,* 86–99.

Shaw, D.S., Owens, E.B., Vondra, J.I., Keenan, K. & Winslow, E.B. (1996). Early risk factors and pathways in the development of early disruptive behavior problems. *Development and Psychopathology, 8,* 679–699.

Shore, R. (1997). *Rethinking the brain: New insights into early development.* New York: Families and Work Institute.

Slade, A., & Aber, J.L. (1992). Attachments, drives, and development: Conflicts and convergences in theory. In J.W. Barron, M.N. Eagle, & D.L. Wolitzky (Eds.), *Interface of psychoanalysis and psychology* (pp. 154–185). Washington, DC: American Psychological Association.

Slater, A., & Butterworth, G. (1997). Perception of social stimuli: Face perception and imitation. In G. Bremner, A. Slater, & G. Butterworth (Eds.), *Infant development: Recent advances* (pp. 223–245). Philadelphia: Psychology Press.

Snyder-Joy, Z.K., & Carlo, T.A. (1998). Parenting through prison walls: Incarcerated mothers and children's visitation programs. In S.L. Miller (Ed.), *Crime control and women: Feminist implications of criminal justice policy* (pp. 130–150). Thousand Oaks, CA: Sage Publications.

Sorce, J.F., Emde, R.N., Campos, J.J., & Klinnert, M.D. (1985). Maternal emotional signaling: Its effect on the visual cliff behavior of 1-year-olds. *Developmental Psychology, 21,* 195–200.

Spangler, G., & Grossmann, K.E. (1993). Biobehavioral organization in securely and insecurely attached infants. *Child Development, 64,* 1439–1450.

Spieker, S.J., & Bensley, L. (1994). Roles of living arrangements and grandmother social support in adolescent mothering and infant attachment. *Developmental Psychology, 30,* 102–111.

Spieker, S.J., & Booth, C.L. (1988). Maternal antecedents of attachment quality. In J. Belsky & T. Nezworski (Eds.), *Clinical implications of attachment* (pp. 95–135). Mahwah, NJ: Lawrence Erlbaum Associates.

Sroufe, L.A. (1988). The role of infant–parent attachment in development. In J. Belsky & T. Nezworski, *Clinical implications of attachment* (pp. 18–38). Mahwah, NJ: Lawrence Erlbaum Associates.

Sroufe, L.A. (1996). *Emotional development: The organization of emotional life in the early years.* Cambridge, England: Cambridge University Press.

Sroufe, L.A., Cooper, R.G., & Marshall, M.E. (1988). *Child development: Its nature and course.* New York: McGraw-Hill.

Sroufe, L.A., & Fleeson, J. (1986). Attachment and the construction of relationships. In W.W. Hartup & Z. Rubin (Eds.), *Relationships and development* (pp. 51–71). Mahwah, NJ: Lawrence Erlbaum Associates.

Sroufe, L.A., & Fleeson, J. (1988). The coherence of family relationships. In R.A. Hinde & J. Stevenson-Hinde (Eds.), *Relationships within families: Mutual influences* (pp. 27–47). Oxford, England: Clarendon Press.

Sroufe, L.A., Fox, N.E., & Pancake, V.R. (1983). Attachment and dependency in developmental perspective. *Child Development, 54,* 1615–1627.

Steele, H., Steele, M., & Fonagy, P. (1996). Associations among attachment classifications of mothers, fathers, and their infants. *Child Development, 67,* 541–555.

Stern, D.N. (1974). Mother and infant at play: The dyadic interaction involving facial, vocal, and gaze behavior. In M. Lewis & L.A. Rosenblum (Eds.), *The effect of the infant on its parent* (pp. 187–213). New York: John Wiley & Sons.

Stern, D.N. (1985). *The interpersonal world of the infant: A view from psychoanalysis and developmental psychology.* New York: Basic Books.

Stern, D.N. (1989). The representation of relational patterns: Developmental considerations. In A.J. Sameroff & R.N. Emde (Eds.), *Relationship disturbances in early childhood: A developmental approach* (pp. 52–69). New York: Basic Books.

Stern, D.N. (1995). *The motherhood constellation: A unified view of parent-infant psychotherapy*. New York: Basic Books.

Stifter, C.A., & Braungart, J.M. (1995). The regulation of negative reactivity in infancy: Function and development. *Developmental Psychology, 31,* 448–455.

Stipek, D., Recchia, S., & McClintic, S. (1992). Self-evaluation in young children. *Monographs of the Society for Research in Child Development, 57*(1, Serial No. 226).

Straus, M.A. (1994). *Beating the devil out of them: Corporal punishment in American families*. Lanham, MD: Lexington Books.

Straus, M.A., & Gelles, R.J. (1986). Societal change and change in family violence from 1975 to 1985 as revealed by two national surveys. *Journal of Marriage and the Family, 48,* 465–479.

Swain, I.U., Zelazo, P.R., & Clifton, R.K. (1993). Newborn infants' memory for speech sounds retained over 24 hours. *Developmental Psychology, 29,* 312–323.

Sylwester, R. (1995). *A celebration of neurons: An educator's guide to the human brain*. Alexandria, VA: Association for Supervision and Curriculum Development.

Tatum, J., Moseley, S., Boyd-Franklin, N., & Herzog, E.P. (1995). A home-based, family systems approach to the treatment of African-American teenage parents and their families. *Zero to Three, 15*(4), 18–25.

Teti, D.M., & Gelfand, D.M. (1991). Behavioral competence among mothers of infants in the first year: The mediational role of maternal self-efficacy. *Child Development, 62,* 918–929.

Teti, D.M., & Gelfand, D.M. (1997). Maternal cognitions as mediators of child outcomes in the context of postpartum depression. In L. Murray & P.J. Cooper (Eds.), *Postpartum depression and child development* (pp. 136–164). New York: The Guilford Press.

Thomas, A., Chess, S., Birch, H.G., Hertzig, M.E., & Korn, S. (1963). *Behavioral individuality in early childhood*. New York: New York University Press.

Thompson, R.A. (1994). Emotion regulation: A theme in search of definition. In N.A. Fox (Ed.), The development of emotion regulation: Biological and behavioral considerations (pp. 25–52). *Monographs of the Society for Research in Child Development, 59* (2–3, Serial No. 240).

Thompson, R.A. (1995). *Preventing child maltreatment through social support: A critical analysis*. Thousand Oaks, CA: Sage Publications.

Thompson, R.A., & Calkins, S.D. (1996). The double-edged sword: Emotional regulation for children at risk. *Development and Psychopathology, 8,* 163–182.

Thurston, L. (1982). *Life skills for women*. (Available from Survival Skills, Education and Development, 2801 Claflin Road, Suite 150, Manhattan, KS 66502; www.ssed.org)

Trevarthen, C. (1993). The function of emotions in early infant communication and development. In J. Nadel & L. Camaioni (Eds.), *New perspectives in early communicative development* (pp. 48–81). New York: Routledge.

Tronick, E.Z., Ricks, M., & Cohn, J.F. (1982). Maternal and infant affective exchanges: Patterns of adaptation. In T. Field & A. Fogel (Eds.), *Emotion and early interaction* (pp. 83–100). Mahwah, NJ: Lawrence Erlbaum Associates.

Tronick, E.Z., & Weinberg, M.K. (1997). Depressed mothers and infants: Failure to form dyadic states of consciousness. In L. Murray & P.J. Cooper (Eds.),

Postpartum depression and child development (pp. 54–81). New York: The Guilford Press.

Trout, M. (1987a). *The awakening and growth of the human infant [videotape series]*. Champaign, IL: The Infant–Parent Institute.

Trout, M.D. (1987b). *Working papers on process in infant mental health assessment and intervention.* Champaign, IL: The Infant–Parent Institute.

Trout, M. (1997). *Multiple transitions: A young child's view of foster care and adoption* [videotape]. Champaign, IL: The Infant–Parent Institute.

Tulkin, S.R., & Kagan, J. (1972). Mother–infant interaction in the first year of life. *Child Development, 43,* 31–41.

Tymchuk, A.J., & Feldman, M.A. (1991). Parents with mental retardation and their children: Review of research relevant to professional practice. *Canadian Psychology, 32,* 486–494.

van den Boom, D.C. (1989). Neonatal irritability and the development of attachment. In G.A. Kohnstamm, J.E. Bates, & M.K. Rothbart (Eds.), *Temperament in childhood* (pp. 299–318). New York: John Wiley & Sons.

van IJzendoorn, M.H., & Bakermans-Kranenbrug, M.J. (1997). Intergenerational transmission of attachment: A move to the contextual level. In L. Atkinson & K.J. Zucker (Eds.), *Attachment and psychopathology* (pp. 135–170). New York: The Guilford Press.

van IJzendoorn, M.H., Goldberg, S., Kroonenberg, P.M., & Frenkel, O.J. (1992). The relative effects of maternal and child problems on the quality of attachment: A meta-analysis of attachment in clinical samples. *Child Development, 63,* 840–858.

Walden, T.A. (1996). Social responsivity: Judging signals of young children with and without developmental delays. *Child Development, 67,* 2074–2085.

Ward, M.J., & Carlson, E.A. (1995). Associations among adult attachment representations, maternal sensitivity, and infant–mother attachment in a sample of adolescent mothers. *Child Development, 66,* 69–79.

Waters, D.B., & Lawrence, E.C. (1993). *Competence, courage, and change: An approach to family therapy.* New York: W.W. Norton.

Waters, E., Matas, L., & Sroufe, L.A. (1975). Infants' reactions to an approaching stranger: Description, validation and functional significance of wariness. *Child Development, 46,* 348–365.

Waters, E., Merrick, S., Treboux, D., Crowell, J., & Albersheim, L. (2000). Attachment security in infancy and early adulthood: A twenty-year longitudinal study. *Child Development, 71,* 684–689.

Weinfield, N.S., Sroufe, L.A., & Egeland, B. (2000). Attachment from infancy to early adulthood in a high-risk sample: Continuity, discontinuity, and their correlates. *Child Development, 71,* 695–702.

Wekerle, C., & Wolfe, D.A. (1998). The role of child maltreatment and attachment style in adolescent relationship violence. *Development and Psychopathology, 10,* 571–586.

Welle, D., Falkin, G.P., & Jainchill, N. (1998). Current approaches to drug treatment for women offenders. *Journal of Substance Abuse Treatment, 15,* 151–163.

Weston, J. (1980). The pathology of child abuse. In R. Helfer & C. Kempe (Eds.), *The battered child* (3rd ed., pp. 241–271). Chicago: University of Chicago Press.

Wieder, S., & Greenspan, S. (2001). The DIR (developmental, individual-difference, relationship-based) approach and intervention planning. *Zero to Three, 21*(4), 11–19.

Youngblade, L.M., & Belsky, J. (1990). Social and emotional consequences of child maltreatment. In R.T. Ammerman & M. Hersen (Eds.), *Children at risk: An evaluation of factors contributing to child abuse and neglect* (pp. 109–146). New York: Kluwer Academic/Plenum Publishers.

Zahn-Waxler, C., Cole, P.M., & Barrett, K.C. (1991). Guilt and empathy: Sex differences and implications for the development of depression. In J. Garber & K.A. Dodge (Eds.), *The development of emotion regulation and dysregulation* (pp. 243–272). New York: Cambridge University Press.

Zanarini, M.C. (Ed.). (1997). *Role of sexual abuse in the etiology of borderline personality disorder*. Washington, DC: American Psychiatric Press.

Zeanah, C.H. (1996). Beyond insecurity: A reconceptualization of attachment disorders of infancy. *Journal of Consulting and Clinical Psychology, 64*, 42–52.

Zeanah, C.H., Benoit, D., Barton, M., Regan, C., Hirshberg, L.M., & Lipsitt, L.P. (1993). Representations of attachment in mothers and their one-year-old infants. *Journal of American Academy of Child and Adolescent Psychiatry, 32*, 278–286.

Zeanah, C.H., Jr., & Boris, N.W. (2000). Disturbances and disorders of attachment in early childhood. In C.H. Zeanah, Jr., (Ed.), *Handbook of infant mental health* (2nd ed., pp. 353–368). New York: The Guilford Press.

Zeanah, C.H., Boris, N.W., Bakshi, S., & Lieberman. A.F. (2000). Attachment disorders of infancy. In J.D. Osofsky & H. Fizgerald (Eds.), *WAIMH handbook of infant mental health* (Vol. 4, pp. 91–122). New York: John Wiley & Sons.

Zeanah, C.H., Finley-Belgrad, E., & Benoit, D. (1997). Intergenerational transmission of relationship psychopathology: A mother–infant case study. In L. Atkinson & K.J. Zucker (Eds.), *Attachment and psychopathology* (pp. 292–318). New York: The Guilford Press.

Zeanah, C.H., Jr., & Scheeringa, M. (1996). Evaluation of posttraumatic symptomatology in infants and young children exposed to violence. In J.D. Osofsky & E. Fenichel (Eds.), *Islands of safety: Assessing and treating young victims of violence* (pp. 9–14). Washington, DC: ZERO TO THREE.

Zedlewski, S.R. (2000). *Snapshots of America's families II: Family economic well-being*. (Available at http://newFederalism.urban.org/nsaf/index.htm)

Zeifert, M., & Brown, K.S. (1991). Skill building for effective intervention with homeless families. *Families in Society: The Journal of Contemporary Human Services, 72*, 212–219.

Zeskind, P.S., Klein, L., & Marshall, T.R. (1992). Adult's perceptions of experimental modifications of durations of pauses and expiratory sounds in infant crying. *Developmental Psychology, 28*(6), 1153–1162.

Zeskind, P.S., & Lester, B.M. (1978). Acoustic features and auditory perceptions of the cries of newborns with prenatal and perinatal complications. *Child Development, 49*, 580–589.

Zuckerman, B. (1998). Women's health: Key to a two-generational approach to child health and development. *Zero to Three, 18*(5), 5–9.

Zuckerman, B., & Brown, E.R. (1993). Maternal substance abuse and infant development. In C.H. Zeanah, Jr. (Ed.), *Handbook of infant mental health* (pp. 143–158). New York: The Guilford Press.

Appendix

Disorders of Attachment in Early Childhood

Disorders of Nonattachment

Nonattachment with Emotional Withdrawal

"In this pattern, important attachment behaviors like comfort seeking, showing affection, reliance for help, and cooperation are remarkably restricted"; there are also disturbances of exploratory behavior. "Affected children not only demonstrate no preference for an attachment figure, they also are emotionally blunted, avoid or fail to respond to social overtures, and demonstrate serious problems in emotional self-regulation. This symptom picture has been described in samples of institutionalized children and neglected children."

Nonattachment with Indiscriminate Sociability

"In this pattern, children also fail to exhibit a preferred attachment figure, but instead of failing to seek proximity or comfort, they seek it indiscriminately, even from strangers. In addition, these children lack the expected social reticence around unfamiliar adults that is typical of children in the second through fourth years of life. Factors that limit the opportunity for young children to develop selective attachments, such as frequent changes in foster care or institutionalization, are linked to this form of nonattachment." "Infants and toddlers who meet criteria for this disorder also may demonstrate serious problems with the ability to protect themselves."

This appendix is adapted from Zeanah, C.H., Jr., & Boris, N.W. (2000). Disturbances and disorders of attachment in early childhood. In C.H. Zeanah, Jr., (Ed.), *Handbook of infant mental health* (2nd ed., pp. 353–368). New York: The Guilford Press. Adapted by permission.

Secure Base Distortions of Attachment

Attachment Disorder with Self-Endangerment

This pattern "is characterized by expected ventures away from the attachment figure for purposes of exploration; however, the exploration is unchecked by the opposing tendency to maintain proximity or to return to the putative safe haven of the attachment figure. In addition, the child may engage in a variety of exceedingly dangerous and provocative behaviors in the presence of the attachment figure, such as running out into traffic, deliberately running away in crowded public places, climbing up on ledges, etc. Accompanying behaviors include aggression that may be self-directed or directed at the caregiver, especially if the aggressive behaviors are displayed in the place of comfort-seeking behaviors. Bold, active, or uninhibited children may exercise poor judgment at times, but their provocative and self-endangering behaviors constitute signs of an attachment disorder only if they are severe, persistent, and relationship-specific." Children with attention-deficit/hyperactivity disorder (ADHD) may exhibit behaviors similar to this pattern.

Attachment Disorder with Clinging/Inhibited Exploration

Young children exhibiting this pattern "do not venture away from the attachment figure to engage in age-expected exploration. Here, the secure-base function of the attachment figure appears to be deficient, and the child's willingness to venture away and explore the object world is impaired. Curiously, this inhibition is not pervasive but rather situation-specific. The inhibited behaviors and high levels of accompanying anxiety are observed when the child is in the presence of the attachment figure in an unfamiliar setting, or especially in the presence of the attachment figure *and* an unfamiliar adult." "This type of attachment disorder is relationship specific, whereas behavioral inhibition as a temperament trait is generalized."

Attachment Disorder with Vigilance/Hypercompliance

This attachment disorder is also associated with strong inhibition of exploration, but in this pattern, there is no clinging to the caregiver. "Instead, the child is emotionally constricted, vigilant of the caregiver, and hypercompliant with caregiver requests and commands. Instead of fearing to leave the caregiver as in the clinging/inhibited pattern, the child instead gives the impression of fearing to displease the caregiver . . . . Although the behavioral pattern is specific to interactions with the attachment figure, it is not necessarily always evident. It is likely that certain cues trigger the response in young children, such as displays of intense or prolonged anger and frustration by the caregiver." This pattern has been observed in children who have been abused by their caregivers.

Attachment Disorder with Role Reversal

In this pattern, "the attachment relationship is inverted . . . instead of the caregiver providing emotional support, nurturance, and protection to the child, the emotional well-being of the caregiver is a preoccupation and even responsibility of the child. To a developmentally inappropriate degree, the child assumes the emotional burden of the relationship. This may be associated with the child's efforts to control the caregiver's behavior, either punitively, oversolicitously, or in some other role-inappropriate manner."

Disrupted Attachment Disorder

This general type of attachment disorder is associated with the sudden loss of the attachment figure. The rationale for the inclusion of this as a disorder for young children is that the loss of the attachment figure for an infant or toddler is so devastating that it is qualitatively different from loss at another point in the life cycle. Young children experiencing such loss may exhibit a sequence of behavior moving from protest to despair to detachment. The presence of another attachment figure may buffer the loss for these children.

Index

Page numbers followed by *t* indicate tables.